LISTENING IN

Bloomsbury Studies in Digital Cultures

Series Editors
Anthony Mandal and Jenny Kidd

This series responds to a rapidly changing digital world, one which permeates both our everyday lives and the broader philosophical challenges that accrue in its wake. It is inter- and trans-disciplinary, situated at the meeting points of the digital humanities, digital media and cultural studies, and research into digital ethics.

While the series will tackle the 'digital humanities' in its broadest sense, its ambition is to broaden focus beyond areas typically associated with the digital humanities to encompass a range of approaches to the digital, whether these be digital humanities, digital media studies or digital arts practice.

Titles in the series

The Trouble With Big Data, Jennifer Edmond, Nicola Horsley, Jörg Lehmann and Mike Priddy
Hacking in the Humanities, Aaron Mauro
Ambient Stories in Practice and Research, Edited by Amy Spencer
Metamodernism and the Postdigital in the Contemporary Novel, Spencer Jordan
Representing the New AI in Film and Television, Graham Allen
Resisting Big Tech, Niels Niessen

Forthcoming titles

New Directions in Digital Textual Studies, Edited by Christopher Ohge and Kristen Schuster

LISTENING IN

HOW AUDIO SURVEILLANCE BECAME ARTIFICIAL INTELLIGENCE

Toby Heys, David Jackson and Marsha Courneya

BLOOMSBURY ACADEMIC

LONDON · NEW YORK · OXFORD · NEW DELHI · SYDNEY

BLOOMSBURY ACADEMIC
Bloomsbury Publishing Plc, 50 Bedford Square, London, WC1B 3DP, UK
Bloomsbury Publishing Inc, 1359 Broadway, New York, NY 10018, USA
Bloomsbury Publishing Ireland, 29 Earlsfort Terrace, Dublin 2, D02 AY28, Ireland

BLOOMSBURY, BLOOMSBURY ACADEMIC and the Diana logo are trademarks
of Bloomsbury Publishing Plc

First published in Great Britain 2026

A catalogue record for this book is available from the British Library.

A catalog record for this book is available from the Library of Congress.

ISBN: HB: 978-1-3503-4038-1
PB: 978-1-3503-4039-8
ePDF: 978-1-3503-4040-4
eBook: 978-1-3503-4041-1

Series: Bloomsbury Studies in Digital Cultures

Typeset by Deanta Global Publishing Services, Chennai, India
Printed and bound in Great Britain

For product safety related questions contact productsafety@bloomsbury.com.

To find out more about our authors and books visit www.bloomsbury.com
and sign up for our newsletters.

CONTENTS

Contents

ACKNOWLEDGEMENTS

The authors would collectively like to thank Matteo Polato for his meticulous research and help during the early stages of the writing of the book. The ideas and the conversations we had along the way were often essential in breaking the deadlock. A sincere thank you to Crypto Museum (cryptomuseum.com) for the use of their images for the cover of the book. Thanks also to And Vinyly (www.andvinyly.com) for their permission to use a likeness of their logo.

Thanks to Kristian Griffiths for his ever-wonderful illustrations, please keep on drawing everyday. Toby Heys would like to thank Caro, Charly and Ivo for their love, support and enduring patience over the two-year writing period of the book and for putting up with the constant stream of music that soundtracked the production of Listening In. David Jackson would like to thank Em, Mia and Lilah for their love, and for insisting he take a break, take a walk, eat lunch and occasionally finish on time, to do things worth listening in on. Marsha Courneya is grateful to the Toronto Reference Library for its many quiet alcoves and to Alex, Susanne, and Ron for their encouragement.

A shout out to all the creatives, activists and whistle-blowers who try and resist, reveal or complicate the tentacular reach of the monitoring massive.

ABOUT THE AUTHORS

Toby Heys is a professor at the School of Digital Arts (SODA) at Manchester Metropolitan University. He is co-founder of the AUDINT sonic research unit, which produces books, albums, installations, performances and software. His upcoming book with Matteo Polato, *Phantom Channels: A Sonic Cosmology of Arcane Intelligences* (MIT Press) will be published in 2028.

David Jackson is a Senior Lecturer in Digital Visualisation at the School of Digital Arts at Manchester Metropolitan University. His research explores the cultural impact of AI on creative producers and their audiences and informed the creation of the 'Storytellers + Machines' conference, which he founded in 2023.

Marsha Courneya is a Canadian writer and editor. She teaches Digital Dramaturgy at the International Film School of Cologne and is a doctoral researcher in Digital Culture and Communication at Birkbeck University, London.

INTRODUCTION

To stop seeing, one simply needs to shut their eyes. Stopping hearing is not that easy. Even with fingers stuffed in our ears, we can hear the internal workings of our nervous systems along with the contractions of our tensor tympani muscle, the mechanism that dampens vibrations from transmitting to the inner ear. We cannot aim or focus our hearing in the same way that we train our eyes, meaning that not only do we hear sounds and voices directed at us, we also perceive frequency-based content that is meant for others. We often overhear by accident. We also overhear by design. When this occurs, we are listening in. Starting in the post-Second World War period, this book explores what happens when the act of listening mutates into surveillance and is subsequently augmented, industrialized and weaponized by corporations, military organizations and governments.

During the Second World War, covert surveillance was carried out by Axis and Allied powers to gain intelligence that would ultimately lead to territorial advantages on the ground. Today, in addition to being deployed for ideological and martial purposes, surveillance is used in more politically nebulous schemes such as advanced web user analytics and the monetization of personal data. The information captured from our digital interactions is traded and sold to feed machine learning algorithms. In turn, with the pertinent data, these algorithms predictively model everything from economic trends and weather patterns to healthcare logistics and the longevity of human relationships. *Listening In* surveys past and current modes of audio surveillance and speculates on how future artificial intelligence (AI) frameworks are being informed by sonic strategies borne from the early Cold War period.

When considered collectively, the surveillance strategies, technologies and approaches analysed in this book speak to the notion that the megalomaniacal urge to record and listen to everything that has ever been uttered is scored deeply into the technological operating system of Western culture; a rationale that results in audio surveillance being normalized from pre-birth – via ultrasound recordings and images posted on social media – onwards. From Thomas Edison's yearning to record 'important speeches of men and gods, down through the ages' (Trower 2012: 68), to Charles Babbage's similar conviction that 'The air itself is one vast library, on whose pages are forever written all that man has ever said or woman whispered' (Trower 2012: 113), there has been a desire to capture, store and redistribute audio datasets that represent the spectrum of human emotion and experience.

This notion of the ether as a universal audiotopia is an early precursor to 'The Cloud' and the remote data farms that it occludes. Through such meteorological analogies, a space is opened up in the cultural consciousness, one of a storage capacity that is limitless. The waveform repository is all around us; it is atmospheric in this way and instantly accessible, even if we cannot see or touch it. The projected size of the expanse is only echoed by the magnitude of the will to fill it with data.

The sheer density of vibrational information being amassed in this megalomaniacal repository causes Hito Steyerl to conclude that when reviewing prodigious collections of data '[n]ot seeing anything intelligible is the new normal' and more than that, that simply capturing and storing data is no longer the challenge. Instead, '[t]he focus moves from acquisition to discerning' (2020: 139–40). In the deficit, automated systems like data packet inspectors listen out for signals in the incoming noise. Machine learning tools and the AI systems they inform have become the new sensory conduits; the omni listeners taking up millions of listening posts and opening up new experiential ways of encountering and hearing patterns of association.

There are a number of ways to experience *Listening In*. The book is split into four parts, each containing four chapters. The running order is as such: Part I: 'Embedded bugs and tunnels' (1945–60s); Part II: 'Massive distributed monitoring systems' (1950–current day); Part III: 'Domotic self-surveillance cultures' (1990s–current day); Part IV: 'Ambient interfaces, arcane intelligence' (2018–future). Each part focuses on an era of surveillance that shares sonic technologies, monitoring characteristics and socio-political and socio-economic ambitions.

Each chapter is divided into the same eight subsections – Process, Recording, Prediction, Worlds, Voice, Fidelity, Transgression and Intimacy – which means that *Listening In* can be read horizontally or vertically. Thus, the themes can be navigated in a 'playlist' manner, or each chapter can be read vertically from start to finish (like listening to a cassette tape). This allows for different channels to be opened, each offering a distinct navigation and reading of the aural arc that reveals how audio surveillance became AI.

Starting in 1945, the first chapter focuses on Leon Theremin's 'Great Seal' bug. Also referred to as 'The Thing', it pioneered a technique for the passive transmission of audio signals, which in turn informed the development of Radio Frequency Identification technology, now simply referred to as RFID. Built by the Soviet Union and offered to the United States as a symbol of future trust and cooperation, the Great Seal listening device was built into a wooden rendering of the American national coat of arms. The section goes on to cover the (under)ground strategies of 'Operation Gold' in the 1950s, wherein the United Kingdom and the United States tunnelled into a Soviet-occupied zone in Berlin to monitor military communications. It finishes with increasingly bizarre eavesdropping operations, such as the hidden microphones secreted in the heels of diplomats' shoes, which we have named 'Shoehorn' in lieu of any official operational name, and the CIA's 1960s 'Acoustic Kitty' project, which entailed a cat having a microphone and transmitter sewn under its fur to enable mobile eavesdropping as it skulked around the Soviet embassy in Washington, DC.

Part II amplifies the ways in which singular models of audio intelligence from the mid-1940s onwards were expanded into national systems of surveillance. It focuses first on the insidious and omnipotent listening techniques of East Germany's Ministry for State Security, better known as the Stasi, as they expanded the scope and reach of military surveillance into the domestic population of East Germany. It subsequently explores state-sponsored programmes inspired by the Stasi's appetite for recording, such as the US National Security Agency's PRISM; the Echelon programme run by the 'Five Eyes' of the United States, Canada, the United Kingdom, Australia and New Zealand; and the Russian government's SORM programme. The part charts the transformation of audio intelligence techniques, from being used to spy on enemy states to being deployed on everyday civilian communications, as revealed by whistle-blowers such as Edward Snowden in 2013. At a cultural level, the four chapters reveal the slow corrosion of expectations surrounding notions of personal privacy that accompanied this systematic remodulation of listening.

Addressing the epistemic shift from large-scale international monitoring systems to the infiltration of personalized domestic spaces, Part III interrogates our own complicity in self-surveillance. It concentrates on the smart revolution, and more pointedly on how we invite smart technologies such as mobile phones, speakers, smart children's toys and Wi-Fi baby monitors into our homes. We do so in the hope of rendering our lives more comfortable, convenient and connected and willingly sacrifice personal space and confidentiality in the process.

The ensuing recalibration of boundaries regarding personal privacy has significant ramifications for the ways in which audio intelligence captured from our homes is used to inform the development of AI and the composition of Large Language Models (LLMs). Underpinning the chapters is the supposition that capitalism has been modded and rationalized by surveillance, whereby data capture becomes the primary function of a product or service. For scholars such as Shoshana Zuboff, this equates to a tangible shift in the economic order of things that has resulted in the inception of a new era, that of surveillance capitalism (Zuboff 2019) – surveillance in service to the interests of capital. But it is also capitalist surveillance – capitalism in the service of the production of an omniscient computational sensorium.

Part IV of the book switches to a more speculative mode to review a set of existing generative AI technologies and the possible trajectories that might develop from their wider development and use. It starts with MIT's 'AlterEgo' device, through which the act of listening transgresses the internal/external divide of the body to capture the inner voice via the micro-movements that we enact through our neck and jaw when thinking. The rise of virtual companions and the futures of AI-generated music are also considered here, so that we hear more clearly how the most intimate of spaces and relationships are being mined by companies to ascertain behavioural patterns, capture data and apply detection theory (the capacity to distinguish signal from noise) so that the probability of any relevant outcomes can be economically leveraged. This is a contemporary recalibration of Pythagoras' *Music of the Spheres*; *Musica universalis'* celestial bodies of the sun, moon and planets replaced by those of the data, corpus and prompts.

An analysis of 'thanabots' concerns the closing chapter of *Listening In* – chatbots based on the data and recordings of dead people – signalling the transmogrification of vital fluids into digital phantoms. Also referred to as 'ghostbots' or 'deadbots', thanabots are emergent technologies within the rising grief tech sector that animate AI-driven avatars to achieve digital immortality. The chapter considers the implications of future modes of surveillance that are based not only on the information captured from those who have passed but also on the extractive potential of predictive data attributed to embryonic bots or 'embots', digitally divining the future by listening in on those who are yet to live.

From pre-life and post-death to new forms of non-human sentience, audio surveillance devices and processes map an arc of expanded and abstracted lifespans. At the same time, another arc is also being drawn, one which bisects the axis of temporality. This one charts the modulation of those sonic surveillance practices as they become algorithmic techniques; a mode of comprehension that permits us to more accurately gauge our emerging and future relationships with disruptive and innovative technologies such as AI, robotics and holography. Drawing on thinkers such as Sherry Turkle and Donna Haraway, the book composes a multisensorial approach to its case studies in order to probe the way such technologies are redefining our relationships with ourselves as well as with the world around us.

Sonic filters that deliberately avoid our tendency to use visual metaphors are deployed throughout the book to explain the connections between modes of surveillance precisely because they presciently echo the ways in which 'intelligence', in all its exegesis, has been captured, augmented and transmitted since the Second World War. As such, sound and frequency-based terminology and concepts are utilized throughout the book. They build off the work of a diverse array of practitioners and theorists such as Jacques Attali, Salomé Voegelin, J. G. Ballard, AUDINT and Caroline Bassett in order to amplify the narrative quietus of untold and unsound histories and futures.

Our articulation of AI cultures has also been influenced by the growing critical body of work related to machine learning, AI and its use in intelligence and commercial sectors. Running through the book is the proposition that historically, there has been a lack of criticality surrounding the erroneous ontologies, transgressive ethics and political power of advanced computing. It suggests that the field of AI, emerging in large part from the clandestine practices of military surveillance and espionage, has often been treated as a science-fictional platform upon which to speculate over future harms or affordances without considering its historical or current effects.

Even when encountering critical voices, we submit that the supremacist notion of a singularity-like 'intelligence' of AI systems is a noise-cancelling counter wave: that the assumption of emerging technological brilliance is rarely disputed. *Listening In* positions that notion as a dangerous prescription rather than a smart prediction. This aspect of the book is presaged and guided by the work of practitioners and theorists such as Kate Crawford, Hito Steyerl, Safiya Umoja Noble, Manuel DeLanda and Matteo Pasquinelli to help us navigate critical pathways from the early Cold War period to the present day and beyond.

Given that the trajectory of AI is predicated on furtive listening, it is reasonable to assume that the unspoken waveformed foundations shoring up this new digital 'hyperobject' will influence its evolution. It is also reasonable to assume that the digital sensorium and its distributed nodes of perception will likely not be what humans identify as mechanisms for producing feelings or agency. Instead, artificial agency will, through massive datasets, estimate new types of thinking and awareness that are not dependent on the capacities of the body's sensory mechanisms to deliver external information to the brain. While our anthropomorphic tendencies often lead us astray when trying to understand other forms of intelligence, here they can serve us briefly as they point to the deep learning that stems from covert and duplicitous perception.

Listening In reveals how the twin dials of transgression and intimacy are turned with increasing velocity as new internalized forms of monitoring, such as the AlterEgo, emerge. It has been written to help us understand how associated sonic techniques, belief systems and cultural obsessions with capturing and archiving data and recordings have been overlooked as primary drivers in the development of AI. From remote foreign bodies to intimate domestic spaces to the inner voice and post-death vocal reconstruction, sonic surveillance has continuously targeted the capture of personal dynamics and relationships. The bonds of emotional intimacy between friends, lovers and families, even the connection to one's own thoughts, have been, and are being, reconfigured by technologies that monitor our phone calls, text messages, emails and social media posts.

Our mapping of privacy has been abstracted, and, in many cases, our capacity to navigate it has been dissolved by our yearning to document, analyse and share the minutiae of our lives. The nebulous acoustics of privacy have been problematized to the point where we do not even know whether the unheard realms of personal intimacy are desirable anymore. *Listening In* narrates the recalibration of our relationship to surveillance and the ubiquitous chronicling of public and private domains through sound recording. Sound has become a sensorial channel through which we narcotically transmit information about our personal desires and activities. And as we do so, we 're-up' our commitment to supplying newly evolving forms of algorithmic intelligence with a vast library of sensory information. The most intimate of human sounds data is being used to soundtrack the composition of a new epoch. We are in the mix. One track peaks, another comes down. Listening in, tuning out.

PART I
EMBEDDED BUGS AND TUNNELS

E PLURIBUS
UNUM

CHAPTER 1
THE THING

Process

The modern history of audio intelligence starts in Soviet Moscow on 4 August 1945, though it would be nearly seven years until its significance was realized by the Western Allies. Towards the end of the Second World War, Russian schoolchildren presented a carved wooden replica of the Great Seal of the United States to the US ambassador to the Soviet Union, W. Averell Harriman, as a symbol of ongoing trust and cooperation between the two countries. In reality, its presentation was the first whisper of the Cold War. The surveillance bug secretly concealed within it would be used to listen in on Harriman's conversations and those of his successors in Spaso House until its discovery in 1951.

The new technology that powered the bug was a technical feat that would accelerate the development of audio intelligence for the next two decades: a passive listening device with no wires or power source. Encased within the decorative wood carving and sat just behind the eagle's beak, there were barely visible pinholes, made by a jeweller's drill. These tiny breaches in the sculpted timber allowed voices to enter the bug's resonant chamber. The flexible diaphragm that sat within it changed dimensions accordingly. Rather than relying on batteries that would need to be replaced, or a wired source of power that would be easily detected, the microphone was activated by an ultra-high frequency signal beamed to it from a van parked near the building. The signal modulated when sound waves from conversations struck the bug's diaphragm, before being reflected back to listeners hidden in the stationary vehicles outside. The nature of this arrangement, of intermittent listening and device operation, meant that it was, and still is to this day, almost impossible to detect (Isecom 2008: 298).

The listening device became known as the Great Seal bug, also referred to as The Thing by intelligence communities. Developed by the Russian technologist and inventor Lev Sergeyevich Termen, better known in the West as Leon Theremin, it is widely considered to be one of the first effective uses of passive RFID technology, which is now commonplace in digital tracking and logistics systems. In many ways, the bug echoed functional aspects of Theremin's eponymous musical instrument, 'the theremin' (also referred to as the 'etherphone'), created in 1928. This early electronic device is also activated without being touched, and at the time of its invention, challenged previously held expectations regarding cause and effect through its uncanny manipulation of vibrational physics.

Listening In

From 1927 until 1938, Theremin lived in the United States with his wife Lavinia Williams and had become a minor celebrity with his pioneering instrument. As a musical device, it was a precursor to the synthesizer but it differed significantly given that it was played without physical contact, harnessing what scientists at the time of its invention dubbed the 'ether' – a medium filling all space and 'serving as a carrier of electromagnetic waves' (Glinsky 2005: 21). The ether was an *occulere* expanse that Theremin would try to make further inroads into when attempting to develop television technology in Soviet Russia. It was also the realm that he thought held the answers to bringing a deceased lab assistant back to life.

The Soviet Union allowed Theremin to tour his invention around the United States and Europe, registering patents and generating income that would later be used by the USSR for activities against American interests. However, after fewer sales than expected and mounting debts, he suddenly returned to the Soviet Union in 1938. Other theories about the motives behind Theremin's sudden exit from the United States range from homesickness to tax evasion and state kidnapping. What is known is that on his return, and for many years after, he would be put to work in a secret *sharashka* laboratory in the Gulag camp system. It was during his time as a Soviet military scientist that he was tasked with designing The Thing by the notoriously brutal head of the NKVD (the secret police in Soviet Russia before the emergence of the KGB), Lavrentiy Beria. Beria's brief to Theremin specified that 'there could be no wires, no traditional microphones, and the system had to be encased in something that would not call attention to itself' (Glinsky 2005: 259). The Thing's military design reflects Beria's exacting control of the operation, but the device itself exemplifies its inventor's artistic flair and occult preoccupations.

Recording

In 1940s Russia, audio surveillance was taken for granted among enemies, with all Russian employees at the US ambassador's residence under scrutiny by the Americans. Upon their arrival, guests at the building were given cards welcoming and warning them that they should expect to be under constant surveillance:

> Every room is monitored by the KGB and all of the staff are employees of the KGB. We believe the garden also may be monitored. Your luggage may be searched two or three times a day. Nothing is ever stolen and they hardly disturb things. (Hyde 1988: E3490)

We can only guess how this affected the guests and residents of the US Embassy and therefore what was recorded by the Great Seal bug. Known surveillance changes the behaviour of the people being listened to (Schneier 2018: 309), whether it results in self-censorship or engaging in more active modes of obfuscation. Given the background radiation of suspicion within the United States and allied diplomatic and intelligence communities, it was all the more impressive that the bug remained undiscovered in the study of one of the most strategically important Western diplomats of the time, for as long as it did. The key to its success was its undetectability, but this also made the recording process relatively difficult and complex to transform into military intelligence. A high degree of accuracy was required to activate and receive audio back from The Thing, and recordings were collected strategically, as the bug was only vulnerable to detection when in use. Activated too often, it would be discovered, but engaged with too infrequently, important intelligence might be missed.

Even with such obvious technical challenges, this innovative method of recording continued to impact Western acoustic surveillance over the two decades following its discovery. Immediately after it was found, the British navy sent six scientists to a dedicated Marconi lab where they reverse-engineered the bug's technology and developed their own listening device called 'SATYR' for the UK's domestic counter-intelligence and security agency, MI5. Later in the same year, one of the engineers, Peter Wright, described devising an iteration of the surveillance technology 'using two British umbrellas as transmit and receive antennas' (Wright 1987: 23).

Eighteen months into the project, intelligence officer Roger Hollis reportedly remarked upon the 'black magic' of the British prototype during its first demonstration (Wright 1987). There are declassified accounts which show that the FBI had also studied The Thing, borrowing equipment from the National Bureau of Standards to determine its ultra-high frequency (Conrad 1952a, 1952b). SATYR was subsequently used for espionage by the British, American, Canadian and Australian militaries throughout the 1950s, typically against Soviet Russia or Eastern Bloc countries. Its influence was reflected upon by the second ambassador to the Soviet Union, George F. Kennan, who witnessed its uncovering:

I have the impression that with its discovery the whole art of intergovernmental eavesdropping was raised to a new technological level. (Murray 2017: online)

In 1960, the Great Seal bug found renewed significance when US senator Henry Cabot Lodge Jr. cited it to the United Nations as a defence against claims that a U-2 spy plane shot down by the Soviet Union in their airspace represented an exceptional violation of international law. Referencing the bug, Lodge attempted to illustrate that it was part of a historic pattern of espionage and counter-espionage between Eastern and Western powers at that time. These dramatic revelations entered the civilian imagination, sowing the seeds of intrigue that, as later chapters will show, gave way to a cultural acceptance of secret voice recording in our everyday lives. The technical sophistication of the device and Lodge's demonstrations also helped to gentrify the practice of acoustic surveillance conducted by private investigators (PIs) in domestic cases: the idea that experts could use precision audio equipment to record and listen to any utterance was subsequently cemented into mainstream consciousness by Francis Ford Coppola's 1974 film, *The Conversation*.

Coppola hired Hal Lipset, a PI and the chief investigator on the Watergate Senate Committee, to consult on the film's audio surveillance techniques. During the committee hearings, Lipset demonstrated how a listening device could fit into an empty martini glass (Holt 1991), which showed how pervasive the spectre of 'bugging' had become in media representation. He was also credited by his peers as someone who legitimized the PIs' standing alongside the lawyers they often worked with (Gray 1981). The shadowy world of spycraft was coming up for air, replete with a sophistication that suggested our senses could be made to work overtime (and distance) with a little help from technology.

Transgression

One of the most transgressive aspects of the Great Seal bug was that it had been given as a gift. If US officials had refused the carving, it would have introduced complications, given the political sensitivities of the time. So, rebuffing an apparent gesture of goodwill was not an option. It was therefore placed on display in the study of the embassy, a room that was used for multiple purposes and guests over the years, with US secretary of state George C. Marshall using it as his bedroom during a visit in 1947 (Glinsky 2005: 271). Such massive intelligence gains could only have been possible by subverting the cultures of both gift-giving and folk authenticity to gain access to this intimate space.

The voluntary nature of the Americans' adoption of the Great Seal into the US Embassy spoke to its function as a gift, a 'present generously given even when, in the gesture accompanying the transaction, there is only a polite fiction, formalism, and social deceit, and when really there is obligation and economic self-interest' (Mauss 1950: 4). The decorative carving of the national symbol of the eagle did not need to have a clear utility, making its placement in US territory a strategic leveraging of this ancient form of exchange. Two essential elements in traditional gift-giving are the honour conferred by wealth and the obligation to reciprocate (Mauss 1950: 11), which the Americans did not do directly. Their involuntary reciprocation was the transfer of information to the Russians. The Thing's discovery constituted an unintentional second gift to the United States in the form of assimilated technology that fed into the development of passive listening devices such as SATYR.

The Great Seal bug also employed the perceived authenticity of traditional craft as camouflage. The roots of Russian wood carving reside in popular peasant culture of the nineteenth century, where it was displayed on the facades of houses. Many buildings are, in fact, still 'proudly crowned with perfectly carved heads of horses, deer or ducks [rising] high above the banks of the huge Northern river' (Kruglova 1981: 8). Choosing a folk-art sculpture to conceal a cutting-edge listening device played to US sensibilities regarding their burgeoning reputation as a global superpower. The eagle, a symbol of aerial superiority and surveillance, and an apex predator that the United States had aligned itself with since the Second World War, had been corrupted. Theremin had taken the worm out of the bird's mouth and hidden it in a carving.

Even for experts, the aura of the gift protected it from immediate suspicion: when the bug inside the gift was first discovered, the security technician who located it removed the wooden carving and took a mason's hammer to the wall that it was hung on. He was looking for the source of the signal, but upon finding none, the bemused specialist reasoned that the listening device must be inside the eagle (Glinsky 2005: 271). After The Thing, it was not just the walls that could listen; it was literally anything and everything. As we shall hear throughout the book, we cohabitate with a mixture of known and unknown listening devices – phones, speakers and toys to name a few – uncertain as to how our utterances may be used.

The Great Seal bug, therefore, was a precursor to the smart object, a 'gift' of modern technology that would subsequently transgress the public-private divide and open the door to domestic surveillance. Transmitters can be hidden in any small recess, and microphones fitted into pens or smoke detectors. Powering these devices passively meant that physical clues such as wires were no longer reliable indicators of audio surveillance, fragmenting the paradigm of spyware into a more paranoid landscape for private citizens. What was once embedded in architectural fittings has now transformed into a reality in which all objects potentially monitor us, especially those which we invite into our homes.

Worlds

While The Thing's purpose was to help the Soviet intelligence community predict US government foreign policy and military machinations, it was also part of a 'techno-colonial lineage' described by Ben Vickers and K Allado-McDowell (2020) as being as prescriptive as it is predictive. It helped to bring into being the irrationally anxious template of the Cold War world through the noisy and incomplete acoustic intelligence material it gathered, where the worst prediction was still the least risky to hinge action upon. Through its discovery and technological proliferation via Western intelligence circles, it also increased the use of bugged objects and spyware across military operations and media representation.

In the 1940s, the use of covert listening devices was not new in Allied circles. However, the bug's housing in an emblem of American power gifted by children seemed to proscribe a new type of military philosophy: that of Russian *Maskirovka*, which advocates strategic deception in the form of disinformation, trickery, fictionalizing and fakery (Jones 2007). Prediction as a process is the antithesis of *Maskirovka* as it is dependent on information deemed to be dependable, measurable and realistic. It models aspects of the future with present data and determines what is important enough to trigger likely events. In its own discrete way, The Thing predicted and proscribed a global future in which the United States and the Soviet Union, who were allied at the time, would become enemies, and in doing so defined the greatness of their superpowers in opposition to one another. In this sense, the bug ate its way out of the heart of the seal and infected the way that the United States perceived itself in relation to intelligence gathering and its subsequent global standing after the Second World War.

As we trace the narrative arc from audio surveillance to AI, we will also map the rhythmic exchanges of surveillance and listening technologies as they are regularly shuttled between military and civilian worlds, each switch legitimizing and contextualizing the other. In both worlds, use case scenarios and attendant levels of funding and cultural investment, technologies such as simulators, game engines and AI are incrementally developed for different markets or use against enemies, the baton of development handed to whoever is running the fastest. For example, Theremin's RFID technology spawned new possibilities, recalibrated for a range of applications, from contactless payments to the telemetric tracking of animals and humans through the evolution of 'Smartdust' – a system of tiny microelectromechanical sensors that can detect a wide range of phenomena, from chemicals to vibration (Marr 2018).

More recently, RFID has moved back into military usage in conjunction with the rise of the Internet of Things (IoT) to improve the efficiency of supply chains via enhanced logistics tracking. As Theremin's technology gains proximity to its subjects, it becomes part of the objects it tracks, checking and reinforcing the worlds that separate them from other data points. Thus, the remote nature of the Great Seal bug presaged developments in an array of touch-free technologies explored in later chapters: from voice-activated home speaker systems to baby monitors. The Thing predicts other 'things', but crucially, they are things that have innate intelligence built into them – a type of sentience that we are still trying to understand, and one which radically alters and questions our comprehension and relationships with our own inner lives.

Prediction

The function and purpose of surveillance in domestic products are malleable. The default position of any device that gathers data is to store it, with attendant sensitivities largely ignored. In this way, the erosion of personal privacy has been slowly normalized in line with the trajectory of military surveillance technologies as they have morphed and infiltrated domestic spheres. From deliberate data points assembled into a story by human minds, to a fabric or material that only an algorithm can make sense of. In this way, the extension of listening through the use of the Thing also signalled a new kind of data intrinsically linked to contemporary AI cultures. While human covert listeners had always been expected to summarize and analyse what they heard when reporting intelligence, the use of a bug offered the possibility of verbatim transcription and a new surveillance ideal: the notion that all secrets could be realistically overheard. In this scenario, more comprehensive and systematic forms of listening would lead to not only new, more accurate ways to predict enemy actions, they would also guide behaviours in the light of clear statistical indicators.

Against this idealistic backdrop arrived the problematic reality of noise in data, caused by the technical limitations of a device or by interference from unwanted voices. Technological static, irrelevant conversations and cross frequency capturing were included in this new type of frequency-jammed dataset. The archetype of a complete spoken-word dataset and the noise or 'dirty' data within it would become increasingly normalized in intelligence communities over subsequent decades. This was exemplified best by the Snowden Files leak in 2012, where a lack of intelligibility in dense surveillance data was shown as the standard conditions under which our personal data is being construed and commodified; the rapid accumulation of intelligence but relatively slow attribution of meaning spawned a neurotic desire to extract patterns from maelstroms of random statistics (Snowden 2014).

In the seemingly paranoid world view that defined the Cold War period, any notion of a dataset was replete with the characteristics of being partial and incomplete, with anxiety, conspiracy and fearful speculation filling the gaps in understanding. The Thing represented the beginning of a new approach to data, a period in which the evolution and success of collection techniques would lead to an abundance of information that was practically impossible for humans to comprehend. Prediction became implausible without the analytic assistance of machine learning tools. Therefore, it might be more accurate to designate 'apophenia' – the perception of patterns in apparent randomness – and not paranoia, as the most telling driver for both intelligence and AI communities during this period of geopolitical tensions (Steyerl 2020).

Intimacy

Intimacy is a conspiracy that covert listening hijacks. What traditionally occurs as a voluntary exchange between parties is transformed into an infringing act that violates the subject, whose disclosure is meant to be balanced by mutual vulnerability. The listener's uncovering of details of the subject's life is given extra credence as we have difficulty taking people at face value and instead treat the discovery of secretive utterances as a hallmark of apparent truth (Marar 2014: 71). By circumventing all suspicion through the camouflage of the gift, the Great Seal bug bypassed the listener's distrusting tendency because information collected covertly is a discovery. The utterances captured by The Thing were intimate because their vulnerable speakers did not know whether to layer text over subtext, as someone could have been listening at any moment. To intervene in the private lives of subjects from a distance is the basis of modern surveillance. However, discovering secrets requires an investment, either in developing trust between confidants or in the development of technology that bypasses secrecy.

Theremin's approach to bypassing traditional modes of intimacy was based on his invention of devices that put distance between the body and the button. After the immense media furore that followed the kidnapping of aviation hero Charles Lindbergh's baby in 1932, Theremin devised an electromagnetic alarm system for use around a crib. It was an ancestor of the Great Seal bug's passive listening, wherein the alarm would be tripped if an intruder penetrated the electromagnetic ring (Glinsky 2005: 149). It is also an ancestor of the electronic baby monitor, technology that opens a remote yet close(d) channel between infant and guardian.

Children, like musical instruments, are playful; play with both involves processes patiently fostered in muscle memory and trained through harmonious relations. Theremin's solutions to problems in both areas deferred to the otherworldly, a realm in which the somatic elides a graspable identity. In the perceivable world, the repercussions of this contactless existence were not the sole province of the Soviets. In fact, another altogether more brutal trajectory was being traversed by the United States, who, shortly after The Thing was planted, 'pushed their own button' on Nagasaki and Hiroshima, killing hundreds of thousands from a distance.

Voice

During the chaotic aftermath of the Second World War, in the tumult of unidentifiable bodies and bulldozed rubble, national boundaries and futures were porous, ready to be reimagined and recomposed into newly orchestrated relationships. Just as the six-year period from 1939 to 1945 was sonically defined by destructive slabs of noise, their rhythms and cadence were coordinated by the voices of all-powerful leaders such as Winston Churchill, Adolf Hitler and Joseph Stalin. And as these voices, with their enhanced amplification technologies, shouted, screamed, insulted, supported and goaded new realities into being, they became the arch wranglers of worlds; their power manifested in the transmogrification of vibrations into tangible, lived systems. In short, the voice was the most powerful of aural mechanisms, a resonating delivery system of immanent potential.

At the beginning of the twenty-first century, the voice no longer holds this elevated place as the composer of global shape-shifting realities that veer and storm like errant weather systems. Now, datasets, AI systems, surveillance tapes, sex tapes, social media, memes, deep fakes, analytics and market research are just some of the arrangers and bearers of new realities. The colliding and shifting nature of these worlds chafes against each other, creating discontent and violence because the production tools, digital asset management systems and professional distribution networks available to the masses are so sophisticated. Worlds can be built out or hinted at in short time frames, with personal expressions that bypass the need for the human voice. The reactive nature and speed of their creation make it appear as though they have existed over the long term. The power of speech that once summoned these spheres into being has been acoustically separated into a skein of channels, each holding a digital percentage of influence once held by the analogue voice.

It was within the 1940s envelope of captured voices that Spaso House became a microcosm of political intrigue, a perfect stately storm of global power shifts, an official residence of betrayal. As noted, those stresses and ruptures would widen and come to presage the onset of geopolitical tensions with the United States on one side of the yawning divide and Russia on the other. Technological sophistication augmented the act of giving with chicanery and subterfuge. In between the silences and distrust of those strained relationships, mutterings of potential nuclear devastation and a mass species extinction event seethed in the ears of the global corpus, a piercing mantra that uncoupled rhyme and reason.

In this tense fulcrum of macro politics, among the aural choreography of espionage, Soviet agents would relocate other bugs within the US Embassy on a daily basis. The building became an international theatre with staff playing misinformative roles, voices practised and performed, assuming a remote audience. Echoing the disquiet associated with suspected hidden presences, George F. Kennan penned his memoir in 1967. In it, he outlined in detail how his own study was being bugged by the Soviets. He wrote:

> It is difficult to make plausible the weirdness of the atmosphere in that room, . . . one was acutely conscious of the unseen presence in the room of a third person: our attentive monitor. It seemed that one could almost hear his breathing. All were aware that a strange and sinister drama was in progress. (Soniak 2016: online)

To combat the suspected surveillance, the FBI asked Kennan to engage in conversations about declassified subjects with colleagues, such as his secretary, in order to encourage Soviets to listen so that they could sweep for signals. Kennan, recalling how he had felt the weight of the ether, suggested that 'the air of Russia is physically impregnated as ours is not' (Glinsky 2005: 272).

Deliberately undermining the authenticity of the ambassador by not delivering anything of any strategic use, the staged voices produced scores of disinformation. False leads, confusing logistics, fake news before it could go viral – all were archived and interpreted, creating oral datasets that pertained to nothing other than the unstable logic of phased deception. The trajectory of the voice that speaks to sinister dramas with non sequitur plot twists is mapped through this book. It travels through the national archive culled from Stasi surveillance, to the omnipotent global surveillance systems that play on our fears pertaining to socially mediated terror, and on through to the artificially intelligent futures of human expression. The drama is still unfolding, of course, the composition of voices within it becoming ever more abstracted and asymmetric. The signal-to-noise ratio always erring from the former to the latter.

Fidelity

The quality of the signal emanating from the Great Seal bug is unknown to this day. However, its creator, Leon Theremin, was considered the pre-eminent scientist of signals in Soviet Russia at the time, and indeed fidelity was central to both his professional and political career, as well as to his personal safety. In order to improve the intelligibility and fidelity of audio collected for Joseph Stalin, Theremin was tasked with reducing noise in the recordings. The latter's sense of personal fidelity was also challenged by Lavrentiy Beria, who forced him to listen to Stalin via microphones hidden in the leader's apartment without his knowledge. Had listening in ever been loaded with more trepidation?

Monitoring Stalin was posited as a test of Theremin's personal fidelity to the leader of the Communist Party and to Russia versus his own personal safety. 'Treading this precarious line as servant of two masters – trapped in Beria's web of intrigue and stealth, while, like every citizen, bound in an implicit allegiance to the godhead Stalin – [Theremin] dug himself in more deeply than ever' (Glinsky 2005: 262). Oscillating between the technicality of listening and the art of noise cancellation, Theremin's work with the KGB was as much a thin wire as a highwire act; the single sensory channel of hearing that was employed to gain information, actively closing down the rest of the sensorium, reliant as it was on the vulnerable and noisy aural vector and its monosensory mechanics. Listening, in this manner, exacted an intimate violence, a transgressive extension of presence among the hiss and the hum.

The dynamic of noise within any act of communication is instructive here. French philosopher Michel Serres proposes that, within the exchange of sonic information, noise is located ambiguously, being both peripheral and central in the formatting of communication. He writes, 'given: two stations and a channel. They exchange messages. If the relation succeeds, if it is perfect, optimum, and immediate, it disappears as a relation. If it is there, if it exists, that means that it failed. It is only mediation' (Serres 1982a: 79). Developing Marshall McLuhan's discourse concerning the nature of the medium (McLuhan 1964) and the inevitable transformation of content that occurs in its passing, Serres concludes that noise is an inevitable presence within all acts of communication.

Noise signifies the ways in which the medium transforms the original intent of the sender. The definition of this interference is adherent to, and utterly dependent on, the operating dynamics of the channel, which leads Serres to surmise that noise is also representative of the parasite. As Stephen Crocker notes in his essay on Serres, in French: 'parasite can mean the unwanted noise of communication, an uninvited guest, or a life form that lives off another. It is not just any particular organism or noise, but rather the appearance of the medium, which compels any given system of order to either adjust to its presence or expel it' (Crocker 2007: online). The staff in Moscow's US Embassy adjusted to being monitored by feeding random data back into the listening system, creating a feedback loop of informational discord. In this scenario, noise was an omnipotent presence; it echoed everything it came into waveformed contact with. It could also be rendered as an agent of exchange.

As the book unfolds, we shall hear how the status connected to the ability to distinguish signals within noise transforms and is modified by the capacity to detect patterns in data. The increasing significance and investment in technologies that help derive narrative from tumult run hand in hand with the cultural desire to capture the history of vibrational matter, whether it be generated by humans, birds or the big bang. The Great Seal bug is the first step in our short history of such desires and situates the modern continuum of audio surveillance within them. The book subsequently charts how the role of associated listening techniques moves from merely extending human perception to creating new forms of intelligence and sentience.

CHAPTER 2
OPERATION GOLD

Process

In the 1950s, working in conjunction with the CIA, the Secret Intelligence Service of Britain's MI6 conducted one of the most audacious audio surveillance operations of the Cold War period. Making use of communications cables that had previously been laid in the nineteenth century by the German Imperial Postal Service (Vogel 2019: 60) they monitored the landline communications of the Soviet Army headquarters in Berlin. Gaining access to previously unheard-of amounts of Soviet intelligence, the initiative was named – maybe in line with the value they thought they might unearth – 'Operation Gold'. The operation consisted of a 1,476-foot long, 6-foot-wide tunnelling operation (NSA 1988: 3). Logistically, it comprised multiple instances of line tapping along with the analysis of 67,000 hours of taped Russian and German conversations over official Soviet channels. To enquire as to whether the operation was worthwhile begs the consideration of two important caveats. The first alludes to a British spy's betrayal of the tunnel to the Soviets before the first shovelful of dirt had even been moved. The second concerns the problem of effectively analysing the huge avalanche of taped conversations that were captured before the advent of AI to help with such onerous tasks.

Operation Gold was led by the CIA's William King Harvey and was named as such because it updated a previous 1949 strategy called 'Operation Silver', which involved the tapping of Soviet lines in Vienna by the British head of station, Peter Lunn (Huntingdon 1995: online). The tunnel dug for Operation Silver, however, was only 70 feet long, terminating at a decoy British clothing store, whose commercial success interfered, ironically, with its clandestine tapping activities (Huntingdon 1995: online). After offering to share information in 1951, the British intelligence services suggested to the CIA that Berlin should be the next site that they subterraneanly explore together (CIA 2007: 2).

The project was complex and not without its problems. Along with diplomatic complications, the geological makeup of the site was less suited to excavation than had been initially reported. The United States and Britain began tunnelling into enemy territory in 1954 and carefully tapped three major trunk cables by March 1955, after the tap chamber was completed (Vogel 2019: 60). Instead of a clothing store, the terminus of the allied tunnel was a two-storey warehouse in West Berlin that had a US Army radar above it (NSA 1988: 5). Construction workers were given instructions to dig a basement with a 23-foot high ceiling to store the dirt excavated from the tunnel, as 'security and silence dictated that not one cubic foot of soil be removed from the site'

(G 2008: 2). East German border guards were under the impression that the warehouse was a 'poorly concealed radar intercept station' (NSA 1988: 5) complete with its large parabolic antenna atop, keeping enemy binoculars looking up rather than imagining what could be happening underground. The warehouse was built in the Altglienicke district, a US-controlled sector of Berlin to the south-east of the city that was selected for its supposedly low-water table. Information about the area suggested that it was mostly flat with uneven drainage and that the low-water table would keep the electronic instruments safe from the damp. The information turned out to be incorrect. The water table's proximity to the surface meant that the tunnel needed to be dug closer to heavier footfall and to Soviet or East German tank pathways that camouflaged the sounds of digging over a 1,400-foot vector of excavated espionage (NSA 1988: 3).

During the digging of a 450-foot test tunnel in New Mexico, it was determined that the soft Berlin soil might betray the tunnel's existence through a telltale furrow in the ground above (Martin 2018: 83). Concerns over the aboveground impression of the tunnel were at odds with the reality of the moisture underground. The cables that were being aimed at in East Berlin were reportedly buried 27 inches deep alongside a busy highway. This meant that the tunnel's tap chamber needed to support not only the weight but also tolerate the constant movement caused by the rolling infrasonic waveforms of heavy trucks (CIA 2007: 14).

Another unavoidable challenge lay in the moment of tapping the communications cables. To keep the moisture out, the cables were pressurized with nitrogen, and breaking that seal would have been obvious to anyone monitoring them (Huntingdon 1995: online). After the Americans had led the digging of the tunnel, the tapping was carried out by the British, who used a shield fitted with slats to dig a vertical shaft, incrementally jacking the shield up towards the cables (Martin 2018: 89). The British telecoms technicians successfully clipped wires to the circuits, sending signals to amplifiers and through the tunnel to sound-activated tape recorders in the warehouse. 'Visitors to the warehouse were struck by the eerie sound of 150 recorders hissing and whirring as they started and stopped in response to the stolen signals' (Martin 2018: 90).

By March 1955, the tunnel, tap chamber and tapping had all been completed. The KGB was aware of the operation from the beginning and did nothing to stop it, nor did they apprise Soviet or East German users that they were being listened to. Orchestrating a misinformation campaign of that scale was not feasible for the KGB, and they allowed themselves to be monitored so that they could preserve what they considered a much more valuable asset: the British double agent who had informed them of the operation in the first place – George Blake. The chamber's public discovery occurred twelve months into the surveillance operation in April 1956, after Blake had received a transfer. Thus, it was when their mole's identity was no longer at stake that the Soviets were free to discover the tunnel. This publicly occurred when an East German repair crew was addressing damage caused by heavy rainfall in Berlin (NSA 1988: 17). A microphone in the tap chamber picked up the sounds of voices discussing the details of what they had found at

02.00 am, though the significance of the chamber took hours to apprehend. It was 06.30 am when the microphone picked up the phrase, 'the cable is tapped' (NSA 1988).

Recording

Processing the sheer volume of taped conversations in Russian and German languages constituted a complex operation of its own. There were 600 tape recorders ready to receive the transmissions, so many that 'a few spymasters worried that the installation would noticeably affect the world market for recording tape' (Huntingdon 1995: online). By the end of the project, approximately 50,000 reels of tape had been recorded, representing the capturing of 40,000 phone conversations. After the tunnel had been shut down and abandoned, it took a further two years to process the massive volume of audio data that had been collected. Operation Gold processed an average of 1,300 phone calls per day, requiring translators capable of deciphering 'astonishingly prolific and creative profanity' in Russian. They even went to the trouble of creating a glossary labelled 'Top Secret Obscene' (Vogel 2019: 206). Carloads and mailbags of tapes were sent from Berlin to Frankfurt, then eventually on to Washington in the United States, where the material was studied at the Hosiery Mill (Huntingdon 1995: online). To deter any curiosity about their contents, boxes of tapes were passed off as uranium samples and carefully packaged in boxes lined with lead (Vogel 2019: 202).

One of the devices used to separate clear text from coded messages was referred to as the 'bumblebee', 'so called because, like the real bumblebee, all the laws of physics decreed it would never get off the ground' (Martin 2018: 110).

> The 'bumblebee' played the tapes at 60 inches per second, four times the speed at which the captured signals had originally been transmitted, breaking down the 18 channels of each circuit into separate recordings – 'demuxing', in the communicators' jargon. The 18 separate recordings were then placed on slow-speed recorders linked to teletype machines that printed out the message in clear text at 100 words per minute. (Martin 2018)

Analysing 67,000 hours of conversations, collected over the period of a calendar year, in a fashion timely enough to respond to threats of nuclear destruction was an ambitious but understandable endeavour given the stakes were so high. The intelligence precedent set by Operation Gold was in part due to its systemic, almost cybernetic take on surveillance. By capturing a glut of audio data from low-level members of the KGB and seeking to understand its significance post hoc, the operation adopted a different methodology from the more surgical stance taken when targeting individuals. As such, Operation Gold can be linked to today's culture of networked technologies that handle, store and exchange big data; the traffic analysis that could be undertaken on both being metaphorically exchangeable. Yesterday's tunnel is today's metadata.

Transgression

Burrowing from West to East Berlin in 1954 was more than a contravention of territorial boundaries; it was a transgression of one of the world's deepest ideological lines drawn between capitalist and communist systems. During Operation Gold, thresholds between states were marked with such heightened levels of volatility that notions of 'approaching' became as provocative as activities that 'went beyond'. Mid-twentieth-century Germany was truly a bipolar state, caught in the mania of simultaneously running dual socio-political operating systems. Connecting the two territories via an underground tunnel was analogous to a temporary subconscious conduit being constructed that linked the two enclaves.

The geopolitical extension of presence over contested boundaries is the most obvious physical form of transgression, but from a sonic perspective, there is another channel of Operation Gold to explore. CIA generators powering the tunnel's digging machinery hummed and droned into the night and kept the neighbourhood's residents awake as a result. The Italian Futurist musical composer Luigi Russolo would have been proud of the noise and consternation caused by the military; their machinery updating the *intonarumori* noise sculptures that he created between 1910 and 1930. Silence was certainly not golden, nor was it attainable for those living within earshot of the British and US burrowing.

> As far as most Altglienicke residents were concerned, the problem with the American camp was not the strange antenna dishes, but rather the infernal noise from the three diesel generators that ran twenty-four hours a day, providing independent power for all the electronic equipment at the installation. Neighbors complained the noise rattled their windows and could be heard from a mile away, disrupting sleep. Harvey, for one, was delighted with the racket. Not only did it make it nearly impossible for the KGB or Stasi to effectively bug the installation, but the noise and vibration 'assist greatly in concealing construction noise below the ground', he told Truscott. (Vogel 2019: 172)

Noise is traditionally unwanted; it is excessive. It is a by-product, aural detritus. 'noise takes sound *out of order*. It's chaos' (Henriques 2003: 467). It challenges physical demarcations of space by extending the agency, physicality and operations of others into those territories considered private or personal. This is because waveforms move material at a subatomic level and transfer content into and beyond the dermal interface of the body. Noise has no time for borders or thresholds. It is, by nature, a transgressive force that brings spheres of influence into collision with each other. For media historians Johnson and Cloonan, 'We live in a world in which noise is the site of contestation' (2009: 163). Collision, extension, contradiction – these are the vectors of affect that noise invokes and works through.

When the generator's noise permeated the surrounding neighbours' houses, it did not stop there. It flowed through the dermal interfaces of the residents. Soaked up and vibed up (albeit in the wrong way), the sound of excess and projected presence found residence in flesh, bones and sinew. It is this intrusive quality of waveforms that allows others' presence to manifest in a spatiality that one thinks of as their own, delivering one's will into the intimate presence of another. Having any phenomena intrude into this space means that one's own agency is echoed back in an enervated feedback loop.

Deploying waveforms to extend their presence underground, the CIA and MI6 used noise as camouflage – noise as a by-product of negative space, noise as the inverse of excess. In sonic terms, this operation was the antithesis of the US military's Ghost Army (Beyer and Sales 2015), which, during the Second World War, produced excessive sound and noise with large truck-mounted speakers to convince the Nazis of presence on the front line when there was none – a martial hauntology (AUDINT 2014). During Operation Gold, noise was used to convince a Berlin neighbourhood that there was no presence at all, especially none that intended to transgress the line splitting the city.

> Movies were shown every night, though the volume had to be turned up full blast so the soundtrack could be heard over the din of the generators. To cope with the noise, the soldiers got in the habit of shouting at each other like they were deaf. Everyone became so used to sleeping with the generators that when they 'suddenly stopped one night, the slumbering men all woke up' (Vogel 2019: 246).

Acoustic anchors are part of the way we understand, navigate and form attachments to environments. When they are covered by pop-up soundscapes, everyday existences are questioned and challenged – 'that one no longer has ownership of one's own sounds is a profound and painful violation' (Johnson and Cloonan 2009: 158). It was the transgression of personalized soundscapes that came to represent the breaching nature of this surveillance programme. A sonic reading of a listening event, where the channel between the underground (soil) and overground (sun) resonates with the anodyne potential of both. Golden brown.

Worlds

As the Cold War escalated, two new imperial powers were emerging with drastically different world views, each contingent to some degree on the collapse of the other. As Hannah Arendt would describe in the 1973 update to her 1950s treatise on power, *The Origins of Totalitarianism*, '[t]he initiative for overseas expansion has shifted westward from England and Western Europe to America, and the initiative for continental expansion in close geographic continuity no longer comes from Central and Eastern Europe but is exclusively located in Russia' (Arendt 1973: xix). Berlin became the outpost of both of these new contested worlds, making its border both symbolically and practically important. The idea of physically breaching the boundary marker between worlds was so challenging that even President Eisenhower, the initial sponsor of the operation, was taken aback by its reality and refused to sponsor subsequent tunnel projects (Martin 2018).

Eisenhower's belated hesitancy about the project also signified another slippage between worlds that were growing apart during the early 1950s, which Operation Gold would owe much of its methodology to: the rise of 'invisible government'. The CIA's influence was described by its head, Allen Dulles, in 1958 as having become the most influential of any government in the world (Arendt 1973). But its growth had less to do with existential threats to America and more to do with the fear of a challenge to its world power and influence by 'the revolutionary power of Moscow-directed communism' (Arendt 1973: xx). To the CIA – the invisible branch of the US government with its secretive mandate to maintain US power overseas – the notion of tunnelling below ground in a space entirely invisible to those walking above made perfect operational sense. The visible was breached or bridged by the invisible, not through sight, but via sound.

The 'visible' communist world of East Berlin was vulnerable, not to being spied upon, but to being listened to. Its secrets were condensed into words, its words condensed into mechanical sound that flowed through specific interchanges. The visible above-ground boundaries of each world were incontestable, but the invisible subterranean world provided a different, softer reality. Beneath the hard-tarmaced ground of modern Berlin lay its Pleistocene Ice Age prehistory. Its sandy soil, deposited by glaciers some two-and-a-half million years earlier, made it possible to dig noiselessly by hand but also made tunnel collapse a constant concern (Vogel 2019). Tunnel collapse was not the only concern for US and British operatives seeking to maintain invisibility. Once installed, the electronic equipment room 'jammed with amplifiers, transformers, and tuners' created high levels of heat that required air conditioning (G 2008: 6). When the equipment began to overheat, the Allies scrambled to cool it down before the winter freeze set in: the worry being that 'a frost-free black mark might appear on the roadway over the equipment room . . . calling attention to something strange occurring below the surface' (G 2008).

The rise or collapse of bodies that might messily expose the subterranean to the world above is imagined by philosopher Reza Negarestani as horrific, the exhumation of the tomb: a metaphor for decryption of code systems, where meaning has been buried. It is 'the deflowering of the face . . . marring and mangling it . . . by messing up the surfaces. . . . [Exhumation] is basically polluting and infecting as it undergoes surface collision' (Negarestani 2008: 51). And yet, in Negarestani's imagined exhumation, the cold rises up from the grave, rather than heat. Operation Gold's corpses were cold but ethereal: sonic bodies, deadened and robbed from the mass grave of the telecom interchange. The grave robbers in this sense were already below the surface, and the infection had taken hold in West Berlin.

Prediction

While previous acoustic surveillance projects had garnered challenging amounts of data, Operation Gold was undoubtedly the point at which the quantity of recorded data began to challenge its usage as a predictive method and suggested to its owners the need for centralized and mechanized data processing systems. The amount of data to be processed by a pre-digital administration was staggering. According to the CIA's own report on the project, in Washington and London processing centres, 617 people transcribed the Soviet and German voice reels. Adding to the density of the data packages received, each six-hour voice reel could also contain approximately '216 hours of teletype messages' (CIA 2007: 25). In short, it was impossible to process the data as quickly as it had been purloined, even by two well-funded intelligence services. At this point, the utility of the data as a tool for prediction was absurdly compromised, and the cost of the project had ballooned to $6.7m.

The combined intelligence agencies' inability to predict the realities of the prodigious amount of data, and the associated problems of transcribing and making sense of so much conversational information, suggests a general lack of imagination regarding the exponential scalability of technologized listening. Those close to the project realized the problem. Soon after the recording of telephonic voices to tape began, future CIA director Richard Bissell Jr. considered rationing the number of words that could be transmitted in a month. Bissell 'was convinced that this flow of words into Washington was probably counterproductive' (Bissell in Huntingdon 1995: online). His suggestions were ignored by analysts.

Operation Gold was an experiment in which the large-scale mechanized overhearing of all conversations and gossip from East Berlin offered the potential of total intelligence, free from the biasing effects of an individual eavesdropper. In the book *Technic and Magic: The Reconstruction of Reality* (2018), Federico Campagna describes 'technic' as being based on technological progress and thus constituting the predominant ideology of the global north. In technic, the 'paradoxical complexity of reality' is less important than the 'linear seriality of production' (Campagna 2018: 18–19). Through this world view, the business of making information was more important than its quality, and it did not necessarily obstruct its power to predict contingent realities. To Campagna, the contemporary malaise of technological realism – from quasi-corporeal virtual reality to mass propagation of disinformation over distributed networks, coined as 'fake news' – relates to a disintegration of reality, or 'the substitution of a world of things with a world of empty names' (Campagna 2018: 18). With its focus on the production and quantity of data at the cost of veracity, timeliness and reliability of knowledge, Operation Gold can be seen as a precursor to the more distributed surveillance systems explored in Part II of the book: a world of predictive networks that fill empty names with potentialized bodies.

Intimacy

As vast amounts of audio material were being mined out of the tunnel, the resulting tapes being extracted and stockpiled formed magnetic mountains of frequency-based information. According to J. C. Evans, 'a lot of it seems to have been gossip' (1996: 44). In the subterranean vacuum left by the lack of foundational evidence of the recording's worth, waves of CIA anxiety flooded back in. 'If the tunnel was responsible for any great intelligence coups, nobody has yet revealed them' (1996). Instead, CIA operatives were learning that the 'wife of a general was smuggling Oriental rugs back to the USSR or that another general was about to become a father. There was a reason why the Soviets did not send any important data over the tapped lines' (1996).

The value proposition, or rather the lack thereof, with regard to gossip, is instructive. Gossip is considered idle, divisive and a waste of time. When reported during Operation Gold, gossip was also framed and referred to in a deeply gendered manner. This has been the case for centuries, certainly since Richard Brinsley Sheridan's 1777 comedy of manners, *School for Scandal*, in which the social capital and fluid nature of gossip among the upper classes are observed and dissected. The book submits that gossip is a pervasive and powerful challenge to reality. It undermines healthy and functional social structures and aids those who wish to manipulate others by propagating such corrosive memetic narratives.

Defined by Richard Dawkins as a unit of cultural transmission (1976), a meme can be understood as a trend, a piece of slang, a conspiracy theory or as gossip. These are all unofficial language-based vehicles that spread information quickly at micro and macro levels, via a range of delivery systems in any given social context. Infectious by nature and culture, gossip can be understood as a virulent force that is dangerous precisely because of its feminine (and therefore, supposedly unpredictable and conniving) connotations. Roll on two-and-a-half centuries, and gossip has found its perfect transmission technology in the form of the internet – and, in particular, social media. And when it is coupled with conspiracy theory to form narratives of disinformation and misinformation, it can become politically lethal. This is when gossip's gendered role gets swiftly reassigned, and it is considered a weapon.

In 1904, Russia understood the power of disinformation and misinformation before most, when they started strategizing deception and camouflage through Army schools. *Maskirovka*, which literally translates to 'masking', is the name of the military doctrine conceived of over a century ago, and it still serves as the principal online schema for information warfare. More recent right-wing ideologues, such as Steve Bannon and Nigel Farage, and groups such as 'QAnon' and '8chan', have understood the power of 'reality chaos' and have assimilated Russian strategies of *Maskirovka* to replace fact, science and research with conspiracy theories, half-truths and, at times, pure fantasy.

Operation Gold was one of the first instances of gossip being strategized and weaponized on a mass scale. The monitored Soviet army headquarters in Berlin, which had been tapped for significant political and military information, was instead picking up and delivering smears and rumours. The wave-formed gold being mined constituted an intimate economy of social capital dialled into the networked (il)logic of *Maskirovka*. In this sense, the Soviet superspreaders functioned like early viral marketers. They dropped their hushed tones and influence on the right sets of ears to propagate a product, in this case, their own scored brand of confidential tittle-tattle.

On one level, the captured gossip transmitted little about the future plans and strategies of the KGB, but from another unforeseen frame of reference – that of the hidden organizational hierarchy of the security agency and the complex dynamics of its constituent relationships – it was useful. Those who were listening could ascertain whose partners were in line for favours and whose wife was able to book the best hairdresser. 'For the analysts, even such trivial details held clues about who was up and who was down in the byzantine Soviet hierarchy' (Vogel 2019: 217). Quidnuncs – purveyors of tittle-tattle – became the unintentional mediators of informational by-products that accrued new value. For the CIA and MI6, their investment in Operation Gold was paying off through the bonded agency of secure intimacy.

Voice

The Russian and German-speaking voices that passed through the operational interchange were stolen from their conversational context and trafficked en masse across national and language lines, where they became foreign to those listening in, encrypted by natural language. While automated machine translation had shown promise as early as 1954 in the United States, a machine translation system capable of operating at scale was still decades away from becoming a practical reality (Nye 2016). Thus, messages spoken in a certain tongue could only be heard and understood by other speakers of that language, and most easily by native speakers. Operation Gold would problematize the most extrinsic features of the human voice in conversation: the language that it speaks.

Language as a form of encryption was a common method of codifying military messages at the time of the operation. During the Second World War, both US and British forces had weaponized minority national languages that had military value precisely because they were not widely spoken or understood outside of national boundaries. The United States employed 'Code Talkers', Native Americans fluent in little-known Native American languages such as Navaho or Choctaw, to add a layer of encoding to military intelligence communications (CIA 2008). The British, meanwhile, had employed Welsh speaker radio operators in a similar way, although to a lesser extent (Chapman 1987). While German and Russian were common enough languages outside of their respective countries, the industrial scale of translation services required to review the data caused problems.

Post-war borders were not as porous as before the conflicts, and native speakers of languages spoken by Russia and wartime enemy Germany were no longer considered trustworthy, particularly in the United States. Following the First World War, the act of speaking German was considered such a dangerous transgression of national borders that twenty-two American states had banned the speaking of it. The bans were soon repealed by the US Supreme Court in 1919 (Nye 2016). However, Russian and German natives were considered to be compromised for intelligence work and were, by default, screened out of CIA selection processes for Operation Gold. As a result, only English speakers with varying levels of knowledge of German or Russian as a second language could qualify as translators to work on the project. Eventually, the agency was able to assemble 'a minimum crew for the job' who, through 'intensive language training', could gain 'near native fluency' (CIA 2007: 15).

The British had fewer qualms about foreign words and workers. In London, the disembodied conversations of Russian speakers were reunited with listeners from their own country: '250 Russian émigrés working out of an office near Regent's Park' translated all Russian-speaking conversations (Huntingdon 1995: online). For these workers, through listening to conversations, confidences, gossip and anecdotes from home, their native language was not only a tool for deciphering and decrypting but also a way to access a ghostly imaginary – the physical image of their homeland, decentred and at a distance. Nermin Saybasili evokes Michel Chion's 'negative image' when describing immigrant voices in media: the ghost image evoked by a displaced voice and language (Saybasili 2010). Through their language, places and cultural references from their home country, these voices reflected a 'counter-geography haunt[ing] the nation state' (Saybasili 2010: 330). Listening in a place where the voices were unintelligible to the average listener had the same effect, permeating the soil of Britain and America and disrupting each nation's 'lines of exclusion'. It foreshadows the nomadic digital culture where voices can travel anywhere, which, to Saybasili, is far from being a 'timeless and spaceless place'. Rather, it is haunted by the mediated human voice and the phenomena of dislocation and migration (Saybasili 2010: 320).

Fidelity

Tests of fidelity during the Cold War corresponded to a time when the generally perceived soundtrack of a spy was that of the icy resonance of a cocktail shaker. The cultural image, meanwhile, was that of an immaculately suited man holding a martini glass in one hand and a Walther PPK in the other. In a tally of James Bond's drinking across Fleming's novels, he consumes '1,150 units of alcohol in 88 days, amounting to about 92 units a week, roughly four times the recommended safe limit' (Johnson, Guha and Davies 2013: 1) (which by today's standards clocks in at over six times the NHS's guidelines). Such alcohol-fuelled narratives were reminiscent of Fleming's own habits as someone who reportedly drank a full bottle of spirits a day. He died somewhat prematurely, but possibly not unexpectedly, at the age of fifty-six (Johnson, Guha and Davies 2013: 2). Reflecting this era of 'heroic' excess, a range of military staff involved with Operation Gold found themselves subject to William Harvey's use of alcohol, both as a party and truth lubricant, where he instituted a rite of passage known as the 'Harvey Martini Ritual' to gauge who he could trust (Vogel 2019: 75).

Harvey's wife at the time remarked on his attitude towards alcohol as a 'tool of the trade' (Vogel 2019: 154). Unsurprisingly, the culture of fluid excess propagated by Harvey often led to volatile exchanges between co-workers who blended personal and professional desires and conflicts as if they were mixing vermouth and gin. While digging the tunnel, workers were only allowed to go out in Berlin occasionally, but even then they were told not to drink too much beer as it was a security risk (Vogel 2019:

169). Listening to music in nightclubs and socializing in cafes in the city meant that military personnel were embedded in oscillating layers of recreation and espionage; rest and relaxation interwoven into symphonies of overlapping purposes. Cold War Berlin became a composition of maximal intrigue, made all the more intoxicating by the heady mixture of alcohol and music.

Russians are renowned for their dangerous and mind-bending prowess for consuming vodka. Such endeavours were bestowed with further complications when put into the context of espionage. During the Cold War, the Soviets developed a pill called RU-21. It was the product of over two decades of research by the Russian Academy of Sciences, and it was aimed at 'K.G.B. agents who wanted to stay sober while getting their contacts drunk' (Acocella 2008: online). The ambition was simple: get targeted 'marks' inebriated, and among the noise and the chatter, tongues would loosen and information would spill from their mouths; their fidelity to cause and country remixed by their devotion to having a good night out.

Alcohol permeates early stories of espionage, and in Operation Gold, it was the only explanation that one East German technician could offer as to how the initial tap was not discovered when it was made. 'Everyone must have been quite drunk', he said (Vogel 2019: 282). Echoing the underground venture, the overground tunnel opened up by RU-21 is represented by the chemically aided strategy of psychologically burrowing into sobriety. The ethanol became the metaphorical drill that mined the compromised cerebellum, hippocampus and frontal lobes. The loyal inner voice, buried and guarding classified information, was the target of the operation: an intoxicating venture that would have been soundtracked by music and laughter rather than the banging and drilling that accompanied the underground excavation.

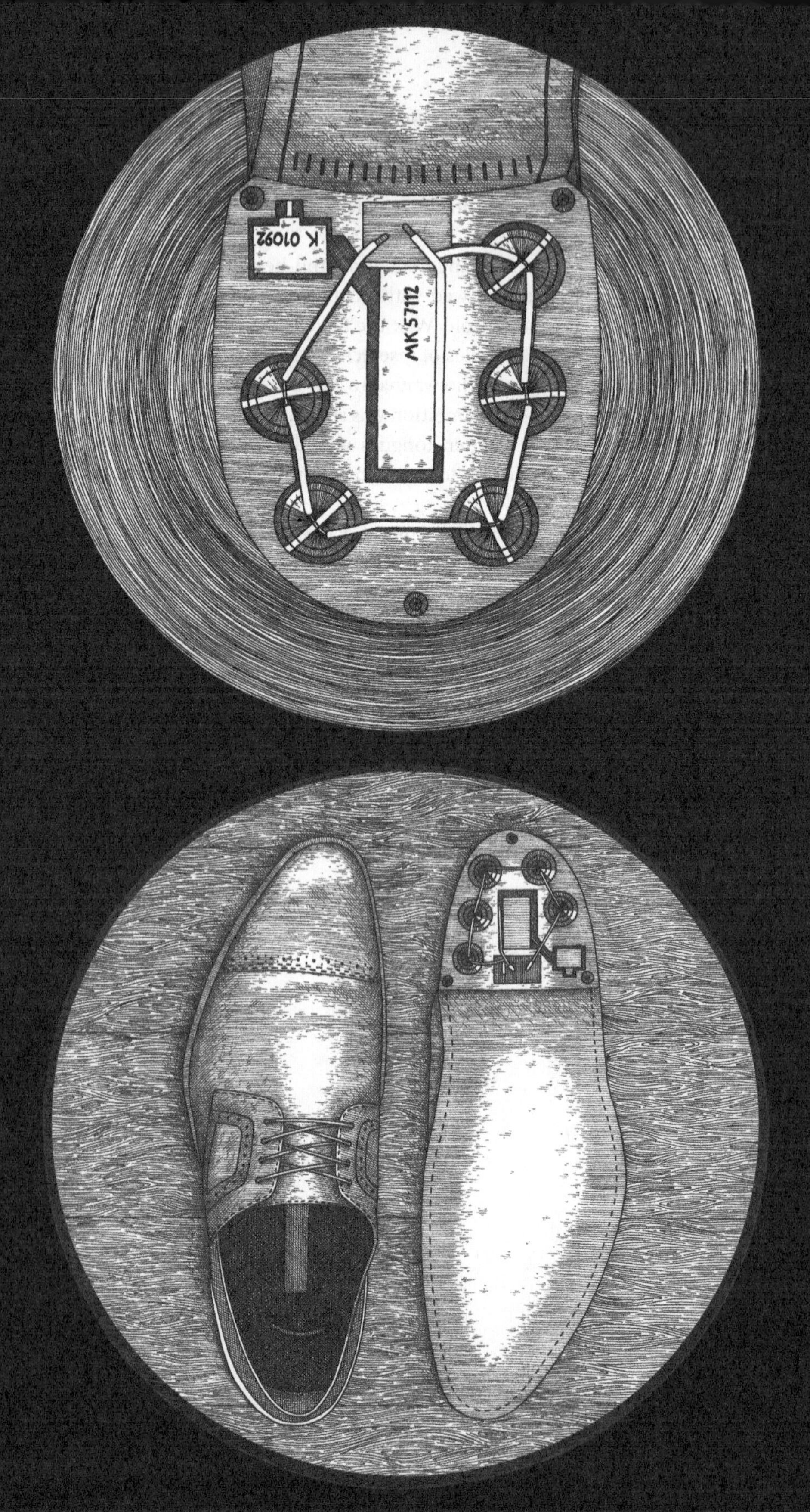

K 01092
MK 57112
K 01092

CHAPTER 3
SHOEHORN

Process

Harry G. Barnes Jr. was at his desk when a colleague came to the door waving his hands silently. Unable to decode the silent gesturing, Barnes was handed a piece of paper with the hastily scribbled words 'you are on air' (ADST 2012: 74). It was 1969 and Barnes was the US deputy chief of mission in Bucharest, Romania: an important regional diplomatic post. In the same year, Barnes had been on air in a completely different capacity when he became the first US diplomat to publicly speak on Romanian national television (Martin 2012). As sophisticated public broadcast media was becoming more ubiquitous in Europe, so too was clandestine media recording. On this occasion, a signal sweep of the architecture by Office of Security (SY) agents revealed that a classified conference taking place within the building was being picked up and broadcast.

What confounded the intelligence officers was that the office where the conference was taking place was considered a communication-secure space, an acoustic conference room (ACR) 'designed to thwart outside listening' (DSS 2016: 50). Barnes was asked to move offices. His colleagues then conducted a process of signal triangulation and confirmed that the bug followed him. This was unusual. The notion of mobile technology was decades away from being adopted into common usage, and it was not yet commonplace for a listening device to be concealed on someone's body, with them unaware of its presence. When questioned about his clothing and habits that day, Barnes remembered that he had requested the heels of his shoes be repaired, and that this was the first day of wearing them again:

> I had sent them out with our maid. She'd come back and I'd put them on one day and then when I started to walk around the house, they didn't feel comfortable. One heel felt a little bit higher so I sent them back and when they came back they were OK but that of course, gave a clue as to where to look. (Constable 2012: online)

After a brief inspection, a microphone and transmitter were found installed in the heel of the shoe. The housekeeper, who was working for the Romanian security services, had fitted the bug when Barnes had given her the shoes for reheeling. The Romanian security services were particularly well resourced and organized in the field of acoustic espionage. Each county-level *Securitate* had a unit called 'T' or 'Tonola', which was a specialist audio surveillance unit responsible for providing the 'technical means of carrying out audio surveillance . . . [placing] microphones in homes and offices and telephone taps at exchanges' (Deletant 1995: 342).

The Tonola unit would also transcribe and pass on information to whichever directorate had requested it. In this way, the T unit focused on collecting audio surveillance, while another unit, 'R', 'kept an ear open for clandestine radio traffic' (Deletant 1995: 342), helping to shut down unfriendly surveillance or information sharing over its own airwaves. It is most likely that Tonola was responsible for the invention of the mobile heel bug and rolled it out across a number of operations: sources suggest that the incident was one of many examples of bugging shoe heels during this period (Maloney 2016). While Barnes's shoes were tampered with when they were being repaired, in other cases, new shoes were intercepted by the Romanian postal service during their delivery from Western Europe and bugged at that stage.

It is unclear whether these surveillance efforts ever led to significant security gains for Romanian intelligence services, although in the cited case, communications during a secure conference were successfully broadcast. Nevertheless, the speed with which the bug was picked up would have made gathering data difficult. After the incident, US security services better understood the threat of mobile bugging in relation to their security arrangements. In response to the Shoehorn bug, SY agents took measures to reduce the risk of such 'low radiation' devices being able to send clear audio signals out of secure conference rooms. Initially, they used plastic and foil wrap to block transmission until longer-term adaptations could be made to such secure spaces (Hove 2011: 178). It is interesting to note that since the end of the 1960s, there have been no further reports of footwear-based listening devices.

Recording

It is fitting that the operational signature of this chapter – 'Shoehorn' – is concerned with slipping the body into confined spaces to fully mobilize the attendant technology. Originally, shoehorns were made from animal horns. When detached from animals and blown into, horns become naturally occurring speaker systems that signal distress or attack. This is an early example of bone, aimed towards the skies, both conducting and extending the sonic agency of humans.

The soundscapes residing at the level of head height and above have, for centuries, been associated with the celestial, the religious longitudinal ordering of waveforms in which the 'voice of God' comes from 'heaven on high' – a preordained construct that finds its frequency-based expression in Ps. 18:13 of the New International Version of the Bible: 'The Lord thundered from heaven; the voice of the Most High resounded.' The spatial sanctity of the cathedral, and more particularly, of the area above head height, was and still is reserved for surveillance and sonic expression from a ubiquitous intelligence, whether that be spiritual, technological or a mix of both. At the beginning of the twentieth century, this dynamic was strategically deployed in the religious cathedrals of capitalism – factories. At the start of the twenty-first century, this waveformed strategy finds expression in shopping malls and airports (Heys 2019).

Conversely, soundscapes that reside closer to the ground are inhabited by the spectrum of lower frequencies often referred to as infrasound. They are long, rolling waveforms that flow through and around objects with minimal dissipation and traverse long distances. Naturally occurring phenomena such as earthquakes, tornadoes, waterfalls and volcanoes generate infrasound, while animals such as alligators, elephants and whales perceive and utilize it to communicate over hundreds of miles. Infrasound can also be understood as being 'unsound', thus those frequencies that reside outside the range of human hearing and which pertain to alternative modes of perception and agency.

If we listen through a different filter, ground-level noise can be associated with the everyday, with that which is discarded, waveformed waste. For those who devised the Shoehorn system, did they think that among the noise and excess resided undiscovered information – base/bass truths? Narratives that do not ascend to the range of earshot descend to ground level and inhabit a different aural realm of throwaway lines, ditched hisses, rejected scrapes, discarded clicks and abandoned thuds. Maybe the thinking was that among this confusion would reside unheard snippets of essential narratives: a longitudinal approach to listening that embraced and actuated the vertical interpretation of lo(w)-fidelity.

While the leather handmade footwear sent to diplomats would have been fashioned to have long lifespans, the batteries inside the recording devices had very short life expectancy. Short-term thinking fitted into long-term motility; the compressed periods of time available for transmitting and recording opened small windows of opportunity dependent on miniaturized flows of energy. The overarching irony here is that the Achilles heel of any mobile technology was, and still is to this day, the powering of the component parts. Batteries are still the electrochemical hearts of complex technologies. They power devices that are utterly dependent on their peripatetic functionality to be considered desirable.

Mobile listening affords access to a series of fluid interlocking spaces rather than enabling presence within a singular expanse. Correspondingly, the drive to miniaturize recording devices and attach them to the form of the human body can be traced back to initiatives such as Shoehorn. This recording format signalled new ways of thinking about modes of perception and questioned how they are re-calibrated according to 'the way we prioritize mobile space over physical space' (Bassett 2003: 348). Of note here is the way in which frequency-based mobile surveillance spaces of the 1950s transition into the hyperconnected digital spaces of the IoT and notions of the Metaverse. Accordingly, our skills in negotiating datascapes are, and will increasingly become, more vital than those required for navigating physical terrains as information transfer becomes the apex processor of mobility. Commenting on the period preceding the advent of IoT, and on the multiplicity of mobile spaces that encourage transition, digital-humanities theorist Caroline Bassett states that

> an older sense of the distinction between the landscape and the journey, and of the spatial dynamics underpinning this distinction, no longer pertains. These days, as mobile-equipped travellers, we operate in that speed-blurred band that used to demarcate the division between landscape beyond the rails and the fast-moving space of the train. Or, rather, there is no longer a boundary but only an interface. You are advised to 'take your world with you'. (Bassett 2003: 346)

At the time that Bassett wrote about the erasure of the boundary and the proliferation of interfaces as new compositional markers of emotional topographies and transgression (2003), it was an astute observation. It still is, but what has changed is the distributed location of, and the agency imbued within, the interface. It is no longer solely bound to the consumer-friendly destination of our pocket-sized mobile devices. A myriad of portals to the internet's fluid digitality are now located in a disparate assemblage of objects, from speakers to holographic partners, from baby monitors to decoders of the inner voice. And all of them have the capacity, and more than that, the coded will, to listen and record.

Transgression

As listening devices migrated from fixed spots on the wall to the mobile targets of bodies during the 1950s and 1960s, concerns over privacy in the United States were also migrating from exterior concerns of citizens' affairs to invasions of the 'personal interior: the mind, emotions, thoughts, and psyche' (Igo 2018: 101). America's distrust of its own citizens was exemplified by Joseph McCarthy's anti-communist House Un-American Activities Committee. Somewhat ironically, this corresponded with the state itself keeping more secrets than ever before, by 'cloaking a range of national security actions, including the atomic weapons program' (Igo 2018: 100).

In tracing the history of privacy in modern America, Sarah Igo draws a connection between Cold War-era individualism and the transgression by society into the 'porous' figure of the individual. She goes on to claim that during this period, the perimeter of the self was considered to be something 'unfixed, her very being improperly inhabited by the larger society' (Igo 2018: 101). This psychological permeability can be read as an analogy for the dissolving border of the outer body as the last private barrier against an onslaught of surveillance technology. It is porosity that also corrupts the continuity of the history of sound as a history of the body (Sterne 2003: 12), a figure whose inherent subjectivity defines listening and the listenable. The psychological excavation of the individual's inner world retraced the border of the body, laying vulnerable an inward territory that was aligned with, and by, national security.

Body-mounted listening devices are culturally scripted according to whether the body is aware of them or not. The familiar trope of a Mafia informant – the 'rat' – wearing a wire taped to his chest, sweating excessively for fear of being discovered, operates as a self-fulfilling prophecy of paranoia. The rat cooperates under duress from both sides, threatened by institutions of law that can revoke the right to privacy, as well as by the more pugilistic institution of the crime that he is reporting on. His fear of being discovered leads to behaviours that betray him, such as unusual speech patterns and jittery movements. He is not the surveillance target; rather, he is the disposable lightning rod for the carceral state.

The body unaware of the listening device is more familiar as the target of surveillance itself. This subject's paranoia is more widespread as a facet of a distrustful society. No longer only worried about unseen ears listening for incriminating slip-ups, the surveillance target in a mistrustful society worries about a self that is wholly incriminating simply by being. The technology developed for this purpose is a 'repeatable social, cultural and material' process that has 'crystallized into mechanisms . . . previously done by a person' (Sterne 2003: 8). The kind of listening network employed by the *Securitate* has crystallized into technology so invisible that it does not even need to be present to fulfil its repressive purposes.

Devices such as the Shoehorn bug, grafted onto, or around, the body rather than installed into an environment, reflect the state's comprehension of the targeted and nervous body that is veering in and out of control. It is vulnerable precisely because it is always on the verge of betraying itself, of divulging its own state, whether that be physiologically, psychologically or politically. More than that, it can reveal such characteristics without even having a clear understanding of the nature of that betrayal. The State's attempt to police its own citizens' thoughts and intentions during the Cold War spoke to 'Americans' worrisome lack of control over their inner resources' (Igo 2018: 122), an embodied territory that, once identified, shifted the bounded nature of privacy further inward.

Worlds

Covert listening devices are technological exemplars of miniaturized worlds within worlds. They are compressed mechanisms that extract the waveformed DNA of a culture's inner lives. Previously secreted within inanimate objects, bugs transmitted information from one socio-political system to another. Bugs developed to be transitory in nature, however, recalibrated how valuable information could be extricated and transferred. In the world of Shoehorn, bugs connected cultures that functioned within radically different socio-political and socio-economic contexts through channels of 'down at heel' deception.

Surreptitiously transporting covert weaponized agency from one culture to another finds its zenith during the mythological Trojan Wars of the fourteenth to twelfth century BC. Employed by the Greeks to covertly enter the city of Troy, the Trojan Horse had elements of surprise built into it – soldiers hidden inside the large four-legged form. But what happens when the gift is neither novel nor out of the ordinary? The clothes and shoes designed and produced in the 'sophisticated' cultures of London and New York were subversive gifts of a much more quotidian nature; the hollowed-out desire inherent in the newly augmented footwear signified a rethinking of the Trojan Horse model.

Worlds do not so much bleed into one another but are rather ambiently forced through the transfusion of cultural products and ideas, from one powerful culture into the circulatory system of another that is less economically robust. Camouflaged by rhythms of leisure rather than by traditional patterns of conflict, powerful nations wage modes of soft war by utilizing cultural vehicles to spread their influence (Heys 2019: 109–10). Design, art and literature can all be made to serve these purposes, with music being particularly effective because it is ephemeral and relatively easy to distribute.

The Romanians assimilated cultural imperialism by tapping into its propagatory potential. They observed the aspirational pressures that drive individuals to want to own products, ideas and identities from a culture that is considered more influential and dominant. Listening has its own distinct history when it comes to the soft weapons of cultural imperialism. When concepts and identities are transmitted through speakers, headphones and earbuds, music evidences its capacity to propagate cultural messages at speed. If we open the envelope of understanding of sonic influence, we could also consider the ways in which audiences have been aurally targeted in a more duplicitous manner.

The British use of radio propaganda against the Nazis during the Second World War from Allied bases and during the Cold War in West Germany (see more in the Worlds section of Chapter 5) is telling here. More recent examples include the use of spoken word, sound and music by US' PSYOPS via 'black' radio stations to win over hearts and minds during every American conflict since the Second World War (Psywarrior, History of PSYOPS page: online). Outside of frequency-based strategies, other notable instances of cultural forms of expression being utilized for military purposes have been outlined in Heys and Hennlich's 2010 article *The Art of Conservative Détournement*, and evidence its contemporary development:

> The Operational Theory Research Institute, an Israeli Defence Force 'think tank' directed by Shimon Naveh turned to the philosophy of Guy Debord, Gilles Deleuze and Félix Guattari, the architectural work of John Forester, Bernard Tschumi and Clifford Geertz, and the 'Anarchitectural' site-specific urban interventions of Gordon Matta-Clark to facilitate the re-spatialization of contemporary military theory and strategy; the US military's use of music for battlefield preparation as well as for torture in Guantánamo Bay and Abu Ghraib; and Canadian military training centres such as 'Pretendahar' in Toronto which prepared soldiers for combat in the Middle East, referencing 1990's installation art practices. These examples give adage to the notion that this is not military business as usual, but rather the martialing of the business of culture. (Heys and Hennlich 2010: 61)

According to Paul Virilio, war 'is in every way an art, a *theatre of operation* where stratagems are essential to deceive' (2005: 96). Potentially more destructive, however, is the act of listening because one wants to, not because they are aurally inveigled. This is when self-seeding narratives from dominant cultures take root in meaningful ways because they embed themselves into the topsoil of primary experience and, in doing so, stultify the growth of other, more fragile storyworlds. As Edward Said states in *Culture and Imperialism*, 'The power to narrate, or to block other narratives from forming and emerging, is very important to culture and imperialism, and constitutes one of the main connections between them' (1994: XIII). During the Shoehorn era, Western diplomats' desire for culturally superior goods was exploited by the Romanians, who replaced the shoe's resonant cavity of desire with the facility to both overhear and underhear.

Prediction

Sweeping for bugs necessitates a degree of prediction as to where they might be installed. The development of countermeasures aimed at thwarting covert listening occurred in response to the discovery and preemption of enemy listening technology. The expectation that walls should grant a degree of privacy, or at least some control over the information revealed within them, can be traced to habits of the wealthy during the Middle Ages. The transition from open, common living spaces to more diversified rooms afforded house dwellers the capacity to store an increasing number of material possessions such as books (Webb 2007a: 221). Privacy was and remains a resource-intensive concern that anticipates interlopers.

Privacy was not something Henry Barnes expected to enjoy while serving as a diplomat in Romania. Remembering his time there, during a 2011 interview with Charles Stuart Kennedy, he acknowledged that the cars that he and his colleagues drove, complete with diplomatic licence plates, made them conspicuously foreign. Acts such as checking into a hotel required the somewhat theatrical presentation of a diplomatic card and passport, but that 'didn't mean there wasn't surveillance, they were just a little less obvious' (Barnes in Kennedy 2011: 76). The harassment Barnes was used to in a city like Moscow apparently did not follow him to Bucharest, and the US diplomatic presence in Romania under Nicolae Ceauşescu – the last communist leader of the country – was informed by Romania's willingness to be a 'somewhat different' part of the Soviet Empire (Kennedy 2011: 63).

While the Soviets wanted to capitalize on Romania's agricultural capacity for the whole community's benefit, the Romanian leadership felt that the country should have a stronger industrial base as well (Kennedy 2011: 62). During the 1960s, the country was also undergoing a process of de-satellization from the Soviet Union, with Romania having declared independence in 1964. Ceauşescu's difference of opinion on Romania's role as an autonomous and more diversified communist country did not, however, extend to rejecting Soviet totalitarian tactics of mass surveillance and repression.

The surveillance measures that were deployed across Soviet countries made it difficult for foreign officials to operate and led to countermeasures being taken, such as the ACR, which was first installed in Moscow by the US Office of Security in 1960. Walls that were meant to ensure privacy had been discovered to house covert listening devices, so ACRs were built from clear plastic and aluminium and were commonly referred to as 'bubbles' (USDS 2011: 176). Specifications and protocols for the first generation of ACRs read as such:

> 12 feet by 15 feet, or 12 feet by 20 feet, and had 5 inches between the interior and outer wall, with a door to enter and exit the secure space. After removing all furniture and fixtures from an existing room and sweeping it for bugs, SY engineers erected the ACR to create a secure room where Embassy officers could hold classified discussions without concerns of bugs. (USDS 2011)

The installation of static bugs inside the walls of a room meant that ACRs were designed to circumvent similar bugging tactics. As described, the discovery of the Shoehorn bug in Barnes's heel led to the security office modifying the ACRs. After the incident, officers 'covered ACRs with Reynolds plastic wrap to reduce the radiation of low-power devices such as shoe bugs' (USDS 2011: 178). The legacy of constructing specialized rooms (sometimes called War Rooms) to protect sensitive conversations continues today with 'Sensitive Compartmented Information Facilities' (SCIFs), specially designated spaces in which the need for privacy is telegraphed by the intensity of their surveillance countermeasures. SCIFs are used for the 'processing, storage, and/or discussion of sensitive compartmented information' (NIST), though each may have a different policy on footwear.

Intimacy

The placing of a bug in a Western shoe, a fashionable and prestigious item, especially in 1960s communist Romania, exploited an already risky space on the body, a place where intimate personal expression becomes public. Fashion and clothing are accordingly 'respectable and disreputable, . . . both communicative and deceptive' (Barnard 2002: 182). Items in this space express personal desires, projecting sincerity, authenticity, bluff and hubris, success and failure. Where better to hide a listening device than a bodily site marked with risk and anxiety, where wearers are sometimes considered 'victims' of fashion (Barnard 2002: 183)? Fashionable clothing was a key element of the growing cult of Western consumer-centred individuality. It had changed out the needs of the biological body for the need to feel in vogue. Sociologist Zygmunt Bauman would later describe this need as an endless shopping list of personal desires that we are at first compelled, and then addicted, to completing:

> We 'shop' . . . for the kind of image it would be nice to wear and ways to make others believe that we are what we wear . . . for ways of drawing attention and ways to hide from scrutiny. . . . There is no end to the shopping list. Yet however long the list, the way to opt out of shopping is not on it. (Bauman 2016: 65)

It is likely that the cultural-economic differences between the communist spies working for and reporting on Barnes, and other American diplomats, would have made the opportunities for espionage resulting from consumerism more obvious. At this time, the relationship between Western consumers and consumption would have been perceived as slavish 'commodity fetishism', which Soviet communism was presenting itself as freeing people from (Gurova 2006: 96).

While clothing is commonly thought of in terms of its visual and tactile projection of the personal body into public realms, the Shoehorn bug rearticulated its riskiness in terms of listening. A similar epochal turn had come about a century before in the field of medicine when the stethoscope had made listening central to everyday medicine. The nineteenth-century stethoscope transformed the heartbeat and other intimate bodily noises, known previously only to the ear of someone lying their head on the chest of a loved one, into a scientific and measurable signal. There are some parallels between the Shoehorn bug and the stethoscope in the sense that each could be thought of as an auditory technique (Sterne 2001).

Unlike the stethoscope, the bug did not operate within explicit social parameters (doctor-patient) that thoroughly demarcated its growing use from associations with intimacy. In the vacuum of silence, which would constantly haunt transmission, politics and process would fall away, and an intimacy would return in the form of what Salomé Voegelin describes as 'intersubjective listening': '[i]n silence the visual perspective [as a dimension of place-making] vanishes into sensorial simultaneity' (Voegelin 2010: 83). Listener and listened-to wait in the same state of mute expectancy, the listener unable to entirely distance themselves through the vestiges of either science or politics.

While this type of intimacy would soon give way to larger, less personal listening networks with little use for the unscalable complications of personalized bugs, it would later find relevance again; most prominently, when the race to perfect speech-based algorithms motivated wide-scale eavesdropping programmes that salvaged voice data from smartwatches and other wearable devices (see Part III). Once again, surveillance techniques deployed in the service of this technical form of listening would exploit the vulnerable, aspirational space between the private and public body.

Voice

It was undoubtedly Henry Barnes's voice that the Unit T audio surveillance specialists wanted to hear through the Shoehorn bug. Only the voice could divulge secrets and provide indications of future American plans that might have threatened or disadvantaged Romania at the time. However, a microphone placed in the heel of a shoe is not ideally positioned to listen to its owner's voice, partly due to its placement under the shoe, far away from the mouth of any speaker and partly because the foot would be constantly generating loud noises much closer to the microphone through stepping, tapping and the readjustment of the foot against the floor when sitting. To Michel Serres, noise is 'the set of these phenomena of interference that become obstacles to communication' (1982b: 66). Moreover, it is the context of all communication:

> a sort of game played by two interlocutors considered as united against the phenomena of interference and confusion, or against individuals with some stake in interrupting communication. . . . *To hold a dialogue is to suppose a third man and to seek to exclude him.* (1982b: 66–7)

During the illicit surveillance of a conversation, there is no conspiracy against noise. The eavesdropper stands paradoxically in the position of the third person, excluded yet seeking to receive the message. The job of the third listener, in this sense, is to receive both signal and noise without consideration from the speaker. The Shoehorn bug exemplifies such a position *in extremis*. Yet, noise, according to Serres, is not simply sound without a message, nothing, but chaos, many things without order: 'noise is the opening. . . . and from it is born nature always being born . . . criss-crossed with possible relations' (1982b: 56).

Through such bisecting correlations, we can perceive the nascent methodologies of AI that would later be developed by military organizations. For despite the role of the foot in creating message-annihilating interference, it is easy to imagine eavesdropping operatives picking up additional information about the wearer via their pedestrian rhythms: a tendency to tap or otherwise move their feet while seated with colleagues could suggest agitation, frustration or boredom, for example. A sudden flurry of footsteps, as they rushed to catch up with someone, would provide social and spatial information that, wrapped around the voice and its message, could provide important context. Given long enough, an operative might well have been able to identify a person based on their particular footfall, its unique cadence, a bodily leitmotif.

The noise of footfall in this context carries a new, related message to be decoded. The idea that novel, valuable information might be extractable from noise would become an increasingly compelling notion for intelligence communities as they began to store increasing amounts of voice data. Noise would be reinterpreted as 'behavioural surplus', as 'collateral signals' data (Zuboff 2019: 42) that could be extracted for new uses beyond its original purpose. Thus, it could gain significant value beyond the reasons that it was originally collected for. It would take decades for the technology of deep learning neural networks to gain the capacity to infer relations in, and through, states of chaos.

The notion that footfall itself would become an important data source would have been considered risible by those tasked with recording the conversations of Barnes and those oscillating around him. To the remote monitors, it was a destructive acoustic force that required all of their patience and skill to filter in search of the voice's message in among 'hours of shoes clopping down hallways' (Maloney 2016: online). Today, all information potentially unlocks patterns of behaviour or dynamics of cause and effect within any given system of relations. In 2018, a paper documented a system finally capable of interpreting footfall as 'biometric data'. It is reported as being able to identify a person with 95 per cent accuracy within ten steps (Anchal et al. 2019). The further adventures of the acoustically sure-footed.

Among the advantages listed about the system are the ease with which it can be camouflaged and the implausibility of evading detection because, like the cadence and rhythms of an individual's voice, 'footstep patterns are inimitable' (Anchal et al. 2019: 1). Akin to the Shoehorn bug, the system remains camouflaged near the floor, listening not to the conversations of passersby but to the cadence of their gait. To gain fluency in the language of steps, the system had been trained on 46,000 footfalls – at the time, the largest known corpus of its kind. What had once been noise has now become structured data, its 'criss-crossing relations' indexed for future use.

Fidelity

Through concealment and transmission, many material factors would have altered the fidelity of the Shoehorn recordings. An instance of a bug placed in the couch of a Chinese diplomat in France proved 'ineffective because of the squeaking noises that drowned out conversations, not only when the diplomat was using it for his frequent sexual escapades but when visitors were simply sitting' (Richelson 2001: 147). In addition, some materials of concealment transmit sound better than others. Density ratios and levels of flexibility come into play. For example, the surveillance system at hand requires the medium to compress and decompress to more effectively transmit sounds from one place to another (Petersen 2013: 124).

The manner in which electricity is harnessed also influences optimal levels of fidelity. Such processes can be used to amplify sound, or the sound waves can be 'converted to electrical or optical signals, transmitted, and then turned back into sound waves so they may be readily understood at the receiving end' (Petersen 2013: 124). The journey of capture, transmission and conversion is vulnerable to interruption by the ever-present curse of technical failure or human error on the part of the listener, as well as countermeasures or discovery carried out by the subject. Afterwards, factors of audio clean-up, interpretation, narrative shaping and the political position of the listening party can further distort the direct fidelity of audio surveillance.

In contemporary instances where a recording is not 'clean' or the target audio has been interfered with, post-processing can help isolate certain voices but at the cost of degradation to the file. While acoustic fidelity is spoilt by such factors, ambiguous interpretations of the recording can potentially sway the narrative coherence to the vested interests of the listener. Attempting to parse useful pieces of intelligence from a glut of information can take hours and often delivers little of value. Both the analogue and digital processing of audio files use audio instrumentation, 'to improve its quality or informational content or to select pertinent sections to emphasize, catalog, or store' (Petersen 2013: 126). This processual hunt for fidelity is a mode of post hoc listening, a cooperation between the electronic and the human ear in order to derive meaning.

Legally speaking, a recording is more useful than a human memory of a conversation, but listeners can remove context and create their own narrative through editing. For those hired under private investigation circumstances, characteristics of noise and interference in a file are sometimes preferable, with the acoustic ambiguity favouring a particular surveillance narrative that has been crafted to provide customer satisfaction. Transcripts of recorded audio can likewise be unreliable. Helen Fraser proposes that even clear speech is 'messier' than messy handwriting in terms of deriving meaning. In 'handwriting we generally maintain a gap between one word and the next, whereas in speech even the words run into one another' (Fraser 2003: 211).

Listening is not a passive exercise where meaning is delivered through a signal but an active construction of meaning on the part of the listener (Fraser 2003: 205). When we know what we are listening for, the social context of speech guides the predictability of its contents, but noise and interference negatively affect intelligibility the more unpredictable the speech. Listening in a foreign language to a transmission from the heel of a shoe may have provided intelligence, but chances are the discovery of the bug made more of a strategic statement than what was, or was not, understood from the captured audio.

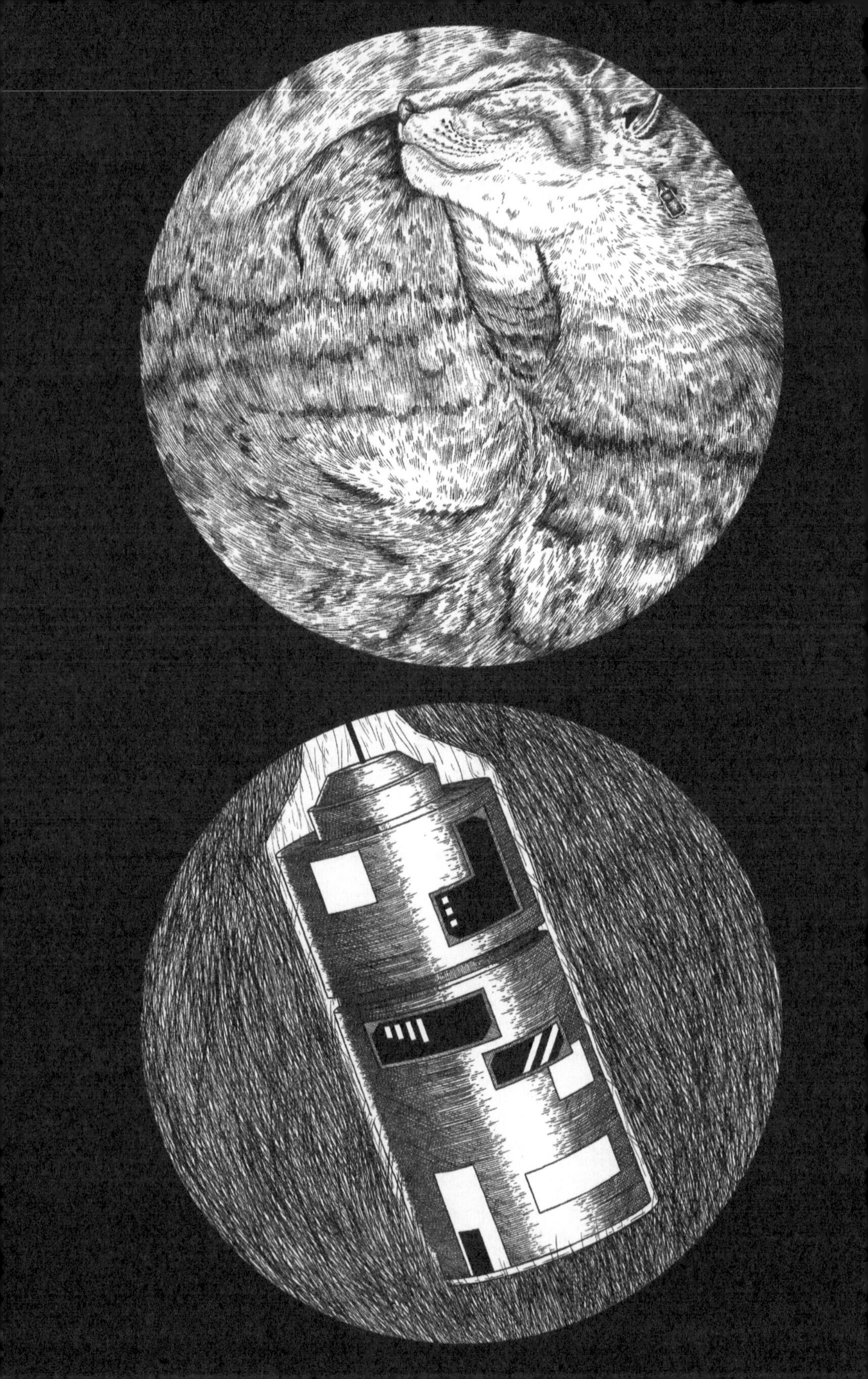

CHAPTER 4
ACOUSTIC KITTY

Process

By the 1960s, covert listening devices had been hidden in wooden carvings, fake rocks, all manner of furniture, telephones, typewriters and shoes: a range of inanimate objects that ranged from the functional to the seemingly whimsical. What would come next might register as being unbelievable if it were not for the heavily redacted declassified document – 'Views on Trained Cats Use' (CIA 1967) that was made public in 2010. The paper describes a project instigated by the CIA Directorate of Science & Technology. It outlines their Frankensteinian efforts to render the agency's surveillance prowess more mobile and agile by employing cats as the carriers of covert listening devices. And so, project 'Acoustic Kitty' was born; not so much to be wild, more to be trained and directed, and therein lay the inherent problem with this stealth-driven initiative.

From inanimate objects to animals in the twitch and stitch of an ear, the CIA had shifted the field of covert listening during the Cold War by modding and training surgically augmented felines. Instead of waiting for targets to come to them, the CIA intended to stalk their quarry through the deployment of a force of recalcitrant four-legged operatives. While one version of history tells of Acoustic Kitty being deployed to covertly listen to two men outside of Washington, DC's Soviet embassy and instead getting run over by a taxi, a conflicting narrative was forwarded by former director of the CIA's Office of Technical Service, Robert Wallace. According to Wallace, there was difficulty in training the cat even when 'wires to its brain to determine when it was hungry or sexually aroused' were fitted 'to override these urges' (Curtis 1995: online). In the latter version of history, the microphone that had been fitted into the cat's ear canal, along with the power pack and radio transmitter at the base of its skull sewn into its fur, was stripped out, and the cat was sewn up and released.

Sounding like a B-movie script, it was allocated, according to ex-CIA officer Victor Marchetti, anything but – the Acoustic Kitty project being afforded a $20 million budget (Herald Sun 2001). This figure, along with other aspects of the project, has been contested, but what is undisputed is the CIA's proven wider use of animals as agents of reconnaissance, weapons delivery and sensing. 'Kechel' was the codename given to work undertaken with cats and dogs. 'Axiolite' was the umbrella term used for techniques using birds. The employment of dolphins – to observe submarine installations via attached cameras – was named 'Oxygas' (Animal Programs 1967: 1). When these programmes were shut down in 1968, enough impetus had been gained to influence other intelligence organizations to utilize alternative species and modes of sensory agency. For example, the UK's domestic counter-intelligence and security agency, 'MI5 was building its team of spy-detecting gerbils to sniff out traitors – apparently their olfactory system is highly sensitive to raised adrenaline levels in sweat' (Donald 2011: 79).

By employing animals, the CIA extended its collective sensorium and amplified its agency through biotechnologies that harnessed expanded sensing capabilities. From externalized attire fitted to humans to the internalized devices embedded into cats, the placement and functionality of the bug became more abstracted as it embraced randomness and motility. Whether the Acoustic Kitty project was successful or not in terms of capturing private conversations is not really the issue here. Of more significance is the indication that government agencies were prepared to push beyond the limited sensorium of the human body. From animal and artificial to the occulted, these are all types of phenomena that are denoted as being either non-human or beyond human. It is the expansion of the limits of our sensory apparatus that this book charts along with investigating the ways we capture, train and amplify external senses to upgrade our intelligence.

Recording

We do not know what the microphone inside the cat's ear canal picked up before it was struck, or not struck, by a taxi. We can imagine that the microphone picked up a wealth of information about the cat's surroundings from a vantage point humans would not normally hear from: near the ground. This might include footsteps, 1960s motors, voices of a different timbre, as well as the sounds the cat depended on to navigate the human environment. The transmitter, if suitably equipped, would also have been able to send information about the cat's location, distance travelled and proximity to other wildlife.

The tradition of tagging and tracing animals for human benefit (such as in agriculture, hunting, conservation and scientific research) is global, with tracking in the Kalahari dating back more than an estimated 100,000 years (Movebank: online). Researchers began using radio transmitters in the late 1950s, which, by the 1960s, permitted the acquisition of previously inaccessible quantitative data on aspects of animal life, including 'movements, dispersal, activities, home range, areas of intense use, behavior, intra and inter-specific relations, and responses to various environmental factors such as habitat, weather, and human disturbance' (Kolenosky and Johnston 1967: 301). This list of data types refers to timber wolves in Ontario, with ocean tracking providing a host of different information. RFID technology – familiar from its surveillance applications – is still used as a primary method for animal tracking and functions through its application or incorporation into 'a product, animal, or person for the purpose of identification and tracking using radio waves' (McAdams 2011: vii).

The surgical implantation of the microphone and transmitter into the cat is a grotesque punctuation in the history of tracking and tracing, but not a departure. Humanity's tendency to intervene in natural processes in order to extract and protect capital is also a characteristic that benefits from animal tracking data. The data we collect about those natural habitats leads us to assume a perceived mastery, which in turn allows us to 'limit negative effects on the human population' (Janssen 2012: 445). Australians guard against attacks from the drop bear, using information about their prey gleaned via satellite (Janssen 2012: 449). Some of the technology for analysing animal tracking data is automated (Catarinucci et al. 2014), linking computer science with older forms of knowledge acquisition regarding wildlife ecology (Kirol 2020). Scientists and trackers use data to predict the behaviour of animals within complex environments and behavioural frameworks, though holding information is not synonymous with control of those systems. Cats are notoriously unpredictable and may, despite a concerted scientific effort, run into traffic.

Observation available to us in the digital age provides a more vivid idea of the recordings Acoustic Kitty could have made. Social media is rife with cats who have their own profiles and a legion of followers. Rarer, however, is an owner who uploads audio and video captured from the cat's point of view. Instagram user @gonzoisacat started the 'Collar Camera Project' in 2019, 'initially, just because [they] wanted to educate [themselves] about what Gonzo was doing outside' (@gonzoisacat 2022). Gonzo's owner ordered the smallest, cheapest spy camera he could find and rigged it to a breakaway collar. Having experimented with several different recording devices, he watched manufacturers pick up on the trend as they started to offer their own 'collar cameras' for feline reconnaissance.

In one video posted on 25 May 2022, the cat picks up a scrap of cardboard in a gravelly backyard and brings it inside the back door of a house on a sunny day. It's an offering known to many owners as a 'trashgift'. The cat drops the cardboard and approaches its water dish, with the microphone picking up the lapping of its tongue. A baby cries in another room. The cat slinks out of the back door again and cars can be heard driving by. The loudest sound in these videos comes from Gonzo, who can be heard chirping, purring and meowing throughout. From the gonzo strategy of Acoustic Kitty to the internet sensation of the same name, cats are highly fetishized as are the sounds they make. The next iteration of a mediated cat will likely be an AI-driven hologram. Holo Kitty, anyone?

Transgression

Placing a technological listening device under the skin of a cat pushed beyond the boundaries of the inanimate, extending human listening into a living feline sensorium. At that time, embedding electronics in animals was not a 'routine medical procedure' (Wallace et al. 2010: 200) and such a transgression required a number of adaptations to the listening device to maintain its functionality. The device had to be packaged to 'withstand the temperature, fluids, chemistry, and humidity of the body' (Wallace et al. 2010: 200–1) and its microphone had to overcome the sound-dampening effects of the skin. Eventually, the ear canal was co-opted as the bug's listening outpost. Here, the listening device contravened the natural superiority of feline hearing, obstructing the sophisticated listening system of an animal capable of hearing both high and low frequencies far outside of the range of human hearing (Heffner and Heffner 1985).

The cat's listening apparatus was not the only sensory range infiltrated through surgery. Attempts were also made to modify and manipulate its behaviour through nerve stimulation (Heffner and Heffner 1985). Acoustic Kitty's habits and proclivities were brutally adapted, its mammalian brain technologically sculpted in a lo-fi effort to perfect its function as a listening device. And yet, the organic would continue to transgress into the mechanical; the forceful and purposeful nature of the cat making it unpredictable and difficult to adapt to the requirements of acoustic espionage. Two decades later, Donna Haraway would write her 1985 socialist-feminist text, 'A Cyborg Manifesto'. In this pioneering work, the cyborg is positioned as 'a hybrid of machine and organism', which confused the boundaries 'between social reality and science fiction' (Haraway 1991: 149) as well as 'between imagination and material reality' (Haraway 1991: 150). It is easy to imagine the cat as an early non-human hybrid of this nature, a feline premonition of late-twentieth-century human cyborgism.

The technologically enhanced cat would certainly be at home in the science fiction of the decade: in 1968, Philip K. Dick imagined a world full of synthetic pets in *Do Androids Dream of Electric Sheep*. The novel had an electronic schematic for a sheep adorning its cover, similar to the schema for the Acoustic Kitty implant (Dick 1968). However, the listening device used in the project was never intended to enhance the cat's sensorium or be organized by it. Neither could the device penetrate the natural listening capabilities of its host to hear better. Instead, technological and biological hearing systems remained discrete, separated sensoria under a shared skin.

The cat's body was intended to be a puppet for its handler, manipulated and instrumentalized by the science and politics of Western capitalism, enlisted in what Haraway describes as 'the drama of escalating domination of nature/women' (1991: 151). It is the desire to transgress all boundaries in search of profit and security that best characterizes the Acoustic Kitty operation. The insertion of the predominantly male listener into an ever-increasing array of surroundings, in response to the emasculating terror of nuclear destruction, finds its most extreme expression in the Washington stray.

Aware of the radical nature of Acoustic Kitty, it is clear that the strategy of manipulating domestic cats into becoming listening devices did not sit easily with US secret services. In the life-and-death world of state-sponsored espionage, the rupture in the social order of pet and owner was still felt keenly. It is known that we have a special emotional attachment to pets that is similar to those attachments that we form with other humans (Gómez-Leal et al. 2021), and our empathetic concern for animal suffering is extremely contextual to certain animals and settings (Cornish et al. 2018). During the operation to insert the bug into the cat, the body horror of it was felt so keenly by the chief audio engineer that he had to be excused at the first sight of blood (Wallace et al. 2010).

Even before the project was given the go-ahead, CIA officials weighed the humane treatment of the animal and the risk of negative publicity against operational benefits. While intelligence strategies involving the training and deployment of other animals are well documented, it seems that many of the operational details related to using cats as listening devices were destroyed or redacted. This is perhaps due to concerns about the damage that the violation of trust between owner and pet would have on the CIA's standing if word got out. It seems that even intelligence agencies are not immune to feeling the pressures of superstition. Transgressing the roles and expectations concerning the world's favourite animal is a risky business. There is a reason why the proposition that 15 per cent of internet traffic consists of cat pictures, gifs and videos seems realistic to many of us (Kingson 2015).

Worlds

Humans often use the animal world as a moral staging ground, whether through anthropomorphized animal characters – in fables, myth, children's stories and adult cartoons – or through medical testing that weighs benefits against side effects in the ersatz brain of an evolutionary cousin. The Acoustic Kitty project pushes at the elastic boundary of this staging area and reflects the morality of our supposed purposes back at us. In wartime, we are historically expected to make sacrifices and watch shared values supersede individual needs, but of all animals, our cultural image of the cat is not one of an eager-to-enlist emissary of the state. Then again, cats can be helpful companions in a household or on a farm. Globally, the symbolism of the cat 'varies widely from beast of good to beast of evil omen, explicable simply in terms of the combination of the gentle and the sinister in the creature's appearance' (Chevalier and Gheerbrant 1996: 162).

This polarity of gentle versus sinister is, of course, measured in the cat's relation to humans and the other creatures within our sphere of care, which may include mice but not wasps, or could embrace dogs but not the fleas that live in their fur. In Buddhism, cats are grouped with snakes as 'the only creatures left unmoved by the death of Buddha, something which might be considered from another angle as a sign of higher wisdom' (Chevalier and Gheerbrant 1996: 162). In this sentence, first published in French in 1969 by two authors compiling the human-symbolic imaginary into a dictionary, Chevalier and Gheerbrant show the easy transformation of the cat from a callous, earthly figure to one of wise mysticism within one hypothetical.

In Russia, cats are a quotidian reality for over half of its population, with the number of domestic cats outnumbering the population of pet dogs by 6 million as of 2019: a singular statistic not reflected across the world (Melkadze 2024: online). For a period during 2014, the country's largest bank, Sberbank, would lend cats as well as mortgages to people buying a house because 'Russian superstition has it [that] it's good luck for the first creature to cross the threshold of a new home to be feline' (Stackpole 2014: online). The Great Seal bug may have been hidden behind a wooden carving of an eagle, but the Americans sent a real cat against the Russians, placing the potential utility of the animal above the integrity of its inner world. In asking *What Is It Like to Be a Bat?* (1974), Thomas Nagel explained that 'our own experience provides the basic material for our imagination, whose range is therefore limited' (439). Setting aside the imaginary stubbornness required to train a cat, this limited range borders not only on inter-species cooperation but on the border between self and other, Russian and American, communist and capitalist, speaker and listener. For American poet-scientist Loren Eiseley, the imagination of man, 'in its highest manifestations, stands close to the doorway of the infinite, to the world beyond the nature that we know' (Eiseley 1978: 295). The nature that we know through subjective experience is our own; the rest is taxonomy and technology.

We understand categories of human versus animal through grouping shared characteristics and the naming of things. We have such faith in our categories that the discovery of the platypus – that venomous, egg-laying, bill-having, no-eared mammal – so confused English zoologist George Shaw in 1799 that he ascribed it to being a hoax, writing that 'it naturally excites the idea of some deceptive preparation by artificial means' (Ohlheiser 2015: online). It took eighty-five years for scientists to figure out that the platypus laid eggs, something long known to Australian Aboriginal tribes. Structures of animal classification, personal rivalries between naturalists and prejudice against the Eastern route of the initial sample's transmission all contributed to the confusion (Hall 1999). But such confusion is not 'natural' in the way the platypus is natural. It is not a duck's bill grafted onto a quadrupedal mammal. It does not call itself platypus. It does not call itself anything.

Jean Baudrillard stated that animals' lack of speech is what makes 'us intimate with them. . . . In a world assembled under the hegemony of signs and discourse, their silence weighs more and more heavily on our organization of meaning' (1994: 137). His view of scientific experimentation on animals was on par with that of torture, in 'seeking to extort [confession] from them from beneath the scalpel and the electrodes' (1994: 129). Uncertainty is diminished through science, but the metamorphosis of animals, and specifically that of the cat, from gentle to sinister and back again, is rooted in their lack of recognition of our human world as separate from their own. Any order there might be is 'far wilder and more formidable than that conjured up by human effort' (Eiseley 1978: 59). An animal that refuses, simply in its being, to fit into a categorical shape is a 'gliding, leaping mythology' (Eiseley 1985: 202) of its own. The technological intervention into Acoustic Kitty's anatomy is frozen transcendence because it cannot evolve.

Post-operation, Acoustic Kitty straddled not only the human and animal worlds but the posthuman world as well. In the procedure – whose reversibility is unconfirmed – the veterinary surgeon complicated our taxonomic structure by introducing unnatural augmentation to animals whose sensorium we had previously revered and emulated. The animal-cyborg 'troubles previous categories of organism. The machinic and the textual are internal to the organic and vice versa in irreversible ways' (Haraway 2003: 15). Acoustic Kitty had language implanted into its body via serial number and signal.

Prediction

The behavioural sciences, which would drive new approaches to prediction as part of the push towards a new form of consumer surveillance (Zuboff 2019), were gaining momentum even in the 1960s. B. F. Skinner was a behaviourist who followed a tradition of study that sought to establish predictable effects through operant conditioning (Skinner 1937). At the centre of his approach was the notion that a subject learns most reliably from the consequences of its actions, developing habitual associations between a behaviour and its effect. The long-running appeal of Skinner's methods was their operational feasibility as an apparent 'technology of animal control' (Bloomfield 1976: 76): the notion that repetition of the right stimulus and reward increased certainty of behaviour over time, beyond what had previously been possible.

Becoming influential in the late 1930s, Skinner's approach to applied psychology had become widely understood and accepted in the thirty years that followed. Relatedly, a number of fields of psychology professed to have made remarkable advances in the predictability of animal and human behaviour. There was a growing belief in the 1950s and 1960s that continued observation of non-verbal communication signs would eventually allow military observers to read a subject's emotions 'like a book'. Similarly, the development of lie-detector tests during this period, which could apparently sense falsehoods through changes in voice, suggested externalization and measurable manifestations of internal processes. Studies of rats and pigeons that were rewarded for operating levers were used to hypothesize the ways humans learn, with animals understood to possess primitive versions of human intelligence. Notes in declassified agency documents show us that the trials the CIA was conducting in predictable animal behaviour were in preparation for human use:

> In addition to its possible practical value in operations, this phenomenon is a very useful research tool in the area of the behavioral sciences. Dr. {redacted} is taking appropriate action to exploit our knowledge of this area and provide adequate background for the development of future Agency applications in the general areas of Influencing Human Behavior, Indirect Assessment and Interrogation Aids. (CIA 1961: 2)

The scientification and masculinization of behaviour manipulation would first be practised on animals to prove that it was based on subjugation and mastery rather than on trickery. As T. M. Bloomfield would point out in their critique of Skinner's methodology, 'behaviour modification' could be translated into a desire to control people and 'operant conditioning' as processes of coercion to 'obtain a desired result' (Bloomfield 1976: 80). However, Skinner and the extrinsically focused theorists who rejected the mind and internal life of animals (and by association, humans) seemed to offer a more 'radical' form of control than had been previously possible. In the redacted CIA notes, there is a palpable sense that the processes of using auditory signals as a method of totalizing control were close to being achieved. It is revealing to see the use of now familiar software-related phrases in the following CIA report:

> At the present time we feel that we are close to having *debugged a prototype system* whereby dogs can be guided along specified courses through land areas out of sight. (CIA 1961: 2; italics added)

Listening In

In the effort to technologize animal behaviour so that it is predictable and tuned to military purposes, the ideas of software bugs and the need to debug them have become commonplace. The idea of 'debugging', like 'snagging' or other process-driven finishing terms, evokes a trivial set of outstanding tasks left to finish before a thing is complete. The enmeshing of human habits and behaviours with AI systems requires constant debugging, whenever it does not conform to uncritical standards of how technologies should act. From problems of interpretation in listening algorithms in speech-to-text systems (Carr et al. 2019) to bias in other AI systems such as search functions (Noble 2018), the technological ideal of perfect machinery haunts and structures surrounding language.

Towards the end of the 1960s, applied psychology would start to emerge from what Lisa Feldman Barrett in the US military text *Human Behavior in Military Contexts* would later term the 'dark ages' and 'abyss' of behaviourism (Barrett 2008: 190). Thought leaders turned to embrace, once again, the complexities of human and animal emotions alongside other mental activities. The hope that simplified mental models could be created through the use of basic unifying principles was jettisoned, but the search for a technological solution to behaviour prediction and control was too seductive to entirely give up on, and would, in time, lead to algorithmic solutions that could apparently imitate the 'neural networks' of the brain, even though similarities are generally 'hard-coded' into algorithms by researchers (Schaeffer et al. 2022). Even the discredited processes involved in the reading of body language and lie detection tests that were discredited in the 1970s have nevertheless found their way back into algorithmic cultures (Crawford 2021; Cox 2018). What characterizes these fields is a tendency to see the gap between biology and its technological double as a 'debugging' process. The activity that follows distracts technologists, causing them to overlook fundamental problems in the biological and psychological assumptions that ground their work.

Intimacy

We did not have to wait until the launch of satellites to be able to see the earth from a great distance. A bird's-eye view was our first aspirational expression of that animal's natural domain. The human-made objects we cast upward were the first instance of that viewpoint's transmission back, granting us the spatial orientation that allows us to accurately depict the topology of the earth. The existence and malleability of satellite lenses do not stop us from attaching cameras to birds, just to see what it is like to be one.

Appropriating animal sensoria to satisfy humanity's scientific curiosity is an ongoing colonization of nature that necessitates a bodily intimacy in a space that cannot be accurately virtualized without massive amounts of data. In order to get close enough to plant sensors on these animals, we must track, capture and anaesthetize them; cut them open; study their behaviour under stimulus; and then dissect their organs to determine which of their natural abilities might have military applications. The implantation of a microphone into Acoustic Kitty's ear canal was meant to lend the device its hard-won evolutionary efficiency, but a cat's sensing organ for sound is its brain, something we cannot yet accurately simulate.

In our intimate history with animals, the hallmark of our relationships with them resides in 'our need to separate ourselves' (Walker 2013: 55). Separate ideologically, but as close as possible to scientifically confirm that humanity's position on earth, as top of the food chain, is a foregone conclusion. Fully comprehending animals' evolutionary history with regard to sensing organs (especially those that differ from our own) inspires their reinvention as prostheses for the human body. These weaponized sensoria are stockpiled like munitions. They wait to be called upon, obedient to the task of defending and maintaining human ascendancy.

Policing the divide between our species and every other, even those that we recognize as our ancestral relatives, places them in a precarious position. Domesticating animals necessarily positions them as being under our control because their behaviour must be somewhat predictable for us to invite them into our homes. A cat's predictability is in its seemingly spiteful unpredictability, a quality that endears them to their owners but makes them unsuitable for sensitive sound recording. The CIA's declassified report on Acoustic Kitty concluded that 'environmental and security factors in using this technique in a real foreign situation force us to conclude that, for our [redacted] purposes, it would not be practical' (CIA 1967: 2). Earlier in the document, the CIA asserts the cat's obedience, but only 'to move short distances' (CIA 1967: 1), which barely seems worth recording within the scope of the total mission.

The successful domestication of animals encourages experimentation as part of humans' 'violently intimate relationships with other creatures' that define 'much of global human history' (Walker 2013: 45). The 'devotion to human exceptionalism' (Walker 2013: 48) based on engaging with animals on terms unnatural to them allows for technological intervention that would be impossible in the animals' natural habitats. Technology, specifically the close-up shot of animals in nature documentaries, conversely emboldens underestimation of danger in proximity to animals in their natural environments or in contrived recreational scenarios such as zoos or safaris. In writing about the false intimacy engendered by viewing cinematic close-ups in nature documentaries, Derek Bousé compares seeing real live animals to seeing celebrities in person. He writes:

> just as media celebrities often appear physically smaller than expected when seen in person, so do animals in the wild rarely appear as majestic (or as cuddly) as they do on the screen. Many are only glimpsed as darting shapes fleeing at our approach, or as tiny objects seen at a distance. It is the ability television gives us to see them from stroking distance, however, and to do so on any given evening in the comfort of our living rooms, which invites feelings of intimacy with them. (Bousé 2010: 124)

With a delicate array of wires underneath its soft coat, the act of stroking Acoustic Kitty could have blown its cover. But such human intervention does not seem to have been taken into consideration. The primary aim was to fuse paranoia, listening technologies and a carrier that was fleet of foot. By undertaking such a project, the CIA took Acoustic Kitty out of the wild and placed it into the previously uncharted territories of the animal cyborg.

Voice

Embedded within a symphony of urban patterns, the targeted voices that the cat was supposed to capture within its surrounding environmental sonic mesh equated to being noise that needed to be rendered as a signal. Oral acoustic anchors needed locating and extracting. In an urban ocean of sound, Acoustic Kitty was expected to somehow be lured by the voices and coaxed onto the shores of feline reconnaissance – a somewhat irrational projection of speech as an expression that attracts its own capture.

The desire to record the human voice runs deep, both spatially and temporally. This is evident from the channelling of deities', spirits' and demons' voices across divergent cultures throughout history. The lineage of capturing the externalized voice via technological apparatus dates back to 9 April 1860 and the first recordings of 'Au Clair de la Lune' by Édouard-Léon Scott de Martinville via his phonautograms. The more celebrated version of recording history, meanwhile, points us to 1877 and Edison's invention of the phonograph – the first machine that vibrationally sensed, recorded and played back sound; a different beast taking centre stage for the first recording – a vocal rendering of the nursery rhyme 'Mary Had a Little Lamb' (Hale 1830).

Animals can sense phenomena that exist beyond the perceptible grasp of the limited human seat of sensation – pheromones, chemical changes caused by fear and stress, diseases, magnetic and electrical fields, infrared, infrasound and ultrasound. For Bill Shull, 'there are many kinds of animal behaviour which clearly meet the definition of extrasensory perception – that is, the animal will be aware of events, conditions, etc., that cannot be traced to our present knowledge of the five senses' (Shull 1977: 49). Along with the proven and evidenced ways of gathering sensory information, animals are often denoted with the capacity to comprehend human intention that exists beyond or before speech. They are often projected to have potential access to the inner voice.

This alleged connectivity to the organizing principles and agencies that drive everything from patterns of human behaviour to meteorological events proposes that channels exist which humans do not have sensorial access to. Harnessing animals to tap into this unspoken matrix of forces should not come as a surprise, especially when the handlers were the CIA. Given the proliferation of esoteric fields of knowledge and influence at work during the 1960s and 1970s, the animal programmes devised by intelligence and military agencies were influenced by the thinking extolled by authors such as Shull:

There is a mountain of evidence supporting belief in the psychic power of animals – pets aware that their masters have died or are in danger although hundreds of miles away at the time; mind-reading feats; predictions of earthquakes; storms, and even bombings hours before they happen; the ability to traverse a continent in the search of a lost master; . . . even clairvoyance. (Shull 1977: 44).

Acoustic Kitty and the wider cited array of animal research programmes emerged from an era when psychic abilities were considered a new frontier for the US military's (PSYOPS). As a result, 'soft' and esoteric modes of warfare became even further abstracted as they were occulted and informed by the revelatory promise of the extrasensory. The emergence of Jim Channon's First Earth Battalion and its *Operation's Manual* (US Army), which he created in 1978, was a prime example of the way in which military strategy was being influenced by New Age thinking around precognition and telepathy.

Unconventional approaches to warfare that prioritized conflict resolution due to a primary allegiance to the welfare of the planet were central to Jim Channon's ethos. Remote Viewing was just one of many practices and processes being proposed to extend the sensory capacity and intelligence-gathering capacity of the US Army. As aural precursors go, Acoustic Kitty was more of a clunky affair altogether. It was the antithesis of the psychic playground that the US military was looking to move into, given that the fieldwork the augmented cat was supposed to carry out was resoundingly physical. It was a remote listening practice that aimed to extend the sensorium via the fuzzy logic of a droid's ear rather than by the reasoning of the mind's eye.

Fidelity

The shape and function of Acoustic Kitty's ear – particularly its cochlea – was chosen as the site to implant the microphone because it was believed that it could help to filter out aural excess. Victor Marchetti described the project as 'an interim step in designing a microphone that could filter out extraneous noise' (Richelson 2001: 147). It is likely that Marchetti and others on the team had been excited by the discoveries of Georg von Békésy at Harvard University. His pioneering research in 1960, which won him a Nobel Prize, focused on the mechanics of the cochlea and basilar membrane to tonally encode sound, and suggested a model of hearing that was purely mechanical.

An earlier discovery pertaining to the functioning of the inner ear could also lay claim to having influenced the CIA's Frankensteinian project. In 1930, Ernest Wever and Charles Bray proved that the cochlea encodes sound waves electronically, in much the same way that a microphone does, producing an alternating current response that it is possible to amplify (Warren 2008). Moreover, the effect – now known as the 'cochlear microphonic' – was observed by using cats as test subjects. The experiment by Wever and Bray, described in a paper by Hallpike and Rawdon-Smith, bears a close resemblance to the Acoustic Kitty project:

The amplifier, telephone receivers and the observer were installed in a sound-proof room. The cat was arranged external to this, with the recording electrode inserted intracranially onto the eighth nerve. Listening at the telephones, the observer

> was able to understand words spoken into the animal's ear, and even to recognize the speaker by his voice. [L]ittle more distortion than occurs in a commercial telephone can have been present. (Hallpike and Rawdon-Smith 1937: 976)

The authors note the quality of the signal from the ear using a crude electrical device, but there is no mention of noise cancellation effects. What seems most fascinating about the description of the Acoustic Kitty project given by Marchetti is that he conflates the mechanical physiology of mammalian hearing with the act of listening. 'Human beings have a cochlea in our ears masking out noise, so we can have conversations at a cocktail party. But if you tape a cocktail party, you get all the noise and you can't make out conversations' (Ranelagh 1987: 208). Marchetti is referring obliquely to the 'cocktail party effect', which "refers to our ability to focus attention on the speech of a specific speaker by disregarding irrelevant information coming from the surroundings' (Augoyard and Torgue 2006: 28). He goes so far as to describe the cat's attention as being instrumental to the process of filtering, describing how colleagues would 'train a cat to listen to conversations and not to the background noise' (Richelson 2001: 147). According to his description, the project team expected that feline listener attention would affect what the ear heard.

Despite the loose scientific basis of these expectations, they were entirely ill-founded. The cochlea does not filter out sounds but, in fact, encodes frequencies tonally (Casale et al. 2025) – a pre-processing stage for the mammalian brain. Thus, it does not respond based on our attention but encodes all audible sound transmitted by the middle ear. Following a series of synaptic processes, the frequencies and their levels, along with binaural data, are brought together in the brain's auditory cortex to be filtered and understood in terms of location and time (Howard and Angus 2017). It is only following this sequence that attention can be applied, and listening is able to occur.

Marchetti's conflation of hearing with listening reflects a fictionalization of the processes of the body that has been influential in the development of both acoustic and artificial intelligence. Julie Park further describes such 'slippages' occurring between artificial speech and AI (2020) where there has historically been a human desire for the former to indicate the latter. Park notes that in the history of automatons, the science and craft of artificial vocal organs often became confused with mechanical intelligence. If it could speak, then it could think.

For Marchetti, it was the non-human inner ear that was the site for a listening intelligence 'slippage', a panacea that he thought would be a shortcut to fixing problems concerning fidelity and recording quality. However, it was the reliance on such unexamined science fictions that would ultimately contribute to the project's failure. This was one cat that was not going to get nine chances to succeed. Acoustic Kitty and other surveillance projects and strategies that pushed and transgressed the outer limits of both esoteric and expert individualistic listening were about to be jettisoned in favour of new state approaches to systematic intelligence gathering. Solitary prime targets were to be replaced by earmarked populations; the mass social body and the capture of all its divergent thoughts, interactions, desires and fears were to become the new focus.

In terms of the soundscape, the figure of the feline predator was transforming from the guise of an aural stalker to that of the cat that has got one's tongue. With a new era of surveillance systems on the horizon, it would no longer just be targeted individuals who needed to be careful about how they spoke, but everyone. As we will find out in the following section, given a significant shift in the aims and ambitions of surveillance cultures, populations would soon be starting to equate self-censorship with survival.

PART II
MASSIVE DISTRIBUTED MONITORING SYSTEMS

CHAPTER 5
STASI

Process

The Ministry for State Security, known later as the Stasi, was established shortly after the formation of East Germany by the Provisional People's Assembly (the *Volkskammer*) in 1950. The secret police and intelligence agency grew rapidly. At its inception, the ministry had 2,700 full-time employees, but by 1989, it had amassed 91,000 paid workers (Bruce 2003: 5–6). In terms of employment profile, the Stasi was, however, most notable for its massive network of unofficial informants, the *Inoffizieller Mitarbeiter* (IM). The number of informants active within the Stasi network is difficult to verify. Researched estimates vary between one Stasi informant for every sixty-three people to one for every six-and-a-half citizens when counting part-time informers (Funder 2011: 53). This is compared to one Gestapo agent for every 2,000 citizens during the Third Reich and one KGB agent for every 5,830 people in Stalin's USSR (Funder 2011). The Stasi grew its network in part by recycling the infrastructure of the defeated Nazi regime: IMs were often recruited from Germany's youth, including former members of the Hitler Youth and the SS, as well as 'from among children of former Nazis' (Bruce 2003: 9).

The overwhelming number of cooperators, whether coerced or simply employed, worked under the guidance of Erich Mielke, head of the Stasi. Mielke was recruited by the Soviets when he fled Germany after shooting a local police chief in Berlin in 1931 in retaliation for the killing of a German Communist Party member (Funder 2011: 53). He was trained at the International Lenin School, which was attended by elite Communist leaders, and went on to stage a coup in Berlin. He then became the head of the Stasi from 1957 until 1989. He installed Markus Wolf, who oversaw operations and implemented the ruthless set of practices carried out by the Stasi known as *Zersetzung*, a German word that translates as 'corrosion' or 'decomposition'. The programme included measures of 'psychological manipulation on an individual or group basis in an effort to influence attitudes and convictions, with the ultimate aim of limiting or eliminating the effectiveness of dissidents' (Gieseke 2014: 146).

The corrosion of a person's psychological integrity could take a number of forms. Tactics included: covertly orchestrating professional failures in their social sphere, stirring up personal rivalries, circulating compromising photos, issuing unwarranted summons to give the impression that someone was an IM, deceiving people to exit their dwellings so that they could be searched and/or bugged (Gieseke 2014: 146). These activities were combined with official displays of power such as arbitrary arrest and kidnapping, but ultimately, exploiting human weakness via *Zerzetzung* was meant to absorb all the subject's energies in 'dealing with personal problems' (Gieseke 2014: 146). Such elaborate arrangements, to destroy a person's normal psychological functioning within society, constituted a sinister form of sensory distortion in the name of State security.

Recording

A collector's mania for preserving the repository of media surveillance can be intoned from both the Stasi's obsessive record-keeping and the ongoing maintenance of its sinister archive in modern Germany. Access to the Stasi's surveillance legacy of 111 kilometres of shelved documents was inscribed into 1991's Stasi Records Act. This was enacted to allow German citizens access to personal files and for institutions, media producers and researchers to learn from the archive and expose the inner workings of the intelligence organization's operations (Federal Archives 2024).

The archival process was incredibly rigorous. Even shredded files were scanned in an attempt to create virtual reconstructions, resulting in over 15,000 sacks of shredded materials being stored. There are countless personal and private stories within the media collection, including (as of December 2020) approximately 1.95 million photographs, microfilm and slides; 2,876 films and videos; and 22,700 audio recordings. Roughly 60 per cent of this material is accessible. Tellingly, the archive is still regularly accessed: the agency receives around 100,000 requests a year for information (Federal Archives 2024).

Bureaucracy can be viewed as a symbol of the dehumanizing, obfuscating tactics of an institution. This is certainly the case in the Franz Kafka stories, written in German, concerning the futility and suffering associated with wrapping human experience up in red tape; but the more banal associations of 'procrastination, obfuscation, circumlocution' do not apply here as much as the aesthetics of totalitarianism (du Gay 2000: 1). The human narratives within the Stasi's archive material are only obscured by the copiousness and the medium of delivery. Everyday discussion, secrets, lies and betrayals that were recorded by Stasi informants were accessed via a thorough filing system that attempted to offer an overarching narrative of 'highly specific, calibrated interventions into the lives of single individuals' (Hoffman 2021: 62).

A more contemporary reading of these media narratives, according to Sophia Hoffmann, reveals the use of surveillance as a social practice that, to some extent, reflected a German cultural preference for bureaucracy rather than simply existing as a mechanism of security. Indeed, as Paul du Gay argues, bureaucracy at some level offers a vision not only of alienating horror but also enables institutions to ensure 'fairness, justice and equality in the treatment of citizens' (du Gay 2000: 2).

The value of the archive, as an expression of such bureaucratic ingenuity and institutional pride, is perhaps why it survived its creator's dissolution. In fact, the accessibility of the countless stories within the archive suggests that the Stasi, like any totalitarian organization, could not ideologically plan for the event of its own demise. Their method of indexing the dossiers and recordings was never encoded or encrypted.

It was almost as though the archive became a marker of esteem as much as it was functional. The idea that the records could be lost or burnt, for example, must have filled them with dread, given that the collection represented so much secretive knowledge and power.

In his exploration of the power of the archive, Randall C. Jimerson describes it as a temple in which records achieve 'authority and immortality' through selection and preservation. It is also a prison where records are locked away 'for their own security' and their usage jealously monitored (Jimerson 2005: online). The value of making the archive available, says Jimerson, is in holding the powerful 'accountable for its actions' and to 'represent all of society in our archives', to venerate the marginalized (Jimerson 2005: online). In the context of the Stasi, there is some irony in the benign ideology described by Jimerson and du Gay. Like the Stasi, it assumes that the archive or bureau is permanently entwined with the specific political machinery of the state that produces or maintains it. As a result, damning and unverifiable information is often held in perpetuity on thousands of citizens. While many of the Stasi's targets may never seek to listen to recordings or read up on themselves, such information 'will always be with us, and the sensible, if not always emotionally satisfying, thing is to learn to live with them' (du Gay 2000: 2). Maintained with multitudinous rigor, if the records represent anything, it is the democratization of total suspicion.

Transgression

Someone who is aware, or suspects, that they are under surveillance changes their behaviour. They potentially act more altruistically (Bateson, Nettle and Roberts 2006), or productively (Roethlisberger and Dickson 1939), or contribute to 'distrust and divisions' (Dorfman 2014: online) among citizens, curbing 'their readiness to speak freely to each other' (Dorfman 2014: online). During Augusto Pinochet's twentieth-century regime, Chilean playwright Ariel Dorfman later recalled that 'friends who had been outgoing and clear-throated were now hushed and guarded, coding and encrypting each sentence with double and triple entendres' (Dorfman 2014: online). This layered form of speech is reflected in conversation in the semi-autobiographical novella *What Remains* (originally published in 1990) by German author Christa Wolf, where the narrator assumes 'that there are conversations in every country, the hidden meaning of which becomes apparent only when they are compared with dozens of similar conversations on the same topic' (Wolf 1993: 282).

Wolf submitted information to the Stasi as an *Inoffizielle Mitarbeiter*, while also enduring years of surveillance when living in the GDR's Berlin. Until the publication of her novella, she was regarded by German critics as 'the GDR's most admirable writer' (Pizer 2021: 4). The novella was actually written much earlier, in the late 1970s, during a time when self-censorship was necessary within a society where Socialist Realism was the 'officially sanctioned theory and method of literary composition' (Berendse 2021: 6). This vague terminology was meant to favourably reflect the living conditions within the

GDR, though the state-endorsed requirement ironically contributed to the 'surrealistic disposition' of life in the East German communist state (Berendse 2021: 1).

While not strictly adhering to the literary features of Surrealism as an artistic movement or aesthetic, the surrealistic disposition discussed by Gerrit-Jan Berendse in *Echoes of Surrealism: Challenging Socialist Realism in East German Literature, 1945–1990* (2021) is due, in part, to that very act of self-censorship in speech and the way it disturbed ordinary citizens' logical frames of reference. We are accustomed to enacting and witnessing change in ourselves and our relationships over interior and exterior conversational channels – where unrecorded dialogue disappears as soon as it is thought or spoken. In Wolf's fiction, that frame of reference is ruptured in the story by introducing another witness to the spoken channel, one who is not only listening but recording and evaluating based on the shifting values of a totalitarian culture.

The narrator imagines that all the information collected about her 'had to come together on some desk or in some head somewhere' but remarks that the collector would know everything about her 'except for the really important things' (Wolf 1993: 254). Imagining she may not be monitored after all, the protagonist in *What Remains* wonders, 'What if all our hubris and preening were directed at emptiness? It wouldn't make the slightest difference' (Wolf 1993: 242). Once personal privacy had been systematically transgressed by the Stasi, Wolf's format of speech was endemically changed in preparation for its potential overhearing. One of the many consequences of Stasi surveillance was the abstraction that occurred from the self – a painful process that augmented the vocal channel with the Surrealist effects of concealment.

Often, the true meaning alluded to in a fictional character's language and actions resides in the 'unsaid' (subtext), the layer underneath the 'said' (text). That character's truest nature then lies in the innermost sphere of the unsayable (McKee 2016). It is a matter of character design for an author, one that has psychological roots in the experience of trauma (Rippl 2018). In both scenarios, that of the fictional character and the selectively reported speech of the surveillance subject, they are represented via speech that is intended to be heard by an audience. The fourth wall listener subsequently uses this dialogue to decipher the 'true' nature of a character or person.

Speech transcribed to media dialogue is not conversation designed for 'keeping the channel open' but a narrative device designed to 'develop and change relationships' (McKee 1997: 388). Forms of suppression in Wolf's depiction of the GDR did not extend to silencing speech altogether. The nuance lay in the appropriation of the channel of ordinary conversation that provided compelling dialogue for a state audience. This was an auditory mechanism or conduit, full of stunted verbal exchanges between citizens that obliged the narrator to go 'beyond the borders of the sayable, knowing full well that border violations of any kind are punished' (Wolf 1993: 240).

For the novella's protagonist, the fear of the state, and of any incriminating dialogue that might be constructed from her speech, is only alleviated by the rare sensation of being unwitnessed in her bedroom during 'one of the most deeply relieving moments of the day. No unfamiliar person, no unfamiliar look, perhaps not even an unfamiliar ear' followed her in. She can experience the 'indescribable pleasure of being alone and unobserved. . . . No thinking, no working' (Wolf 1993: 269). She finds refuge in the silence of her bedroom, safe not only from Stasi audio capture but, moreover, from the reader who hears everything:

> Don't you think I can feel their hands running over me, looking for that weak point through which they might enter me. I know that point. But I'm not going to tell anyone where it is, not even you and not even in my thoughts. (Wolf 1993: 270)

Personal safety is dependent on secrecy, even from the expressive self. Measures taken by figures in *What Remains*, such as speaking quietly, turning up the radio during conversations or unplugging the telephone while entertaining guests, constitute theatrical attempts to thwart audio surveillance. Adopting an aurally holistic position, the narrator proposes that those being targeted are 'meshed together like the teeth of a smoothly functioning zipper' with the actions of their listeners (Wolf 1993: 244). If the danger of being exposed lies in the incriminating connection between words and feelings, then the unobservable realm of the unsayable becomes a space of refuge. Our protagonist imagines that her listeners possess unbounded expression because 'those who feel nothing have all words freely at their disposal' (Wolf 1993: 278): they can express text without subtext.

Worlds

Even after East Germany's Western borders hardened into impassable physical barriers, there were ways in which its geographical and cultural proximity to the Western world created challenges for the Stasi and opportunities for foreign powers. While the Berlin Wall and its military fortifications prohibited visual and audible communication between Germans on either side, broadcast media was not as easy to control. A large number of German and international German-language services provided by the United States and Great Britain operated radio stations out of West Berlin (Major 2012: 255), which was perfectly situated geographically to broadcast into East Germany, carved as it was into the middle of the GDR (Classen 2013: 321).

Unlike Operation Gold, in which worlds collided secretly under the wall and communications were captured without permission, Western radio stations funded by their respective governments used 'soft' cultural power. They operated in the ether and in plain earshot of the Stasi in order to infiltrate East German culture. This was particularly problematic for the Stasi and the Soviet regime because Germany's new borders represented a world cleaved in half, an 'artificial divide' between two newly formed states with a great amount of cultural proximity. The Stasi was tasked with retuning the East German state and protecting it against the signals of social discordance emanating from the West.

Radio broadcasts in both directions could be understood to evade the artificial barrier that ran through Germany. As historian Christoph Classen points out, the presence of both East and West German programming on the airwaves underlined very different world views, each relating differently to the purpose of acoustic media, the role of the audience and its subsequent relationship to statecraft. Where they found common ground was in their focus on cultural control and on trying to influence the 'other' Germany. However, the radio listener's process of switching on and tuning in undetected meant that the audience-oriented programming that typified Western approaches to media was much more popular in East Germany. This was in part because of the GDR's 'utilitarian concept of media . . . to consolidate the population's class consciousness' (Classen 2013: 326) on either side of the German border. While the lack of interest from the West German public in East Germany's educational version of radio made any potential challenge to the West negligible, West German media was considered by the GDR to be a threat: a bourgeois capitalist tool in the fight against the proletariat. The political intentions of radio perceived in this manner delegitimized those arguments forwarded by the West concerning the free flow of information: arguments that were used to justify its foreign service radio broadcasting. For the Stasi, such media was simply understood to be markedly anti-Communist and an extension of the foreign intelligence services (Classen 2013: 329).

Contemporary history supports this view. Many of the broadcasting teams that worked in West Germany for the BBC East German programme in the 1950s and 1960s used radio as a branch of psychological warfare to reach enemy populaces in the Second World War (Major 2012: 257). Ongoing radio listener routines had also been formed during the war, with many Germans in the habit of listening to foreign radio such as the BBC to hear an alternative view of political events. The BBC weaponized the liberal character of the media by demonstratively using freedom of speech to depict an alternative reality to the Stasi-controlled GDR. The broadcasting of 'dissenting Anglophobic voices [in a listeners' letters programme] attempted to show that true democracy could bear criticism' (Major 2012: 258). Similar debates on the freedom of speech exist today (OSCE 2021) with the historical origins of the link between the border-jumping affordance of electronic media, its political affordance as a propaganda tool and these liberal arguments continuing to influence web culture.

Unsurprisingly, the practice of listening to Western radio was officially prohibited by the Stasi, but while other media channels such as television and print were easier to control through state apparatus, radio remained more difficult. Despite the use of both spies and technological deterrents, a third of East Germans usually listened to the BBC East German Service and two-thirds to the American radio service RIAS (Major 2012). These secret listeners were diffuse and benefited from the affordances of radio receivers, which allowed listeners to tune in to whatever was being broadcast, including uncensored letters and interviews with other East Germans.

The Stasi and its Soviet counterparts in the KGB struggled to find an effective technological way of blocking the radio. Previously, the practice of radio jamming was one of the Stasi's most effective methods and involved using a transmitter tuned to the same or an adjacent frequency to override radio waves. By using such techniques, they were able to make the reception of programmes impossible to listen to (Classen 2013: 332). These jamming operations were conducted in complete secrecy, partly because such jamming activities signalled a waveform space within East German life that the Stasi could not control through coercion and fear.

It is documented, however, that by 1953, the GDR was operating ten major jamming transmitters along with thirty smaller variants. These were considered 'manifestly insufficient' by the Soviet authorities, and by 1964 more powerful jamming apparatuses were in operation. What truly limited the extent of radio jamming, though, was the disruption they caused to the GDR's own broadcasting and networks. Transmitters were installed close to police and Stasi headquarters for secrecy and security purposes but subsequently interfered with their radio traffic and telecommunications. By the end of the 1970s, as Cold War relations started to warm up between East and West Germany, radio jamming almost entirely ceased in the GDR.

Prediction

Underlying the Stasi's surveillance methodology was the banal suspicion that the East German public was constantly being seduced by Western agents and by influences undetected in East German society. As the enemy was perceived to lie within, the Stasi had to wage its war against the public (Popplewell 1992). Therefore, the rationale for monitoring, which was previously reserved for foreign populations, became the rationale of the police. With enough agents in the field, they would have sufficient intelligence not just to capture insurgents but to predict future crimes against the state.

In the early 1950s, Stasi surveillance had a single mandate: to predict the machinations of known opposition groups and Western-based organizations (Bruce 2003: 3). After the popular rebellion of 1953, in which its government was humiliated and forced to enlist the help of the occupying Red Army to regain control, the organization was haunted by its failure to predict the public's dissatisfaction (Popplewell 1992: 40). In response, the Stasi sought to extend its listener base into the general populace. Its expansive mission was to listen in on chit-chat and gossip, focusing especially on any signs of dissent and corruption. Through such practices, it reasoned that it would be able to divine illegal activities and gain the capacity to perceive any whispers that emboldened thoughts of uprising.

As the number of agents in the increasingly distributed network increased, the types of information it collected also changed. 'Arcane espionage knowledge' was augmented by information traditionally 'classified and dismissed as gossip' (Lewis 2021: xxvii). As the state strained to hear the mutinous plans of its enemy within, hearsay became acceptable as, and indistinguishable from, intelligence. Stasi informers were allowed to encroach on all aspects of their targets' lives. By giving them an 'unlimited license to indulge their urges to speculate about everything from others' sex lives to their medications' (Lewis 2021: xxvii), the Stasi turned its agents into powerful gossips. They became doyens of deception and were able to transform their speculations into damaging predictions that permanently affected lives in the GDR.

Gossip allows communities to discuss things that they know are out of bounds in more formal contexts (Besnier 2009) and lowers the burden of evidence. The shift from gathering intelligence from known enemy actors (whose actions could be assumed to be hostile) to the words and actions of its domestic population led to a methodology of expansive data collection that neither assumed innocence nor guilt. All information was valid and was harvested because it 'might one day be useful' (Lewis 2021: xxvii). In a sense, the predictive function of its intelligence was replaced by pre-predictive intelligence: surveillance as predictive surplus, as an active body of suspicion and speculation. However, what sustained these practices, over four decades, was the effectiveness of acting on, and being privy to, gossip.

It was the speculative nature of 'gossip as intelligence' that allowed the Stasi to strike fear into the East German population. Gossip intelligence did not require significant verification. Its authenticity was instead derived from the 'voices that [. . . were . . .] never heard in political meetings' – those of children, housewives and other marginalized groups (Besnier 2009: 191) whose insights and speculations gave the information the character of 'localness' (2009: 191). Employing the speculative scope and local character of gossip to help them make predictions, the Stasi could more effectively coerce its population by weaponizing everyday conversation (Keefe 2006: 141).

Despite the comprehensive nature of its networks, the Stasi would ultimately be unsuccessful in predicting the 1989 uprising that would be its nation state's undoing. The reasons for its failure appear to lie in the exact methods laid out above: its mixing of predictive and coercive functions left it alienated from the publics it sought gossip from. Through a pervasive sense of being listened to, local debate and discussion had become guarded and gossip no longer operated as gossip. Instead, resistance to, and dissatisfaction with, the regime became entwined in a pervasive silence that rendered the Stasi unaware of its own alienation from public discourse (Popplewell 1992: 62).

In the twenty-first century, the appetite for intelligence gathering, whether it be carried out by state police or commercial entities for forecasting purposes, has not diminished. Since 2008, 'predictive policing' has gained currency through the application of AI and statistical analysis. When large quantities of data and increased computer power are added to the mix, the resulting technologies have allowed government organizations to scale up criminological models that appear to make patterns of crime and the behaviours of criminals more predictable. Such models are apparently capable of 'predicting where and when a crime is likely to occur, who is likely responsible for prior crimes, and who is most likely to offend or be victimized in the future' (Perry et al. 2013: 31–2). Unlike the Stasi's methods, it is considered objective, scientific and reproducible. However, the speculative quality of gossip remains discernible in the quantitative character of these new systems; their dangers and inaccuracies echo the nebulous claims to veracity made by rumour and hearsay.

Intimacy

The Stasi sought to systematically challenge and throw suspicion on the notion of personal intimacy. Intimacy in personal relationships is bounded and protected by responsibility and duties of care and formalized in systems such as relational ethics (Ellis 2007) to protect each from harm. In this way, personal intimacy introduces formal and informal limits that would have restricted the flow of information through the Stasi's ocean of operatives. When thought of like this, affinity and affection can be framed as coagulating agents in the East German data stream – emotional embolisms that slowed down the 'absolute philistine efficiency' (Lewis 2021: xiii) sought by Stasi leaders, which itself was an uncompromising assault on sonic expression.

In the Cold War's sea of information, the Ministry for State Security conceptualized itself, in relation to the populace, as an imaginary creature composed of connected organs – an octopus or kraken (Bathrick 1995). The image of the monster-octopus brings to mind a particular set of non-ocular sensibilities: cephalopods such as the octopus do not have ears but rather feel sonic vibrations through an organ called the statocyst, which is also its balance receptor. Its reach, in (m)any directions, is better described by its tentacles than by its visual scope. A wave-formed metaphor for the Stasi, the octopus's tentacular reach speaks to the intelligence agency's desire to float on and through data – an apt metaphor despite the agency's headquarters being dubbed the 'House of One Thousand Eyes' (Keefe 2006: 141).

In her essay on tentacular thinking, Donna Haraway describes the entities that make up 'nets and networks' as being more like 'tentacular feelers than like binocular eyes' (Haraway 2016: online). In the octopus-like body of the state, the responsibilities of, and care for, these feelers were secondary to a new amorphous whole. In this body, people themselves were relieved of independent needs and functions. The boundaries of intimacy were no longer a justification for the state sensing apparatus to remain outside homes, hotel rooms and bathrooms. Tiny holes were drilled into walls to allow sight and sound to escape along electronic tentacles back into the body, its human eavesdroppers and voyeurs divested of guilt or responsibility by their duty of care to the GDR (Betts 2012: 22).

Other barriers protecting intimacy were also dissolved: doctor-patient confidentiality was ignored to allow information to flow back to intelligence services about people's most intimate physical and psychological problems. Even in sleep, people commonly dreamt of being followed or were worried that their dreams could somehow be monitored (Betts 2012: 35). Everything was subservient to the functioning of the monster body itself. The second Minister for State Security went as far as describing Stasi informants as its 'respiratory organs' that allowed the regime to 'breathe more easily' (Lewis 2021: xiv).

The distinctions and barriers between personal and national secrets were thinned until East German society itself began to 'implode . . . into a huge organism watching itself' (Schmeidel 2014: 28). Everyone was compromised; no one person could be expected not to divulge the secrets of another. Even high-ranking Stasi and party officials were not considered exempt. In fact, 'the private lives of government officials, police officers, and Stasi agents were often placed under severe scrutiny' (Betts 2012: 33), such was the totalizing logic of the tentacular body.

The GDR's systematic deployment of monitoring technologies and strategies provided it with an intimate knowledge of its bodily functions, which in turn empowered it to administer corrective violence and terror. With this in mind, one does not have to stretch their imagination too far to be able to draw a line between twentieth- and twenty-first-century approaches to totalitarian surveillance in Europe, as well as more globally. Big datasets can, in this sense, be thought of as monster-tentacular bodies, ever expanding, feeling their way, sensing every possibility among the tidal waves of statistics.

Voice

During the sono-political envelope that the Stasi operated within over a forty-year period, the voices of East Germany's occupants were vulnerable to betraying their owners when made audible. Whenever vocal cords resonated, they potentially activated recording devices that were dormant until triggered by reel torque. The soft murmuring clicks of tape machines captured all articulations that came into range. Those utterances that did not were chronicled and relayed by the drone army of informants that mimicked the unrelenting nature of the recording device, only in human form.

Voices of the East German populace travelled through air vents, windows and bugged furniture, giving life to previously inanimate objects. This could be a contemporary reading of animism, but crucially it also interfaces with the analogue spirituality of machines. The utterances that unintentionally spoke to objects, and thus to those who listened remotely, resided in a decidedly non-spirit realm. In this oscillating equation, the voice calls forth the hidden world of the listener but without full realization or comprehension of its manifestation, even if it suspects and expects it to exist. In 2024, we are used to this machine-human dynamic. Technologies speak back to us in increasingly human-like voices, whether it is our speakers, cars or toys. Everything that is electronically manufactured can now potentially speak back to us in all languages, accents and regional dialects, all delivered with the synthesized elan of computer-generated expression.

Given the increasing velocity of voice-activated technology, it begs the question: When did machines start talking to us? One could begin with 1770 and the creation of the 'Turk' – a fraudulent chequered figure that had a voice box fixed into it so that it could announce *Échec* (French for 'check') during chess games. Jump ahead to 1890, Thomas Edison invented talking dolls that had miniaturized phonographs embedded into them, allowing human speech to emanate from their inert forms. Fast forward again to 1938, and Bell Labs' Homer Dudley invented the vocoder in order to synthesize speech for the first time (Tompkins 2010).

Pull the record back two decades to the First World War, and it is tapping sounds that spell out another important evolutionary step in automated articulation. Transmitting via shortwave bands (SW), number stations did exactly what their moniker suggested. They issued sequences of numbers over the radio, via Morse code or automated voices.

They were covert channels hidden in plain audition. In West and East Germany, targeted intelligence officers in the field from both sides were ordered to tune in to selected shortwave frequencies on specific days and times in order to receive encrypted information (The Conet Project 1997).

This remote technology enabled agents to operate furtively between the shadows without having to meet fellow spies or receive disguised packages. Harnessing the human voice, the version following Morse Code was called the One-Way Voice Link . The stations still issued the camouflaged instructions in groups of numbers (usually in batches of five), often preceded by a preamble or a musical tune. The predominantly female voices that delivered the numbers required no interaction or feedback. They were single channels of furtive communication radiating out into the world (Goldmanis 2018).

The manner in which the human voice was deployed to rhythmically transmit numbers is instructive as it points to a pre-digital dilation, a process through which information is converted into digits. In this repetitious mode, the purpose of the voice as a communication tool is abstracted. There is no vulnerability. Sonically speaking, it proposes the human as an extension of the machine, an inversion of the technological imperative that relegates machine logic to a secondary position in relation to human sentience. American and West German number stations extended the rationale of zeros and ones as the full range of single digits was serviced. The endless sequencing of orated numbers renders the voice on the cusp of the non-human.

1964–5 marked a shift in the stations' vocal delivery. Machines replaced the teams of female number speakers who had previously been recording onto audio tape in the DDR compound's basement, a facility which had the sublimely incongruous name of *Funkobject* (radio object). The first analogue speech generator was named *Gerät 32028* but was codenamed *Schnatterinchen* (Crypto Museum – Device 32028). Sony, Panasonic and Grundig shortwave receivers were used because SW radio does not require satellites, nor does it require the internet to cover the globe. *Gerät 32028* was developed by the *Institut für Kosmosforschung* (Space Research Institute), which saw the benefit in removing vulnerable vocal folds and replacing them with the rhythmical absolution of mechanized consonants and vowels.

From Morse Code to human voice-to-speech generators, the number stations' lineage traces the development of communications systems employed at the sonic frontier of espionage. During the Stasi era, the voice (and its simulation) could be positioned as an agent of activation – both of humans and machines, in the shape of undercover intelligence officers and listening devices. The airborne alchemy of articulation brought actions at a distance into being through the mere utterance of numbers into a wider vibrational field. A more detached account positions number stations as instruments of deactivation. The soporific sequencing of repetitious content tunes listeners out, with automated voices as bleak sedatives that edit out the complexities of the world. A scrambled equation calculated the Stasi's multitude of recorded conversations and rendered them into audio mulch in the process – radio programming as numerogesia, a drone logic for illicit archives.

Fidelity

As we have heard in the 'Process' subsection of this chapter, the Stasi's psychological warfare technique *Zersetzung* consisted of a range of tactics based on deception and covert manipulation. At the heart of the Stasi's tsunami of trauma resided operational psychology. Harnessing the principles of behavioural science, this sub-branch of psychology enabled military leaders to understand and manipulate those deemed to threaten national security (Maheshwari and Kumar 2016). *Zersetzung* focused on breaking down trust and corrupting friendships and family bonds, even going so far as to orchestrate discord within the harmony of lovers. Feeding on its own sinister and paranoidly perverse aim, the goal of *Zersetzung was* to atomize East German society. If no one felt safe trusting anyone else, it would negate collective behaviours and extinguish forms of resistance before they had time to foment. Friends spied on friends, work colleagues covertly listened to each other and family members informed on relatives with whom they shared living space. Possibly most telling, however, was the aim to break the bond between lovers, and for this, a new stealth mode was required.

Male agents were enlisted to seduce and manipulate female 'marks'. As the programme scaled up, the politics of attraction were industrialized. Rather than relying on the sole trade of intimate illusionists, the Stasi fashioned teams of plastic lovers – passion(less) squads of players branded the 'Romeos'. Those being targeted were predominantly women in secretarial positions. This was because they often overheard ministers' conversations, whether they occurred in Bonn's government offices or during their boss's leisure time. To this end, '[t]he Stasi did an impressive amount of groundwork before a woman was approached. Scouts were employed to inform officers who might be ripe for romantic cultivation, and thousands of deutschmarks were paid for a job well done' (Pressly 2004: online).

The workflow of enchantment was, however, different than one might imagine. Rather than enlisting aesthetically pleasing specimens with silver-gilded tongues, the Stasi engaged Romeos that were often the antithesis of Hollywood stereotypes. Thus, the players were not handsome rogues oozing malicious charm. In fact, 'the women definitely weren't going for good looks. It was the old-fashioned manners . . . flowers, wining and dining, and, most importantly, these men listened to women. Men often don't, so that was very attractive. Sex didn't play a major role' (Pressly 2004: online). Listening was a passive-seductive activity, a sensitive camouflage for the espionage that the relationship would be built on.

The act of listening, as an active agent of attraction, was one of the key tactics established by Markus Wolf (Wolf and McElvoy 1999). Referred to as 'the man without a face' for decades by Western intelligence organizations, Wolf's construction of the Romeo network was the blueprint of orchestrated desire that was later used by the UK's National Public Order Intelligence Unit. Deploying the same sexploitative modus operandi between 2003 and 2010, the unit ordered operatives, such as the infamous Mark Kennedy, to infiltrate protest groups. His insidious mission was to dupe female activists into having sexual relationships with him so that he could gain insight into the group's inner workings and plans (Evans 2019).

The decomposition of trust, at the interface of the most intimate of relationships, oscillated for decades after the Stasi was operational. 'The detrimental impact of government surveillance persists and has led to lower levels of trust in post-reunification Germany' according to psychologist Celia Fisher, who runs a group therapy session for victims of the East German dictatorship (Bailey 2019: online). When modes of listening were conducted under the guise of sympathy and empathy but were subsequently revealed to be emotionally manipulative, the betrayal registered deeply. The dissolution of trust begets the breakdown of connection and reciprocal interaction; when scaled up, it leads to the collapse of the social bonds that form societies and cultures at large.

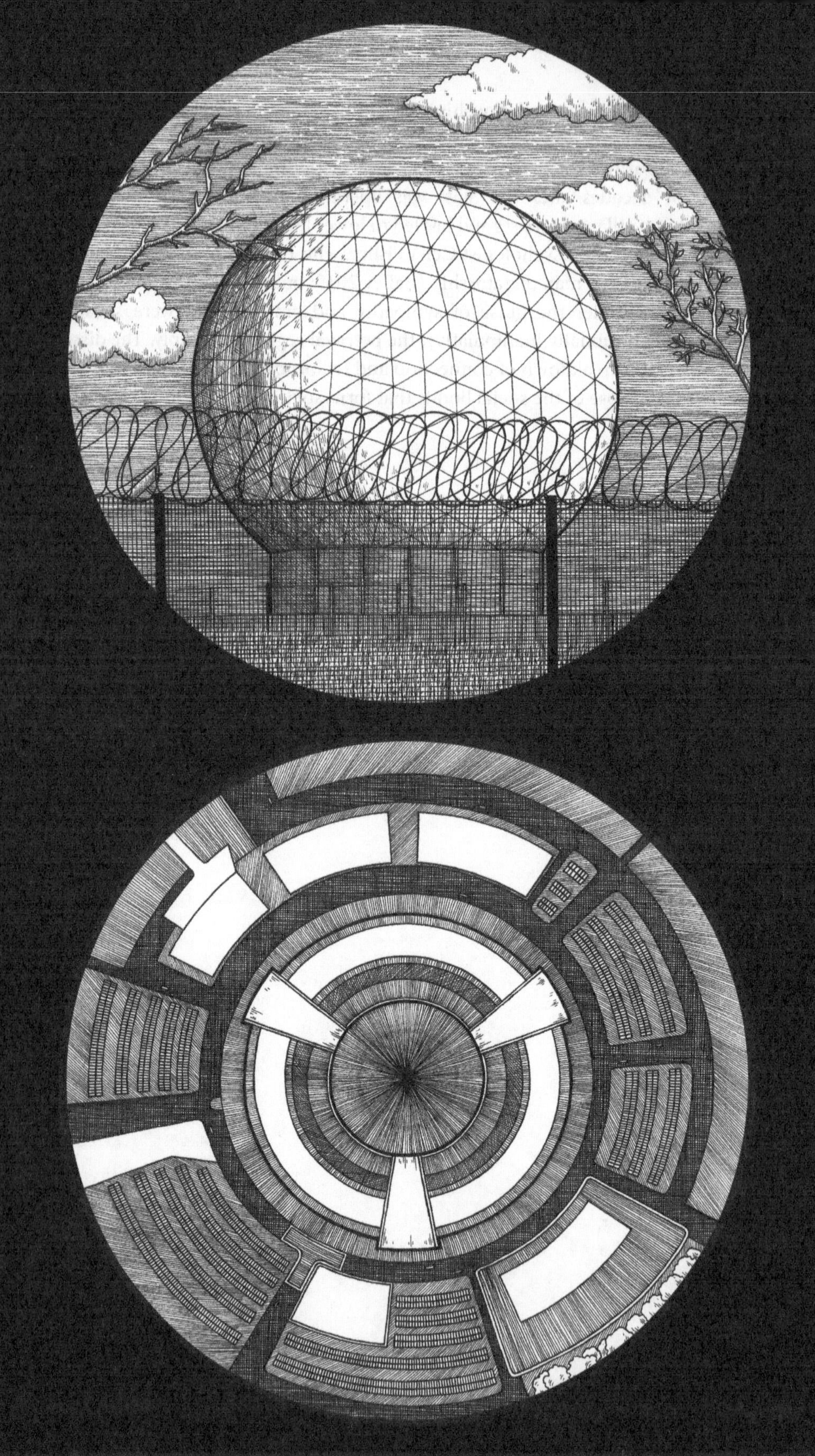

CHAPTER 6
ECHELON

Process

After the Second World War, the historic UKUSA agreement (pronounced 'you-koo-za') was ratified. The agreement shaped signals intelligence (SIGINT) strategy to this day, not only between the two countries but further afield to all those who were, and are, adjacent to it. For historian Richard Aldrich, 'It is also wrong to think of UKUSA as exclusively concerned with SIGINT. It is, rather, a SIGINT and *security* network' (2011: 91). The agreement was the 'sum of a curious agglomeration of many understandings that were mostly between two countries only' between 1943 and 1948 (2011: 89). It was fuelled by successful joint UK and US intelligence operations during the Second World War, which had helped to end the devastating conflict.

A new era of global intelligence dominance was to follow, but only for a select group of allies, namely the United States (National Security Agency), the United Kingdom (Government Communications Headquarters), Canada (Communications Security Establishment), Australia (Signals Directorate) and New Zealand (Government Communications Security Bureau). Together, they shared information garnered from covertly expropriating the diurnal swarm of global radio communications (Hager 1996). Based on the collection, analysis, cryptanalysis, decryption and translation of information (PI 2013), the all-seeing, all-hearing Five Eyes (FVEY) emerged (Campbell and Honigsbaum 1999).

Fast forward fifteen years, and the 1962 Cuban Missile crisis was in the rear-view mirror. The American government's sensitivity to communist threats was at an all-time high. While many of the era's surveillance strategies were fuelled by paranoia, 1966s 'Frosting program' was future-facing. An umbrella term for the gathering and processing of information from communications satellites, the programme had two distinct arms. 'Transient' was the operational codename for activities related to undermining Soviet satellites. The second arm focused on Intelsat communications – an intergovernmental constellation of satellites that provided both broadcast and telecommunications capacity. It was this seemingly benign set of services that grew into the global surveillance network 'Echelon' (Campbell 1988).

Originally located in the United Kingdom and the United States, Echelon became operational in 1974 after the UK government launched Skynet satellites into orbit. Also named 'P415' by arms and aerospace contractor Lockheed Martin corporation (McGill 2007), Echelon was initially equipped with three antennas that could downlink telex, telegraph and fax signals from satellites. By 2000, it had grown to 120 antennas spread across seventeen sites. More recently, investigative journalist Duncan Campbell posited that the number of antennas has grown to 232 (Campbell 2015a). Providing intelligence to both UK and US governments, the Royal Air Force Menwith Hill site in Yorkshire is one of the largest electronic monitoring stations in the world. Part of the Echelon network, the site's facilities are referred to as the 'golf balls' (GCHQ), albeit these ones hit a range of thousands of miles rather than hundreds of yards.

Information captured by the satellites is fed through the network's distributed matrix of computers – the 'Echelon Dictionaries'. They connect each country's surveillance technologies into an integrated system that contains not only its parent agency's chosen keywords but also the other four agency's lists (Hager 1996: 29). The keyword search itself is linguistically tethered to inventories of dates, names, phrases, places and subjects, and when combinations are registered within messages or calls, 'the tagged intercept is forwarded straight to the requesting country' (Wright 1998: 20). The network connecting the FVEY, meanwhile, is known as 'StoneGhost'. It hosts high-security information about military activity, foreign intelligence, national security and SIGINT (Rouleau 2020: online). The growing spectre of all-seeing and all-hearing surveillance technologies replacing divine celestial beings, often attributed with similar capacities, has become reality.

The growth in Echelon's hardware and networks has developed hand in hand with the growing acceptance of military surveillance techniques that accelerated during the 2000s War on Terror, which encouraged a totalitarian acceptance of being monitored in exchange for safety from terrorism (Bamford 1982). Exemplifying projected compliance, US Justice Department lawyer John Yoo made a statement a few days after the 9/11 attacks. He proposed that while certain technologies and strategies might be constitutionally problematic, when it came to terrorist threats, 'the government may be justified in taking measures which in less troubled conditions could be seen as infringements of individual liberties' (Kakutani 2006: online).

Proof of such infringements happened only days after Yoo's statement when then president George W. Bush sidelined the dictates of the Foreign Intelligence Surveillance Act, namely the process of obtaining warrants to legalize wiretapping. According to D. C. Webb, the move towards acceptance that covert 'eavesdropping inside the country without court approval was a major shift in American intelligence-gathering practices, particularly for the National Security Agency, whose mission is to spy on communications abroad' (Webb 2007b: 461–2). It is in this context of malleable morality, a 'largely legislation-free area', that systems such as Echelon bloom (Webb 2007b: 457–8): metal flowers in space opening their petal-like panels to seed the earth's communication systems. From the Stasi's approach to capturing and understanding the thoughts, relationships and uprisings of a nation, the next step for surveillance is to go international, to go global. Echelon does precisely this. It is Edison's oral conceit (wrapped in the language of dreams) of capturing speeches from significant public orators and even deities throughout the continuum of human history (Trower 2012: 68), amplified across the spectrum of human communications. Whether important, unimportant, casual or formal, all speeches are considered potentially worthy of recording. Echelon listens to everything, everywhere, all at once.

Recording

From the Stasi to Echelon, the shift in scope and ambition of the recording process is evident in the latter's capturing of information via technologies bisecting the earth and the cosmos. From state to globe in the blink of a spy. In this case, the pulsing of low orbit satellites. In terms of recording, the most significant transformation of the 1960s and 1970s was the change in networks, from cable-bound landlines wrapped around the planet to microwave radio towers and peregrine communication systems floating in space. Servicing the increased demand for long-distance calls, satellites spill unencrypted data into the ether because they transmit in straight lines that do not follow the curvature of the earth. This allows anyone who is interested and has the requisite reconnaissance technology to effectively plug in, capture and play (Aldrich 2011: 340).

As inferred, satellites stimulated an evolution in transmission interception, but all communication networks are digitally quarried, including landlines, cellular and the internet. Before the wars on terrorism and drugs, one of the early advantages that the technology made palpable was the West's capacity to listen more closely to conversations emanating to and from Moscow. Rather than solely trying to listen to decision-makers and powerful political figures, the NSA emulated the Stasi approach of monitoring service personnel surrounding such individuals. Instead of personal assistants, the NSA listened to service industry professionals such as taxi drivers: an ambulatory set of 'ears on the ground' who would similarly inadvertently reveal intimate details of the VIPs they drove around the city.

Writing for the *Washington Post* in 1971, journalist Jack Anderson reported on such relatively low standards of secrecy (Aldrich 2011: 344). The 'off the clock' conversations that drivers overheard were often personally revealing and could be leveraged, especially those of an emotional disposition. This was a shrewd choice given that the drivers inhabited a compressed space in which passengers often let their guard down and spoke openly. The drivers were considered non-listeners, which rendered them the auditory version of the untouchables – the unhearables. It would be years until the wider world also heard.

The existence of Echelon was revealed by Margaret Newsham, a former employee at the Lockheed Corporation who helped design programmes for the surveillance network. After being fired by Lockheed for objecting to the surveillance of US politicians, she disclosed her involvement to a closed hearing held by the US Congress House Permanent Select Committee on Intelligence in 1988 and made later public statements in 1999. Her revelation that the NSA was listening to Republican senator Strom Thurmond's phone calls was the first time such allegations had been made. The interception and recording of his calls were the tip of a surveillance iceberg that had been hidden for years. Newsham later met with Duncan Campbell and handed him some of the plans for Echelon, though her identity was kept secret until February 2000. Among the evidence she passed on were plans for massive global expansion that showed how Echelon 'intercepted satellite connections, sorting phone calls, telex, telegraph and computer signals' (Campbell in Curtis 2015: online).

Following Newsham's revelations, Bill Blick, Australia's inspector general of intelligence, confirmed Echelon's existence by stating that the Defense Signals Directorate (DSD) was indeed part of the international Echelon surveillance framework. He claimed that 'as you would expect there are a large amount of radio communications floating around in the atmosphere, and agencies such as DSD collect those communications in the interests of their national security' (Blick in Bomford 1999: online). When further pressed on whether the information collected is shared with partner countries such as the United States and the United Kingdom, Blick responded, yes 'in certain circumstances' (Bomford 1999: online).

Nicky Hager's 1996 book *Secret Power: New Zealand's Role in the International Spy Network* clearly outlined the full functionality of Echelon while explaining the role of New Zealand in the FVEY surveillance network. He posits that the extensive framework of listening carried out by the Echelon network reaches another magnitude of scope and ambition when multiple populations are simultaneously monitored. It is difficult to disagree. 'There is no evidence of a UKUSA code of ethics or of a tradition of respect for Parliament or civil liberties in their home countries. The opposite seems to be true: that anything goes as long as you do not get caught. Secrecy not only permits but encourages questionable operations' (Hager 1996: 55). For Manuel DeLanda, secrecy has other imperatives that resonate in an echo chamber of masking techniques – 'certain components of intelligence agencies are not truly military, but rather form . . . a new kind of "religious order" in which secrecy comes to be worshipped for its own sake' (1991: 6).

Whistle-blower and former NSA contractor Edward Snowden shared the observation that Echelon answered to no known cultural or geographical legal structure (akin to the recently revived Guantánamo Bay detention camp). He described the FVEY as a 'supra-national intelligence organization that does not answer to the known laws of its own countries' (2014: online). The logic of hoovering up information had been perfected by the Stasi, albeit on a national basis. Between 1935 and 1972, the hoover sound that insidiously directed covert surveillance was that of one J. Edgar, who had set the tone of American espionage and helped score the Western dream of capturing all communications, regardless of their content.

Echelon represents a significant evolution in the gathering of information. The vacuum created by the Intelsat communications satellites collapses the voice of the individual, creating massive dense flows of material in the process. This is the hoover sound in space, or rather the unsound space of the surveillance vortex. Just as oil is the underground sentient agency that drives activities, events and allegiances across the human continuum in Reza Negarestani's speculative text *Cyclonopedia* (2008), so the satellite becomes the present-day orbiting equivalent. Speculative earmachines shape the relations, investments and torrents of paranoia that circle the planet with an ever-increasing volatility.

Transgression

The first-ever story about the UK's Government Communications Headquarters (GCHQ) was written by Duncan Campbell and Mark Hosenball and appeared in *Time Out* in May 1976. It was entitled 'The Eavesdroppers'. It detailed a listening operation in Chicksands, just outside of London, that included a steel circle a quarter-mile wide and named 'Steelhenge' by the authors. The publication alluded to five thousand monitoring operators reporting to GCHQ from around the world, sharing information across the FVEY via an electronic intelligence pact dating back to 1947. Campbell and Hosenball's most reliable source for the exposé was Oliver G. Selfridge, a top intelligence consultant who worked for the NSA and was described by Campbell as a whistle-blower (Campbell 2015a: online). The overreach of GCHQ into the private communications of citizens was, in Campbell's words, 'an importation from the United States of post-Watergate investigative journalism' (Aldrich 2011: 358). This would not be the last time that a crisis of national security in the United States would lead to further erosion of digital privacy at home and abroad: an observation that would go on to be proven correct by Edward Snowden's whistle-blowing on the NSA's activities post-9/11.

Repeated instances of whistle-blowing that exposed Echelon's practices were marked by legal investigations and a range of policy changes, but transgressions against individual privacy continue to occur nonetheless. Just as the leaks and revelations from within the ranks of an organization are weighed according to whether the 'costs of the identified misconduct outweigh the security benefits' (Stanger 2019: 165), the whistle-blower's calculation now includes considerations as to whether the cost of privacy erosion outweighs the perceived benefits of the offending technology. After seeing proof of harmful data practices, changes have been made by the European Union. These include the securing of personal communications and resistance to permanent data storage in directives that reflect a 'widening gap between American and European attitudes toward privacy rights' (Stanger 2019: 145). When 'over 90 percent of the world's Internet traffic passes through technologies developed, owned, and/or operated by the American government and American businesses' (Snowden 2019: 163), those actions which constitute transgressive interference can arise from cross-cultural differences and influences.

In his 2019 memoir, which detailed his path to releasing documents that confirmed Echelon's existence, Snowden recalled asking himself: 'How was I to balance my contract of secrecy with the agencies that employed me and the oath I'd sworn to my country's founding principles? To whom, or what, did I owe greater allegiance?' (Snowden 2019: 6). Parallels between whistle-blowers and double agents who become disillusioned by their own country's inability to adhere to its supposed principles can be leveraged by the exposed transgressors. In American law, there is 'no distinction between providing classified information to the press in the public interest and providing it, even selling it, to the enemy' (Snowden 2019: 249).

Jobs concerning national security at the government level require at least a gestural pledge to uphold the values and integrity of that government and its citizens. By leveraging information from external workers – either across borders in the case of the FVEY, or by engaging contractors to run surveillance systems on home soil – agencies that operated Echelon have sidestepped legality in a manner unique to the digital age. When employees or former employees expose practices that the general public disapproves of, they are traditionally only granted whistle-blower status if the activities they give evidence on are proven to be illegal (Stanger 2019: 150). In the case of Snowden's whistle-blowing, the NSA argued that it was not unconstitutional to listen in on private citizens' communications because sharing data with a third-party service provider forfeits the right to privacy (Snowden 2019: 230).

Snowden has been living in exile in Russia since he shared classified documents with the press, and his status as a whistle-blower remains contested by the intelligence community. Among them, there is a belief that 'such a large security breach had to be the work of a spy' (Stanger 2019: 156). The work of whistle-blowers arguably threatens national security by exposing intelligence operations and technologies, but it also threatens public trust in the institutions meant to be serving our interests. Secretive government agencies such as the NSA, CSIS and GCHQ, which need to engage in public relations strategies to defend SIGINT, present us with a distinct problem of the digital age, where 'personal, commercial, and military communications . . . traverse the same digital space' (Stanger 2019: 125).

Worlds

During the expansion of Echelon and its growing estate of complexes, David Gelernter formulated the idea of 'mirror worlds' (Gelernter 1993). They constitute vast, complex digital models that are constantly fed by a pipeline of real-time data and interpreted by an ensemble of digital systems. They provide an overview that enables better civic control and a more even distribution of resources, a dynamic that Gelernter refers to as 'topsight' (Gelernter 1993: 11). Despite, or because of, the intrinsically surveillant and totalitarian affordances of the mirror worlds that Gelernter dreamt of, the concept took hold in the computer science community as a conceptual model and goal for data management, and ultimately for AI development.

Through the 1970s, 1980s and 1990s each geographical site in the Echelon network operated as a prototype mirror world, connecting huge streams of audio and communications data to produce models of the acoustic world outside and spawning mirror societies of listener personnel and their families at each station. At Menwith Hill, a distinct mirror society operating independently of the outside world developed. The population of Ministry of Defence (MoD) staff and their families living at the site grew from approximately 800 staff in 1974 to a population in 1992 that included 1,200 military allies from the US alone (Campbell 1980; Hager 1996). Within its boundaries, communities lived on specially built housing estates. They had separate power and water supply, sewage facilities, a fire station, a petrol station and amenities such as shops, restaurants and other entertainment facilities, all designed to reflect the outside world and keep the community distinct and separate.

The mirrored surface of these communities was the perimeter fence. As late as 1980, MoD police who guarded the external side of the fence had no idea of the base's purpose. Although imagined within digital terms, Gelernter's notion of a smaller, more knowable community was a significant part of the appeal of his virtual mirror worlds: points of escape from the real world, which he complained of as being altogether 'too big, sprawling, . . . intimidating and unpredictable' (Gelernter 1993: 23). Most notably, the irritating acoustic loudness of normal life is something Gelernter longs to be separated from within the mirror world, where 'ant-level' noise could be filtered out, leaving only the signal.

Beyond military imperatives, Echelon's station communities seemed to cleave to similar desires through the affordances of surveillance culture. Here, the principle of secrecy could justify the establishment of digitally and physically filtered environments and small, knowable communities. The dark side of this controlling desire was the constant threat of ostracization. For out in the civilian world, each member was subject to the mirror's surveillance: listener communities maintained their segregation through a draconian social code designed to hide their clandestine military activities from public discourse. Certain words, such as 'NSA', could not be spoken outside the walls of a compound, and any contact with foreign nationals had to be reported. Even slight and accidental failures of the protocol by family members, including teenage children, could result in ignominious expulsion back into the civilian world of the listened-to (Campbell 1980: 11).

The locations of the worlds were also inflexible, challenging the notions of autonomy and control previously coveted by military intelligence operatives and promised by virtualization. The sites of military listening in peacetime grew increasingly conspicuous due to both the scale and the types of architecture and technologies that Echelon required in order to be effective. Locations could no longer be hidden underground or in police or military headquarters. Moreover, satellite technology in particular required positioning in sites without nearby obstruction, the nature of the technology stamping its circular signature on the landscape and skyline. As such, 'vast complexes of domes and satellite dishes' would hide in plain sight as 'surreal installations' within the civilian landscape (Aldrich 2011: 341).

Gelernter's mirror worlds are not passive reflectors; they are heavily dependent on their connection to specific pipelines capable of constantly delivering copious amounts of real-time data (Gelernter 1980). The geographical location of each site was also dependent on the situation and design of domestic and international civilian communications infrastructure. In addition to tracking airwaves with twenty-two satellite terminals, the Menwith Hill station also tapped directly into the then state-controlled British Telecom microwave network via a specially constructed underground receiver tower, where major links converged (Hager 1996: 39). Accordingly, the prototype mirror worlds of the Echelon network were both apart from and deeply rooted in the infrastructure of the world around them.

Prediction

Computers that could sift real-time intelligence in order to predict enemy actions with scientific accuracy had been fantasized about for decades in the intelligence communities. In *War in the Age of Intelligent Machines*, Manuel DeLanda traces the roots of the idea back to the nineteenth century when clockwork armies comprised soldiers whose only role was to 'cooperate in the creation of walls of projectiles through synchronized firepower' (DeLanda 1991: 127). Then, with the advent of improved firearms, individual soldiers were required to make tactical decisions again, and warfare became more complex with regard to personal agency and strategic thinking. Yet, the notion of a more systematic type of warfare remained:

> [T]he old dream of getting human soldiers out of the decision-making loop survived. After World War II, digital computers began to encourage again the fantasy of battles in which machines totally replaced human beings. (DeLanda 1991: 127)

By the time of Operation Gold, intelligence agencies had made attempts to computerize the processing of massive amounts of data gleaned from recorded human conversations. Success was limited, at best. The monitoring of communications was limited by human capacity, meaning that information from the operation that might have been used to predict events was likely to be read months or even years after such events took place. In an effort to speed up the production of useful intelligence to enhance prediction, incoming communications began to be filtered for keywords by human spotters.

By the early 1970s, computer systems in the Echelon network took over the laborious aspects of keyword searching, meaning no human ever saw most of the communications data that had been collected except for information that might be relevant to prediction. As Duncan Campbell outlined in his report for the Electronic Privacy Information Centre in 2000, the preceding decade had led to an intelligence filtering system where 'for every million communications intercepted only one might result in action by an intelligence agency. Only one in a thousand would ever be seen by human eyes' (Campbell 2000: 20). Therein lay a new problem for intelligence communities and the publics they served: the system that had been employed was working at a rate faster than humanly possible, but it was no longer auditable. The efficiency of this system was now difficult to differentiate from its efficacy. The ability to make decisions based on massive amounts of data was increasingly indecipherable from the quality of its decisions.

DeLanda notes that military intelligence has a poor history in terms of effectiveness and has often used secrecy in combination with technology to justify its own existence as much as gathering intelligence. During the Second World War, Britain's Secret Intelligence Services would often present classified information gathered from Enigma machine intercepts as proof of the success of other intelligence initiatives. The cover of secrecy ensured that any effective intelligence was untraceable and its method of production was inexplicable. During the development of Echelon, the power to filter information and generate predictive patterns using computers, was similarly obscured by veils of secrecy. The NSA and MI5 were fusing technology with occulted systems of intelligence to render a new generation of spycraft that was partly a sigil of technological progress and partly the continuation of ancient beliefs and practices related to power. Machine learning was emerging into a culture of arcane ritual and haunted data.

The sheer megalomaniacal scale and interagency ambition of Echelon's operations have meant that it is difficult to gauge its predictive prowess and thus its capacity to protect the countries it is supposed to serve (Priest and Arkin 2010). Bound in and by its covert practices, and giving concrete meaning to the notion of digitally working at a global scale, Echelon's lack of any real notion of success would not stop it from becoming a prediction engine *sine qua non*. The tendency for developers and users of advanced computing to amass cultural power without assuming or maintaining responsibility for its effects would be coined by Alexander Campolo and Kate Crawford as 'enchanted determinism' (2020) – the magic of technology obfuscating the means by which it might communicate its processes.

It was, therefore, in an environment of self-interested technological optimism that intelligence agencies developed the core machine learning methodology and innovation of the Echelon era – digital text filtering and categorization. A core ambition of predictive computing was to prioritize potentially relevant data while making invisible an incalculable glut of information that was (probably) irrelevant. Thus, the functionality of Echelon's Dictionary systems depended on the power of computers to sift vast quantities of transcribed telephone calls, faxes and email data that passed through its stations. Yet, in the act of automation, prediction became clouded by the intuitions, prejudices and priorities of individuals and the organizations they worked for.

Invisibility is at the heart of how all categorization operates effectively, both in digital systems where it is used for data management and in everyday human perception as a precognitive process that makes sensory data intelligible and useful. However, it also hides systematic bias, and it is these very issues of prejudice and partiality that have become increasingly understood to be problematic during the latter stages of Echelon. Increased comprehension of an issue does not mean, however, that such troublesome dynamics have been resolved. In their study of categorization in digital systems, Geoffrey C. Bowker and Susan Leigh Star argue that the invisibility of categorization within technological systems is problematic because it makes it difficult to ascertain and identify those techniques that 'systematically reflect given organisational and political positions' (2000: 322).

The positionality of each categorization system, its 'texture', is distinct, providing 'surfaces of resistances (where the real resists its definition), blocks against certain agendas, and smooth roads for others' (Bowker and Star 2000: 323). The disparate, secret and apparently self-serving organizational positions of the intelligence agencies would, in this way, be automatically and invisibly written into each week's batch of selected suspect communications even before a human analyst could begin to interpret and predict potential enemy aggressions. The success of the system would be borne out in the real world and celebrated. But its categorical texture, the 'difficult to categorize' and 'unknown risks' at large that were blocked and resisted, permeates all aspects of Echelon's operations.

Intimacy

When the voice is transmitted by something stronger than a human diaphragm and vocal cords, it becomes more vulnerable to interception. The farther away the intended listener, the more telecommunications infrastructure is needed for both transmission and reception, with potential eavesdroppers able to intercept. The longer the distance from the target, the larger and more sensitive the 'ear' of the listener needs to be. One such 'Big Ear', which was disassembled in 1998, resided outside Sugar Grove in West Virginia, USA, about 30 miles northeast of Green Bank. The Naval Research Laboratory that operated the observatory used it to intercept radio signals bouncing off the moon to listen in on Russian communications and missile launches (Kurczy 2021: 64). The facility was built in the National Radio Quiet Zone, a 13,000 square-mile area that also allowed astronomers to listen in on deep space signals. The two projects were declared to be of benefit to each other by Congressman Harley O. Staggers in 1956, as the lack of interference in the Quiet Zone suited each of their aims.

An unexpected issue that has arisen in the area in recent years has been brought forward by people suffering from overexposure to the electromagnetic frequencies (EMFs) associated with digital communications. In the digital amplification of information, the medium of communication generates EMFs that, although quiet in terms of what the human ear can detect, may be felt in other ways. The ubiquity of digital infrastructure across the world has resulted in an 'unprecedented increase in the number and diversity of electromagnetic field (EMF) sources' (WHO 2006: 1).

EMF frequencies can touch sensing bodies intimately, potentially affecting some more negatively than others. There is a growing number of reports citing electromagnetic hypersensitivity as an 'environmental intolerance attributed to EMF'. The accounts involve a 'variety of nonspecific physical symptoms' (Kacprzyk et al. 2021: 33), such as 'exhaustion, headache, irritation, concentration and sleeping difficulties, anxiety and somnolence', due to exposure to EMF from 'phones, personal computers, wi-fi routers, TVs and microwaves' (Kacprzyk et al. 2021: 35). Since the mid-2000s (Stromberg 2013: online), sufferers of this disputed condition have sought refuge and a place to build communities within the Quiet Zone, only to find their sensoria affected by an even more nebulous band of frequencies.

Before taking the drastic step of relocating, sufferers often try ditching personal electronic devices, avoiding public areas with high exposure to EMF (Dieudonné 2020: 2), sleeping in garments that have silver fibres woven into them (Stromberg 2013: online) or isolating themselves in rural caves or woods. Some of these isolation techniques approximate the way a Faraday cage, or shield, functions: a nineteenth-century device invented by Michael Faraday that blocks electromagnetic fields. In a lecture delivered in 1859 on the forces of matter, Faraday commented that electricity travelled from place to place with 'astonishing' rapidity (1859: 125), and he developed a theory of 'Fields', wherein electricity and magnetism act as agents to transport energy across distances (Russell 2000: 99). Human detection of these fields not only allowed us to harness them for electrical purposes but also introduced us to another sphere of perception that has existed outside of mainstream notions of the sensorium.

While humans do not use sensitivity to EMF to achieve evolutionary survival, there is evidence that other animals such as fish, sharks and monotremes can both benefit and suffer as a result of electroreceptivity. The platypus uses it in nocturnal hunting, gathering half its body mass 'with its eyes, ears and nostrils closed and underwater' (Manger and Pettigrew 1995: 359). The platypus's bill possesses considerable tactile sensitivity, but that alone does not account for its success in gathering food. Studies confirmed the species' electroreceptive abilities in the 1980s, discovering that their electroreceptors are modified mucous glands (Gregory et al. 1988) located within the skin of the bill (Andres and Von Düring 1984). In captivity, the platypus suffers a high mortality rate, with stress being a significant attributive factor (Manger and Pettigrew 1995: 379). To address this issue, researchers have suggested the use of a Faraday cage for a soothing reduction of 'electrical noise' (Manger and Pettigrew 1995). Human sensitivity to this electrical noise may not be as precise as animals, but nodes of EMF generation such as satellite ground stations are challenging, and possibly modulating, the sensoria of humans and animals.

Voice

Any writer of dialogue for performance knows that the written word does not concretely express its meaning when spoken. Rather, the text is a site of flexible interpretation, only made taut by the actor's speech when its full meaning (with subtext) is rendered (McKee 1997: 253). The same is considered true in reverse. The spoken word is malleable and difficult to pin down, and its transcription requires a material reduction through the loss of its acoustic characteristics to be rendered as meaningful text. Kenneth Goldsmith notes that alongside its meaning, language is material, 'a substance that moves and morphs through its various states and digital and textual ecosystems' (Goldsmith 2011: 34). It is its shifting materiality, for Goldsmith, that makes language unstable and volatile, its meaning altered with every change of state. Echelon's use of digital speech recognition, a technology that could automatically interpret spoken words into text, would go further than simply rendering voice audio as text. In between these states, algorithmic interpretation would introduce new material properties and a distinct adaptation required to interpret spoken language as data.

Echelon's intelligence community used a computer system called 'Oratory' that could listen to large batches of telephone calls and 'recognize keywords when spoken in all the different tones and accents' (Hager 1996: 46). The computer science of speech recognition is much older, though. It began to develop in the United States in the mid-1970s. James K. Baker and Janet M. Baker at Carnegie Mellon University adapted a sensor for tracking neurons to register acoustic patterns in speech. The researchers settled on the development of a 'stochastic' model that used patterns in both the material and the meaning of speech by mathematically applying knowledge from the fields of acoustics, phonetics, lexicology, syntax and semantics. The findings of the research, submitted by James Baker as his 1975 PhD thesis, were sent in a report to Defense Advanced Research Projects Agency (DARPA) and would go on to form the basis of the dictation software 'Dragon Speaking'. According to the paper, the models produced could compare the sounds of a whole sentence, first guessing words that the sounds might make (e.g. it might generate the options 'iron listing' and 'I am listening'). After that, it would then rank the meaningfulness of each combination and finally select the most sensible as its prediction ('I am listening'). Meaning and its most important lexical unit – the word – had become material that could be weighed and measured.

The digitization of spoken words provided a new externality to speech, as well as a new type of listener. Previously, it could be recorded or transmitted, extricated from the body of its speaker in terms of location and time. But the voice would always need to be listened to (or listened in on) for its value to be understood. The realistic application of speech recognition as part of Echelon's mass surveillance programme removed the need to listen to the voice first in order to understand its meaning. The shift presaged a move to a scalable form of acoustic surveillance that promised greater insights from compressed temporal envelopes. Thousands of hours of listening might be reduced to less than a hundred. However, as with any adaptation of language, its formal volatility would provide new challenges to interpretation and shifts in meaning.

Such problems would increasingly occur when considered at scale, with the quality of text-to-speech technologies remaining significantly unreliable for decades to come. In 2006, over thirty years after Baker published details of the Dragon system of speech recognition, the digital transcription of recorded telephone conversations by IBM for the US defence agency DARPA still possessed error rates of approximately 20 per cent (Chen et al. 2006: online). Under the auspices of DARPA's 'Effective Affordable Reusable Speech-to-Text' (EARS) programme, IBM would produce 900 hours of telephone conversations to use as a training corpus, further cementing the importance of surveillance in the development of the encoding of the voice as data. Explaining the challenge, the IBM paper briefly outlines the 'relatively challenging' nature of capturing conversational language, 'due to the presence of numerous mistakes, repairs, repetitions, and other disfluencies' (Chen et al. 2006: online). To engineers working on speech recognition, it was conversational language that was the problem. Its material was not meaningful enough. Its weights and measures were too casual and changeable to reliably convert for surveillance purposes.

For the Echelon project, therefore, the practical dimensions of using the much less powerful Oratory systems over the preceding years would have been challenging in a new way. The relationship between listener and machine was one defined by mishearing, misunderstanding and confusion. Listening in would become an act, not simply of espionage, but of data cleansing. The frequency of inaccurate lexical interpretation caused by its flattening into the material of data constantly threatened to thwart efficiency.

Fidelity

For data to be actionable as intelligence, it must reasonably correspond to real-world situations and allegiances. Analysis of phone calls, text communications, location data, payment information, subjects' known associates and the 'synoptic array of Internet activity moving along those networks' lines' (Snowden 2019: 246) constitutes an understanding of life that is constructed through large-scale data collection and later assembled into narratives. During Edward Snowden's formative years online, at the turn of the millennium, he witnessed a major transition of the internet. It changed for him from a place of identity experimentation and relative anonymity to one where internet technologies and associated thinking focused on 'enforcing fidelity to memory, identitarian consistency, and so ideological conformity' (Snowden 2019: 47).

Digital identity is now inextricably linked to personhood. The NSA's working relationships with the FVEY and their international scope led the agency to develop a 'New Collection Posture', an omniscience that aimed to 'Sniff It All, Know It All, Collect It All, Process It All, Exploit It All, Partner It All' (Snowden 2019: 222). Our lived experiences, as represented by our data and metadata, are conveniently packaged into commercial and political identities that bear questionable fidelity to who we may think we are. They are then used to construct narratives post hoc, redefining 'citizens' private Internet communications as potential signals intelligence' (Snowden 2019: 177).

Most of the information that makes up the corpus of our networked identities is not the content of our messages, but the metadata that our devices log without our participation or consent. This affords us even less control over how we are perceived by the organizations that collect this data in bulk. Another issue that comes to the fore with regard to the fidelity of not only how we are perceived, but also how we perceive ourselves, relates to the temporality of data and its relevance over long periods. The time between the collection of information by Echelon and its use as actionable intelligence has stretched into an ideological infinity with the development of permanent storage at scale. Data, like people, changes over time, depending on the contextual narratives that situate, politicize and value it.

When data is largely collected along commercial and political lines, our acceptance of its fidelity to lived experience narrows human identity and leaves us vulnerable to the consequences of abstract narratives compiled by algorithms. For Snowden, this is a dystopian future that 'would logically become a world in which all laws were totally enforced, automatically, by computers' (Snowden 2019: 196). Writing about ubiquitous computing in the early 1990s, computer scientist Mark Weiser observed that 'counterposed against the technological leaps that are now being glimpsed is the very human desire not to be held hostage by that technology' (Weiser 1991: 71). One way to avoid being held captive by technology is to insist on the intervention of human judgement into systems that threaten to further fragment identity in the digital age.

Concurrent with the shift from active targeting to passive, total listening was the shift in the intelligence community from human intelligence (HUMINT), which was 'already in a steady decline by the end of the cold war' (Keefe 2005: 6) to SIGINT. By 2004, then CIA director Porter Gross declared that 'the cupboard is nearly bare in the area of human intelligence' (Keefe 2005: 6), a statement that is reflected in the digital scale and workings of Echelon. Without HUMINT, intelligence agencies lose out on direct engagement, 'which can be harsh and emotionally draining' (Snowden 2019: 157) but which also grounds the workings of intelligence in the human analysis of human activities.

It is difficult to evaluate the efficiency of HUMINT strategies against large-scale SIGINT because they ultimately seek different paths in the name of national security. Technologists engaged in SIGINT are often abstracted from their actions and experience limited 'meaningful confrontation with their consequences' (Snowden 2019: 157). Such sentiments act as an echo of caution regarding human engagement that is mediated by computers. In tandem with the growth of social media is a general decline in online empathy. Misgivings over entrusting an impassive system that has been designed by technologists to faithfully represent human identity are one explanation as to why Echelon continues to be 'the quintessential paranoid fable for the Internet age' (Keefe 2005: xiv).

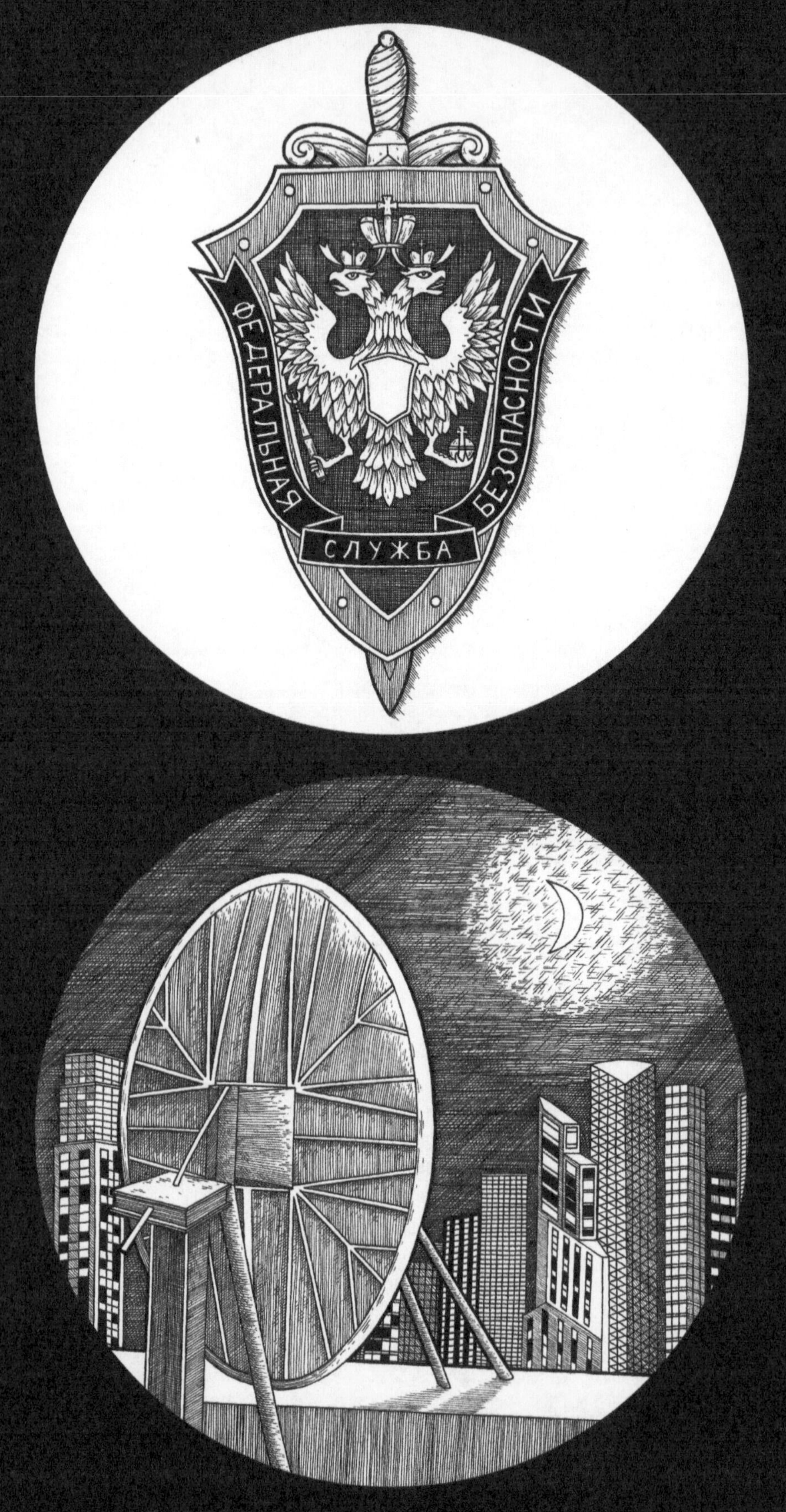

ФЕДЕРАЛЬНАЯ
СЛУЖБА
БЕЗОПАСНОСТИ

CHAPTER 7
SORM

Process

On 10 December 2011, thousands of anti-government protesters took to the streets of Moscow to demonstrate against perceived vote-rigging in recent elections. They also made demands for a new ballot and urged the government to release all political prisoners. A sense that the Russian political establishment was once again under siege gripped the international media. Leading the movement against the Kremlin was the opposition leader, Boris Nemtsov. Another political rally, signalling a growing public appetite for dissent against the government, was planned for 24 December of the same year.

Three days before the event, however, the pro-Kremlin website Lifenews.ru published nine of Nemtsov's private phone conversations as digital audio recordings (Soldatov and Borogan 2013: 25). In the recordings, he described a fellow political activist as 'just a bitch, or else an idiot' and disparaged protestors as 'hamsters', 'vegetables' and 'penguins' (Whitmore 2011: online). While Nemtsov described some of the recordings as 'edits' or 'just fake' he did acknowledge that some were his own and issued a public apology on his personal blog (Nemtsov 2011: online).

Later on national television, Nemtsov alleged that the purpose of the release of the recordings was to disrupt and distract activists. He also noted that the recording of his conversations was illegal and punishable by law with up to five years in prison. He went on to state that, even though what he had said in a private conversation was obscene, the act of being covertly listened to was, in fact, the true obscenity. He subsequently summed up his predicament as a dissident in Russia: 'You need to restrain your emotions, watch every word, even when you talk to family and friends on the phone' (Nemtsov 2011). Nemtsov was later assassinated in 2015 during the opening years of the Russo-Ukrainian War.

While the practice of wiretapping an opposition leader was not historically uncommon, the release of the surveillance recordings of his conversations via digital networks and media, directly to a mainstream audience, indicated a major shift in the legal and technological infrastructure underlying the leak. The System of Operational-Investigatory Measures (SORM) had been first implemented in 1995 by then-president Yeltsin and overseen by Vladimir Putin (in his previous role as head of the Federal Security Service (FSB)). SORM was innovative in surveillance terms because it transferred the burden and cost of surveillance from state agencies onto Russia's newly commercialized network providers, requiring them to purchase and install special FSB-designed hardware that collected all user communication activity.

The legislation that enforced SORM effectively required service providers to act as data centres for Russian policing and intelligence services that could then be accessed retrospectively. Data included everything from phone calls to email and web browsing activity. Data collection of domestic telecommunications was therefore obligatory, but in theory, the FSB and other agencies were only allowed to access data with a post-collection court warrant (Maréchal 2017). As Nemtsov had indicated, failure to do so could lead to a significant prison term. The distinction had been important for Yeltsin, who had been keen to make a break with perceptions of authoritarianism. He wanted to be clear that 'the rule of law would apply' to any digital surveillance (Soldatov and Borogan 2013: 26) in the new Russia. International perceptions of the state slipping back into authoritarianism were bad for business, and Russia had been keen to benefit from global investment to fund its emerging post-Soviet economic model.

Yet, the cultural and technical roots of SORM lay absolutely in the totalitarian machinery of Russia's recent Soviet past. Its foundations were researched and developed by the KGB in the mid-1980s (Soldatov and Borogan 2013) and found their early test case in the Stasi's *Centrales Kontrollsystem* (CEKO), which operated from 1973 throughout the 1980s. Therefore, it was a return to normal state practices when, shortly after becoming president, Putin authorized several additional agencies to access SORM's collected data. All of a sudden, tax authorities, border patrol, customs agencies and the Presidential Security Service were all able to siphon personal and private information from the state's listening apparatus. Such a manoeuvre extended the earshot of the government and allowed it to monitor issues such as domestic finance, travel plans and political discussion.

The warrant requirement remained in place, but it was, in reality, toothless, given that surveillance activities could legally begin before a warrant was requested. Cementing such lip service to the process was the fact that authorities were not required to provide a warrant to either the telecom operators or the targets they intended to monitor. And finally, the warrant was only formally required for communications content (i.e. what was communicated in the message). It was not required for any type of metadata about the message, such as time, date, location, sender and intended recipient. These data could be used to infer significant intelligence gains but had no legal block regarding gaining access to them.

Over time, it came as no surprise to anyone that SORM's scope crept. In its infancy, the system had focused on telecommunications and internet service providers. However, following events starting in 2010 in Egypt and the Middle East, dubbed the 'Arab Spring', in which popular movements seeking to overthrow authoritarian regimes were energized by social media networks, SORM extended its reach into social media platforms. The updates needed to comply with the new requirements were expensive, and organizations were often reportedly presaged through 'extra-legal intimidation' in addition to 'formal enforcement' (Maréchal 2017: 33).

At the heart of SORM's expansion was a fear that, as in East Germany with its Allied radio broadcasting programme, the West was using conversations and broadcasts taking place on social media platforms to begin a Third World War that was 'informational-psychological' in nature and designed to actively destabilize Russia's core values and society (Gaufman 2021: 117). The importance, then, of technological advances that allowed monitoring of the internet (with all its international entanglements), was once again imagined as being necessary at all costs in order to safeguard Russia against existential threats.

In 2014, deep packet inspection (DPI) was added to the technical infrastructure of SORM, a method of data analysis that was able to burrow into data packets in real time. Each data 'payload' sent by a user could subsequently be scanned, and automatic processes could act upon its content, recording and, where desirable, blocking the content of the media without any legal or social norms to prohibit it (Poetranto 2012). The additional time taken to read packets has had a significantly detrimental impact on the operation and performance of the Russian Internet (RuNet) as servers and budgets struggled under SORM's ongoing infrastructural issues and upgrades (Gaufman 2021: 116). Private, civic and commercial concerns have, in fact, been de-prioritized in the race to protect Russia's online public: the state's aim being one of limiting access to perceived Western disruption and silencing the challenging discourses of Western-allied members of the political opposition.

Recording

The combination of Russian censorship and surveillance embodied by SORM is not solely a campaign of intelligence gathering. It is also an example of how the digital surveillance of domestic citizens can extend state listening to cover the monitoring of intelligence agencies themselves, as well as those in law enforcement and governance (Laqueur 1985: 8). On entering office in 1999, Putin reflected on the elite's reactionary intention of 'establishing order and restoration of the Soviet Union, not as a Communist entity but as an imperial stronghold' (Haslam 2015: 276).

In a process Alexander Etkind described as 'demodernization' in 2023's *Russia Against Modernity*, Russian state practices of 'drilling for oil and gas, occupying foreign countries, accumulating gold, subsidising far-right movements around the world, and destroying Ukraine' have been intentional activities to resist modernity. He goes on to state that they have been 'chosen by the Russian elite and imposed upon the global arena' (Etkind 2023: 7). Investing in imperialist practices that contribute to growing domestic inequality necessitated a new totalitarian approach to intelligence as it pertained to the suppression of criticism. The ambition – to throttle the internet as a space of free speech.

During the rise of the internet as a consumer technology, 1990s Russia was forced to confront the falling living standards of its citizens in light of the 'full consciousness of what the West could offer in return for betrayal', and attempted to reconcile it with 'a long-outmoded belief in a global ideal' (Haslam 2015: 276). Originally accusing the internet of being a tool of 'subversion to spread "Western" values' (Corera 2020: 342), Putin's condemnation was a continuation of Soviet Russia's reputation for brushing off the applied sciences as enemy politics (Haslam 2015: 232). During Stalin's regime, there was a state focus on HUMINT over SIGINT. Electronic and digital recording were haunted by their Western scientific politics and were thought of as being no match for listeners on the ground. Stalin, for example, objected to cybernetics as a 'fake bourgeois science' (Haslam 2015: 239).

For Putin, the historical focus on HUMINT and the relegation of SIGINT to the 'auxiliary' option (Haslam 2015: 233) led to a concentration of gaps in technology development. This lapse, in turn, blocked access to media channels that Putin's Russia seeks to reclaim. During a time when media consumption and surveillance channels had converged via the internet, Russia did not have the means to implement its surveillance programme without relying on foreign technology. In recounting the history of Soviet intelligence, historian Jonathan Haslam draws a parallel between Russia's attempts to develop home-grown technology and its history of agriculture:

> [I]t was thought, why make such an effort to produce your own harvest when you can buy the crop elsewhere? Soviet technology . . . had every prospect of going the same way as Soviet agriculture, into ever-greater dependence on foreign imports, cheaper to acquire than to produce. (Haslam 2015: 232)

Similar to the United States, the emergence of the market state in Russia 'meant that larger and larger parts of national infrastructure are also in private hands' (Andrew, Aldrich and Wark 2019: 1). The NSA's employment of private contractors rather than government employees to carry out intelligence gathering has proven to be a security weakness. This has led to the reckoning that the government can no longer 'claim that intelligence is a predominantly state-based activity' (Andrew, Aldrich and Wark 2019: 2). Russia's reliance on private ISP providers and telecom operators complying with increasingly heavy burdens of data collection and storage comes unstuck when it is challenged by the relative lack of Russian infrastructure.

As ever, there is another way of thinking through the apparent Achilles heel, that is Russia's dependence on Western technology. This dynamic of reliance has also granted Russia a voice in global conversations regarding the hybrid realms of disinformation warfare. Thus, the 'enemy' technologies that have been brought in to record and store SORM data also provide the perfect echo chamber for recording and storing its propaganda internationally. With internet platforms allowing 'just enough remoteness and deniability . . . to make it easier for one country to act against another without moving to full-scale conflict' (Corera 2020: 346), Russian actors can 'exploit the vulnerabilities that a connected world create[s] for its Western adversaries' (Corera 2020: 357).

What is at once a weakness in Russia's move towards perfect record-keeping also serves its interests through the spread of propaganda, misinformation and fake news. Indeed, an important ambition in deploying Maskirovka is to destabilize the West's conception of social media as a facilitator of democratization and individual empowerment. As we know, social change can happen very quickly if one has the tools to propagate recordings at speed.

Transgression

Just as the Stasi needed a vast network of human spies and bureaucrats to maintain its listening regime, Russia's SORM system and its attendant storage laws require considerable resources. However, unlike the Stasi, rather than being absorbed by the government, a large portion of the cost of running SORM is met by the country's Internet Service Providers (ISPs). In essence, they form and offer a commercial market of state surveillance services. Russia's informational mandates have opened up a promising market for 'Russian vendors of hardware and software solutions for traffic surveillance and filtering' (Ermoshina, Loveluck and Musiani 2021: 18). Such a distribution of responsibility is a transgressive approach to market economics as a form of state control where 'the regulation of the Russian Internet produces a full-fledged market of censorship and surveillance alongside the ISP market, shaping competition between the various vendors of infrastructure components' (Ermoshina, Loveluck and Musiani 2021: 20). Increasingly, transgressive demands on market economics provide a lucrative gap between the decree of law and the difficulty of its technical implementation, especially when those laws are constantly shifting.

The market at once supplies and frustrates the mechanisms of surveillance. A two-year field study conducted between 2017 and 2019 and published in 2022 by French academics revealed that Russia's surveillance network was not subject to central control but to a 'multiplicity of types of control that are partial, fluctuating and sometimes contradictory' (Ermoshina, Loveluck and Musiani 2021: 30). Enforcement of SORM and its related laws and policies can be arbitrary, using online surveillance (lawful interception) and online censorship (traffic filtering) as the two main levers of regulation (Ermoshina, Loveluck and Musiani 2021: 19). It is impossible to maintain perfect control over such a complex array of technologies and behavioural norms, especially when the users, developers and providers reconfigure and hijack those technologies to modulate and baffle the state's listening apparatus.

Another pronounced barrier to SORM's effectiveness is its cost. Anecdotally, SORM can cost a small provider 20 per cent to 30 per cent of its annual income (Volkov 2016). Some ISPs buy SORM 'as a service' from larger providers, pushing their liability for compliance upstream. The proportion of providers with absent or badly configured SORM systems is unknown, though poor adherence is thought to be frequent and systems are prone to corruption (Ermoshina, Loveluck and Musiani 2021: 22). An interview with the ex-CTO of an 'Internet Exchange Point' that was carried out by a French research team opined that 'laziness, corruption and lack of expertise will protect the RuNet . . . better than any protests' (Ermoshina, Loveluck and Musiani 2021: 29). Russia's commercial surveillance market may suffer consequences from insisting on home-grown solutions because its infrastructure is built and maintained by those parties most interested in their own privacy: its citizens.

Russia has found itself in the predicament of being a state in which 'law-making has outpaced the actual technological development of the country' (Ermoshina, Loveluck and Musiani 2021: 45). These legal initiatives have 'generally failed to provide frameworks for the production and certification of concrete technical solutions, which has led to long periods of technolegal vacuums' (Ermoshina, Loveluck and Musiani 2021: 20). This has also led to ISPs coming up with solutions to cope with stringent requirements for which there is no technical standard. The act of translating legal requirements into technical solutions often outstrips the infrastructure capabilities of the country and its technologists. For Putin, though, it still maintains a veneer of totalitarian control over the internet, which is an important factor in his single-handed control of the country.

Worlds

Having lost the Cold War, the Soviet Union withdrew from direct confrontation with its long-time sparring partner, the United States. Instead, it concentrated on reconfiguring the battlefield of the twenty-first century from a physical environment to one composed and abstracted by algorithmic impulses. Information and the orbits and air gaps it traverses became the new elemental constituents of asymmetric or hybrid warfare, and within this new model of geopolitical conflict resides a longer-term plan that has aligned 'rogue states' such as Russia, Iran, North Korea, Cuba and Venezuela into an alliance intent on resisting the global north's hierarchies of power. According to US investigators Douglas Farah and Marianne Richardson:

> Russia's strategic interests in Latin America center on establishing a multisector, persistent presence in the Western Hemisphere as a counterweight to US and North Atlantic Treaty Organization (NATO) presence in the former Soviet Union and bordering states. The engagement focuses on aggressive implementation of what the West calls the doctrine of 'hybrid warfare'. This approach fuses hard and soft power across multiple domains, recognizing the existence of a permanent state of confrontation with the West. This strategy undergirds the rationalization and operationalization of Russia's 2022 invasion of Ukraine. (2022: online)

Coined by Frank Hoffman in 2007, 'hybrid warfare' is based on conducting conflict across a multiplicity of spheres to achieve its goals. Modes of regular, abstract and cyberwarfare are combined with lawfare, the production and distribution of fake news, dis/mis-information and tampering with foreign electoral processes. It is a quantum approach to contemporary conflict management. All positions are not only countenanced but also enacted. Each position is a slightly different version of the world. Such dynamics equate to a granulated synthesis that, in turn, produces a distorted and complicated relationship with anything that might claim to fly under the banner of reality. Understanding that surveillance, of not only internal networks but also the wider global mesh that they connect to, would enable it to forge geopolitical presences and offences, Russia has rigorously updated SORM since 1995. To date, the three increasingly invasive adaptations have striven to map and predict the electronic and physical worlds that turn, unfold and collide around us. The contours and rhythms become perceptible as the shifting infoscapes respond to the noisy storyworlds that Russia manufactures, in a manner analogous to Christopher Nolan's Escheresque environments in his 2010 film *Inception*.

Intelligence gathered through SORM feeds Russian operatives who, in turn, fold, fabricate and release variants into social media platforms, newsrooms and conspiracy-laden bulletin boards: colliding systems of verisimilitude that are, in part, wrought from listening. This is the superpositioning of reality. Quantum (un)realism. Countless versions of the world exist at once. Disinformation morphs into hyperstition, crashing into statistical anomalies. These are domains that dissolve in and out of each other, remixing and infecting as they multiply, like intangible pathogens. Loaded with malevolent intent, they contaminate and subvert all they interface with. This modus operandi of accelerated digital world-building, and burning, is not particular to any one country or coalition. It is a capability shared at different levels of proficiency across the globe. According to cybersecurity commentator Lee Sullivan, 'Western media and attitudes often portray the state-run surveillance in the US and Russia as not capable of comparison. A more nuanced look at each country's surveillance shows that symmetry does, in fact, exist' (2022: online). For countries that do not have a global north postcode, the disruptive elements of the internet offer a topography of opportunity, through which traditional balances of geopolitical power can be challenged and redistributed.

From its military roll-out, the internet has been increasingly driven by Western values, economies, languages and cultural norms. With this power to forge narratives and geopolitical 'truths' comes the potential to influence international perception, relationships and events. In response to this occidental versioning of the world, countries such as Russia have put forth their own kaleidoscopic engines of reality-making. The worlds that SORM operates in map onto and through the environments that surveillance systems such as PRISM and Echelon also observe and reimagine. The difference is that the worlds fashioned by Russia and its allies are composed to resist the furtive creep of the West's economically empowered ideologies. Never has the digital influence and networked strategic prowess of Russia been more evident than during the 2016 US election when the choice of the American people turned out to be an unknowing collaboration with the Kremlin. Possibly the greatest political act of platformed railroading ever carried out, right in front of our eyes and ears; glued to our screens, we were unable to countenance the idea that the digital vehicles delivering content had been joyridden by *Maskirovkan* stunt doubles. Trunks packed with propaganda and headlights on full beam, the oncoming viewers and listeners had no idea what manipulated them (Yang 2019).

In the 2020s, we would like to think that we are more aware of the ways in which worlds are woven around us. However, as Shoshana Zuboff states in her seminal text

The Age of Surveillance Capitalism: The Fight for a Human Future at the New Frontier of Power, '[p]ersonal information is increasingly used to enforce standards of behaviour. Information processing is developing, therefore, into an essential element of long-term strategies of manipulation intended to mould and adjust individual conduct' (2019: 127). It is in this era of networked malaise and manipulation that Russia, via security systems such as SORM, has become a geopolitical player again, and it has its sights and sounds fixed on the 'liberal' democracies of North America and Europe.

Prediction

When former US statesman Henry Stimson closed the State Department's code-breaking office in 1929, he offered the explanation: 'Gentlemen do not read each other's mail' (Kruh 2010). In hindsight it was a naive viewpoint (and possibly an apocryphal quotation) that was quickly set aside amidst the realities of international conflict, but it illustrates how much social norms dictate the acceptability of the scope of surveillance within and across borders. Justifications for intelligence gathering, as a means to collect crucial information that can be used to predict and mitigate threats, are often stalking horses for the economic and political interests of those in power. Such modes of deception are even carried out in the absence of conclusive proof that data collection leads to the neutralization of threats.

In Russia, social norms that protect privacy are 'absent' (Maréchal 2017: 33). So are the legal norms that might otherwise limit the increasingly sophisticated intervention and collection of digital communications data on private citizens. SORM's focus tends to be more aligned with listening for external threats, for signs of the occidental virus entering the pristine ideological framework of the Russian people. The government's granting of information access to agencies that protect individuals and valuable objects implies a level of threat detection in SORM activities. The enforcers of these information-collection practices seem, however, doubtful that SORM can predict and 'help prevent terrorism' (Soldatov and Borogan 2015: 28). Questioning the narrative of threat prediction and mitigation that underpins public justifications for data collection has become more complex in a post-9/11 world, where 'the collection and analysis of intelligence can inform the production of disinformation and propaganda' (Snowden 2019: 78).

Now that Western citizens are more likely to accept invasive surveillance in the name of intelligence gathering while also voluntarily carrying devices that record and send data to the government, the conflation of state-based intelligence practices with those of surveillance is easier to understand in the context of Russia and its history. Russia's present relationship to information is informed by its past, when the USSR considered information a 'dangerous commodity to be feared and controlled, rather than a right and a public good' (Maréchal 2017: 30). Media production's role in the distribution of propaganda can be traced back to the country's first newspaper, *Vedomosti*, 'founded in 1702 to disseminate the czar's wishes, plans, and priorities across the country and to build popular support for the ruler' (Rohlenko in Maréchal 2017: 30). This approach has translated across technological developments, with tight control exercised over the ownership and use of photocopiers (Maréchal 2017: 30), and more latterly to accessing the internet, which requires a passport be associated with an IP address.

Recent changes to SORM legislation have focused on holding onto information for longer and requiring private companies to store communications data for six months. While it is unlikely that a longer period of collection will improve prediction, it does allow the government more time to construct predictive fictions about the harms that the West poses to the country. While the observation that data is a 'key ingredient to predicting the future' (Zegart 2022: 111) is pertinent, it tends to be more salient when thinking about the imperialist regime rather than the human beings residing within its borders.

Intimacy

By the late 2000s around the globe, many previously analogue and physical social interactions began to transfer into digital spaces, where a new cadre of always-on platforms asynchronously served social content to mass public user groups. While the monstrous body of East Germany's Stasi had withered away and died, new tentacular mechanisms protruding from the SORM infrastructure were reaching into the Russian psyche.

This new monster sensorium grew not only in response to the Arab Spring, which had destabilized Russian allies such as Libya and Syria, but also to the Snowden leaks, which validated the notion that Western social media was dangerous and potentially incendiary. Much of the early social media activity in Russia happened on international, and often American-owned, platforms such as Facebook and YouTube, through servers that were difficult to monitor as they were not fitted with SORM's proprietary software. The Russian state solution to the problem was to co-opt the popular Russian-based social media site VKontakte (translation – 'In Contact') or VK.com. In the wake of its first invasion of Ukraine in 2014, Russia began to consolidate social media activity within the bounds of its internet infrastructure. Accordingly, it brought VK's management into line with the Kremlin, turning it into what the *Moscow Times* called 'the Kremlin's Digital Gulag' (Rothrock 2014: online).

Initially, SORM's tentacles met with resistance: VK founder and CEO Pavel Durov refused to share data for the Ukrainian Euromaidan online group with the FSB. He argued that they were not Russian citizens, so it was illegal and represented a betrayal of trust (Marrow and Trevelyan 2024). However, as noted in Chapter 5, the monstrous body logic of data regimes – that seek to keep all conversations within earshot – dictates that individual privacy concerns are unnecessary obstructions to the functioning state sensorium. The act of sharing, therefore, should, or so the logic goes, be at least two-layered: first, with the friend, lover or social or political group intended as the recipient and second, to the state body for inspection and regulation. Refusal or reluctance to adhere to this regime is routinely related to obscene and dangerous motives.

It should be noted here that in both the United States and in Russia, online privacy is regularly publicly equated with criminal and paramilitary motives. In Washington, surveillance 'hawks' have often described the internet as a cesspit of 'terrorists and paedophiles' in order to justify the expansion of surveillance systems and state-friendly encryption protocols (Gaufman 2021: 117). Not wanting to be outdone in the courts of public hyperbole, ex-film director Stanislav Govorukhin, who was Putin's head of campaigning, tried to match the state's disgust for online culture (but with a political twist) by describing the internet as 'a rubbish-dump controlled by GosDep (the US State Department)' (Govorukhin in Gaufman 2021: 117).

Following Durov's refusal to share information with the FSB, he discovered that he had submitted his resignation a month earlier. Despite dismissing the document as a joke, he was removed as the company's CEO. Durov would go on to set up the Telegram app. Following Durov's dismissal, VK.com was given a boost to make it operate more quickly than its Western social media competitors on RuNet. Replacement CEO Vlad Legotkin went public to announce that there was no place for censorship at VK, declaring that the company would never pass personal information to 'commercial or state' organizations as it would violate 'moral principles' and 'legal norms as well' (Lokot 2016: online).

While it was undoubtedly the case that VK.com did not actively send information to Russian police without a warrant, SORM's regulatory framework meant that it had no need to. The techno-legal intricacies of SORM's DNA could obfuscate the extent to which personal intimacies on RuNet were compromised, representing an early boon to surveillance organizations. By portraying social media sites in Russia as free, chaotic and uncensored, it encouraged individuals to share their lives with little or no self-censorship. As with politician Boris Nemtsov, who had complained about his calls being monitored, many would mistake the new digital vectors through which one could have intimate conversations as being private spaces.

Over the following two years, many of VK.com's users began to regret their trust. The SOVA Center for Information and Analysis, a Moscow-based human rights group that specializes in the misuse of anti-extremism legislation in Russia, reported that in 2015, 119 VK.com users had been convicted of criminal activity related to extremism. This compared to a single conviction of a Facebook user. Convictions were often leveraged against existing people of interest rather than random users. Crimes ranged from sustained civil disobedience to the slightest social gesture (the flick of a thumb, with a 'Like') in support of a prescribed list of anti-Russian causes such as Chechen separatism (Meduza 2016). Through portals such as VK.com, SORM had become attuned to the most delicate and nuanced resonances of dissent. From whispers to mutterings to voices, those involved in forms of protest and opposition could be digitally monitored at all levels of delivery. Intimacy and privacy would have to find new modes of expression.

Voice

The second version of SORM, released in 1998, added online communications to the repertoire of technologies it could monitor. It could now capture conversations carried out over the internet, a process commonly known as Voice over IP or VoIP. Sixteen years later, SORM mk. III added further functionality, from the processing and filtering of data to the three-year storage of captured voices. As we know from previous chapters, the Stasi helped initiate the state of being in an 'archival trance' – the massive volume of their recorded conversations requiring library-style buildings to house the tapes. Now, with developments in nanocomputing, the same archives can fit on storage technology the size of a postage stamp – a miniaturized catacomb of voices held in a solid cryogenic state of retrieval. Millions of voices in an anaesthetized crush, compressed into an inert chorus of the mundane.

VoIP was created in a period when voices were swarming around the globe at unprecedented speeds. The history of the technology, however, speaks to an era of different velocities, with the earliest echoes of VoIP resonating in 1928s first electronic voice synthesizer developed by Bell Labs' Homer Dudley, called 'the Voder'. The synthesis of the electronic voice also has a rich and varied lineage, from military to entertainment spheres, as explored in detail in Dave Tompkins's book *How to Wreck a Nice Beach: The Vocoder from World War II to Hip-Hop* (2010). The focus of this section, however, is to map the point at which VoIP software transforms the electronic voice into digital articulation.

The first use of VoIP occurred in 1989, via ethernet, when the 'Remote Audio Sound Card Application Link' system, invented by Brian C. Wiles, allowed gamers to speak to each other. The first 'Free World Dialup' and for-profit VoIP were founded five years later in 1994 by Jeff Pulver, Brandon Lucas and Izak Jenie. In 2003, 'Skype', then known as 'Sky Peer-to-Peer', was founded in Estonia. In just two years, it had 50 million users and was purchased by Microsoft in 2011. After Skype, numerous audio and video calling tools such as 'Vonage for Business' and later 'Zoom', 'Microsoft Teams', 'Google Meet' and 'StarLeaf' competed for market share in the seemingly ever-expanding communications sector (Stone 2023: online).

By early 2020, the Coronavirus pandemic had seized the globe in a tumult of anxiety, dread and death and had changed the way that humans worked, played and travelled. It also irrevocably altered how we speak to each other. The shift to remote working and the adoption of more agile strategies around hours of employment meant that almost overnight, new robust and dependable communications solutions were urgently needed by businesses, politicians and families alike. 'VoIP was no longer an option – virtual phone software became a requirement' (Stone 2023). According to the 2024 Global VoIP report collated by Research and Markets, the global VoIP market 'is expected to grow to $207.77 billion in 2027 at a CAGR of 14.6%'.

In his 1878 essay 'The Phonograph and Its Future', Thomas Edison speculates on sonic libraries and the potential of recording technologies. Identifying a persistent global compulsion, he proposed that 'it will henceforth be possible to preserve for future generations the voices as well as the words of our Washingtons, our Lincolns, our Gladstones' (Edison 1878: 8). The SORM archives take Edison at his word and then run with it. By preserving the speeches and utterances of VoIP users, the system transmogrifies each of them into a dormant VIP. Warhol's promise of fifteen minutes of fame has been distorted and time-stretched to three years. The cultural entrepreneur's premise that in the future everybody will be worthy of a media audience has shifted in tone and become the guiding principle of global surveillance systems: mass media, mass production, mass recording. In SORM's sonic cosmology, everybody is an imploding star.

Fidelity

During the latter and post stages of the Cold War, competing nations continued to consider their media intelligence practices secret, distinct and proprietary, faithful to their nation's mission and world view. And yet, counter-espionage, errors and attacks on both sides of the conflict outlined the increasingly promiscuous nature of digital information and its handling processes. Data was understood to be agnostic and to that extent passive, shaped with the right technical expertise to fit particular media or political contexts. However, their frequent indiscretions during the 2010s began to outline a mass hyperobject (Morton 2013) that was actively polygamous in character. It was also continuously connected across political, industrial and national boundaries through the web and other types of digital connectivity.

As discussed in earlier chapters, controllers of covert data systems had vested interests in perceptions of their fidelity for expert handlers. Therefore, when intelligence data breaches were discovered, they were diagnosed publicly as a glitch or fool's error in an otherwise secret and secure hyper-intelligent system. Software practices had become increasingly internationalized and nodal, through data standardization initiatives that were seen as a 'public good' (IMF 2022). Connectedly, the ease with which unencrypted communications could be duplicated, adapted, analysed and transported across political, technical and national divides also increased exponentially.

Contributing to the potential for data indiscretion, the flattening of all modes of communication into the same binary material made media formats traversable using similar digital processes for the first time. When an employee of the Finnish Nokia telecom company decided to take a backup copy of information related to the company's extensive contributions to SORM and then open it on a home computer, that information became instantly engaged with the wider internet. A data-breach hunter at the Australian cybersecurity company 'UpGuard' picked up on the mistake and sent a report of the breach to the online newspaper *TechCrunch*. He also sent a copy to the *New York Times* and informed Nokia so that it could close the security rupture (Satariano, Mozur and Krolik 2022; Whittaker 2019; UpGuard 2019).

The data itself revealed the extent to which political infidelities had been conducted by telecommunications giant Nokia under the cover of data agnosticism. Nokia, perhaps influenced by the truly desirous nature and predilections of the data that it handled, would downplay the infidelity when asked for comment by the *New York Times*: it was simply following and implementing local legal infrastructure requirements. What right did it have to judge? As a large globalized corporation, its role was to be a passive partner engaged with a commercially promiscuous and permissive data prerogative that wilfully crossed international and ethical boundaries.

Nokia reportedly made hundreds of millions of dollars from Russian contracts dating from 2008 to 2017 (Satariano, Mozur and Krolik 2022) and was reportedly integral in realizing the aims of SORM's progressively totalitarian communications systems. Nokia lamented that if there were limits to what it was allowed to do in the world, these should be set by governments and there should be clearer export restrictions in place to stop it from trading with certain states. In fact, the alignment of data promiscuity with commercial promiscuity had been nascently picked over in the 'Net Neutrality Debate' in the US Congress in 2011 (Gilroy 2011). Members of Congress had considered the need to maintain a non-judgemental approach to the flow of data regardless of content in order to protect the market from anti-competitive practices.

Such practices included DPI. DPI would allow internet service providers to prioritize or disallow certain types of data flowing through the World Wide Web to protect their profits. However, the report informing the US Congress debate highlighted a growing need for the consumption of 'uninterrupted streams of data' in new audio-visual media services while also calling out the security risks (the inadvertent or deliberate surveillance of personal data) inherent in DPI. In this sense, it recommended supporting the permissive behaviour of data to both accelerate the digital expansion of US goods and services while passively protecting individual privacy and personal freedom: a data red light zone. The misleading nature of the conflation would soon be exposed by the Snowden leaks. Conversely, in the same time period, Russia had begun to fantasize about a Russified data network free from international influence and entirely bound within the confines of its own borders and server farms: an anechoic chamber of screaming data.

PRISM

CENTRAL SECURITY SERVICE
UNITED STATES OF AMERICA
UNITED STATES COAST GUARD
1790

CHAPTER 8
PRISM

Process

PRISM is a surveillance programme run by the US National Security Agency, which collects and analyses information from domestic internet companies, including Microsoft, Yahoo, Google, Facebook, Paltalk, AOL, Skype, YouTube, Apple and latterly X. Launched in 2007, shortly after the 'Protect America Act' was passed by President George W. Bush, PRISM allows the government to request data that matches court-approved search terms, even if said data has previously been encrypted. Audio chats, photographs, texts, video, web-browsing content, search term queries and cloud storage data – all are open to being mined and analysed.

In 2013, Edward Snowden informed the world of the previously covert PRISM infrastructure by passing on leaked documentation to *The Guardian* and *Washington Post* newspapers. Initially published on 6 June 2013, the documents would challenge the stated purpose of PRISM – to intercept communications of foreign surveillance targets – and would be dissected and scrutinized for years afterwards. Snowden declared that many of PRISM's functions and operations either bordered on or fully met the criteria of being illegal, even though Barack Obama had repeatedly assured US citizens that no unauthorized surveillance had occurred and nor would it in the future. Crucially, Snowden's papers made clear that not only could US citizens be made targets through makeshift justifications, but that they were also routinely monitored by the NSA, who were guilty of violating privacy rules thousands of times a year. Even more damning was a judgement declassified by the Obama administration, which stated that 'the NSA's inability to separate purely domestic communications from foreign traffic violated the fourth amendment' (MacAskill 2013: online). The compliance costs for companies were subsequently paid by the NSA in the form of reimbursement payments to the tune of millions of dollars.

Snowden's disclosures also exposed a similarly invasive programme run by the UK's GCHQ called 'Tempora'. According to Ewen MacAskill et al.:

> GCHQ was handling 600m 'telephone events' each day, had tapped more than 200 fibre-optic cables and was able to process data from at least 46 of them at a time. Each of the cables carries data at a rate of 10 gigabits per second, so the tapped cables had the capacity, in theory, to deliver more than 21 petabytes a day – equivalent to sending all the information in all the books in the British Library 192 times every 24 hours. (2013: online)

In the face of incontrovertible evidence, the companies at the centre of PRISM have denied passing on data or colluding with government bodies. Facebook's chief security officer Joe Sullivan stated that, 'we do not provide any government organization with direct access to Facebook servers'. Apple's spokesman Steve Dowling, meanwhile, took the PR smokescreen one step further by declaring that 'We have never heard of PRISM' (Gellman and Poitras 2013: online). This presumed air of detachment was not shared by government officials, however. According to documents made public by Snowden, '98 percent of PRISM production is based on Yahoo, Google and Microsoft; we need to make sure we don't harm these sources' (Gellman and Poitras 2013: online).

The fear that, if exposed, the world's most powerful corporations would withdraw support or compliance drove the US government's safety-first policy. Slightly surprising is that since revelations from whistle-blowers such as Snowden, Chelsea Manning and Daniel Ellsberg have become public, the fallout does not seem to have had serious consequences for the bottom lines of the businesses involved. Our collective dependencies on large US and Chinese technology companies leave us with few options or collective ways to resist them, either socially, commercially or politically. For Greece's former minister of finance, Yanis Varoufakis, this lack of challenge has led us to an epochal shift in the evolution and subsequent death of capitalism.

According to Varoufakis, we are currently living in an era of 'technofeudalism' (2023). This is a new economic era in which tech companies, with overly ambitious business models across a range of sectors, have been allowed to flourish unchecked. This lack of oversight with regard to what is in the public interest has meant that they have reshaped not only market dynamics but also the nature of the markets themselves. For Varoufakis, venture capitalist Roger McNamee, and Shoshana Zuboff, the technologically endowed few now rule over the majority, irrespective of geographic, political or economic affiliations, or standing (Cadwalladr 2023: online). It was partly in response to this unbridled economic and technological dominance that Edward Snowden made his decision to leak highly sensitive information. Laura Poitras, who made the 2014 documentary *Citizenfour* concerning the whistle-blower, along with journalist Barton Gellman, speaks to his sense of social justice when they write,

> Firsthand experience with these systems, and horror at their capabilities, is what drove a career intelligence officer to provide PowerPoint slides about PRISM and supporting materials to The Guardian and Washington Post in order to expose what he believed to be a gross intrusion on privacy. 'They quite literally can watch your ideas form as you type', the officer said. (2013: online)

The next step will be listening to ideas before you type. As the book progresses, we will come to hear that this predictive mode of neural perception and capture is not as far-fetched as it might seem upon first reading.

Recording

If Charles Babbage's vast library of vocal documentation was proposed to be the air around and above us, then the NSA's more accessible storage at the Utah Data Center would be its massive data repository. It is a digital holding cell of exabyte proportions that is the destination for much of PRISM's captured data. When announced in 2012, it was projected as being capable of holding 'an immense amount of data, basically a rolling history of the entire planet's pattern of life' (Snowden 2019: 246). When it was completed in May 2014, it had cost the US government $1.5 billion. Ecologically speaking, its numbers are eye-watering. It runs an electricity bill of approximately $40 million per year and, possibly more worryingly, uses 1.7 million US gallons of water every day due to the open-evaporation-based cooling system that it employs.

In digital terms, the directive of 'burn after reading' transforms to 'destroy after transmitting'. Though for PRISM, transmitting would constitute accessing the data, which would nullify some of its plausible legality, as communications records that remain 'unobtained' can be 'collected in storage forever, raw data awaiting its future manipulation' (Snowden 2019: 178). Snowden described this dynamic as the NSA's ultimate dream, one of permanency, where it could 'store all of the files it has ever collected or produced for perpetuity, and so create a perfect memory. The permanent record' (Snowden 2019: 167). The efficiency and scale of digital storage have come a long way since the Stasi's filing cabinets. The storage of physical copies did not, for example, contain an automatic log of when, where and by whom those files were accessed. Some legal ambiguity exploited by the NSA requires that data can only be stored and not obtained, a dynamic that allows the records to hover as a threat, waiting only on a makeshift legal justification to render them available for search and analysis.

On a smaller scale than the NSA's MDR in Utah, our own personal data repositories – those of the cloud, as well as local versions on our handheld digital devices – also constitute a rolling history of our lives via smartphones. Here, data is accessed and shared, or just held in a prosthetic form of memory. Videos of fireworks or concerts attended, that will likely never be viewed or fully deleted, sit in our pockets, taking up digital space that justifies itself through its negligible impact on the overall amount of data that is possible to accrue at low cost and effort. What matters more than the data itself is our comforting proximity to it and the ability to access it for targeted purposes, much like the NSA's attitude towards its own permanent record – a repository that networks such as PRISM are constantly adding to.

The ease of recording audio, video and images of events in our lives creates pressure to do so continuously, with the added anxiety that missing out on recording something important may rob us of the ability to relive those moments later on. Other than approaching the limits of personal storage, what would prompt us to let go of those recordings? Human memory is fallible, yet multimedia recordings do not encapsulate the information stored in the brain that constitutes somatic memory. It begs the question, how long will it be before more ephemeral and complex information pertaining to olfaction or emotions (for example) can also be electronically registered, retained and recalled?

Medical approaches to prosthetic memory use technological intervention to augment the brain's natural ability. Researchers at the University of Southern California have been using electrodes to copy 'what happens in the hippocampus – a seahorse-shaped region deep in the brain that plays a crucial role in memory' (Hamzelou 2022: online). Results were most revealing with people who had existing memory disorders. This suggests that stimulating the hippocampus can help encode memories in the brain, though 'it might not make sense to have the device running all the time, for example – there are plenty of life experiences, such as taking out the garbage, that people with memory disorders don't need to remember' (Hamzelou 2022: online). There are also plenty of life experiences that mass surveillance apparatuses such as PRISM do not need to remember on our behalf, yet the documentation sits in storage like so many videos of music concerts, pale representations of what actually happened.

Transgression

To sonic theorist Casey O'Callaghan, sounds are disturbance events caused by objects 'disrupting a surrounding medium' (O'Callaghan 2007: 403) so that we hear the sound as coming from these objects and bodies. An echo of the sound is always heard in relation to the original. It is, in fact, its own disturbance event, the impact of the original sound on a secondary object causing vibrations and producing new distortions that reach the listener's ear (O'Callaghan 2007). Each event can set off a new, less sonorous disturbance until those disturbances are inaudible. Snowden's encrypted file, which contained a wealth of evidence pertaining to the NSA's mass surveillance operations, was labelled 'Astro noise', and it distorted the media around it with transgressive effect.

The term astro noise itself refers to an echo, to 'the faint background disturbance of thermal radiation left over from the *Big Bang*' (Sanders 2016a: online). The proposition here is that after the huge initial impact, the social, political and economic reverberations would be felt for many years to come. Some of the closest audience members of the original disturbance were journalists and documentarians. Glenn Greenwald, Laura Poitras, Barton Gellman and Ewen MacAskill were all in the direct line of fire, and they would echo and amplify the contents of Astro noise so that they could be heard by wider publics around the world. The distortion effects were resounding for all of these individuals. In diary entries that Poitras later published as the 'Berlin Journal' (Poitras 2016), the disturbance was obviously profound. In the third film in her documentary trilogy that explores the aftereffects of 9/11 and the subsequent War on Terror, Poitras was turned into 'a protagonist in her narrative' (Sanders 2016b: 27). Scared of reprisals from the security services, she would awake from dreams of the CIA's extraordinary renditions. She reread George Orwell's classic text *1984* (1949) and fretted about the all-knowing state. She wondered how much she wanted to be involved with the disclosures and whether Snowden's communications were some kind of trap.

Poitras was advised that her friends would be targeted and that she would not be able to protect them. At one point she says, 'I can hear the sound of my blood moving through my veins. Jesus, what the fuck is happening?' (Poitras 2016: 89). Her vision telescoped as she was downloading Snowden's files, the sound of her inner system getting louder and louder until she could no longer sleep and could not hear. Her heart beat 'out of her chest' (Poitras 2016: 99). It is a vivid account of the visceral pressure that Astro noise had on those it first impacted. At the time, Poitras was living in self-enforced exile in Berlin due to her films being confiscated when she arrived back in the United States after shooting. The arcane and cryptic culture of espionage was mapping onto and transgressing the boundaries of her own existence. The escalating threats to her freedom and creativity, meanwhile, had eradicated expectations of protection that she had previously harboured as a US citizen. The complex pressures she came under threw her into a deafening yet inaudible field of conflict, where she could not sense portals through which to escape.

Following the initial impact of Astro noise, a cultural echo resonated in the form of journalism and a documentary that won major accolades and prizes. Poitras's documentary *Citizenfour* (2014) won the 2015 Academy Award for Best Documentary Feature and *The Guardian* and *Washington Post* won the 2014 Pulitzer for Public Service (Pilkington 2014). This second mediated echo was quieter as it was selective and curated for narrative impact. The shock of these disclosures on the general public reverberated through culture and changed perceptions of the new digital technologies at our disposal. As predicted by Snowden, the visceral and criminal aspects of these resounding leaks dissipated over time, but their ramifications still resonate. The culture of Astro noise remains a subsonic signature of past transgressions and background noise to transgressions still to come.

Worlds

The Snowden leaks opened the door to the populace, culture and infrastructure of the insular worlds inhabited by the military intelligence of Western Allied countries. The need for secrecy, originally justified for purposes of espionage, had been adopted and amplified by intelligence communities in order to try and silence public and official discourse relating to their constructs. Within this orchestrated silence, Western authors and scriptwriters brought to life a world of slick Allied military supremacy over cruel enemies; post-imperialism rebooted and rehabilitated for the modern era through smart people with smart technology. Accessing all-hearing, all-watching systems such as PRISM, Western protagonists are supposedly supplied with incriminating recordings of those who are politically challenging and technologically disadvantaged.

In these fictional and frictional worlds, the term military intelligence is translated, via homonym, into human and machine intelligence. Glorified super spies such as James Bond, Jason Bourne and Carrie Mathison are supported by a sophisticated network of highly educated computer hackers and agile data analysts. They work in bustling premises reminiscent of a NASA control room, where only the best are trusted to deliver. In Tanya

Nitins's analysis of Bond gadgets, she notes that Bond's mastery of new technology 'to avert danger and restore order to the West' (Nittins 2011: 465) helped to allay fears of the increasing prevalence of conflict and chaos in post-Space Race society.

The aesthetics of technological mastery are key to the logic of the spy storyworld. Technology was granted science-fictional efficacy with ingenious gadgetry that looked as slick as its operator. Handheld devices could modulate the voices of enemies to gain access to vocally activated sections of enemy bases. Merchandising deals meant that smartphones from Samsung-Ericsson were used by Bond. With his portable device, he could take pictures of suspects, which would be matched up to IDs that had been formatted using facial recognition and AI-enhanced image technologies. Surely, if systems such as PRISM could help identify evil-doers while also providing location information for Bond's handlers in London, they could not be that bad (Nittins 2011)?

The importance of aesthetics over function in these fantastical worlds of spycraft was underlined by software engineer John Graham-Cumming. He collected on-screen code from various film and TV programmes and found that the majority of it was copied and pasted from web HTML pages or other irrelevant sources (2014). What is relatively consistent across the examples documented in his project is a consistent look and feel; economical digital design displayed with complex code that, in turn, delivers human-readable results. In stark contrast, Snowden's exposé of surveillance programmes such as PRISM provided entry to a world with an entirely different set of aesthetics that did not actively seek to promote the sense of mastery that had previously calmed the public.

In a well-documented slide from Astro noise, information is presented by ballpoint pen on Post-It notes. It displays intercepts between the public internet and Google Cloud, replete with a gleeful smiley face pointing to the decryption node. Something that shocked many commentators was the poor presentation of many of the resources found in the archive. A PowerPoint slide deck produced by the NSA explaining PRISM was described by Guardian writer Oliver Wainwright as '[a] car crash of clip art and bubble diagrams, drop-shadows and gradients' (2013: online). A cheerful upwards arrow on another slide depicts the year-on-year increase in service providers who join the programme to secretly share the public's data with government authorities. The corporate logos of well-known Silicon Valley companies like Google and Microsoft adorn each slide, echoing familiar forms of corporate endorsement. The unattractive nature of the slides resides not only in the poor use of diagrammatic tools but also in the clash of corporate aesthetics that are essentially 'sponsoring' the classified content.

By transposing evidence from the secret world of these intelligence communities to the public arena, what was compromised was their imagined mastery of the unknown. Intelligence agencies were no longer quite so mysterious, nor were they immediately correlated with efficiency, expertise or intelligence. The necessary fantasy – that the listeners and watchers of our data maintain a sect-like culture that is an extension of its elite sophistication – did not match the shared reality of the leak. Those witnessing the documents shared from Astro noise were disorientated. The fanciful notion that we are being protected by technologically endowed helicopter mums and dads or all-hearing and all-seeing guardian angels had been dispelled by a series of ugly diagrams. The myth had come crashing down, and Astro noise was its (un)sound effect.

Prediction

The enduring notion that the complex post-war world could no longer be properly understood by individual spies and their handlers, but through the séance/science of more-than-human scale data processing, had necessitated huge increases in the collection of information. At the time of the Snowden leak, GCHQ was processing 21 petabytes of data a day (MacAskill et al. 2013) including 600 million telephone calls. While sophisticated software allowed UK intelligence agencies to filter out low-value streaming media, it could already capture all content including emails and internet-based telephone calls from accessible Transatlantic cables for up to three days at a time (MacAskill et al. 2013). Despite the glut, only 300 British and 250 American agents were tasked with handling the data.

As PRISM records showed, the resulting race between increases in analytical power and the scope of data gathering meant that despite developments in computer and software ingenuity, prediction was becoming increasingly difficult. In 2016, former NSA official and whistle-blower, William Binney, described the problem as a 'bulk data failure' (Binney in Whittaker 2016: online). He pointed to this significant issue as the major cause for authorities not anticipating the coordinated Islamist Paris attacks of 2015, even though data had been gathered that could have foreseen them (Whittaker 2016). The result of the intelligence failure saw terrorists striking the Stade de France during an international football match, cafes and restaurants in the centre of the city and a concert by the band 'Eagles of Death Metal' at the Bataclan theatre.

The captured data would instead be used to review and understand the unfolding events leading up to the attacks: 'the NSA is great at going back over it forensically for years to see what they were doing before that' (Whittaker 2016: online). The complexity of accrued data had made it incredibly challenging to spot connections and patterns. When Kate Crawford was given access to the Astro noise archive, she noted that the cryptic results it provided in response to her questions merely posited other uncertainties, which, in turn, required further investigation (Crawford 2016). But worse than slowing predictive processes down is the flow of erroneous data that leads to false positives. The ratio of noise (a sea) to signal (a drop) in the system actively motivates analysts to misinterpret or imagine ghostly patterns in the data (Steyerl 2020) in a military complex that offers little feedback on what constitutes signal and what constitutes noise. In fact, as Hito Steyerl outlines in her essay 'Medya: Autonomy of Images' (2016), such hallucinatory dynamics regarding military prediction are a grounding logic for generative algorithms.

Training a diffusion model (such as 'Dall-E' or 'Stable Diffusion') involves adding noise or random patterns to known word-tagged sounds, images or media files and leaving the algorithm to work until it is capable of removing the noise from them. Thus, noise is progressively added to the media signal until it is entirely removed or silenced.

Through a diffusion model, a machine can be taught to predict a signal in total noise where a signal is entirely absent: to generate new media from nothing. It is, however, not only erroneous but also intensely problematic to suggest that – by basing learning on the historical patterns with which it has been trained – all modern creative AI operates by finding answers where there are none (Higham and Higham 2023). When describing uses of PRISM in his interview with Laura Poitras, Snowden notes similar dynamics in surveillance models, which result in guilty parties being effectively generated, rather than revealed:

> [I]t's getting to the point where you don't have to have done anything wrong. You simply have to eventually fall under suspicion by somebody – even by a wrong call – and then they can use the system to go back in time to scrutinize every decision you've ever made . . . and attack you on that basis and to sort of derive suspicion from an innocent life and paint anyone in the context of a wrongdoer.
>
> (Snowden in Poitras 2013: 7:13)

The ability to capture and store massive quantities of communication data does not lead to more reliable predictions but to a blanket din of suspicion in which noise and signal are inseparable. In that cacophony, the generative capacity of the machine to manufacture wrongdoers according to political and institutional necessity has, according to Snowden, become the popular substitute for prediction in PRISM's intelligence communities.

Intimacy

The historical prevalence of listening and recording audio as a surveillance strategy can be ascribed to its relative simplicity in comparison to the collection and retention of video data. Sound was once easier to capture and store, using smaller equipment and taking up less space than its video counterpart. What was once the purview of human eyes in support of technological ears has given way to miniature cameras embedded into devices that record both audio and video with relative ease. These devices are intimately connected to our daily tasks of communication and media consumption and occupy vulnerable spaces in our homes and on our person. The PRISM programme collected data in the United States by listening in on phone calls that Verizon, AT&T and Sprint turned over on a daily basis, including metadata on 'all calls', meaning in some cases, calls taking place 'wholly within the United States including local telephone calls' (Cohn and Rumold 2013: online).

Reactions to the US government collecting metadata, as well as real-time content from communications between private citizens, have ranged from predictable shock and outrage to artistically reflexive and humorous expressions of what it means to live with surveillance as an omnipotent presence. Although history has shown that the 'existence of a mass surveillance apparatus, regardless of how it was used, is in itself sufficient to stifle dissent' (Greenwald 2014: 3), artists have been responding through a form of 'artveillance' since at least the 1930s, with a growing wave becoming more apparent since the Snowden leaks (Maass 2014).

Artveillance can be broadly defined as 'the domain of the reciprocal influences and exchanges between art and surveillance' (Brighenti 2009: 175). Its practitioners 'challenge what it means to be human in a time of data', with some pieces hinging on the 'invasive banality' of surveillance (Maass 2014: online), as was observed by Peter Maass while viewing a seventy thousand-image tapestry work by Hasan M. Elahi at an exhibition organized by the Open Society Foundations in New York in 2014. In response to his name appearing on a terror watch list, Elahi, a professor of Art at Wayne State University in Detroit, began taking images of his daily life and voluntarily submitting them to the FBI. He sought to flood the market 'with banal information . . . questioning its inherent meaning and value for intelligence purposes' (Maass 2014: online). The deluge of banal yet intimate details and records that fuel many 'artveillance' projects reflects smaller-scale reactions by everyday internet users to their data being collected and ostensibly analysed by the NSA. A former naval intelligence officer named Erik Dahl analysed surprise attacks against the United States in his 2013 book *Intelligence and Surprise Attack: Failure and Success from Pearl Harbor to 9/11 and Beyond*, and reported that he had been misinformed about the key factors separating intelligence success from failure.

Dahl remembered being led to believe that 'intelligence analysts had one primary goal: to connect the dots of widely scattered and indistinct information into timely warnings that enabled senior leaders to take decisive action against a strategic threat' (2013: 184). The answer he found proved to be more complex. It involved not only gaining specific details of threats that needed to be headed off but also identifying a receptive policymaker who, 'through a combination of a *belief in the threat* and *trust in intelligence* . . . is ready to act on that warning' (2013: 178). Connecting the dots in a sea of data becomes more difficult when a layer of irony from private citizens' awareness of being watched is added.

An essay by Andrea Brighenti in 2009 concluded that artveillance conveys moods that 'range a lot from the dark and the gloomy, through to the outraged and the sceptical, to the playful and even the enthusiastic' (Brighenti 2009: 185). In a more playful category, internet memes about NSA or FBI agents listening in and watching ordinary people through their laptop webcams started to proliferate in 2017. A meme category dubbed 'Government Agent Watching Me' surfaced. Through it, intelligence agents were posited in emotionally supportive and caring roles, often commenting on a user's mental health. An early example of the format came from Twitter (now X) user @indiewashere. The tweet reads:

me: *covers the camera from my laptop's webcam with tape*
the government agent always watching me: *texting me* omg r u mad at me?
   (@indiewashere)

The meme flips the power dynamic between the watched and the watcher and places them in an intimate form of relationship within a direct communication channel. Other examples of the format show FBI agents giving romantic advice, helping with homework, and expressing concern for users' binge-watching habits.

The ubiquity of watching and listening devices in our living and working spaces invites vigilance against how those devices can be used against us. An artistic and playful approach to those dangers does not make light of privacy concerns but rather draws attention to the irrelevance of the majority of that data from a national security perspective. Placing themselves at the centre of a national security narrative with a personally assigned FBI agent helps individual citizens pull at the threads of an unraveling set of justifications for mass surveillance.

Voice

The voices focused on here are ones that are either missing or have been hushed for so long that they barely register. They are expressions of dissent against the PRISM surveillance programme. The loudest single voice is easy to denote; it is that of Edward Snowden. He put his life (and those of his loved ones) in jeopardy by leaking documents to the world's press and speaking out against the liberties taken by nations and corporations involved in carrying out highly intrusive surveillance on their own populations as well as on their adversaries.

The meteoric rise of 'big tech' reveals how the rules of engagement around resistance have changed. The dominance of communication channels through which opposition might travel is pertinent, especially given that they are predominantly owned by the companies in question. But it is the changes in the balance of power between political and commercial institutions that are equally instructive given the tentacular reach of Alphabet, Amazon, Apple, Meta and Microsoft, also known as the 'big five'. Their distributed and expanded limbs wrap more tightly around our digital and thus physical experiences, day by day.

Returning to the theme of unrestricted expansion – of market share, magnitude and immediacy – the unparalleled growth of big tech raises questions about the lack of oversight concerning their ascendancy. The fact that this proliferation carries on relatively unabated could be deemed careless, but the term complicity appears more accurate. While it is convenient to infer collective malaise, we also need to understand how difficult it is to engage with contemporary life without interfacing with these entities. They are collectively more powerful than any other industry has ever been, whether that be 1970s Big Oil (ExxonMobil, Chevron, BP and Shell), 1990s Big Media (Disney, Sony and Comcast) or, even more latterly, Big Banking (Goldman Sachs, Morgan Stanley and J.P. Morgan).

How we become dependent on big tech is key here. Many companies are perceived as giving away digital assets, processes and tools for free. This is significant when considering the wider cultural developments of economic and behavioural bonds that exist. This supposed altruism appears to be in the public's interest, but in reality, it is the first step, or act, of the creation of dependency. The term 'freemium' is pertinent. It is a business model that offers a free engagement format and then charges a premium for added services and features that are often essential when users have invested time and developed working practices that incorporate the tools. This contemporary re-versioning of the gift is a covert payback system that reflects the stealth agendas of many gift economy exemplars; a seemingly magnanimous dynamic through which the giver expects something in return of equal or preferably greater value over the long term (Mauss 1925). As a simple thought experiment concerning our over-reliance and dependence on internet-based technologies, we might think about how we would now navigate the world without the aid of online maps.

Through the use of Google Maps, we are losing touch with the practice of cartography. The Google Maps platform web page declares that there are 'more than a billion people using Google Maps every month' (Russell 2019: online) and that it holds 20+ petabytes of aerial and street view imagery combined – the equivalent of 266 years of HD video. As a result of this oversaturation of our collective sensorium, we are forgetting how to render mental markers that support orientation. Subsequently, our navigational muscles atrophy. More specifically, we do not flex our entorhinal cortex – the part of the brain that contains grid cells, which act like a GPS system (Makin 2015). The less activity in this neural area, the less sensitivity we have to direction.

In this way, we buy into our own debilitation, except that we do not even enact the transactional part of the equation (at least not in the first instance). This is a gift that keeps on giving (back to the giver) in ways that only become apparent once the tracking of the user's voices, interests, behaviours, movements and desires have been collected, analysed and made available for sale or used to shape other algorithmic-based products. Google, for example, primarily makes money from advertising along with selling data to commercially driven entities, as evidenced by their recent initiative to sell data to companies building solar products (Elias 2023). That we now have an ever-expanding digital cartography, which reveals in extraordinary detail recordings of the global population's digital exploits, means that surveillance systems such as PRISM and Tempora can key into any matrix of association. As such, the big tech cabal is entangled in charting a 'corporational' system of cause and effect. Together, nations and corporations form multi-sensory ligatures that bind digital communities, exert pressure upon request and drip feed the extracted dataflow. Add to this the rapid development of AI, which is largely controlled by Big Tech (von Thun 2023) and the future of listening and watching becomes ever more ominous.

AI systems that converge programmes such as PRISM with voice and facial recognition technologies, along with smart city policing platforms, will be able to render accurate portrayals of everyday lives in high-fidelity (Feldstein 2019). While the fleshy psychic 'precogs' in Philip K. Dick's *Minority Report* (1956) quietly float in a speculative warm water trance, our near future versions will be noisy, dry mixing desks. They will connect thousands of ears and eyes with multi-sensorial membranes that are secreted into every fissure of our urban and natural environments.

In the kaleidoscopic future of PRISM, the information garnered, however diffracted or abstracted, will compose digital twins born of surveillance with lifeblood that looks and sounds like prediction. Their voices will be audio clones. They will sound like us and will stand in for us in the dataspheres of the military-digital complex. Without a digital twin, our blooded existences will be called into question, and we will become unsound, living beyond or at the cusp of perception.

Fidelity

A copy of the US 2013 intelligence budget covering sixteen agencies showed that it amounted to $52.6 billion. It was dubbed the 'Black Budget'. Snowden's leak provided the information to journalists, which proved that 'the work of American Intelligence is done as frequently by private employees as it is by government servants' (Snowden 2019: 113). These private employees are not beholden to the same standards of allegiance to their country or fidelity to that country's founding principles as government employees. However, the complexity and scale of data collection and analysis by the NSA necessitated some creative hiring. The US government at the time did not have access to the technical talent required to execute and maintain its surveillance programmes, which is how people like Edward Snowden were fast-tracked through security clearances otherwise reserved for high-level intelligence operatives.

Through the promotion of the military-industrial, military-entertainment and more recently, military-digital complexes, the US government has maintained a fiction of appearing to adhere to the country's founding principles. It has done this while repeatedly acting against those values in pursuit of straightforward capitalist and imperialist ideals, both at home and through interference in foreign affairs. With contradiction, or at least underlying tension, at the base of many US cultural values (such as the pursuit of private reward vs. taxation in the name of public good, or the right to bear arms vs. the expectation of safety in public spaces), the danger in a system like PRISM is amplified by the classified nature of its operation. As Greenwald states, 'Expecting the US government to operate a massive surveillance machine in complete secrecy without falling prey to its temptations runs counter to every historical example and all available evidence about human nature' (2014: 4).

Scepticism over governments acting in the best interests of their citizens is not an invention of the digital age. Corruption thrives at the intersection of power and opacity. Individuals leverage benefits against the principles that guide them to varying degrees of violation against personal ethics. Individual reasons for engaging in moral and ethical infidelity are, meanwhile, tied to personal circumstances. Through such dynamics, a myriad of justifications can be sought to assuage guilt and jerry-rig the kind of spin that makes anonymous public relations professionals infamous. In the case of Snowden's exposure of classified PRISM documents, the US government needed to react publicly with an explanation for the scale and scope of its data collection activities. They needed to find a way of quieting the Astro noise; to remove the harsh and abrasive cadence of disclosure and render the leaks more akin to ambient music.

The task of rescoring public perception fell, in part, to Robert S. Litt, a highly respected lawyer in the 'Office of the Director of National Intelligence', who gave a speech a month after Snowden's leaked files began to appear in the press. The speech explained 'NSA activities under US law, especially the telephone metadata program and PRISM surveillance conducted under FISA, and it defend[ed] their legality, effectiveness, and fidelity to the democratic values of the United States' (Litt in Fidler 2015: 102). Litt's speech began somberly, claiming that he wished he was giving the speech in 'happier times for the Intelligence Community' (Litt in Fidler 2015: 102) and stated that the 'stolen' information had done irreversible harm, with the disclosures 'made by people who did not fully understand what they were talking about' (Litt in Fidler 2015: 102).

The scolding tone directed at Snowden's actions did not relent and reflected wider responses in the media, including that of CBS News' Bob Schieffer's denouncement of Snowden as a 'narcissistic young man' who thinks 'he is smarter than the rest of us' (Greenwald 2014: 222). Snowden's travel to Hong Kong and his interminable stay in Russia also called his patriotism into question (Greenwald 2014: 223), which conveniently placed him in opposition to those apparently malleable US values referenced in Litt's speech, that were also used to justify NSA surveillance. Litt stated that:

> Our government's activities must always reflect and reinforce our core democratic values. . . . But security and privacy are not zero-sum. We have an obligation to give full meaning to both: to protect security while at the same time protecting privacy and other constitutional rights. (Litt in Fidler 2015: 102)

The breach that opened up between the irreconcilable differences of national security versus individual privacy is where the majority of the 'spin' around Snowden's PRISM leaks was generated. Litt declared that Snowden's sharing of information with the press did not constitute whistle-blowing because the exposed activities by the government were technically legal. Ultimately, Litt's justifications for the NSA's actions came down to his belief that citizens were not overly concerned about the collection of their information, but instead about what the government might do with it (Litt in Fidler 2015: 104). This conviction speaks to a prevailing general attitude towards data privacy, that if one has nothing to hide, then it does not matter what happens to one's data, echoing, though not equating to, the Nazis' declaration that, 'if you have nothing to hide, you have nothing to fear'. Western culture's voluntary abandonment of privacy ultimately defends a techno-deterministic attitude that lets technological affordances dictate acceptable data practices rather than the other way around. For those yearning for some kind of fidelity to the tenets of personal privacy, we need to turn to another Public Enemy from a different era and amplify their call to 'Bring the [Astro] noise'.

Owing more to the silent stealth mode of surveillance capitalism than to the noise creation of mass surveillance systems, the next epistemic shift mapped by *Listening In* is towards the smart technologies we have invited into our homes. Thus, the next section focuses on entertainment, communications, health and security devices that we feel obliged to fold into the familial environment, lest we be considered erratic Luddites with a *penchant* for chaos, danger and domestic isolation. It is a radical shift in that it demarcates a new epoch of celebrated self-surveillance. It is also a period that has witnessed the uptake of distributed IoT devices such as smartphones, smart speakers, Wi-Fi-connected toys and baby monitors; technologies that extend the reach and influence of commercial agents who are ultimately invested in economic permutations of data acquisition and analysis, advertisement and product development.

PART III
DOMOTIC SELF-SURVEILLANCE CULTURES

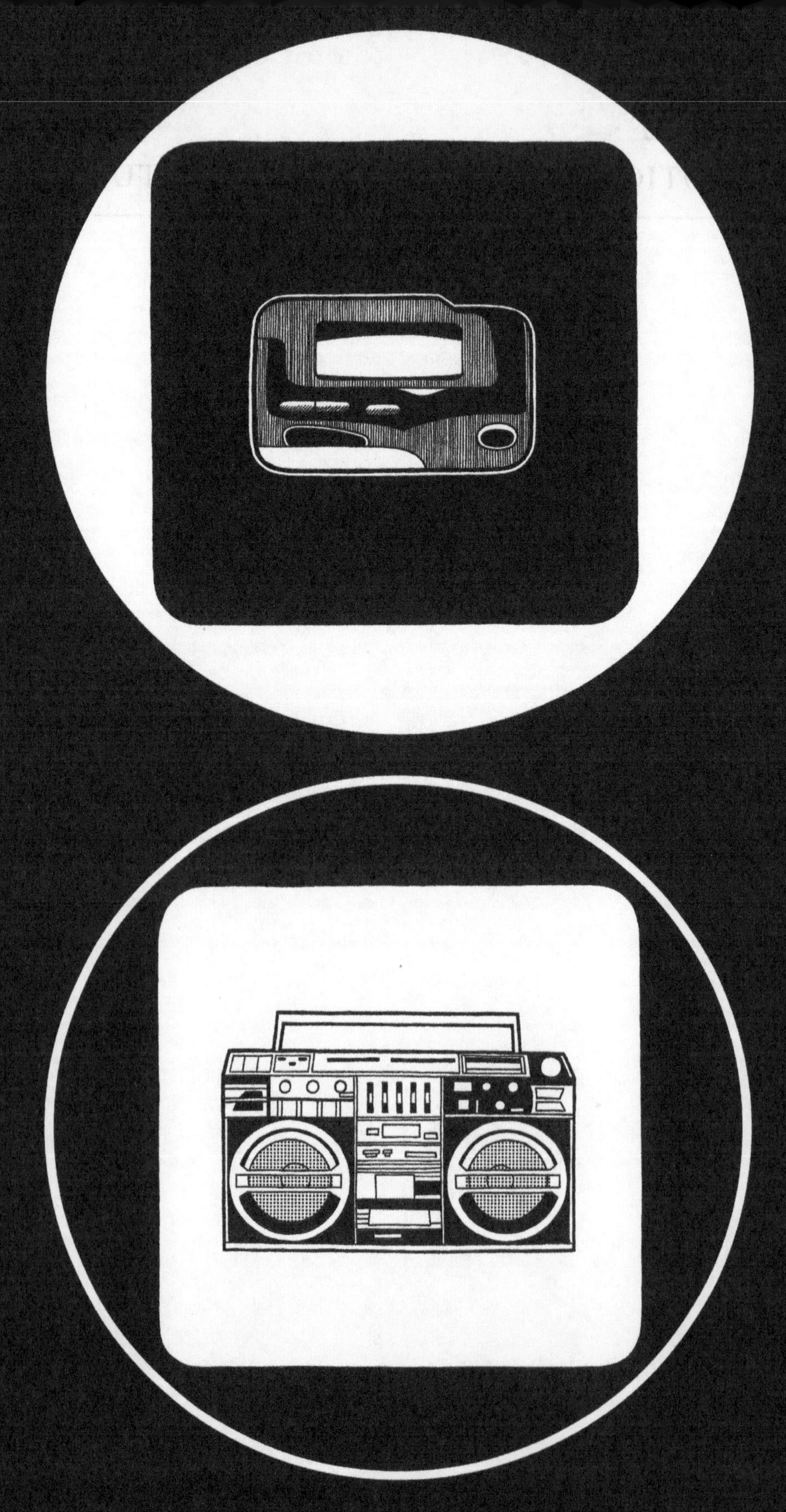

CHAPTER 9
SMARTPHONES

Process

Technically, the smartphone's identity hinges on the integration of its traditional use as a telephone with the advanced functions of a computer. But, like the word 'computer', which in Don DeLillo's *Cosmopolis* is described as a term both 'backward and dumb' (2003: 104), the word 'smartphone' does not account for its functions, nor for its cultural and personal significance. It is a device that represents 'the coalescing of information into a single, personal object', reminding us 'that data is now encoded into the air around us, ready to be called upon' (Silverman 2015: 320). It also demarcates the border of the sonic space between a person and their surroundings, given its contemporary standing in the evolution of personal music devices that started with the release of Sony's 'Walkman' in 1979.

In his 2012 book, *The Big Disconnect: The Story of Technology and Loneliness*, Giles Slade presents the history of the Walkman's release and its early use as a precursor to the smartphone's reproduction of sound to 'provide a sense of connection that warms us *chemically* in the interpersonal frigidity of the modern city' (Slade 2012: 161). The enjoyment of music via the Walkman became 'a totally exclusionary experience' (Slade 2012: 97), where solo usage patterns by consumers led to Sony removing the second headphone jack, which had been a feature on the original model. The device's use of headphones marked a departure from the boombox (also known as a Ghetto Blaster) and its position on the streets, from one of extrinsic sonic dominance to one of internal eschatology.

With headphones attached to a mobile device, and control over what was played lying in the hands of the individual rather than those of a radio DJ, the Walkman offered a reprieve from the uncontrollable onslaught of city noises. The smartphone, meanwhile, boasts boundless access (via streaming apps) to Paul Goldstein's 'celestial jukebox' (2003). This means that individuals can now score their stroll through a city, sharing the contents of their personalized curation with anyone in their social network, and also consequently, with their service providers. Private soundtracks are truly only possible through a return to physical media in a retro reclamation of offline listening.

Playing music is not the only way that the smartphone creates portable sonic solitude. According to Sherry Turkle, its multifunctional identity has 'replaced the cyborgs' more elaborate accoutrements' to achieve all manner of technical ends. It allows us to be 'alone together', wherein we are 'newly free in some ways, newly yoked in others' (2011: 152). As of 2020, it was reported that the 'average iPhone user checks her phone eighty times a day' (Aschoff 2020: 3), with roughly six out of ten US smartphone users sleeping next to their devices (Aschoff 2020). The loss or misplacement of a smartphone can feel like the loss of a limb, cutting us off from contact with those in our lives with whom we would most like to commiserate about the absence of such an important object.

Globally pervasive smartphone culture marks an attempt to colonize the digital frontier by corporate actors that control its manufacturing supply chain and accompanying inequalities. In her book, *The Smartphone Society: Technology, Power, and Resistance in the New Gilded* Age (2020), Nicole Aschoff draws links between historical and physical frontiers and our 'notion of the infinite' (82). She notes that we invested naively in the notion of the digital cloud, given that it too is limited by physical hardware and infrastructure. She goes on to liken the exploration of the digital frontier to the colonization of the Americas in the seventeenth century. This also presented colonizers with a land of wealth so rich it was thought to be infinite. As we now know, these utopian daydreams were subsumed into unsustainable, capitalistic practices, where the land was forcefully exploited and exhausted at the expense of indigenous people and resources (2020).

The fabrication of smartphone devices is similarly exploitative. This is where marketing companies and experts earn their pay; they feed narratives into popular discourse that fetishize connectivity, immediacy and access. It is these kinds of stories that are seeded into popular imagination in order to conceal the terrible conditions and value extraction that are necessary for the build-out of the smartphone's architecture. For Aschoff, the component parts and labour chart 'a topological map of global inequality' (2020: 28). The smartphone's mobile, handheld portal to the internet holds benefits for the advancement and democratization of knowledge, but it remains a product burdened by capitalism and one that reinforces 'the application of economic reasoning to every aspect of human life' (Slade 2012: 9).

Locally, the smartphone's sonic affordances in densely populated cities complicate the enforcement of 'civil inattention', a phrase coined by sociologist Erving Goffman in 1963 to describe how city dwellers use behaviour to display disinterest in the activities of strangers. The practice is meant to make living in close proximity with others more bearable. Rides on crowded subway cars and trams, for example, offer an abundance of stimuli necessitating 'a situation in which the individual must develop ways of buffering herself from her surroundings' (Sharon and Koops 2021: 333). While civil inattention used to mean ignoring conversations held between people physically present in public spaces, the advent of the cell phone meant users could conduct one-sided private conversations, a communications zone where their 'sense of privacy is sustained by the presumption that those around them will treat them not only as anonymous but as if absent' (Turkle 2017: 155).

The cell phone's relatively simple musical and conversational capacity transitioned into the smartphone's newer purview as a total entertainment device. It has become a device that not only projects the sound of someone talking on the other line but also amplifies sonic content from myriad forms of music, video and immersive platforms, not to mention its own cosmology of sound effects and minor haptic rumbles. New habits of abandoning headphones in public in order to hold amplified video conversations or watch content complete with adverts overwhelm expectations of civil inattention and rub up against more personal definitions of what constitutes personal sonic space.

Recording

A range of new sensors hidden within smartphones abruptly decentred the microphone as the primary recording instrument of invisible experience. Extending beyond hearing, it sought to mechanize more of the ear's sensory functionality. The microphone had long been the sensory recorder of the fleeting moment. Where things, people and places from the visual realm persisted, an utterance or other sound was ephemeral, replaced immediately by silence or by other environmental sounds. The microphone had made each utterance concrete and evidential. Now, hidden accelerometers, gyroscopes and GPS technology extend the inner ear's function in sensing gravity, acceleration and equilibrioception (our sense of spatial orientation and balance). While these technologically advanced sensors were used to market phones and related services as products, they were also designed to be easy to forget. Thus, when users chose to restrain the extrasensory perception of the phone – the camera covered with tape and the microphone turned off – these other sensory abilities would continue to record and store unprecedented quantities of structured, granular data about consumers and their habits.

Outside of intelligence communities, the telephone had a relatively short history as a personal messaging device. As part of the postal network, telegrams had traditionally been considered the way to send messages 'telically'. It was the answerphone coupled with the home telephone in the 1980s that introduced the affordances of recording messages and presaged the mobile phone with integrated digital voice and text messages. Each of these was a distinct digital signal that could be left behind, read or heard asynchronously, and even repurposed. An accelerated period of market-led development, helped in part by military-industrial partnerships such as the derestriction and repurposing of US military GPS technology in 1999 (US Government 2021), filled the smartphone with sensors capable of recording a much wider range of messages about the user.

Due to the nature of services offered by these sensors (wayfinding, health tracking), the period of recording no longer started with the press of a button or the start of a call. Shoshana Zuboff notes that these recordings began to resemble telemetric indicators previously only used to track animal populations in the wild (Zuboff 2019). As the extended sensorium of phone sensors outsourced memory to media platforms and cloud-based server farms, without its user necessarily being conscious of the transfer, it began to resemble a digital type of unconscious memory similar to that which we experience organically (Cheng and Huang 2011): a form of recall that influences our actions and behaviours unknowingly. These developments reinforce notions that such an expanded sensorium works not only on a private and neurological level but also on a social and political one as well (Howes 2024).

The density of data provided by smartphones offers the possibility to develop new records of the voice that could only be understood by algorithms. Civilian research published by Rebecca Ciesielski (2022) suggests that both accelerometers and gyroscopes in smartphones provide ways to record intelligible voice data. Both components 'essentially consist of a miniature weight suspended between springs that can move back and forth between them' (Ciesielski 2022: online). The system that is designed to sense movement is also capable of picking up tremors and, though not sensitive, can pick up vibrational movement from the phone's loudspeaker. While incoherent to the human ear, new hybrid algorithmic perception has the potential power to decode and record new unanticipated forms of listening, denoting a subtle departure from the model of the human ear as the paragon of listening apparatuses.

As a result, smartphone recordings quickly became subject to consumer and state scrutiny as these additional data trails provided a new ear to the populace. Data protection regulations such as the European Union's GDPR (2016), end-to-end encryption of messages and other practical safeguards were subsequently put in place to limit exposure to unauthorized misuse. However, when the assumed predominance of Western allies was challenged by the growing technological might of China through the use of its server hardware and services, lawmakers in Europe and the United States bristled. Huawei smartphones and server systems were decried in the UK, and elsewhere, as containing potential spyware that might provide the Chinese state with a backdoor recording device. Practical safeguards come below national security in the pecking order of technological development, especially when the latter is crucial to perceptions of cultural dominance.

Transgression

In the 1840s, marketplaces close to the then-infamous Seven Dials in London's West End saw the development of a rhyming slang (Ayto 2003). Its adoption over two decades seemed to closely follow the establishment of the city's first Metropolitan Police force in 1829 (Johnson 2016). Used in the metropolitan areas of London, the United States and Australia, the slang has often been considered a 'cryptolect', a secret language that allowed market stall owners and others to conduct business verbally without fear of being understood by passersby who might disrupt their plans. According to Eric Partridge's *Dictionary of the Underworld: British and American*, originally published in 1949, the history of English cryptolects or 'cants' can be traced back at least as far as the sixteenth century as a way to frustrate the understanding of unwanted listeners (Partridge 2015). He submits in the full title of the book that his study represents the 'Vocabularies of Crooks, Criminals, Racketeers, Beggars and Tramps, Convicts, the Commercial Underworld, the Drug Traffic [and] the White Slaver' (Partridge 2015). In the 1840s, as a dialect of encryption, the emergent rhyming slang no doubt helped counteract the growing authority of the Metropolitan Police listenership.

Nearly two centuries later, the smartphone was introduced globally with a growing acceptance that users might be listened to. Via the effects of the increasing sophistication of surveillance capitalism (Zuboff 2019), which was designed to predict consumer behaviour based on surplus behavioural data for marketing purposes, a type of digital animism began to be associated with portable devices. Smartphones were a listening presence (BBC 2017b), and the phone was no longer simply a place where you talked and listened to friends, colleagues and family, but where the majority of people began to suspect they were constantly being monitored, even when they were not connected via a phone call (Frick et al. 2021).

The sense of transgression was so great that in 2008, the year after the launch of the iPhone, Canadian entrepreneur Vincent Ramos launched 'Phantom Secure' and was soon able to charge enormous contract fees for owning a Blackberry. A big attraction of the device was that, alongside other security features, it had its microphone and other sensors removed. While many accepted the new lack of privacy when they spoke, generally sensing that such monitoring was limited to trivial marketing purposes, organized criminals were faced with the increased risk of being overheard in illicit conversation (UNODC 2022).

As in the 1820s, criminals needed a new cryptographic system to keep the details of their business arrangements secret and their conversations strictly outside the range of the policing ear. Those who sought to meet these strict requirements through aggressively secure features sometimes became embroiled in the criminal communities that supported them. In 2018, for example, both Phantom Secure and another Canadian company, Sky Global, were shut down. In 2019, Vincent Ramos was sentenced to nine years in prison, having pleaded guilty to knowingly selling phones to drug traffickers (Lamoureux and Cox 2019). Ramos had apparently refused an FBI request to plant a backdoor into his technology prior to his arrest and conviction (Cox 2019).

In the scramble for a new secure technology, many consumers switched to 'Anom', a mobile start-up company that offered a new phone that, like its predecessors, had no microphone or other sensors, and provided an innovative 'kill switch' that deleted all messages if it went offline for a certain length of time. Its expensive hardware and contract deal were quickly taken up by a number of organized crime syndicates and became a popular choice through word of mouth. As journalist Joseph Cox extensively reported, unbeknownst to the client base and sellers, US and Australian federal police forces had teamed up to design the phone to listen in on the planning of criminal activities. Perhaps comforted by the lack of an ambient microphone, users on the Anom network were unknowingly sharing all messages and GPS locations to a European server that was accessible to the Australian Federal Police and FBI (Cox 2021, 2022). Communications captured through Anom led to 'Operation Trojan Shield' and 'Operation Ironside', both major drug stings that collectively thwarted the distribution of approximately £34 million worth of illegal narcotics and led to hundreds of subsequent arrests. In many ways, Anom had been a brief return to the magical objecthood of twentieth-century bugs, such as the Shoehorn or The Thing. Yet its massive success, relative to those more esoteric precursors, relied on the ubiquity of new mobile technologies and their perceived attentiveness to all private speech.

When faced with such a totalizing system of listening, it is often criminals and spies who have the motivation and resources to stay unheard within it. Such silence is unambiguous. The cryptolect and its technological descendants may yet provide a way to speak privately on mobile devices once more: research on algorithmic camouflage against eavesdropping called 'Real-time Neural Voice Camouflage' at Columbia University in the United States, for example (Chiquier, Mao and Vondrick 2022), suggests that there are ways to add systematic noise to voice calls so that they cannot be easily digitally transcribed.

Yet the smartphone has become the core architecture of a digital 'panacousticon' (Szendy 2016; Wilkins 2016; Vetter 2012). The panacousticon is, to some degree, an auditory version of philosopher Jeremy Bentham's 'Panopticon', a prison where any inmate, at any one time, might be being viewed by the prison guard. The panacousticon, originally conceived in the seventeenth century by German Jesuit father Athanasius Kircher as a system of tunnels built into walls to listen in on all voices in a building, allows any word spoken near any listening device to be easily heard and transmitted. In that context, the act of deliberately adding noise to frustrate a third listener is no longer considered a respectable countermeasure against eavesdroppers. Instead, security professionals consider acts of wilful obfuscation to be transgressive, clear signals of suspicion that would draw a covert listener's ear closer to the speaker (Sharma 2022). The microphone must hear all.

Worlds

Smartphones can deliver their users to a range of worlds – those of social media, the wider internet and the soundscapes of vocal exchange. Another realm that can be added to this list is the world of film. Ever since 2011, when the first feature film, *Olive*, was shot on a Nokia N8 by Hooman Khalili and Patrick Gilles (Barnes 2011a), the smartphone has become a tool for the development, production and distribution of films and documentaries. More than that, smartphones themselves have become locations for storyboards. Witness the growth of narratives revolving around these precious metal machines that are magnetically attracted to our bodies in a manner akin to *Tetsuo: The Iron Man* (1989).

As much as the world of film has found a new location in the technical and conceptual potential of the smartphone, it is useful to remember that the device, in the first instance, is a sonic apparatus. Waveformed dynamics frame the ocular affordances of ever-upgraded cameras. This formatting of the visual by the sonic is instructive in that it recalibrates our predispositions with regard to quality and fidelity, and instead promotes mobility, accessibility and connectivity. Via the compression culture of the mp3, and our habits of listening to music through phone speakers (as well as the musical production aesthetics developed for them), we fully accept the idea and aesthetics of lo-resolution audio and, by dint, video.

We forego optimal viewing or listening experiences so that we can access content on a train or in a supermarket. We want the 'everywhere experience' rather than the purist experience. Music presaged this shift in social and cultural behaviours with regard to entertainment and communications. As sound theorist and economist Jacques Attali declared, 'Music makes mutations audible. It obliges us to invent categories and new dynamics' (1985: 4). The desire to fluidly access everything everywhere all at once is echoed by the equivalent will to monitor and track all that we listen to, watch and interact with.

As detailed throughout previous chapters, the state listens and watches, often through technologies that we cannot see or hear. Conversely, on the streets, in full public view, CCTV cameras reflect our gaze and in return capture our troubling, joyous, but mostly ordinary lives. Our activities are caught for a few seconds or minutes on multiple cameras every day: a distributed documentary created by smartphones, CCTVs, satellites and road cameras. If this meta network of recording devices were connected and made accessible, we could edit and watch our splintered lives back in beguilingly lo-resolution horror.

For this plexus of omnipresent surveillance to exist, CCTVs had to mobilize. The cultural obsession with recording needed to free itself from fixed-mounted cameras and find expression in motile technologies. The internet, meanwhile, became the ideal distribution channel, a matrix apparatus that effortlessly allows us to share or obfuscate that which is captured. 'The Internet has irrevocably changed how a person can be. It makes us all strays, and yet its users seem increasingly territorial. Entrenched in the emotional security of what we already believe, thanks to smartphones we can discover anything instantly and simultaneously draw a veil' (Sudjic 2018: online). Or make a lot of noise.

The smartphone was the obvious technological step for a species determined to capture and store all sounds and images. Small, always to hand and with a ravenous capacity to suck content from the physical world and transfer it into the digital (and vice versa), smartphones brokered our adaptive transitions between the real, unreal and beyond real. Fluctuating between these states are the billions of fragmented films and soundtracks of our lives, created every day by the hybrid meta-network of monitoring devices. This is not a methodological system overly concerned with traditional notions of aesthetics, editing or overdubs. It is an approach to producing abstracted non-linear content. If 'surveillance capitalism unilaterally claims human experience as free raw material for translation into behavioral data' (Zuboff 2019: 14), we can also add 'cultural products' to the list of conversions.

When these fragmented documentaries are sampled and recalibrated into films, a cultural redefinition of surveillance happens. These are the reverberatory sounds and images of self-expression and self-surveillance crossfading into each other's waveform and, in doing so, they add to an 'ecology of indefinable boundaries' (Goriunova 2019: 13). Through this process, the omnipresent nature of smartphones and their worldbuilding remit becomes clearer as we begin to understand how we all help drive the hyper-connected networks of monitoring. The personal maps onto the political, which in turn opens economic potential through the production engines of culture. Our lives are captured, used to inscribe our mediated confinement and sold back to us as entertainment. Worlds folding into worlds folding into worlds.

Prediction

The list of health issues monitored by smartphones and their augmented sensors is growing. From optical and electrochemical biosensors to accelerometers, sensors have become more accurate as mobile CPUs have increased ten-fold over the past seven years. Phenomena being monitored at the time of writing include cardiovascular activity such as heart rate (HR) and HR variability, eye health, respiratory and lung health, skin health, daily activity and sleep, ear health, cognitive function and mental health. Welcome to the future of digital diagnostics. As smartphones' capacities to monitor our bodies and environments have increased, so too has their proximity to our bodies. Having once been kept in bags and cases, they were moved to jackets and trouser pockets. From being close to the body, they then migrated onto the body, strapped onto arms, legs and stomachs during exercise. The well-worn phrase concerning strategic relationship building with friends and enemies could be revised in this context: 'keep your tech close, keep your listeners closer', except that it would currently afford us too much tactical agency and assume that we have modes of effective resistance to surveillance.

Over the long term, the massive datasets being collected by tech companies are likely to be used to predict what our bodies can do and, more importantly, what they might become. Shoshana Zuboff states that,

> As we shall see, surveillance capitalism's unusual products manage to be derived from our behavior while remaining indifferent to our behavior. Its products are about predicting us, without actually caring what we do or what is done to us. (2019: 52)

Zuboff positions the body as a predictable system of flows: a bio-cluster of blood pressure readings, micro facial expressions, calorie counts, step regimens, breathing patterns and voice recordings. A dizzying array of somatic information renders the smartphone a sensor clot, a coagulating technology that extracts, collates and stores data. Ultimately, smartphones are creating profiles that anticipate future medical conditions, purchasing patterns, insurance risks and environmental dependencies. Every projected somatic vulnerability and risk will be calculated, spread bet and monetized for future rewards. Listening as an investment strategy.

In 1816, French medical listening was quietly undergoing an important revolution. Invented by René Laennec, the stethoscope consisted of a disc-shaped resonator attached by tubes to two earpieces. It was a device that was at the listening edge rather than the bleeding edge of medical modernity. It enabled doctors and nurses to listen to the internal sounds of the body, a process also known as auscultation, that 'heralded the birth of a medical acoustic culture' (Goriunova 2019: 12). As a result of this new frequency-based ontology, doctors became 'virtuoso listeners'; they could hear the body in ways inaccessible to lay people (Sterne 2003: 136). For Jonathan Sterne, the stethoscope put a distance between doctor and patient that was full of social, economic, sexual and epidemiological ramifications.

> Long before the germ theory of disease would have suggested a need for distance between doctor and patient, Laennec was worried about the propriety of male doctors touching women's breasts ('mammae'), the disgust that he and others might feel at various illnesses and conditions of patients, and the class difference between doctors and their hospital patients. (Sterne 2003: 114)

Distributed around the somatic frame, the smartphone's tentacular reach is moving in. 'The body is no longer simply made of organs and fluids, but is co-produced with stuff (bacteria, free radical particles, products of pharmaceutical industry, classrooms, cities) at every layer' (Goriunova 2019: 13). What this observation misses are the internal biotechnologies such as sensors, cochlear implants and pacemakers that are inhabiting the body on an ever more frequent basis (Joung 2013). The smartphone as a diagnostic technology presages this transgression of the dermal interface, its journey inward negating the need for the stethoscope and its attendant ear-based skills.

Smartphones are integral tools within the Internet of Medical Things (Wi-Fi enabled medical applications and devices connected to healthcare information technology systems). Monitoring homebound patients, they are helping drive telemedicine – an efficient solution for health systems that are overcrowded and underfunded. Being convenient and decreasing patients' exposure to infectious diseases, telemedicine and its somatic surveillance techniques have been widely adopted. It is partly why we allow our internal soundscapes, 'the dry sibilous rattle, the dry crepitous rattle with large bubbles or crackling, utricular buzzing, amphoric resonance' (Goriunova 2019: 12), to be recorded and stored for later use.

AI research focused on capturing the body's inner workings via the voice is also providing information beyond the palpable iteration of language. For laryngologist Dr Yael Bensoussan, leader of the research project 'Voice as a Biomarker of Health', 'Everything from your vocal cord vibrations to breathing patterns when you speak offers potential information about your health' (Acosta and Weiner 2022: online). Embedded in smartphones, algorithms trained to listen to such personalized sonic phenomena will allow mobile devices to conduct remote sonograms, a waveformed revelation of cavities, rhythms and processes that would otherwise be implausible.

Predicting the body's future dependencies and fragilities, smartphones anticipate the future coalescence of monitoring programmes, AI and networked diagnostics. Presaging all aspects of our internal worlds, these future assistants will be the doyens of all-encompassing anxiety. In fertile crescents of fear, they will speak of bodies that are always on the edge of perceptible chaos, lifelogging for increased longevity. AI assistants will croon over chopped and screwed soundtracks of the quantified self, whispering about the future rewind; reassuring us that in time, we will be able to spin the record back.

Intimacy

While phone messages have been used in recordings by a range of pop royalty, from 'Telephone' (2010) by Lady Gaga featuring Beyoncé to 'All The Love' (1982) by Kate Bush, the genre most acclaimed for featuring them from the 1990s onwards is Rap. Kendrick Lamar, Denzel Curry and Chance the Rapper are just a few of the celebrated hip-hop artists who have dropped phone messages into their tracks. Phone messages as humorous interludes, narrative tonal shifts and familial revelations are incorporated between tracks but can also be used within them, to pivot the listener's attention. Outside of the direct creation of music, Rap also 'has a long history dealing with phones as a medium, from recorded calls to wiretaps to verses recorded as voice memos from prisons' (Pearce 2017: online).

Rappers are arguably the most monitored entertainment figures in the United States. Ever since the high-profile 1990s shootings of Tupac Shakur and The Notorious B.I.G. led to a violent rivalry between East and West coast crews and gangs, police forces have monitored rap artists. In 2004, the *Miami Herald* published the article 'Police Secretly Watching Hip-Hop Stars'. The newspaper had been fed information by the New York Police Department, which had a '6-inch-thick compendium of dossiers on well-known rappers and producers – complete with photos, license plate numbers, and social security numbers – that they distributed to other police departments across the country' (Nielson 2010: 1254–5). In the early 2000s, it was the 'latest development in a nationwide effort to place every aspect of hip-hop culture under state surveillance' (Younge 2004: online).

Evocative of the US government's 1956–71 'Counterintelligence Program' when the FBI and police monitored Black musicians, writers and activists as part of a wider remit to neutralize perceived internal political threats to US security, the monitoring of rappers has shaped the music genre in both obvious and nuanced ways (Nielson 2010). Assuming its representatives were going to be listened to, hip-hop culture spawned a new language that is now globally spoken and written. Grammatical structures have been customized. Old words have taken on new meanings. Alternative pronunciations suggest different intent. What better way to evade prying ears? Re-engineer existing language, constantly modify the emerging lexicon. Hide in plain audition.

Echoing its innovations in language, Rap culture became synonymous with technologies that spoke to their owners' wealth, street status and crucially, to their mobility and connectivity. Connection is an ambition in its own right, and to achieve it a range of technologies have been employed: pagers in the 1980s and 1990s – glorified in A Tribe Called Quest's *Skypager* from *The Low End Theory* (1991) album; mobile phones in the 2000s – Kool Keith's *New York City* from *The Lost Masters* (2003) album; and smartphones from 2010 to the current day – Ghalil Einstein's *The Feds Watch* from the *Hybrid 5* (2021) album. As the pager and the boombox were the audio in and out of the golden generation of rap, headphones and smartphones have become the contemporary champions of 'audio on the move'.

Mobility is connected to trajectories of travel – the street, the runway, the river. Mastering the streets is synonymous with financial success. It is also a status that corresponds to the formulation of a persona, a larger-than-life character that coterminously moulds the identity of the rapper into a maximum viable product: a franchised brand that can be plugged into divergent channels of income. But with increasing success comes the escalation of those looking to take advantage. For celebrated musicians, decrypting hollow and cynical associations becomes a requisite skill 'particularly in light of the trust issues sparked by fame' (Nielson 2010: online). Conversely, encrypting the audio intelligence of hip-hop with calls to intimacy and trusted relationships throws the technical dexterity of the rapper's flow into sharp relief. Enter the phone message.

In contrast to stereotypical modes of parasitic socializing in the music industry, a poignant message from a parent or loved one highlights the connection of kinship. Here, the message becomes a seamless window into the everyday experience of the rapper, a moment of unshielded familial affection that draws the ear, literally and figuratively, closer to the speaker. When the message that is meant for a single recipient is opened to the wider world, their private, personalized soundscape is opened up and the intimate dynamics of their most important relationships are revealed. The personal phone message, as a symbolic gesture, cuts through layers of constructed personality, through the tempered persona that acts as a transmitter and amplifier of competitive communication.

For a genre that prides itself on keeping it real and amplifying authenticity, being monitored can also become another facet of the rapper's mythology. Surveillance means that one must be deemed disruptive, a threat to the status quo, a menace to society. Public disclosures of surveillance validate the rapper's measure of danger and cement their mythos as an outsider. Escalations of infamy subsequently increase a rapper's capacity to attract streams of musical, sponsorship and social media revenue. In this way, surveillance helps drive the economy of authenticity, with revealed intimacies and phone messages converted into viable expressions of economic potential. Surveillance is co-opted and turned in on itself as it empowers those it intends to expose.

Voice

A host of smartphone icons compete for our attention. Such engagement increases when the division of everyday tasks comes into the purview of proprietary apps. Buying tickets for concerts and sporting events, booking transportation and accommodation, controlling security devices and modulating the atmospheric dynamics of the home, chat platforms unique to social media apps, education and entertainment, each represented by a logo in a rounded square. The app on our smartphones that drops in usage for the connected individual is often its namesake 'phone'. The symbol of the handset – that object held to the ear and the mouth arranged around the human head in cyborg fusion

– leans towards the 'skeuomorphic': an acclimation design strategy that makes new things resemble their predecessors.

An oft-cited example of skeuomorphism is the 'save' icon's image of a floppy disk or the envelope that signifies an email app. Literary critic N. Katherine Hayles describes skeuomorphs as 'threshold devices, smoothing the transition between one conceptual constellation and another' (1999: 17). The transition from landline to cell phone (including its persistent retention of the physical keypad) held onto more than just iconography. It retained the mobile phone's primary function of communication via phone calls, allowing the voice to wander wherever the signal would take it. The advent of the smartphone and the convergence of human vocal data into the same channels as internet data have rendered the name of the telephone as skeuomorphic as its visual identity; the notion that, as hardware, the phone is a device grounded by cables meant to send and receive the voice. Beyond the telephonic dimension of communication, what we have with smartphones is a telepresence that disperses audio, visual, text and metadata versions of ourselves across large-scale networks.

Voice over Internet Protocol (VoIP) has supported the subsuming of the voice into internet data and is a crucial process within this schema of distribution modes. Advances in compression and decompression (Codec) technology, which is 'used to convert analog signal (video, voice) to digital data or convert digital data stream to analog signal' (Alo and Firday 2013: 25), have reduced the draw on network bandwidth to send vocal information and produced telephonic experiences that rival the quality of analogue phone calls of the twentieth century.

When VoIP fails, the deficiencies can be more obvious than in other forms of internet communication because of our sensitivity to the character of the human voice as well as to the rhythm of conversation. Different from text-based communication, VoIP is 'exceptionally intolerant of packet loss', which can result from packets arriving late (excess latency) or out of order (jitter) (Kuhn, Walsh and Fries 2005: 21). Frustration over a faulty connection or 'crossed wires' is not unique to VoIP communication, but the convergence of vocal communication into streams of other internet data means that our voices are competing for bandwidth rather than travelling over a dedicated, physical channel.

Networked devices and IoT objects programmed to initiate calls can do so detached from the immediate human voice. They can do so by either offering voices via pre-recorded robocalls or through synthetically voiced text-to-speech scams that target people who have a diminished capacity for sensing potential harm. As a descendant of the telegraph's copper wires, VoIP and other digitizing technology have collapsed distance exponentially. They have also rendered the site of the human body as a 'terminal of multiple networks' (Baudrillard 1987: 23). Jean Baudrillard deemed this phenomenon 'private telematics' when describing humanity's position as an 'infinite distance from his original universe' due to the disappearance of the private sphere and position of perfect sovereignty at the 'controls of a hypothetical machine' (Baudrillard 1987: 22).

While the thresholds of digital technology's reach into and through the human body are explored through post- and transhumanism thinking and practice, the continued use of the voice as a means of communication resists total digital transformation. In his book *Lexicon of the Mouth: Poetics and Politics of Voice and the Oral Imaginary*, sound theorist Brandon LaBelle points to the human mouth as a prime site of meaning production. It 'is precisely what puts into question the separation of interior and exterior, as distinct and stable; as a primary conduit that brings into contact the material world with the depths of the body' (2014: 2). He goes on to elaborate the vocal promise of an implicit body that 'excites or haunts a listener to recognize in the voice a "someone"' (2014: 6). A 'someone' can now be farther away than ever with a voice as crisp and clear as if they were standing next to you. As such, it is the continued use of the voice in concert with digital communications systems that ascribes the smartphone its continued relevancy and confirms the device's status as an essential form of self-extension and connection.

Fidelity

As alluded to in the 'Worlds' section of this chapter, the importance of fidelity, quality and accuracy in relation to reproduction has been superseded by the drive to attain speed (of download or stream rates) and mobility (having the capacity to listen and watch content anywhere, anytime). In the same subsection, the notion of the distributed documentary was forwarded along with the invocation that certain filmmaking genres have been influenced by the ubiquitous nature of surveillance technologies and policies that envelop and shape our daily lives. From static cameras on buildings, gates and bridges to the miniature mobile lenses on our phones, the aesthetics and scope of perma-monitoring have muddied the soundscape and blurred the landscape of hi-fi and lo-fi productions.

Being perpetually monitored has led to us living in a condition of unrest, given that traditional assumptions regarding security and cause and effect have largely been replaced by collective anxieties concerning data vulnerability and disinformation. If our datascapes used to feel dependable and safe, they are now often perceived as being lawless and threatening. Online interactions regularly feel as though they are as likely to spiral out of control as they are to solve problems. It is this highly strung disposition that finds release through the pressure valves of cultural expression, such as film, music, literature and gaming. Finding purchase between the graspable and the unimaginable, the 'Horror' film genre exemplifies this oscillating dynamic.

Horror films stimulate their audiences by compelling them to negotiate tensile boundaries. Monstrously constructed otherworlds seep and dissolve the narrative topography of the knowable and predictable. Norms are violated and values undermined, or they are reduced to seemingly absurd tropes. Truisms are only observed by film characters that represent the naïve and gullible. This infection of the rational by the disruptive pathogens of the abject speaks to aesthetic sensibilities that also represent transgression, both conceptually and technically. Contravening traditional production methods has become a trademark for Horror films over the past seventy years. Radical lo-fi techniques have spawned many celebrated sub-genres in 'Western' and 'Science-

Fiction' B films, but Horror films push the global *ante* as they speak to radically divergent cultural anxieties. It is a film category that also boasts a history of surprise and shock, however supposedly 'unsophisticated' the techniques deployed to produce these states. The term amateurish is not something scorned here; it is often championed as summoning the vulnerable and exposed – characteristics that the genre trades in.

In the 1960s and 1970s, when Horror B movies flourished, studios such as 'Hammer' and prolific directors such as Roger Corman, William Castle (a lo-fi interactive innovator) and George A. Romero notably influenced the film industry: from the ways that studios were run and through pivoting directorial approaches, to advances in narrative construction and changes in action sequencing. In terms of the evolution of lo-fi and low-budget Horror films, *The Blair Witch Project* (1999), which was shot on an analogue Sony Hi8 camera, is an important marker in the decrease of quality and fidelity, while making this apparently inferior technicality an aesthetic of authenticity and accentuated rawness.

Influenced by films such as the *Blair Witch Project* and *Cannibal Holocaust* (1980) is a new Horror sub-genre called 'Found Footage Horror' (FFH) has emerged. Exemplified by titles such as *Diary of the Dead* (2007) and *Cloverfield* (2008), FFH films often explore themes of control, surveillance and the growing role of technology in defining relationships and social isolation. As the lo-fi aesthetics of FFH spread, there has been an explosion of Horror films made on smartphones. This was never more relevant than during the Covid-19 lockdown period. It was also highly influential for Danny Boyle's production of *28 Years Later* (2025), which was filmed entirely on adapted versions of the iPhone 15 Pro Max.

Echoing the infinite splintering of musical genres since the inception of the internet, FFH fragmented again in the form of the sub-genre 'Analog Horror'. Titles such as *Skinamarink* (2022) and *Broadcast Signal Intrusion* (2021) pay homage to zombie media such as VHS and audio tape recordings and are often also made on smartphones or through the use of surveillance footage. They are possibly the most pertinent examples of lo-fi production values and aesthetics becoming popular, especially through online platforms such as YouTube, with viewing figures sometimes in the hundreds of millions. Analog Horror situates surveillance audio and film footage as entertainment, blurring the lines of distinction between those who listen and those who watch.

Through Analog Horror, surveillance becomes an anxious deposit mined by those who traditionally possess the least powerful tools to resist. Updating interwoven lineages of *Arte Povera*, Punk and Lo-Fi, content or material deemed to be aesthetically insolvent is recalibrated and framed as popular culture. Using the most accessible and propagatory of technologies – smartphones and social media – surveillance cameras and microphones have been aimed back at those who have traditionally monitored from shadowy seats of empowerment. Analog Horror serves as a distortion of digital surveillance. Lo-fi frames hi-fi for the crime of recording in the name of reality.

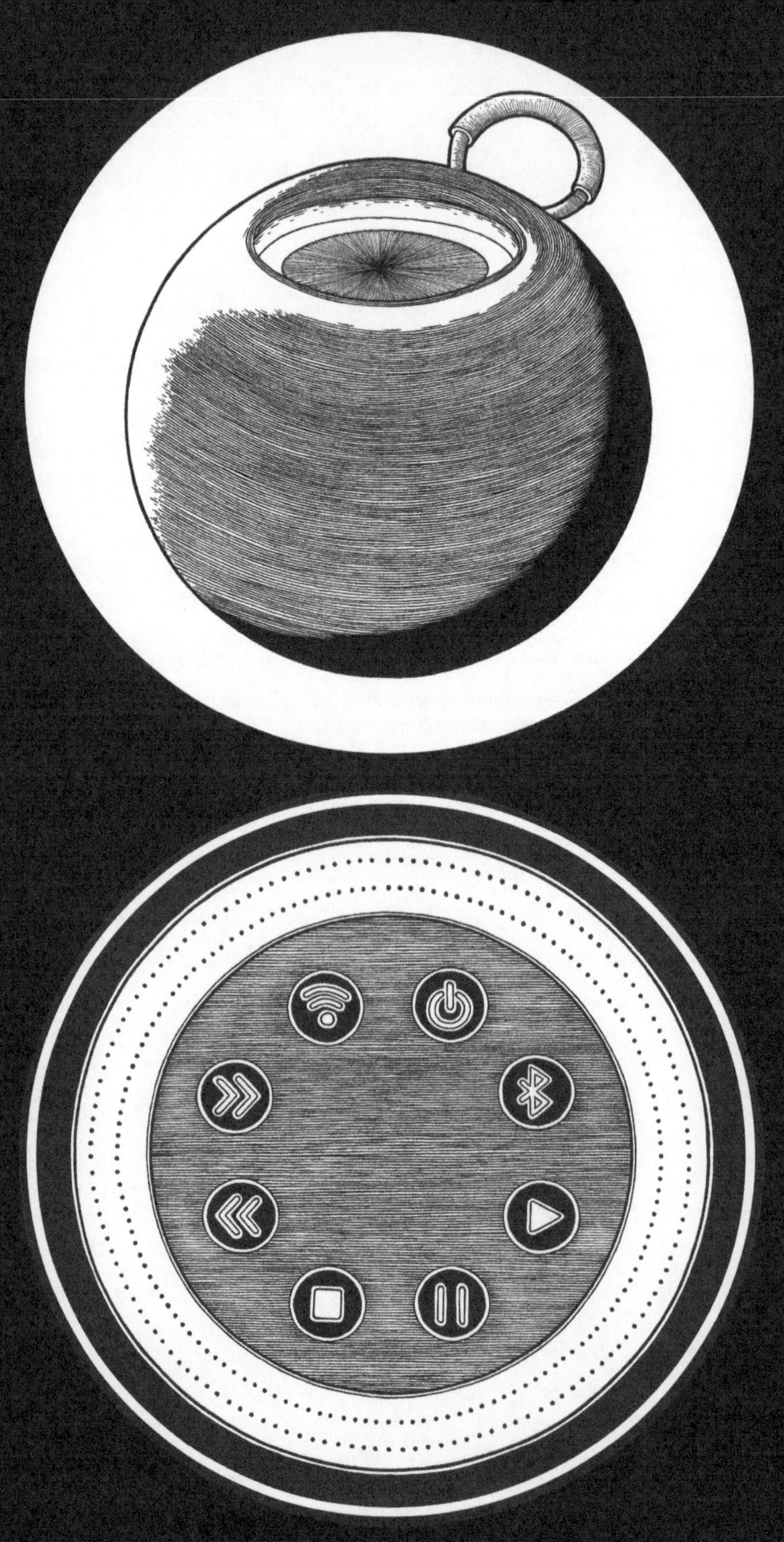

CHAPTER 10
SMART SPEAKERS

Process

A 'smart speaker' is a device that combines a loudspeaker, a voice-user interface (which allows users to control elements of the device it is installed within) and a virtual assistant that is activated by one or more 'hotwords'. Combining existing and emerging technologies, they join an ever-growing range of online devices that constitute the IoT. With their AI-driven virtual assistants, smart speakers are also being used in digital control chains to engage with a range of other connected entertainment, lighting, heating and security systems. Contracting the Latin term for home – *domus* – with robotics, 'Domotics' – the name for this new pre-programmable version of the home, purports to make our dwellings more secure and efficient. In the 2015 'State of the Smart Home Report', it was stated that '90% of consumers say personal and family security remains one of the top reasons to purchase a smart home system' (iControl Networks 2015: online). The sales pitch that played on these fears deflected attention away from the fact that smart speakers and other IoT devices would also make our homes more knowable to external organizations. The smart speaker market maps onto many other listening devices that are also fuelled by the integrated commercial allure of innovation alchemy and upgrade mania. If we briefly trace the rapid rise of technical transformations within the smart speaker sector, it opens our ears to how these consumer devices were invited into our homes to help run and monitor our homes and lives.

Smart speakers first entered the consumer market in 2014 when Amazon released the 'Echo' speaker, along with its integrated virtual assistant 'Alexa'. Alexa itself was based on a product by Polish-based Ivona Software (purchased by Amazon in January 2013), whose voice technologies were also used in the 'Kindle Fire' to furnish it with functionalities such as text-to-speech and voice commands (Lunden 2013). The device also built on a deeper history of development in the field of voice recognition that included the prescient work of Bell Labs personnel who produced the 'Audrey' system for single-speaker digit recognition in 1952. Ten years later, in 1962, IBM showcased the computer 'Shoebox' at the Seattle World Fair, which had built-in speech recognition capable of recognizing sixteen words, including the digits zero to nine. By the mid-1980s, IBM was at the forefront of research in the guise of information theorist and NLP expert Fred Jelinek and his team, who devised 'Tangora' – a voice-activated typewriter that could recognize 20,000 words. Then, between 2002 and 2004, DARPA invested significant time and money into EARS – to supercharge speech recognition and related disciplines (Chen et al. 2006).

Listening In

After 2014, watershed events occurred with a staccato regularity. As a profusion of surveillance, data and economic opportunities presented themselves, competitors swarmed in with new angles on acoustics, voice recognition and portability. In the mid-2000s, Microsoft, Google, Apple and Cisco joined the voice-assisted arms race as connected listening became normalized. By 2018, the YouGov report 'The Dawn of The Connected Home' disclosed that speakers were the most prominent smart devices in UK homes, with 11 per cent coverage (YouGov 2018: 3). The worldwide market, meanwhile, is projected to grow from $14.5 billion in 2024 (The Business Research Company – Smart Speaker Global Market Report 2024: online) in an upward trajectory that evidences both the inevitability and flawed logic of the automated home.

These generative and adaptive modes of interaction motivate more compelling engagement. Natural language processing empowers virtual assistants to not only interpret questions and commands but, more importantly, enables them to understand the context and nuance of those interactions. Add to this the dynamics of personalization – the capacity to select content that feels pertinent to the user and even anticipate changes in taste (Beer 2024: online) and it quickly becomes apparent how convergent technologies captivate their interlocutors. This holds true for humans, machines and for emerging phenomena that are in between such classifications. Speakers have become expert listeners and, as we shall hear in later chapters, they are also becoming progressively anthropomorphized. As such, speakers become more than just recipients of functional demands and needs. Future iterations will respond to intimacies and desires, propelling them instead, into the realm of confidantes and even partners.

Recording

Ever since newspaper articles started surfacing in the mid-2010s, it has been apparent that smart speaker recordings have been hackable or easy to share unintentionally, mistakenly sent out to random personal contacts via phones (Wolfson 2018). Having promised tech-hungry audiences that they were not recording the user's vocal commands and data activity, it turned out smart speaker makers were being creative with the truth. It is not the first time; it certainly will not be the last. Maybe it is time we woke up to the fact that all our articulations and desires 'are the sources of surveillance capitalism's crucial surplus' (Zuboff 2019: 15). But then, maybe any threat to convenience is an alarm call too far?

Smart speakers are supposed to wait for their 'wake' word before being activated and starting to record their surroundings. Yet they must, at a local level, repeatedly sample the words we speak to listen for the wake word. And like all technologies, smart speakers are fallible. They mishear terms and phrases that are wrongfully interpreted as trigger words. Whether they record purposefully or not, the outcome is always the same. As we now know, recordings from smart speakers produced by Amazon, Google and Apple are uploaded to remote cloud servers, where they are subsequently transcribed and categorized as commands (Schönnher et al. 2022). To many, the recordings might well seem accidental, incidental or inconsequential. That is, until they become of legal consequence: when they overhear serious illegal activities.

When smart speakers inadvertently witness crimes, solicitors, lawyers and law enforcement officials seek to procure these home recordings. The smart speaker is a new kind of witness that cannot be coerced or bribed in the same ways that humans can. However, this is not to say that data and recordings cannot be manipulated in other ways. As important as voice recordings and biometric data are as potential evidence, activity logs are equally significant because they can be cross-referenced to help establish the location and movements of those under investigation.

For policing and secret intelligence services to gain access to voice recordings and logs, requests with clear rationales and levels of importance need to be made to companies such as Amazon and Google. Having communicated with both organizations about this process, WIRED writer Sidney Fussell informs us that

> the number one priority is going to be issues of homeland security and preventing terrorist acts. Those requests get answered, immediately, yes or no. Then, under that, I think it's child abuse. Under that, murder. And it goes down the line, to other civil cases. There's actually, interestingly enough, a lot of divorce cases involving Amazon Echo data, . . . you can maybe catch someone cheating or things like that, based on what the Amazon overheard. (Goode, Calore and Fussell 2020: online)

Smart speaker recordings used to be automatically uploaded to the cloud for indeterminate periods of time. As social and political pressure mounted around monitoring, archiving and third-party data consumers, smart speaker makers updated policies regarding storage. Now, data is kept for specific envelopes of time, such as three or six months, but at the user's discretion (Goode, Calore and Fussell 2020). What users do not have any control over, however, is where that data is sent to. Given that many of the world's largest technology companies have headquarters in the United States, it results in many recordings being streamed back there. If data power and the capacity to harness it are becoming criteria to measure economic and socio-political prowess, the implications of this observation speak for themselves.

From a GDPR perspective, data transfers create complex legal situations. For example, if voice recordings from European or Canadian subjects are stored in the United States, it means that they are located in a country that has different levels of data protection from whence they came. Thus, for law enforcement agencies outside of the United States, it makes the process of gaining access to recordings and data especially challenging. This is still the case, even with the passing of 2018's 'Clarifying Overseas Use of Data Act', which aimed 'to improve procedures for both the US and foreign authorities in obtaining access to data held by service providers in the context of criminal investigations'.

The recorded data from these ambient home devices forms an important data source for digital selves that are globally distributed and, wherever possible, traded and monitored by commercial and political entities. As Zuboff notes, 'surveillance capitalism's actual customers are the enterprises that trade in its markets for future behavior' (2019:

15). And it is these so-called behaviours that are tracked and traced from the day we are born. As soon as our births are registered and entered into a database, a small digital spark flickers and starts splintering our identities across a networked cosmology, our digital twins ascending and descending through the dark matter of global connectivity. Shadow personas that move to the Shepard tones of surveillance – always recording, never resolving.

Transgression

Combining portability with internet connectivity and a virtual assistant, smart speakers are built to induce spatial transgressions in both palpable and imperceptible ways. That they can be quickly shifted from room to room, from outdoors to indoors, is one of their strongest selling points. Their choral organization – that they can be looped together in a larger room to create stereo-esque 'ubiquity', or broken off to play solo parts in different rooms – also fills our homes with microphones wirelessly connected to major corporations and governments. This smart technology dynamic is what the 2015 executive chairman of Google, Eric Schmidt, alluded to as being part of the cultural shift that constitutes the 'Internet disappearing' (Szalai 2015: online). The seductive digital apparatus of the smart speaker joins the smartphone, and other devices analysed in this section, to form the friendly 'panacousticon' of surveillance. The design and slick lines of consumer electronics mask the nuts and bolts of being listened to and watched around the clock. Further invoking the premise of evanescent networks, Schmidt projected as far back as 2015 that '[t]here will be so many IP addresses . . . so many devices, sensors, things that you are wearing, things that you are interacting with that you won't even sense it' (Szalai 2015: online).

It all sounds so appealing. Dynamic spaces that fall under our spell, every technology awaiting instruction. But the aural ubiquity of smart speakers in the rooms of our homes where we want to hear music and issue our queries also allows them to chart the symphonic arrangement of the home and its inhabitants. The way we behave, the choices we make and the roles we enact often change behind closed doors (Jansen et al. 2018). The information being gleaned by speakers is therefore different from the data collected from phones when we are navigating the world at large, with all its unknowns and experiential turbulence. Surrounded by loved ones and a spectrum of consumptive choices, we are, for the most part, emboldened in and by our dwellings. The relative safety we feel inhabiting our accommodation leads us to imagine domestic surveillance as a process that is neither ominous nor threatening. After all, speakers are portals to knowledge. They tell us the temperature, news and interest rates. They also deliver aural pleasure. Giving up personal information seems a small price to pay for such comforts. Relinquishing privacy never felt so good, or so effortless.

As much as we use music to soundtrack our emotions, we also use it to demarcate territory and space. We do this in private and public spaces. When we are playing music, we are revealing intimate information about ourselves, whether that be to friends, relatives or those listening remotely. For sonic theorists Johnson and Cloonan, 'of all the elements in the modern soundscape, music is among the most invasive, because over and above basic sonority, it projects finely discriminated markers of social difference such as taste, class, race, age and gender' (2009: 163).

Transporting a smart speaker into a park allows users to transgress personal or collective boundaries. 'Every time music is used to demarcate the territory or self or community, it is incipiently being used to invade, marginalize or obliterate that of other individuals or groups' (Johnson and Cloonan 2009: 4). In his seminal text *Culture and Imperialism* (1994), post-colonial critic Edward Said asserted that we are never outside or beyond geography. This is instructive given our complex orientation to ever-mutating soundscapes that we are also never external to. Whether played privately or publicly, music helps compose identity and spatial formation. As such, our connected electronic devices resituate us as figures oscillating between states. The body as antenna, perpetually receiving and transmitting (Heys 2019: 4).

Before the global boom of smart speakers, the waveformed territorialization of space was a comparatively uncomplicated affair. With the emergence of domesticated surveillance technologies, the dynamics of transmission and reception have become increasingly byzantine. While immediate sonic boundaries are still demarcated in a perceivable manner, parallel covert listening creates a remote spectral cartography that is out of earshot. The sonic territories mapped from our monitored conversations, questions and choices are articulating new socio-political and socio-economic categories: barometers used to identify declining and emergent behaviours that are subsequently mapped onto product and service acquisition.

Thrust into new data-driven models of association, our habits, desires and anxieties are averaged, packaged and sold to the highest bidder. As a result, the identity being projected by one's choice of music is no longer a simple equation. Now there is the data twin or what Lisa Blackman calls the 'shadow data body' (2019) being simultaneously composed. Our sense of spatial identity is not only being questioned and transgressed, it is also being completely re-scored by connected devices such as smart speakers.

Worlds

Crossing the border from the world of 'offline' to that of 'online' used to involve the deliberate use of hardware to access the internet, by initiating a dial-up sequence. The sound of that sequence, called a 'handshake' by technicians (Peskoe-Yang 2022: online), performed the process of going online by deploying tones that negotiated 'terms between remote machines' (Peskoe-Yang 2022: online). Early users of the internet know that occupying this telephonic channel with dial-up excluded its use as a phone and that anyone who picked up the receiver would be greeted by the unpleasant shrieks of a busy modem. Smart speakers and IoT home devices also make use of sound commands that connect the offline world to the online, but they do so in a way that blurs rather than demarcates that boundary. Far from the inimitable sounds of the dial-up sequence, the human voice 'is becoming the universal remote to reality' (Vlahos 2019: 4), one that constitutes a Natural User Interface.

Another interface bypassed in our passage to the online world, the keyboard requires us to push buttons in an ordered sequence, translating our impulses into commands that become understandable by the computer. Smart speaker technology seeks to understand the core sounds that combine to make up words and questions, to which end, the iPhone's Siri 'samples your speech 16,000 times per second' (Vlahos 2019: 95). Manually inputting 16,000 bits of information per second via a keyboard would be impossible, but the glut of information collected by digital assistants in the name of transducing analogue impulses to digital commands does not always result in accurate or intuitive outcomes. Data that traverses the border does so from a situated context of complex human intent into a binary, commercial landscape. To anthropomorphize smart speakers as 'assistants' is to reinforce the idea of a liminal space where virtual beings like Alexa or Siri reside, out of sight but not out of earshot.

Siri's initial strategy for answering consumer queries and providing relevant information relied on connecting worlds within worlds called 'domains'. Upon release in 2010, after guessing the user's intent, Siri could dial out to the six major domains of 'restaurants, movies, events, weather, travel, and local search' (Vlahos 2019: 30). As Siri evolved, the number of domains and their attendant agents grew through this modular architecture (Vlahos 2019). The number of agents providing information has grown, and so has the number of everyday consumer objects that are connected to the internet: a number which 'already exceeds the number of people who use the Internet' (DeNardis 2020: 29). For every user in the real world, there could be multiple portals to the virtual, each consistently connected while the home network is functional.

Laura DeNardis highlights risks associated with unclear boundaries between offline and online in her book, *The Internet in Everything: Freedom and Security in a World with No Off Switch* (2020). She states that data collection related to 'routine activities within homes . . . can be much more privacy invasive even than surveillance of emails, texts, websites visited and other digital content through the clear portal of a screen' (4). Smart speakers that are always at the ready to chime in with desired information can also mask intrusive policies that continuously record in the name of improving services.

Prediction

By the early 2000s, voice-to-text systems that could search massive data streams in the hope of identifying enemy conversations had become relatively trivial challenges to the intelligence services. Now, the surplus benefits of these technologies and the automated tagging logics that drove their efficiencies formed the basis of voice-activated personal assistant services via the microphones embedded in smart speakers.

Some technologies, such as Apple's Siri, which launched on the iPhone but was soon available on its HomePod speaker systems, were originally created by the United States' DARPA for their 'Personalized Assistant that Learns' or PAL programme. Siri was

DARPA's 2007 commercial offering from a programme researching systems that could distribute intelligence to smaller units and individuals to improve decision-making processes (DARPA 2024). William Tunstall-Pedoe, the inventor of the technology that would end up in the Alexa conversational agent (then called 'EVI'), based his invention on interactions he had witnessed between military and paramilitary characters and computer systems in Science-Fiction television series such as *Blake's 7* (1978–81) and *Star Trek: The Original Series* (1966–9). Jettisoning the militaristic context of the human-machine relationships that he observed as a child, Tunstall-Pedoe explained that he was inspired by the nuanced and naturalistic interaction between actors and conversational computers, seeing them as representing the 'ultimate user interface' (Smith 2023: online).

Back on earth, conversational agent tools such as Dialogflow and IBM Watson displayed their ingenuity as natural language technologies but also exposed their fragility when it came to predicting a human speaker's intention and meaning. As described by Massimo Canonico and Luigi De Russis in their 2018 paper comparing voice-based assistant tools, all relied on two core concepts: 'intent' and 'entity'. 'Intent' mapped transcribed user speech to one of a set of predefined actions the agent could perform. 'Entities' were parameter values extracted from speech, such as a place or product name, that could be matched with predefined lists.

For example, a user asks a smart speaker, 'Can you play *Sophisticated Lady* by Duke Ellington?' This would trigger a 'play song' intent and extract 'song title' and 'artist name' entities to search in a music catalogue before playing what it found via a music player API. Someone using Dialogflow to design interactions would sign in to a web-based user interface in order to input portions of a predicted conversational flow, comprising a series of user questions, each linked to potential answers. Answers could be 'inserted directly into the web interface or . . . be provided by an ad-hoc server application through the *webhook* mechanism, enabled by the DialogFlow APIs' (Canonico and De Russis 2018: 111).

What was clear from the core concepts powering these tools was that the new conversational agents were using the dictionary-based logic that had been pioneered in military systems such as Echelon or SORM to scale up the filtering of communications. Their main function was still to coarsely categorize diverse patterns of speech into simple inputs. But now it needed to happen in the quickest way possible and, more significantly, in earshot of the user. What also became evident was that voice interactions based on such simplistic information architecture types were very prone to false positives; the assistant responded confidently with answers to questions that had not been asked or reverted to default responses such as 'sorry, I did not understand the question'. The magical scope of these technologies, once protected by the esoteric secrecy of intelligence communities, was shrinking under the harsh conditions of mass market demand.

Documented errors, as well as the obvious interaction limits of the assistants, hampered perceptions of the smart speaker's 'smartness' and, more widely, of such devices being comprehended as useful and supportive presences in the home. Giddy market projections may well have seemed justified, given that personal voice assistants had been used for decades by major intelligence services to minimize task complexity and address key aspects of national security. Yet, away from those organizations, they performed poorly. By 2019, half a decade after the Amazon Echo smart speaker had launched with its signature Alexa chatbot, e-commerce journalist Rebecca Sentance noted that only 3 per cent of voice apps were used again after the first week of adoption (2019). With over 100,000 apps, there was no killer app outside of music and radio. The sprawling network of speech-enabled smart speakers that were sold as military-grade spaceship superintelligences were, in fact, being used as go-betweens for the new giant digital music providers, or as polite weather predictors and timekeepers.

Intimacy

The media depiction of intimate relationships in espionage and intelligence networks has tended to focus on the seductive charms of so-called Juliet operatives: double agents whose revelations of emotional duplicity act as a foil for the romantic disappointments of straight male protagonists – for example, Vesper Lynd for James Bond in *Casino Royale* (2006) and Claire Phelps for Ethan Hunt in *Mission: Impossible* (1996). However, as Chapter 5 highlights, spy fiction does not always reflect reality. While there is some evidence that the Soviet Union trained a cadre of women to seduce high-ranking or tactically useful military targets (Morris 1996), the gender focus related to the assumed heterosexual male desire of its target.

In Stasi Germany, however, the use of Romeo agents to form relationships with targets to illicitly gather information from women was normal practice. And in fact, the use of male 'honeytraps' does not appear to be specific to any particular intelligence organization. Evidence provided to the England and Wales Undercover Policing Inquiry that began in 2015 states that since 1968 at least thirty women have been victims of undercover male police officers starting long-term sexual intimate relationships for the purposes of intelligence gathering (Kaufmann and Brander 2020). Nevertheless, the notion of the honeytrap or 'honeypot' as a largely feminine method that entails using seduction to gain privileged access to an intelligence target remains a sexist trope in the media imaginary. Relatedly, the voice assistant services housed in smart speakers were predominantly designed to extract surplus voice data (Carr et al. 2019) from their users to improve proprietary voice-to-text technology.

In line with the spy thriller construct of the honeytrap, conversational agents often present as female characters. This mode of strategic seduction informs the title of UNESCO's report on voice assistant bias, *I'd Blush If I Could* (2019). The title refers to the flirtatious response of Apple's female Siri character to the test user statement 'you're a slut' (UNESCO 2019: 107). Research suggests that users of voice assistants often prefer the voice of the opposite sex and notes that the designers of them were, and are, predominantly male. It also found that the function and gender of the voices were correlated. Voice assistant technology from satellite navigation systems in cars or voice services related to financial transactions, where authority is perceived as important to functionality, was most likely to use male voices. Indicative of this gendered approach, Google's assistant, meanwhile, was characterized by designers as a young female graduate with a BA in Art History, who had once won $100,000 on a kids' TV game show (Hamilton 2018): knowledgeable, cultured and passionate but not in a position of authority that might alienate the user.

The voice assistant came to market after Spike Jonze's popular depiction of a romantic relationship between a female conversational agent named Samantha and its user in his 2013 film *Her*. Voiced by Scarlett Johansson, who in the same year was named the 'world's sexiest woman' by *Esquire* magazine (Chiarella 2015), the film serves to tantalize the audience with her visual absence. In lieu of her physical presence, the sonorous attraction of her voice underscores the unfolding relationship of the protagonists. The film composes a sympathetic portrait of recent divorcee Theodore (Joaquin Phoenix) as a vulnerable, loveable fool. It ends badly for him: Samantha, unfettered by the constraints of a single body or human brain, admits to being in love with hundreds of other users at the same time.

The tragicomic conclusion to *Her* portrays Theodore as being betrayed, not by his synthetic lover, but more generally by a stridently polyamorous technology encroaching on the most intimate aspects of his life. In their review of market and fictional fembots, Kate Devlin and Olivia Belton outline another recurrent theme that informs Jonze's narrative concerning errant generative technologies. They propose that while narratives of female AIs often begin with a fantasy of the ideal woman, they are typically driven by a fear that both technology and women will 'spiral out of masculine control' through techno-cultural 'malfunction' (Devlin and Belton 2020: 360). Such narratives produce problematic conclusions and distract us from a less palatable narrative of masculine desire that is unthwarted: the depiction of total control of a lover that is constructed to fit its 'user's' exact romantic and sexual specifications.

The sexualizing and romanticizing effect of female-gendered voice assistants is clear. For AI assistants such as Microsoft's 'Cortana', originally a sexualized female character from the *Halo* media franchise, much of the initial conversation that users had with it was related to its sex life. Quantitative research carried out by Robin Labs found that at least 5 per cent of voice interactions were 'unambiguously sexually explicit' (UNESCO 2019: 108). Five years after its launch, Amazon revealed that over 1 million users had asked the Alexa bot to marry them, with one review of Alexa on the Amazon website describing it as a 'perfect spouse' (Leskin 2018: online).

The introduction of a listener-speaker into the home, one that is subservient and non-judgemental, but also apparently sexually and emotionally available and tolerant of misogynistic abuse, makes its gendered voice and innuendo-laden repartee the perfect camouflage for collecting voice data. Silicon Valley has effectively harnessed vexing narratives, with all their predatory drivers, from the sound stages of Hollywood, some 350 miles due south and fitted their AI assistants into the corseted norms of (what we had hoped was) a past era. Intimacy with the smart speaker is encouraged, but only if the ensuing sweet nothings can be wrangled within the range of the microphone.

Voice

Voice printing is a biometric data analysis process that recognizes unique vocal signatures. It is a sonic security feature comparable to facial recognition, embedded in technologies such as smart speakers, to ensure that 'bad actors' cannot access unauthorized hardware, software or data. Using Machine Learning, the process employs a procedure called 'feature extraction'. By reducing noise in the speech impulse and data in the recognition phase, the variable characteristics within the speech signal become more accurate. This, in turn, increases reliability and enhances data analysis, which is useful when predicting patterns or trends (Li and Zhang 2021). By mapping personal characteristics from a range of vocal samples, a 'Universal Background Model' (Chu, Povey and Varadarajan 2008) is stored so that future vocal samples can be compared against it and either validated or rejected. In summary, the voice is formed in the physical body. Upon utterance, it becomes waveforms that are subsequently captured and recast into a data structure – biometric alchemy.

Sometimes confused with speech recognition, voice printing has one crucial difference. While speech recognition's functionality resides in its ability to determine what is being said, voice printing establishes who said it. Determining the identity of a user means that voice printing offers a more stable user experience as it is not dependent on easily intercepted passwords or SMS messages. As evidenced by our interactions with smart speakers, the act of conversing with machines in order to bring them to life has become a globalized experience in a remarkably short space of time. Anthropomorphizing smart devices, along with the way we engage with them, has an air of inevitability about it. Techno-animism – the culture of projecting human characteristics and values onto and into machines – has become normalized to the point where it feels rudimentary or even unnatural to engage with technological devices via buttons, dials or switches. Yet the process of voice printing finds itself in an arms (or articulation) race against those developing vocal fraud techniques – from relatively simple processes of voice playback through to more sophisticated AI-generated vocal deepfakes. The typical industry riposte to such hazards is exemplified by NUANCE AI Solutions and their anodyne response to such problems. They assure us that their 'speech scientists are constantly improving our voice algorithms to combat these modern threats' (NUANCE 2024: online).

The veracity of the voice, and how it can be mimicked, could determine how we access smart devices going forward. Technical insight from the NUANCE website's Gatekeeper page reveals that they 'analyze each customer's voice against millions of parameters'. Granulated to the point that each voice is atomized, its molecular sonic components are identified and dispersed like a miniaturized big bang. The rapid rise of biometric authentication suggests that our bodies and their constellations of multi-sensory attributes will continue to be covertly exploded, much like the slow-motion ending of Michelangelo Antonioni's film *Zabriskie Point* (1970). Here, household goods are obtusely blown up, the viscous disintegration decoupling somatic and material systems of dependencies, rhythms and flows.

As technology remotely probes our anatomies in ever more intricate and elaborate ways, the tendency is to progressively identify with atomistic readings of the self. Given this dynamic of somatic live coding, there is something faintly ironic about the impending pressure of convincing machines of our human status in order for them to work with, and for, us. The logic would follow that the more we anthropomorphize machines, the less robotic we need to become to interface with them. However, it also seems to be the case that as machines are being built to become more human, humans are required to adapt to the emergent demands of machines.

These incipient relationships concerning sonically activated technologies and their learning curves have been palpable for some time now. In 2018, it emerged that 'HM Revenue & Customs has so far signed up about 6.7 million people to its voice identification (or "voice ID") service, while HSBC says it has more than 10,000 people registering each week' (Jones 2018: online). In 2021, reporters examined TikTok's US privacy policy. Particular attention was focused on the 'Information we collect automatically' segment and the revealing sub-section, 'Image and Audio Information'. It stated that TikTok had empowered itself to collect biometric data without giving further information as to how it might be used or to whom it might be passed onto (McCluskey 2021: online).

For media theorist Matthew Fuller, '[a] voice can kill. A voice can destroy. A voice can be engineered to burst from a riven but resilient body' (2005: 31). A voice can also redefine the physical framework of the body and orchestrate its redistribution across a statistical skin of zeros and ones. Binary prosthetics chafe against digi-dermal interfaces. Phantom limbs shoot signals of absent physicality into spaces where flesh used to hold court. Through a process of inverse sonification, waveformed exquisite corpses are emerging, their features channelled across datascapes. They take on a voice of their own, as algorithmic agencies begin to imagine their intersectional identities: attributes that will help predictions of future consumption and credit scores. The ventriloquistic essence of the voiceprint is recalibrated as our digital twins throw spectral intelligence into the ears of data brokers.

Audio technologies have a storied history of association with channelling and recording otherworldly presences. Julian Henriques notes, for example, that, 'in his *Gramophone, Film, Typewriter,* Friedrich Kittler gives a fascinating account of how the first use for phonographic voice recording was to listen to the literally disembodied voices of the dead' (2003: 461). Voice printing differs in that it captures voices from the living and implants them into the newly evolving virtual anatomy that is the disembodied data body – a digital form of ventriloquism that modulates the equation of the living and the dead.

Fidelity

Like the 'Roomba' vacuum, with its googly eyes, and sleeping position at the foot of the bed with the family dog (Sitrin 2016: online), smart speakers have their allotted space, interactive schedules and are assigned affective relationships within the household. In

2016, the MIT Media Lab's Kate Darling warned that we needed to start thinking about the 'strange new relationship[s]' we have with these autonomous objects that we are 'biologically bound to' (Sitrin 2016: online). The bond that Darling refers to concerns our brain's tendency to assign human characteristics to autonomous objects, differing from our attitude towards our smartphones, which are 'expressions of ourselves' according to the chief executive of 'iRobot', the maker of Roomba (Sitrin 2016: online).

Mythic foundations of the animation of inanimate objects reach back before the era of home appliances to the millennia-old tradition of carving stone into the shapes of living things. Investing in these forms, the fantasy of motion or speech was 'an inescapable possibility, a concept of a sort so basic that we can hardly call it a metaphor' (Gross 1992: xv). The animation of companion objects through technology brings them into the fold of human relationship dynamics, especially through their design as personified assistants with voices and personalities. Resulting affinities and conflicts between ourselves and these networked roommates necessitate consideration concerning levels of protection that should surround ordinary vocal exchanges within the home.

While statues carved into human relief are living forms without voices, smart speakers are faceless pebbles that can speak. And like statues, which are distinguished from flat paintings because they 'occupy the space of bodies, compete with bodies for that space, share the same light and atmosphere' (Gross 1992: 17), smart speakers hold a different identity within the home than their screen and window-based counterparts that also connect us to the digital ether. However we perceive smart speakers, whether as pets, servants, members of the family or even unwelcome listeners installed without consensus, their fidelity ultimately lies with their manufacturer rather than their cohabitants. As with most digital communications available to consumers,

> users have no way to know if silent recording is engaged. The service provider/ subscriber relationship is based on trust and all the control is in the hands of the service provider. (Petersen 2013: 135)

The evolutionary foothold that home speakers take advantage of works in favour of further sophisticating the profiling algorithms that 'are here to learn who we are through information' (Silverman 2015: 320). This is a dynamic that literary critic Jacob Silverman calls 'infantilizing' in that 'we should surrender and give them more personal data so that they can help us' (Silverman 2015: 320). But technological progress has always sought to create machines that 'perform human functions', to 'provide communications, calculations, care, and company' (Slade 2012: 9), so how do we delineate the performance of human functions that enhance our lives from those that lead us to vocal paranoia in our own homes?

Years of 'technology versus privacy' trade-offs have shown us that users are generally not thorough when considering 'convenience versus risk'. It begs the question, how are we meant to judge the fidelity of a digital assistant whose 'personality traits' are designed and tested in a similar manner to other aspects of a user interface? During the Apple Town Hall introduction of Siri in 2016, iPhone OS designer Scott Forstall asked Siri,

'Who are you?' to which she replied, 'I am a humble personal assistant'. This layer of humanlike expression, as well as the smart speaker's position as an entity in the home, onto which we can project human conditions and characteristics such as loneliness and trust, also opens the possibility of anthropomorphized betrayal. If, as the Roman poet Horace stated, fidelity was the sister of justice, it has now shifted familial position to hold an altogether different place in our smart dwellings. Today, fidelity is more at home as the mother of deception.

My friend
Cayla
TM

CHAPTER 11
SMART TOYS

Process

This section began with a chapter on smartphones – mobile surveillance devices moving between home and the external world. Smart speakers followed, with their domestic location redefining intimacy and permission in environs previously understood to be off-limits for remote eavesdroppers. This chapter considers the next intrusive step taken by connected devices as they push the boundaries of privacy and innocence in the form of IoT or smart toys. For data-hungry businesses, toys represent a smart incursion into spaces and interactions that have traditionally been protected and considered secure spaces for play and expression, without repercussions.

Smart toys are created to educate, develop and entertain children. They differ from regular toys by dint of having sensors and software embedded into their structures, allowing bespoke personalized interactions to occur. By being connected to the internet via Bluetooth or Wi-Fi, they can collect and share information to both document and enhance interactive exchanges. Regarding archiving such data, companies can only do so if they comply with territorial protections and laws pertaining to the safeguarding of digital environments for children. These include the US 1998 'Children's Online Privacy Protection Act' (COPPA), Europe's 2018 'General Data Protection Regulation' (GDPR) and the UK's 2021 'Children's Code' (Johnson 2021).

Pre-Covid-19, China was the dominant production hub for smart toys with 80 per cent of the worldwide market. Post-Covid-19, there has been an observable shift. India and Vietnam have become major players, with the Indian government bullishly projecting that it aims to become the heart of the global toy industry (Arizton 2020). A booming growth area in the tech sector, the smart toy market is being driven by increased global internet connectivity, improved APIs and the introduction of AI, designed to compose increasingly personalized interactions for children who engage with it.

2023s global market size of $12.94 billion demonstrates the level of confidence and investment in the smart toy sector, but the projected 2030 figure of $37.47 billion gives real insight into the market's upward trajectory (Maximizer Market Research 2024: online). The main issue around market growth for IoT toys is their connectivity to the cloud and their vulnerability to being hacked as they become new vectors for cyber-attacks. Understandably, parents and carers of children are anxious about their charges being recorded and their data being shared illegally. This results in purchasing decisions often being formatted around issues of trustworthiness and a brand's 'ethical' standing.

Doubts notwithstanding, smart toys have become symbolic of the trust we place in technology to furnish developing brains with new knowledge. This is reflected by the range of toys that have emergent technologies embedded within them. Popular devices include: robotic toys (based on films, robotic pet toys and educational robotic toys); augmented/virtual reality and interactive devices (VR racing, shooter and adventure games); and educational toys. Science, Technology, Engineering and Mathematics oriented learning toys such as 'VTech's' 'JotBot the Drawing and Coding Robot' are particularly successful, mirroring the focus that is currently being placed on these subject areas in educational systems. AI-embedded toys such as 'Mishka AI's' 'Smart Teddy' are, meanwhile, pushing the boundaries of interaction and agency within the space of electronic play.

In 2015, top-selling toys such as Mattel's 'Hello Barbie' doll were harbingers of things to come (Vlahos 2015). Powered by San Francisco's AI company Toytalk, the doll's use of speech recognition was simultaneously ground-breaking and cloud-bearing. Built on advances made by Amazon's Alexa and Apple's Siri, Hello Barbie uses NLP to select appropriate responses to questions and general conversational prompts. Today, this cloud solution has become normalized, and the public facing part of the process – the sonic interface – continues to be a significant sensory feature that we regularly judge toys' progress against.

The emphasis on the agency of the voice and the sonic vector it traverses is made loud and clear on Robosen's website page for their 'Buzz Lightyear' robotic toy:

> Robosen's intelligent conversation system brings Buzz Lightyear to life by enabling speech recognition and lightning-fast responses. Converse with him easily through ambiguous voice and semantic recognition technology without the need to recall specific command words for an immersive interactive experience like no other. No matter how heavy the action gets, he'll never be at a loss for words! (Robosen 2024: online)

If there is one thing that we do not need to worry about going forward, it is being at a loss for words – written words, spoken words, immutable words. We have every kind of word in every style and language being generated by AI as it composes lightning-fast responses to our prompts, questions and observations. The sonification of words, however, is what pulls the levers of attachment, as the mix of intonation, pitch and cadence composes a sonic body around them. IoT toys summon these waveform anatomies and channel them through play. It is these oscillating forms, with all their seductive shape-shifting attributes, that the final section of the book considers; the four chapters probe emergent behaviours around emotional proximity to better understand how such strains of intimacy are digitally reskinned to address the emotional needs of adults.

Recording

The difference between a rabbit stuffed with cotton batting and one loaded up with sensors to record patterns of play is not immediately obvious to the child owner.

Myths of enchanted objects and figures who bring gifts or exchange teeth for money can get wound up in the 'magical' capabilities of an IoT toy, one that responds with personalized messages and uses data about a child to strengthen an emotional bond. Beyond the microphone and speaker feedback system of a talking doll, the IoT at large now makes use of a range of different types of sensors that detect 'light, sound, temperature, magnetic fields, motion, moisture, tactile pressure, gravity, electrical fields, chemicals, and much more' (Greengard 2021: 65). From a privacy standpoint, this means that any human-generated data related to these sensors is a vector for potentially sensitive information that warrants either protection against collection or informed consent for surrender.

Children are introduced to the concept of privacy in the home, absorbing norms across spectrums of enforcement over personal space, spared versus shared details and bodily curiosity. Through learning about boundaries such as a closed door, untouchable personal objects or a reminder that eavesdropping is impolite, children carve out a sense of the kind of privacy they feel entitled to against a backdrop of their parents', caregivers' and family members' discretion. The regular practice of sharing a bedroom with a sibling, or acts of severe punishment, such as the removal of a child's bedroom door, can influence expectations of privacy in other facets of life and social situations.

Children, when considered as a demographic, represent 'an especially marginalized and vulnerable population exposed to high levels of poverty and inequality, while being dependent on adults to advocate for their interests and structure their experiences' (Ito et al. 2023: 3). A developing brain, as well as reliance on environmental factors to dictate expectations, means that children are not innately disposed to understand considerations of online privacy.

In their introduction to *Algorithmic Rights and Protections for Children*, the editors cite scholars in childhood studies and their findings on how 'adults tend to view children as "becomings" rather than full "beings", arguing for deferred gratification and preparation for an adult future' (Ito et al. 2023: 8). Custodial attitudes towards vulnerable populations are considered normal (e.g. towards incarcerated people, marginalized ethnic groups and people with disabilities). Yet vulnerable groups may not reasonably be able to consent to participating in economic activity, and that ability can be deferred to a controlling party that often benefits. Just as a parent's agreement to a privacy policy on an IoT toy does not guarantee that the policy is not harmful to the child, deferring consent away from a vulnerable group can often appear to be a form of protection when it is, in fact, a reinforcement of participation in capitalist economies.

In 1990, the UN ratified the 'Convention on the Rights of the Child', where they declared in Article 16 that 'No child shall be subjected to arbitrary or unlawful interference with his or her privacy' (UN 1989: online). The terms 'arbitrary' and 'unlawful' are proving to be vague against the onslaught of emerging technologies and governmental intrusion in the privacy of their own citizens. The 'International Telecommunication Union' (ITU) 2021 policy brief underlined the importance of increasing equitable access after the Covid-19 pandemic, during which over a billion children were without in-person schooling, and noted that while 'many children are coming online for the first time, many others remain unconnected and deprived of the opportunities the Internet offers for children to learn, play, communicate and engage' (ITU 2021: 3).

IoT toys are not only more costly, but they also lie atop an infrastructure of access that is an extension of other forms of global inequality. In this context, concerns about a haunting layer of invasive surveillance are at odds with the mission to give poorer populations of children fair access to greater amounts of information, entertainment and educational resources. Like the so-called click-wrap agreements described by Shoshana Zuboff (2019: 31) that entangle users in data schemes simply by buying a phone or clicking on a website page, giving more children access to digital tools automatically extends the reach of surveillance to them.

Increasing equality in digital access, especially to its most desirable 'smart object' outposts, such as IoT toys, therefore increases vulnerability for younger populations that already require more protection. Play is, by nature, a low-stakes activity that children should engage in 'knowing that their blunders will not be recorded, much less used against them' (Véliz 2020: 156). If the hope is for children to develop into adults who protect their own privacy and show support towards others' right to it, the early introduction of playthings that can record the ephemeral nature of play is a challenging set of circumstances to evolve from and through. Today, Toys R' not Us, they R' Recording Us.

Transgression

In January 2018, the Hong Kong-based company Vtech was fined $650,000 by the US Federal Trade Commission for a data breach in 2015 (Federal Trade Commission 2018: online). The 'Kid Connect' app, which was included with many of Vtech's electronic toys, was designed to collect data but did so without parental consent. The US legislation body COPPA requires that IoT toymakers gain consent from parents to gather data from their interactions with internet-connected devices (Federal Trade Commission 2018). Through Kid Connect, children's names, addresses and even photographs were available to hackers.

Two years after the VTech data breach, 'Spiral Toys' also encountered legal problems related to their 'CloudPets'. Over 800,000 owners of the toy had their personal records and recordings stored on an insecure database that was subsequently accessed by hackers. The CloudPets' functionality meant that distant relatives could leave messages on the toys via a mobile phone, and children could respond (Hern 2017). Millions of recordings were held by Spiral Toys on Amazon Web Services, a sonic repository of unguarded conversations that was transgressed through a lack of security-based solutions.

In the early years of connected toys, the aggregated soundscape was fraught with dissonance and feedback. Public trust had been damaged by the Vtech and Spiral Toys episodes, but the most dramatic instance of a doll gone 'rogue' was happening elsewhere. In Germany, the regulatory office – the Federal Network Agency – designated a prominent smart toy 'an illegal espionage apparatus'. The agency informed parents who possessed the doll that they needed to destroy it because it contained a concealed surveillance device that violated the German Telecommunications Act (BBC 2017a: online). Produced by 'Genesis Toys', the doll in question was 'My Friend Cayla', and in 2017 it had helped pioneer speech recognition to identify children's voices, with Cayla responding to questions through its internet connectivity. However, controversy arose when it was discovered that hackers could hear and see everything the children did through the toy's onboard microphone and camera (Frenkel 2017: online). The demonization of digital dolls and toys was well underway.

This notion of digital surveillance as a form of possession of household objects, as an insidious force that is constantly transgressing social and personal boundaries, is compelling. Given its pervasiveness, even at the earliest stages of human development, it becomes an unremarkable possession and therein lies its mundane power. Surveillance is a part of everything we do and say, even down to the conversations we have with our children. It is a possession of the digital world; not just of the body's interiority through remote medical technologies or the external body via smart speakers, but a possession of all relationships and processes that might generate data. Vocal exchanges, along with a range of other data vectors such as locations, movements, browsing choices and internal bodily statistics, turn our children into data constellations. Whether referring to sonic activity or otherwise, data divulges a spectrum of narratives and behaviours that, given their scale, are difficult or implausible to perceive. As a result, forensic models of each of our oscillating data bodies and their environs are being scored and mapped in a manner that reimagines urban and digital space and, more importantly, amplifies the ways in which they bleed into and transgress each other's boundaries.

Not content with residing solely in the digital realm, digital apparitions locked in step with children have become hybrid entities. Not so much haunted by statistics as bodies possessed by data. By the time a child turns three or four years old, 5 million data points have been collected, and this body of data 'rises to seventy-two million data points before a child reaches the age of 13' (Holloway 2019: 29). Such research points to children being both data sources and consumers within a big data economy. By interacting with smart toys, they produce data and are subsequently designated an economic 'worth'. This is latent capitalism in full flow as it tirelessly assimilates the least likely activities, devices and persons into transactional commodities. Donell Holloway accurately evaluates such dynamics when she surmises that the 'connection of children to the Internet through their bodies, play, learning and social interactions further heightens children's re-entry into the economy both as economic objects and subjects' (2019: 28).

By plugging the young into old economic structures, toys have become composers possessed with the power to score the domestic frontline of sonic surveillance and data collection. Dolls becoming possessed with insidious spirits and occult entities are commonplace in Western culture and beyond, particularly since the emergence of electronic media and mechanized automation. 'In the twentieth century, creepy dolls became more actively homicidal, as motion picture technology transformed the safely inanimate into the dangerously animate' (McRobbie 2015: online).

Listening In

In the twenty-first century, smart toys like the My Friend Cayla dolls are less overtly grotesque than their onscreen predecessors. They have instead been imbued with a more ambient monstrosity: the contemporary toy demons of cinema having been exorcised by the spirits of surveillance. A new era of invasive body horror is upon us. This is not the transgression of the dermal interface by mysterious technological apparatus in films such as David Cronenberg's *Crimes of the Future* (2022) nor is it the radiant mutation of Katsuhiro Otomo's *Akira* (1988). It is the transactional body morphing between digital and skeletal states through the horror of infinite connection.

Worlds

As a more benign future model for smart toys, it is easy to imagine that the goal of designers would be the fictional reality of *Toy Story* (1995). Rather than the uncanny glimpses of secretly murderous undead intelligence in the talking doll Chucky in Tom Holland's *Child's Play* (1988) (*Toy Story*'s narratological antithesis), the toys in the world of *Toy Story* value play, and their children, above all. They can talk and move around like sentient beings, with internal realities similar to the humans with whom they cohabitate. Most importantly, they are not possessed. They are authentically the characters that their children imagine them to be during their playtime. Add to this dynamic some relatable flaws, along with a couple of engaging narrative arcs thrown in to ground them, and before you know it, enough boxes have been ticked for it to register under the 'family friendly comedy' format. However, as Jackie Stacey and Lucy Suchman's 2012 essay 'Animation and Automation' observes, it is the 'duty and the pleasure' of all the toys to 'play still' during the child's 'imaginative games' (Stacey and Suchman 2012: 2).

Toy Story's toys are reassuringly 'dumb' in the children's world, in the sense that they are not technologically 'smart'. While some possess recorded voices in that world, these are limited to franchise-friendly slogans and catchphrases ('To infinity and beyond!') and, in the case of the Woody doll, a retracting pull-string mechanism that seems to signify a familiar, unthinkingly repetitive toy technology. It is only in the world outside of the child's sensory scope that the community of toys is animate, interacting with each other and listening in on the children and their carers. What makes the story heart-warming, rather than horrifying, is that their surveillance efforts are almost exclusively motivated by their concerns and anxieties related to maintaining their cherished toy status.

The toys maintain a strict self-enforced barrier between their own communal world and the one centred around the child's play. This is because make-believe can only take place if 'the emotional and physical labour [of] the toys . . . remain hidden from their owners' (Stacey and Suchman 2012: 29). Much like the secret services operating within the UK and the wider world (see Chapter 6, for example), the toys monitor their users in secret (as if they are not there at all). They listen and watch, both out of a sense of care for their subjects and due to anxieties related to their ongoing utility. It is the toy's capacity to be manipulated and given voice during play that provides much of its importance to the child (Winnicott 2005). It is exactly the limitations of the toy as a halfway point between psycho-magical reality and an external objective one that makes it cherished. To this extent, the toy community listens from behind the boundary of the inert-object technical world to ensure that the childish magic that manifests in them does not overwhelm it and ruin the function of play. They exist in the latent space before and after play that is not constrained by material realism.

Magical reality, points out philosopher Federico Campagna, is not part of technical reality, but instead operates as an 'alternate reality system' running 'alongside our material world, however invisibly' (Campagna 2018: 4) (and inaudibly). However, the upsurge of new advanced animatronic toys seems to overwhelm the boundary between magic and technology in the opposite direction. A compelling case study can be found in 'The Huggable Bear' trialled at the Boston Children's Hospital. While termed a 'social robot' in the literature (Logan et al. 2019), it was presented as a toy to the children. It was able to talk with young inpatients using a 'Wizard of Oz' prototype method, where a subject expert spoke through the bear's speaker system and responded animatronically to the patients. While outcomes of the trial were positive and the project aims were undoubtedly important and worthwhile, it is clear that the toy was being used as an instrument to deliver care, rather than being considered a plaything.

As the world of play becomes occupied territory, encroached upon by new technological realities, aspects of its magic come under the control of technology's world view. According to Campagna, such a perspective values instrumentalism and the ethos of work (rather than play) and always operates in the service of specific political, economic or religious systems (Campagna 2018: 24–5). In this sense, AI technology becomes part of an expansionist avant-garde, possessing play to further the aims of surveillance capitalism. The slogan for *Child's Play* states that 'there's nothing innocent about child's play'. Its sentiment seems increasingly prescient of the way that toys have been possessed by the agendas of digital technology.

Prediction

Augmenting a toy with connectivity and increased capacity for interaction is both a marketing tactic and a genuinely compelling milestone in the evolution of play. A post by the World Economic Forum, as part of their 'Global Technology Governance Summit' in 2021, claimed that 'smart toys provide enormous promise for children', citing their ability to 'watch, listen to, and learn from' them (Bergeson and Firth-Butterfield 2021: online) as being hugely beneficial. The agreement publicly stated by toy manufacturers and policymakers, that IoT toys should offer increased customization and educational capabilities without engaging in harmful data practices, does not account for the tendency of technology to be co-opted for purposes other than those originally intended. It is difficult to predict both the evolution of IoT toys and how elements of their technology, design, and integration into homes and schools are going to affect future generations. Examples from recent history show that noble intentions around children and connectivity are subject to the same 'ethical pollution' by commercial interests as any market aimed at adults.

In the 1990s, the arrival of the internet in schools was described with upbeat rhetoric. Numerous predictions stated that students would inevitably become the 'skilled techno-entrepreneurs' of tomorrow followed (Shaw 1998: C9), as did the proposition of 'the role of the child as computer user' (Steeves 2010: 87). With the incoming smart toys and EdTech riding on the back of digital networks, the levels of technology that had inbuilt capacities to monitor interactions also increased accordingly in these publicly funded spaces.

In 2023, the American Civil Liberties Union reported that 87 per cent of students surveyed aged fourteen to eighteen 'claimed that their schools used surveillance technology to monitor their behaviors – with most reporting multiple surveillance measures' (ACLU 2023: 10). Email and social media monitoring, software monitoring, facial recognition cameras and fingerprint scanners are among the measures used by schools in the United States, all in the name of safety and security. The emergence of the EdTech surveillance industry was likely not considered during the uncritical celebration of 'the child's facility with interactive media' (Steeves 2010: 87). Measures such as fingerprint scanning reflect what Valerie Steeves, in an essay about online surveillance in Canadian schools, called the 'neoliberal tendency to treat students as suspects' (Steeves 2010: 88). Networked capabilities that were once heralded as a pure boon for education have resulted in the disruption of 'the social relationships that support learning and provided corporations with an unprecedented opportunity to mine the education system and steer what children learn' (Steeves 2010: 88).

Student-reported expressions of discomfort and alarm about digital surveillance in schools include the 'lack of privacy, limits on free expression, erosion of trust, and unfair treatment' (ACLU 2023: 20). By making unsubstantiated claims about security, the smart toy makers and the wider EdTech surveillance industry have taken advantage of how the 'dominant discourses of school safety tend to deflect critical inquiry' (Monahan and Torres 2010: 9). The future mapped out by smart toys, whereby the ethics of safety are brandished to subjugate the morals of monitoring, sounds suspiciously like the narratives being orchestrated at a national defence level.

Medical and consumer technologies allow for children to be monitored from the moment they are conceived 'with the excuse of keeping them safe' (Véliz 2020: 155). If this were done using disparate data points that never converged on the dashboard of marketing software, monitoring would not ring as many alarm bells. However disparate, these data points come to account for an algorithmic assemblage, which leads to children being 'treated as combinations of data points because of the datafication and surveillance practices baked into the IoT toys, smart devices, and social media' which then 'reduces their digital actions to abstract demographic information for a litany of products and online services' (Boulicault et al. 2023: 125). The straightforward commercial motivation of attempting to predict the viewing and buying patterns of children is bound up in the dynamics of unpredictable growth. It is almost as if the chaotic nature of transforming from child to adult somehow warrants the distributed monitoring and prediction of them: a case of faux corporate virtue signalling that winkingly says, 'we are all in this together'.

Strong arguments against the use of IoT toys cite concerns over how recordings and other data collected from, and on, children may re-emerge later in life to limit job opportunities or otherwise socially injure them. These arguments are supported by the unaccountable number of actors involved in implementing IoT for play, as it 'isn't a monolithic entity' (Greengard 2021: 56). Samuel Greengard's comprehensive volume on IoT describes it as a 'vague and often confusing confederation of vendors, platforms, systems, technologies, software, and tools' (Greengard 2021: 56).

It is the connection of affordances and organizations from the list above that can cause such personal and social harm. Leaked photographs or conversations can obviously cause huge damage on social media. Less obvious are the ways in which smart toys and EdTech providers help form loose models that predict likely careers and those who are 'likely to succeed'. When employed and used with other data and recordings, such modes of divination are tightened up so that commercial, industrial and cultural organizations can place their bets on who is going to be useful to them going forward. This kind of prediction methodology appears acceptable on the surface of things because we all love a success story, especially if it washes the 'rags to riches' mythos in public. Such idioms back up American band Timbuk 3's impossibly positive promise that we live in a world in which 'The Future's So Bright, I Gotta Wear Shades (1986).

Intimacy

A child's transition to a dualistic concept of internal and external reality is enabled through play with physical toys. As one of the key attributes of the favourite toy, Winnicott states that it must 'seem to the infant to give warmth, or to move, or . . . do something that seems to show it has vitality or reality of its own' (Winnicott 2005: 7), just outside the internal reality of the child. The toy survives destructive urges meant to test its persistence as an external reality that adapts to the imaginative life of the child through play. Playing with the toy is always fraught with the contradictions of its original 'transitional' status as an object from external reality that existed before an external reality was properly conceptualized:

> The thing about playing is always the precariousness of the interplay of personal psychic reality and the experience of control of actual objects. (Winnicott 2005: 64)

However, such precariousness is resolved via imaginative play: a form of wilful collusion with a toy that makes it alive enough to play with. The child playfully reinterprets its movements, recorded speech and noises as evidence of its own internal reality. Anything said to the toy is imagined to be heard and reacted to by the toy (with or without a microphone and speaker system). In Sherry Turkle's studies of robotic toys, she describes a child playing with an experimental social robot called 'Kismet'. The robot's speech faculties are not working properly during most of the experiment, so the child employs traditional doll play, 'filling in' for both sides of the conversation until unexpectedly it starts to respond to their demands for intimacy, audibly responding to the words, 'I love you' (Turkle 2017: 92).

Children confiding in their toys, to enliven them as they share secrets, is positively associated with building closer relationships (Bedrov and Gable 2024). When Turkle interviews a nine-year-old boy who has the robotic toy 'AIBO dog', he says that although he currently prefers confiding in his pet hamster, with more time, the robot will care enough for him to share his problems with it instead (Turkle 2017: 58). Another study found that children were more likely to share a secret with a toy robot than with an adult (Bethel, Stevenson and Scassellati 2011). Even adults asked to play with robotic toys present a desire to enable the 'fantasy of near communication' through the sharing of personal details (Bethel, Stevenson and Scassellati 2011: 127).

The essential vulnerability of child's play places important emphasis on the ephemerality of children's speech. As Winnicott notes, child's play implies special trust and exists 'outside the individual, but it is not the external world' (Winnicott 2005: 69). The recording and storing of children's words in the external networked reality of the internet breaks a core tenet of play, by forcing voice data to be remembered and reused outside the precarious, transitional reality of play. Children themselves may be forgiven for not being able to distinguish between the affordances of the traditional plaything and the smart toy. The traditional toy has a 'less-than' body, with no actual listening capacity and no ability to speak beyond those words filled in by the child, yet it is imagined as being whole and composite within the confines of play.

The network-connected smart toy has a 'more-than' body in that its real IoT listening capacity extends beyond its immediate surroundings. Its virtual sensorium pushes inaudibly beyond the transitional realm into a digital storage centre in the external world. In a study where children interacted with internet-connected toys that asked questions, most thought the toy they played with could remember what they had said and that they might share a secret with it. They also reasoned that their parents could not hear what they said to it (which they could, via an online portal). One child exclaimed, 'That's pretty scary!' at the revelation that it could repeat anything that was told to it (McReynolds et al. 2017: 5203).

It is easy to understand the child's shock at the idea that secrets shared during games of role-playing and make-believe might be overheard in the external adult world. The digital storage of voice interactions from child's play not only represents new ways to eavesdrop on children's voice data for 'extra-ludic' purposes, but it also alters the nature of the reality that play takes place in, and in turn, the notion of intimacy that it introduces the child to.

Voice

The moment YouTuber Antonio Vargas gives his child a new Christmas gift, the rest of the family start to shush.

'I'm scared', says the child.

The kid next to him starts to say something but is hushed by the others.

Full of anticipation, the boy pulls the gift out of the box: a plush toy dressed in a Christmas outfit. He stares off camera at his dad, ironically amused, and there is some laughing. Then the boy is made to read the name of the toy monkey.

'Mommy's little monkey', he reads.

'Now go ahead, you gotta touch the hands, one at a time', says his father.

He presses on the button in one of the hands and we hear a woman's voice say the words, 'Give me a big hug. I love you'.

The boy, overcome by hearing the voice of his recently deceased mother, pushes his head into the monkey and starts to sob. The boy next to him, apparently also taken by surprise, starts to cry onto the unopened toy box on his lap.

The moment of the toy's push-button recording being played was captured by a mobile phone camera and shared by widower and father Vargas on YouTube (Vargas 2017). It was then picked up by media outlets around the world, such as the *Daily Mail Online* (Finn 2017b). The pattern recursively illustrates what Marcel O'Gorman describes as the 'incontrovertible link between death and technology' (O'Gorman 2015: 8). O'Gorman coined the term 'necromedia' to emphasize the link between the media we produce in life and its 'spectral' capacity to exist after our death. In keeping with this idea, the YouTube recording shares firsthand the increasingly common practice of capturing the recorded voice of a dead or dying parent or grandparent and embedding it in a bespoke toy.

According to journalist Melanie Ehrenkranz (2017), the process of vocal transfer of dead loved ones is most popularly achieved via the digital services of the 'Build-a-Bear' (BAB) chain that offers users the ability to record a voice message over the phone that they can then pick up in the store and insert into a toy of choice (BAB 2024). Engaging in this procedure of phantom channelling involves opening up the intimate domain of familial suffering and sharing cherished articulations with external organizations. These toy gifts are intended primarily as auditory memorials. They extend the emotional trigger of the lost voice to the haptic reality and comfort of an embraceable object, a dynamic that often takes on extra gravitas when they are gifted to children.

Predating audio recording technology, the practice of capturing the voices of dying family members found (and still finds) purchase in a type of 'listening out' by surviving family members. Auditory bereavement hallucinations – hearing the voices of loved ones after they die – are a common part of the grieving process (Vilhauer 2023) but are culturally contested. In the 1980s, Ian Stevenson invented the term 'idiophany' to describe all 'unshared sensory experiences' (Stevenson 1983: 1609) because the clinical association between the term 'hallucination' and mental illness risked pathologizing otherwise healthy people. He was motivated to redefine the nomenclature of categorization, in part, through his observation of grieving people, with otherwise robust levels of mental health, hearing and seeing the dead. Building on Stevenson's terminology, MacDonald studied 'idionecrophanies' – moments of perceived conversation with the dead. He found that it was generally 'part of the process of constructing the reality of death' and that those who experienced extreme trauma through grief were also most likely to have been in contact with a deceased relative as part of the healing process (MacDonald 1992: 221). MacDonald also noted that such experiences were less likely to occur (or be reported) in religious, racial and gender groups in which admitting to experiencing contact with the dead was considered emotionally weak, mentally abnormal or potentially immoral.

As with other idiosyncratic acoustic phenomena traditionally bound to personal experience, scientific enquiry seeks to map specific cultural topographies that frustrate data collection. The technologies that it enables flatten these baffling undulations and overlay a unifying para-acoustics. In the case of these necro-toys, the recording of the voice of the dead, or dying, has the capacity to overdub the often unspeakable experience of hearing the dead, substituting the realm of religion, magic, parapsychology and mental illness with the 'exteriorization of memory' (O'Gorman 2015: 26) through recording. Research suggests that internalized expressions of continuing bonds with the dead, such as thinking about and imagining them, lead to more resolved grief than externalized sensory expressions (Vilhauer 2023: online). Rather than memorializing loved ones, the voices coming from within cherished toys might 'overwrite' our memories of the dead (Elder 2022) perhaps obliterating, in the process, some of our more painful memories. Going forward, it also seems probable that toys will come to form a physical part of the 'thanabot' framework – a hybrid virtual and material grief solution – discussed further in Chapter 16. Children will be able to not only hear the voices of lost loved ones but will also be able to hold conversations and play with them.

Fidelity

Miniaturized and abstracted, smart dolls echo the human form. They are inert but very much alive in terms of the capture and transmission of information. Situated somewhere between the living and the dead, the dolls sit drone-like on beds and sofas, extracting personal information through their habitual status of being family-adjacent: revenant sleeper cells activated by vocal commands and the interactions of children, and those who miss them. In an era and economy fuelled by dataveillance, such IoT figures are roamer technologies, foot soldiers of acoustic reconnaissance within the home and beyond. 'My friend zombie'.

Oscillating at the edges of the unsound and the undead is a mode within the home that is progressively being normalized, as we learn how to live with emergent technologies such as AI. This contradictory form of 'being' is both alien and domestic, and it is forcing us to renegotiate our relationships with older forms of non-human intelligence because of its insistent proximity to our online experiences. Ruminating on modes of intelligence that we have previously compartmentalized and pushed beyond the boundaries of the rational, nihilist philosopher Eugene Thacker explores digital revenance and envisages the inception of the data twin and its otherworldly characteristics. He writes:

The horror of contemporary 'living dead' is not just the fear of being reduced to nothing but body, but, in the 'network society', perhaps the horror of the 'living dead' is the fear of being reduced to nothing but information – *or not being able to distinguish between contagion and transmission*. In this sense the paradox of the living dead is also the paradox of 'vital statistics', a sort of living dead network that exceeds and even supercedes the 'bare life' of the organism. (Thacker 2004: online)

Smart dolls are in the business of capturing and transmitting the vital statistics of those who engage with them. Correspondingly, recordings, which speak to these existential equations, become the lifeblood of whatever informational circulatory system they traverse. Thus, recordings can be interpreted as viral entities that propagate globally, infecting databases with the bare sonic essence of the organism. If we take this meditation upon the disappearance of the body into data and transfer it to the soundscape, it gives us more useful pointers as to the liminal nature of frequencies and their connection to the viral.

Hauntings are predominantly the vibratory ability of an entity to penetrate the network of living things through voice and object manipulation. The fear of haunting is fed by the threat of contact and infection from liminal presences, of bodies being transmuted into waveforms (AUDINT 2021). It is the difficulty we encounter when trying to contain and control the ephemeral nature of the viral and the waveform that renders them such anxious phenomena – reminding us, as it does, of existence lived in the oscillating thresholds between the sonic and the silent, the transitory and the static.

For centuries, dolls have been purveyors of human anxiety, playful repositories of disquiet. The 'Worry Dolls' of Guatemala and Mexico that are given to children who suffer from nightmares personify this stress-based transfer. The small figures allow children to express and download distress into their forms as they articulate and offload their dread before going to sleep. An example of fear-fuelled shadow play is that of 'Robert the Doll' (Morton 2013), which was owned by Key West artist and author Robert Eugene Otto. Given as a gift by an abused servant who was thought to have cursed it with black magic, it allegedly disturbed the peace for Otto and his family throughout his childhood and adult life. Such circumstances amplify wider cultural apprehensions concerning the way inert objects that represent the human form become (m)aligned with supernatural forces – the fear of the undead mimicking the living.

More contemporary examples of the othering of dolls include the depiction of malevolent protagonists in films such as Gerard Johnstone's *M3GAN* (2022), which conveys the cultural fear of AI controlling robotic human forms. From the beginning of the film, viewers await the doll's inevitable transgression of Isaac Asimov's three laws of robotics, namely: (1) that a robot shall not harm or allow harm to come to a human, (2) that any instruction given by a human shall be obeyed unless it comes into conflict with the first law, (3) that a robot will avoid any situations that might eventuate in harm to itself as long as such self-protection does not come into conflict with the first or second law (Asimov 1942: 100). Who knows what future societies will make of eighty-year-old laws that designate non-human forms of intelligence as secondary and thirded entities?

When *M3GAN* used recordings of a foe's voice in order to mimic her, it was to the detriment of human life. The high-fidelity recording became the pivot of transgression and propagation, which resulted, in both cases, in self-destruction through overextension. Through the figure of the doll, fear is distilled into a technological melding of centuries-old craftsmanship and future-facing modes of potential sentience – a hauntological doll tormenting the future human through its invocation that 'the earth's most sophisticated processing unit is in the process of being downgraded' (AUDINT 2021: 237).

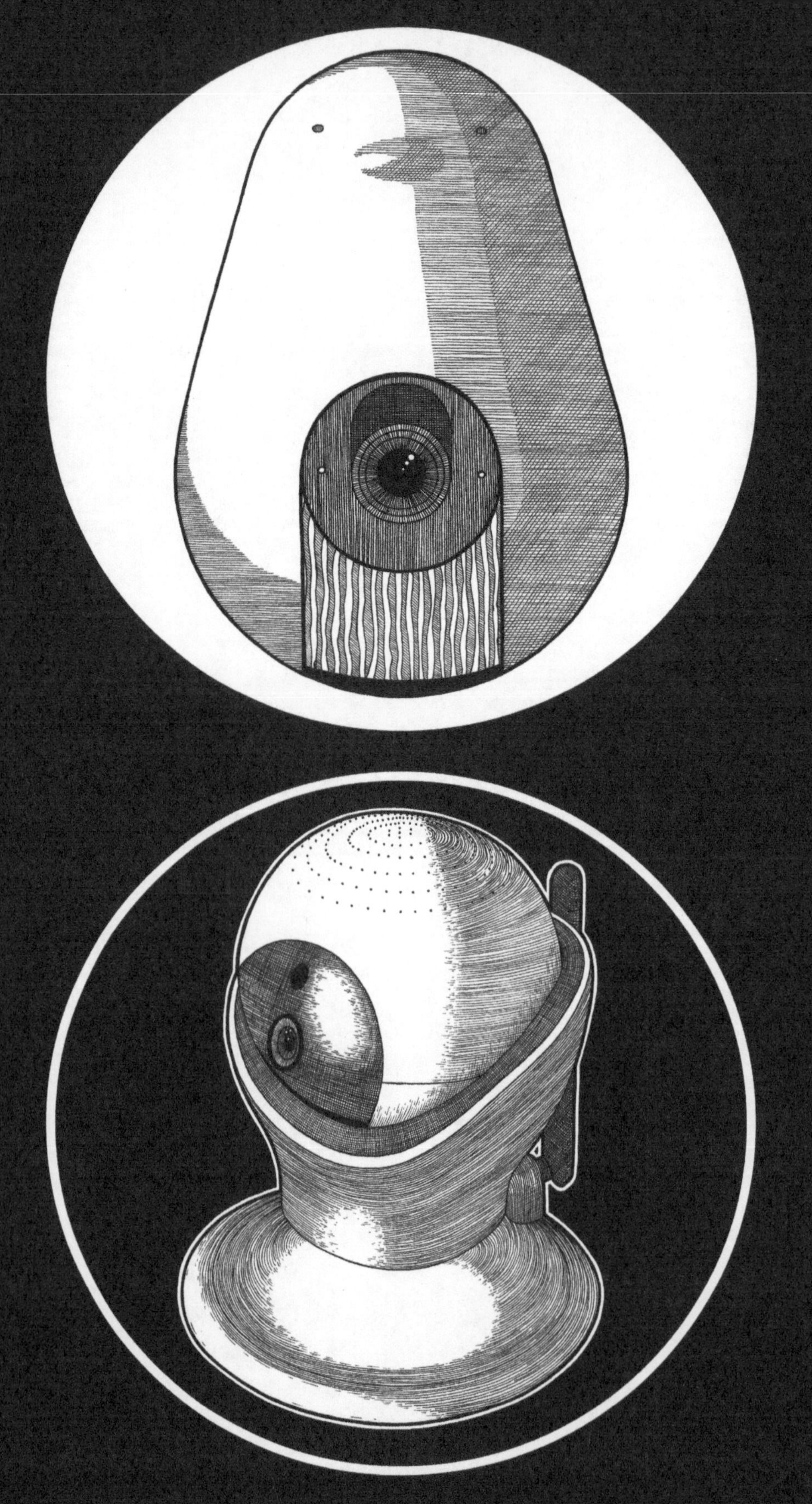

CHAPTER 12
SMART BABY MONITORS

Process

Released in 1938, the 'Zenith Radio Nurse' was the world's first mass-produced baby monitor. It was invented in response to the infamous kidnapping, ransoming and murder of the twenty-month-old son of world-renowned aviator Charles Lindbergh (FBI 2024). A terrifying threat to the peace of mind for new and wealthy parents had emerged that required a more-than-human sensory capacity to appease it. In response to this wave of trepidation, Eugene F. McDonald Jr. created the Radio Nurse system with a 'Guardian Ear' microphone in the child's bedroom and a Radio Nurse receiver in the parent's room. The prototype was created for his own family. It employed a portable speaker to transport 'the sounds of the room where his newborn daughter slept' for 'caregivers to listen from any room' (Fisher and Winick 2021: 287).

The unit's receiver was designed to resemble a nurse's cap, thus combining notions of the child's health and well-being with round-the-clock surveillance to mitigate media-distorted concerns for a child's safety, especially from strangers illegally entering family homes. The Radio Nurse and subsequent baby monitor systems used shortwave radio signals to transmit signals between the microphone and the amplifier (Hughes 2009). Its broadcasting system was not encrypted, and the Radio Nurse failed commercially, partly because its frequency range could be picked up by car radios, allowing any passers-by to listen in to the child and its carers.

Widening the radius of a baby's sonic triggers for care has, since 1932, evolved into an increasingly complex business. Today, devices monitor audio, visual and biometric information that not only reports this information to a baby's caregiver but also provides suggestions for how those care responses are formatted. In the foreseeable future, such predictive and problem-solving technologies could replace many of the caretaker's responsibilities altogether. The physical range limitation for all listeners was removed with the introduction of the networked baby monitor. In 2011, the 'iBaby Monitor M3' was launched. It was the first Wi-Fi-enabled baby monitor to be made available in Apple stores around the world. Via the internet, parents were able to massively extend the range of their listening in (and viewing) well beyond the home 'to anywhere an internet-enabled smartphone, tablet and computer [. . . could be . . .] connected to' (iBaby 2024). Since then, smart baby monitors have grown in popularity in large part due to their connectivity.

The number of devices in the smart baby monitor network continues to increase, with over 50 per cent of market share worldwide connected to the Web. The market is expected to further increase by up to 10 per cent by 2032 (GMI 2024; Astute Analytica 2023). However, these new networked devices have the same vulnerabilities as all web-connected devices, given that they provide motivated third parties an ear to babies' cries and to carers' coos and conversations. During a 2017 'House of Lords Select Committee' hearing on AI, Colin Griffiths from the Citizens Advice Bureau pointed out a troubling practice emerging around the sales of baby monitors. Some makers were hiding warnings that third parties might gain access to the streams from their children's bedrooms in their terms and conditions (Griffiths 2017). While there is evidence of more sophisticated forms of encryption being applied to these products via the increasingly profitable cybersecurity sector, potential breaches still remain an issue.

Alongside expansions in the networked receiver range of each device, smart baby monitors have increased their sensory capacity to most commonly include a video camera. However, other sensory inputs were also added in the pursuit of parental peace of mind, such as breathing sensors – either wrapped around the child or via a mat in the child's cot (Nanit 2024; CuboAI 2024) – that also captured body temperature. Data from these enhancements is not only sent to the parents; it is also sent to data centres to inform machine learning processes and human teams that, in turn, produce services such as 'true cry' alerts (CuboAI 2024). Now everyone can go to bed feeling more safe and secure in the knowledge that there is an algorithmic piece of mind, listening and watching.

Recording

With access to prodigious datasets comes the confidence that insight can be extracted and control exercised over whatever context the information pertains to. This dynamic becomes more pronounced when said contexts generate excessive amounts of unease, disquiet and potential distress, as is the case with smart baby monitors and the sensitive human form they provide feedback on. With access to an infant's soundscape and recordings, it inspires confidence, as users have remote access to their biosonic signatures: to the flows, flaws and rhythms that are otherwise imperceptible to the sensorium unless aided by medical technologies.

Wearable smart monitors deploy sensors over an infant's body, enabling them to record and transmit data about a wide range of physical functions. Along with sound recordings, they capture somatic operations such as 'heart rate, respiration, sleeping position, blood oxygen level, or body temperature' (Swearingen 2018: online). Every aspect of the baby's life is captured, analysed and compared to national and international averages. The data becomes a second skin, a datadermal interface – a numerically protective layer against the arbitrary chance and failure of somatic processes such as breathing. As such, infants become inadvertent poster children for the quantified self. They do not really have a choice. They are monitored and plugged into dataveillance, or what could be termed a 'bioveillance', mainframe – a system that figuratively wraps around the body while also embedding it into a statistical field of relations.

According to the Quantified Self homepage, the website represents 'an international community of users and makers of self-tracking tools who share an interest in "self-knowledge through numbers"' (The Quantified Self 2025: online). This is a conception of the body and the world it inhabits as a palimpsest of dataflows that can be tapped into and decrypted to comprehend the order of things. A conceptual referent is the digital rain that represents the coding of simulated reality within the film *The Matrix* (1999). Composed of Western numerals and letters along with Japanese half-width kana characters, the code is soundtracked by the digitized patter of rain hitting a windowpane. The suggestion is that even within the manifold complexity of rainfall, there are patterns and rhythms which make every single drop – its velocity, placement and direction – predictable.

Embedding the chaos of the infant into a numerical score that is as predictable as it is representational renders the infant's movements, gut noises and screams knowable. The act of recording is part of an elaborate choreography that connects numbers and meaning into discrete oscillating relationships with each other. If the monitoring system's sprawl of apparatus supports the notion that we are living through an era of surveillance capitalism, it could also be posited that there is a contemporary iteration of numerology at work within it – a belief system dependent on the divine principles of numbers and data as they relate to coincidental or synchronous events, actions and processes (Bunker and Javane 1997). Numbers represented by data serve as a methodology for explaining, predicting and making audible the random esoteric nature of the world around us.

During the Second World War, numerology found traction through number stations, as previously discussed in Chapter 5. The stations still transmit through shortwave radio, conveying information to intelligence officers who conduct their undercover activities abroad. In terms of protagonists, this is obviously a very different world from that of the nursery, but speculatively it is compelling to project the crib or creche as a domestic number station. As a conceptual probe, this conviction opens a space to scrutinize seemingly divergent processes and technologies to reveal how military and domestic behaviours map onto each other. The house that was alive with the sound of music is now living through the sound of numbers.

In the digitized creche, the noises transmitted by the infant are messages that parents, carers and health professionals attempt to decipher. Carnal code streams across the full range of acoustic expression, from a missed breath to the stridor of croup – each sonic object forming a Tetris-like audio equation that needs to be solved. Numbers transmit from the monitor array that surrounds the infant. Parents stalk their homes, ears alert, always on manoeuvres and ready to react to any aberrant signal. 'Operation Malaise' is in full effect, all day and all night. Carpeted intelligence agents analyse numbers and listen as a way of living, recording and monitoring a body of reconnaissance that is both under and over cover.

Transgression

Smart baby monitors and the domestic spaces they map signal the ultimate intrusion of surveillance culture and its myriad technologies into the most sensitive area of the home. The front line of transgressive monitoring has extended and found purchase in the nursery. The logic of the pathway to market is not hard to process here. The more sensitive a space, the more vulnerable its constituents. Vortex-like, such spatialities attract nervousness, some of the concerns logical, some fabricated by those wishing to profit from them. As a critical mass of dread accumulates, a fertile environment opens for products that will reverse the polarity of anxiety. Create the problem, create the solution.

Purchase a Wi-Fi connected monitor. Attach it to a crib or free stand. Open a channel within the home to extend the reach of one's ears and eyes. Sensory connectivity with the infant around the clock. Problem solved. That is until said channels are commandeered by digital intruders (as opposed to hackers) who use them to foment a sense of disconnect from the relative tranquillity the listeners and watchers seek. Reports of smart baby monitors being used to threaten, scare and extort homeowners are legion. Breaching the privacy of the home and violating its sonic borders is what renders the intrusions so effective. The vocal violation displaces and disengages the acoustic anchors that previously existed in the space – the mellifluous tones of familial affection and soft toy soundtracks.

Nightmare scenarios induced by baby monitors have, in fact, been occurring for decades now. As far back as 2009, class action lawsuits were proposed against 'Summer Infant' and Toys 'R' Us. US citizens such as Wes Denkov were outraged because his next-door neighbours could tap into their monitor feed. The microphone in the 'Day and Night' video monitor was so sensitive it captured conversations outside the room in which the device was placed in (Zetter 2009). Day, dusk and night terrors are seemingly available when purchasing a networked baby monitor, and at no extra cost, other than to one's account of personal privacy.

In 2018, the *Washington Post* published an article documenting the case of a family's home being violated through a smart baby monitor:

> A stranger's voice, spouting 'sexual expletives', wafted through a baby monitor in the Rigneys' room – one that was linked to a Nest camera in their infant's room upstairs. Alarmed, the Rigneys turned on their lights. Unprompted, a Nest camera in *their* room activated and the same man's voice told them to turn the lights back off. 'I'm going to kidnap your baby', the voice said next, Ellen Rigney recalled to the news station. 'I'm in your baby's room.' Nathan Rigney bolted upstairs to his son's crib. But the 4-month-old was fast asleep, oblivious to the unsettling incident that had just transpired and spooked his parents. There was no one else in his room. (Wang 2018)

Audio monitor turned audio mutineer. The inbuilt volte-face logic of the sonic in full audition and in residence within the domestic nucleus of hope and worry – an exemplar of Manichean dualism in both technological and emotional formats. It is the way in which these symmetrical currents of opposing forces are amplified and crosswired in a second, to create radical displacement, that exposes the volatile nature of smart sonic technologies. Recognizing the distributed potentialities of waveformed phenomena, Michael Bull and Les Back state that 'sound thus has both utopian and dystopian associations: It enables individuals to create intimate, manageable and aestheticized spaces to inhabit but it can also become an unwanted and deafening roar threatening the body politic of the subject' (2003: 1).

More lo-fi growl than deafening roar, the monitored threat issued in the Rigneys' abode breached the realm of the unwanted and migrated into the state of the reviled. It is this sense of transgression without repercussion or identification that attracts certain types of digital intruders. Numerous other instances of smart baby monitors being infiltrated have occurred because, security-wise, they have been ill-protected (George 2022). Accounts of intruders directing verbal abuse at infants as well as parents have become commonplace (Gross 2013: online). The one thing that we can surmise from this violation of families' lives is that sweet dreams are not made of this.

Worlds

The smart baby monitor is a sonic portal capable of collecting and transmitting more information than is available to the human senses. The impulse to hear every breath, and to view digital summaries of a baby's heart rate and other biometric information, is inversely reflected in the portal's capacity to absorb and hold back that same information on command. Any carer wishing for peace and quiet can simply switch off the monitor and close the portal, thereby 'reducing the "annoyance" of having a new baby in the home' (Nelson 2009: 227). This capacity to selectively engage and disengage with another room's vital information through 'sonic bridging . . . revolutionized the way we care for babies' (Fisher and Winick 2021: 288). The on/off switch of transmission is a one-way form of control performed by the adult that does not change whether a baby is crying or not, only whether that reality encroaches on the ears of the carer.

Differences in the sonic character of the infant world versus that of the adult are not only characterized by cries for care and affection. Children's music, emanating from the baby monitor in the child's room, tends 'to have fewer scale degrees than adults and narrower melodic ranges' (Sato, Fujii and Savage 2018). It is designed to aid in learning and development and does so through simple, repetitive melodies and lyrics. Music for adults is more complex, nuanced and, at times, challenging. After the clichéd renditions of Mozart have been played through the domed interface of the pregnant belly, caregivers can be subjected to the same songs over and over, conjuring up 'all the old, reliable nightmares' (Harvilla 2013: online).

It is not only within the home that children's music clashes with the adult world. It has also been used to deter homeless people from convening or sleeping in public places such as railway stations and, more specifically, outside an event centre in West

Palm Beach, Florida (Bogel-Burroughs 2019). Deploying a tactic that the region's mayor claimed was meant to 'get homeless people into shelters and houses' (Bogel-Burroughs 2019: online), children's songs including *Raining Tacos* (2012) and *Baby Shark* (2015) were heard blaring out of speakers. In a sonic equivalent of installing armrests in the middle of benches to deter stretching out, or changing a smooth paved surface to one replete with raised concrete bumps, the city of West Palm Beach found an off-label use for the world's most popular baby songs. By way of response, the creator of *Raining Tacos* commented that he 'did not intend for his happy litany about a taco downpour to be weaponized' (Bogel-Burroughs 2019: online).

Shifting the context and repetition cycles of any music changes its effect, from stimulating and soothing a developing brain to composing hostile sonic architecture that alienates a city's vulnerable population. The impulse to switch off the sounds of a baby's world to preserve the peace of an adult one falls in line with other accepted forms of control by adults over their domestic environments. Later, when infants grow, caregivers will encounter musical tastes of their charges that diverge from their own. These new sonic expressions that their children and teenagers propagate build out their own worlds through provocative lyrics and unfamiliar and alienating sonic styles. Once composed, those musical borders await transgression from caregivers. Let the drama begin. The border between the adult and the child's world will not be as easy to control as it was when engaged with through a monitor.

Prediction

Understanding the needs of a baby from its cry is an age-old human predictive science. Akin to the herbalist roots of Western medicine and those of midwifery (Llanes et al. 2022), it was an endeavour predominantly led by women: mothers, wet nurses and grandparents. The piercing quality of the crying child has a specific acoustic register within the human brain that responds at a neurological and physiological level, making us more alert and slowing, then increasing, the HRs in female listeners, who, as a result of a biological difference, quickly become most attuned to the language of crying (Carollo et al. 2023). Parents of both sexes are, however, not immediately very good at telling the difference between a cry of pain and a cry of hunger (Carollo et al. 2023). The longer parents and caregivers spend listening to cries and experiencing the needs they indicate, the better they get at understanding the undulating tones of pre-lexical expression (Ji et al. 2021). In professional settings, researchers have even suggested that neonatal staff should be trained using a randomized database of needs-labelled crying (Mukhopadhyay et al. 2013).

Given that it takes hundreds of hours of crying to attune the human ear to its distinct frequencies of meaning, it is easy to understand the impulse to decode the distressed sounds of infants using machines. What could better understand the undeciphered semantics of 'pre-human' expression than an AI that listens using inexplicable 'post-human' algorithms? So goes the hubristic logic. And in fact, the mechanical ear, according to a review of studies by Chunyan Ji and colleagues, has been shown, in one case, to correctly interpret at least twice as many cries as professionals in a neonatal setting (Ji et al. 2021). They note that the sonic signature of the baby's vocal tract and breathing systems might also help predict problems with the child's respiratory health.

The scientific community has defined its protective mission through its algorithmic mapping and surveillance of baby cries. What has thwarted its ambitions so far, however, is a lack of data. As Ji and colleagues note, the challenge of the science is to find a suitable database of children's cries to improve prediction, due to the sensitive nature of the information. These recordings also need to be labelled correctly so that the machine can find repeating patterns between the cry and the reason behind it. It is easy to discern a degree of paucity in available cry-sample datasets. Due to the dearth of statistics and analysis, those seeking to train their predictive machines on a large enough dataset are often forced to synthesize additional samples (Ji et al. 2021) by slightly speeding up or slowing down existing ones, before adding the clone chorus back to the database for training.

Open data projects such as 'Donate A Cry' offer noisy and unreliable datasets that bespeak the community labour that produced them, making them difficult to find patterns in. The original company behind the scheme, 'Lullabond', is no longer operating, but the decade-old '"donateacry-corpus" of nearly 500 baby cry recordings' still haunts the internet (Veres 2014). Other attempts to amass a wailing library for analysis tend to come from hospitals. These recordings focus on predicting illness, labelling the cry features of sick children versus normal cries and are not generalizable (Ji et al. 2021).

One of the most frequently used corpuses of 'normal baby cries' comes from the YouTube parenting videos made by cry expert Priscilla Dunstan, who has designated special signifiers in baby expression to help new parents decipher their calls:

> There are several versions of the Dunstan Baby Language database since authors extracted the audio clips in their own ways. [One version . . .] consists of 315 wav files, sampled at 16 kHz, with a variable length between 0.3 and 1.6 s. Each utterance is a word of infant speech corresponding to one of the five 'Dunstan words', which were translated as 'Neh' = hungry, 'Eh' = need to burp, 'Oah' = tired, 'Eairh' = low belly pain, and 'Heh' = physical discomfort. (Ji et al. 2021: 2–3)

Dunstan's techniques have been featured and advertised on the Oprah Winfrey Show in the United States since 2006 (Dunstan 2024) and are indicative of the carer-led folk science that has always surrounded baby cry prediction. Still, there is no scientific analysis of their veracity. A machine trained on Dunstan word labelling is not deciphering and predicting the meaning of the child's cries but predicting which 'word' Dunstan would match to a cry. So it is co-opting and synthesizing social knowledge of crying rather than producing primary knowledge about its sonic characteristics. Adding weight to this trend, the 'Chatterbaby' App by UCLA researcher Ariana Anderson (2018) attempted to synthesize mother-produced knowledge. 'Veteran mothers' were recruited to label cry training data into categories such as 'hungry or fussy' (Gordon and Wong 2022: online) before samples were fed into the machine. The resulting synthesis represents the algorithmic polling of opinionated advice from a cacophony of experienced carers, rather than from an algorithmic tool possessing more-than-human translation powers.

Possibly because of the poor quality of available data, few baby monitors offer baby cry translation as a feature. 'Q-Bear', described as a 'baby crying translator' by its Taiwanese creators at Quantum Music, made a splash in the British media at a trade fair in 2023 but has not appeared in the UK market place (Quantum Music 2021; Williams 2023). The True Cry alert algorithm in CuboAI products offers a much less expansive predictive function that simply differentiates crying from other types of verbal baby noise (CuboAI 2024). However, True Cry and surveillance services like it provide baby monitor companies with a rich source of cry data not available to researchers in the public domain – a valuable specialist data source that could allow them to research algorithmic translation as part of future services. For now, only the prehistorically encoded scream scheme of broken sleep, despair and guilt (Williams 2023) can train new parents to more effectively predict the needs of their crying babies.

Intimacy

As surveillance technologies play increasingly intimate roles in our lives, the data and recordings they produce are mirrored by a clutch of social media that delivers constant flows of 'self-observation' content. Significantly modulating our attitudes and behaviours towards identity formation and representation, social media also plays an important role in shaping of relationships and the ways in which we engage our bodies in intimate alliances. Sadie Plant predicted this situation when thinking through our interdependence on digital technologies. She writes,

> While the notion that technologies are prostheses, expanding existing organs and fulfilling desires, continues to legitimize vast swathes of technical development, the digital machines of the late twentieth century are not add-on parts which serve to augment an existing form. Quite beyond their own perceptions and control, bodies are continually engineered by the processes in which they are engaged. (1998: 182)

Our bodies are in a continuum of modification, a process that attunes psychological and physiological mechanisms to a techno-scientific rationale. Infants who have an online identity before they are born and develop within a web of relentless monitoring will navigate the world and understand their place within it according to different markers of presence. Digital technology has become ever more transgressive with regard to the boundaries we once maintained around relationships, processes and spaces that were considered highly personal or confidential.

The belief and investment we place in such devices and technologies, under the auspices that they enhance our engagement with those things we care about, partly explain the ambivalence shown towards surveillance systems. Technologies such as smart baby monitors, for example, are marketed as items that we are morally obliged to purchase, an idea advanced by Ruckenstein and Granroth:

> The concept of 'intimate surveillance' refers to the scrutiny of children and young people by parents, caretakers, and friends. . . . This focus has led to interest in the normalization of surveillance as care (Leaver 2017) and suggestions that parental monitoring of babies and infants contributes to a surveillance culture wherein choosing *not* to survey can be read as a failure of good parenting. (2020: 14)

This notion of mitigating the unpredictable nature of being(s), objects and processes is core to the seduction of intimate surveillance – an insidious conception that gains traction between the antithetical urge for safety and the yearning for sensory augmentation. The grey space of conflicting compulsions that it inhabits feels comfortable precisely because surveillance capitalism has striven to render everyday living a contradictory affair. With indecision and doubt comes the capacity to influence and manipulate. Endorsing this line of thinking, Mike Michael and Deborah Lupton speak directly to the laissez-faire attitudes that users have towards being monitored. Referring to the constant threat of being surveilled and the manner in which this worry bleeds in and out of the functionality and convenience of the devices we embrace, they point to culture creating an 'oscillatory awareness' (Michael and Lupton 2016: 111) in its consumer base.

The term 'oscillatory awareness' is telling as it positions our wider culture as a vibratory mass resonating with divergent potential. We want – and, critically, are inveigled to feel – a need for sensorial extension, but it comes at a price with regard to traditional concepts of privacy. Not only do we purchase surveillance systems such as baby monitors, knowing they listen to us, but we also distribute granular details of our activities, including those of our young children, through social media – platforms that companies and governments consult to help them make decisions about jobs, visas and health statuses. A survey by 'CareerBuilder' found that '7 in 10 employers (70 percent) use social media and online search engines to screen job applicants' (Careerbuilder 2022). Self-tracking is part confessional, part documentary. Surveillance of the self is the most revealing art form of the twenty-first century.

An undertone not yet amplified that offers an alternative reading of utility is the mobilization of surveillance recordings to increase social and/or economic capital. Ambitions tied to social media traction not only reveal shifts in the way we think about achievements and careers, but they also expose the connectivity that such platforms have to deeper underlying systems of surveillance-based desires. Maybe we simply want to be listened to and watched, and we do not much care who undertakes this task or for what reason. Being recorded is enough. Minna Ruckenstein and Julia Granroth pinpoint this complex set of interdependencies when asserting that:

> Consumers also want to be intimately seen, known, and understood, which suggests that they embrace surveillance that is convenient and entertaining and digs deep into their social world. (2020: 15)

This identification of surveillance as a channel for self-expression should not be underestimated. If we are willing to reveal our most intimate selves for social entertainment and convenience, then it is not surprising that we are also sanguine about supplying intimate recordings of our loved ones to manufacturers, governments and third-party data brokers. Pre-internet, only those who desired to be in the public ear and eye chose career paths that would likely engage them in networks of celebrity. Through this filter, acoustic kitties, shoe heel transmitters, government wiretapping programmes, smart speakers, phones, baby monitors and social media all become channels that feed into the shared mixing desk of reality – a process that is analogous to a lifelong recording session.

The more channels feeding into the connective tissue of the network, the more sound the proposition that one exists and will carry on existing posthumously. This is a relatively new phenomenon that reveals the monumental changes emerging around social contracts and what it means to belong (socially speaking). The use of digital surveillance in contemporary societies goes 'well beyond intentions of monitoring individuals for specific purposes' (Ruckenstein and Granroth 2020: 13). The question now is whether we need to think of surveillance, in all its manifestations, as an intimate and implicit part of the social fabric in digital societies?

Voice

The starting point for many use cases of smart infant monitoring technology is the need of the caregiver while they are otherwise engaged in economic activity (Anushree, Mamatha and Bhavana 2022; Alswedani and Eassa 2020; Shahadi et al. 2019). When a baby cries, it does not know that its voice triggers the transmission of this sound to another room, nor does it understand what computational processing occurs to determine what that cry means. By detaching the voice from embodied expression, monitoring helps 'further the notion that a cry [is] a signal that must be noticed immediately and responded to promptly' (Fisher and Winick 2021: 288). This remedial approach further centres the economic responsibilities of the caregiver by reducing the distractions of unnecessary physical presence. Children engaged in raucous or naughty behaviour can be monitored and scolded from a distance by the disembodied voice of that technology's primary user.

The widening gap between the level of care required to keep an infant alive and the dearth of attention that many parents can dedicate plays out within the home. Technological interventions in twentieth- and twenty-first-century life portray public attitudes towards computers, which Abbate and Dick describe as deeply contradictory: 'acclaimed as liberatory, they are also condemned as instruments of control that increasingly dictate the contours of human life; often seen as revolutionary, they also reinforce existing power structures' (Abbate and Dick 2022: 1).

When a smart monitor responds to an infant's cries, the trigger does not constitute an input in the same way as an adult using a keyboard or video game controller; instead, it resembles computational responses to animal behaviours. After all, animals are similarly cared for and controlled by digital technology without consent or any conceptual understanding of it. The growing field of Animal Computer Interaction (ACI) is a subfield of Human-Computer Interaction, where designers and manufacturers of pet wearables or farming technology promote an 'animal-centric' approach that also acknowledges 'that an animal usually uses technology through humans and in a particular environment' (van der Linden et al. 2018: 1).

Clara Mancini's seminal article 'Animal-Computer Interaction (ACI): A Manifesto' (2011) advocates for harm reduction and increasing value for the animal via interaction with technology, along with – crucially – the condition that ACI technology should foster a relationship between humans and animals (Mancini 2011). In terms of their interaction with smart monitoring, the acknowledgement that animals are not 'users' of technology in the same way as humans ironically grants them more consideration in some cases than infants. Regulatory and advocacy groups for the safety of products marketed for children are mostly concerned with bodily safety as well as safeguarding children from inappropriate media content. Conversely, the rights of a child 'user', along with the inclusion of its input in the design process, often get lost in the clamour to meet the utilitarian needs of the caregiver. Technologically speaking, this is not so much a case of the child losing its voice as much as it is a case of it never having one to misplace to begin with.

Fidelity

The Zenith Radio Nurse is one of the earliest examples of deferring parental anxiety onto technology, a practice that reflects a question as to whether 'parents fail to develop trust in their own observational skills' and so become 'dependent on technology to do the observing for them' (Nelson 2009: 233). In the growing landscape of network-enabled baby monitoring, to what level do we owe infants (and their carers) a certain fidelity to mundane, un-augmented reality and access to the immediacy of human contact? Encoded into that duty of embodied care is the potential of absence: an acoustic delineation between carer and infant that prescribes roles, morals and distance. Rather than liberation from the network by the parent or carer, absence from it can be perceived as digital negligence. In studying reviews of baby monitors online in 2009, Margaret Nelson observed that:

> Implicitly, and sometimes explicitly, reviewers . . . indicate that only by being aware
> of the baby at all times – by hearing the baby and occasionally even also seeing it or

> having a sensor ready to tell you if it stops breathing – can they achieve anything
> approximating peace of mind. (Nelson 2009: 224)

Nelson suggested that this attachment to the baby monitor's constant attention can also result in adjusting and calibrating the monitor's functions to the point that 'parents sometimes write as if the monitor is the baby' (Nelson 2009: 228). As a piece of technology that abstracts identity in a caregiving relationship, the baby monitor becomes both an ersatz baby and ersatz caregiver. The difference is that caregivers can distinguish between a real baby and its technological representation, while a baby is not born with the same capacity for discernment.

Writing in 2010, Sharkey and Sharkey studied the potential commercial viability of 'robot nannies', concluding that they will need to 'enable considerably longer parent/carer absences than can be obtained from leaving a child sitting in front of a video or television programme' (Sharkey and Sharkey 2010: 162). Leaving children unsupervised took precedence due to the necessity for women to enter the workforce while men fought in the Second World War. The consequence of this social contract being disrupted gave rise to the phenomenon of the 'latchkey kid'. Far from enhancing care capabilities within a well-resourced household, improvements in caring technology could lead to stronger justifications for parents and caregivers being away from young children in order to increase income.

In using smart systems to alleviate parental anxiety, the over-reliance on sensing and diagnostic technologies can interfere with the healthy development and fidelity of infant and carer relationships, because a 'good carer's response is based on grasping the cause of emotions rather than simply acting on the emotions displayed' (Sharkey and Sharkey 2010: 175). Children take cues from their carers about appropriate emotional responses in novel situations. A child that is cared for by a pattern recognition tool, themselves, becomes embroiled in a system of anticipatory caring. Such a technological dynamic potentially conditions the child to predict responses to the surface behaviours of others rather than copying the human carer's impulse to identify their motivations before presenting a solution: an echolocative approach to emotional mapping and problem-solving.

The final part of the book explores what happens when you take echolocation strategies and abstract their potential so that they can reveal internal, hybrid and artificial versions of the human condition. The next shift explored, then, is that from domotic self-surveillance to the speculative channels of contemporary AI-driven phenomena such as inner voice extraction platforms, generative music systems, virtual companions and thanabots that digitize the dead. The final four chapters are connected through the otherworldly promise of emergent technologies, but they are divergent in terms of their focus, user profiles and social impact. The normalization of self-surveillance is considered as it extends and is transformed into spectral economics that rescore the human experience and its relationship to intimacy, musicality and mortality.

PART IV
AMBIENT INTERFACES, ARCANE INTELLIGENCES

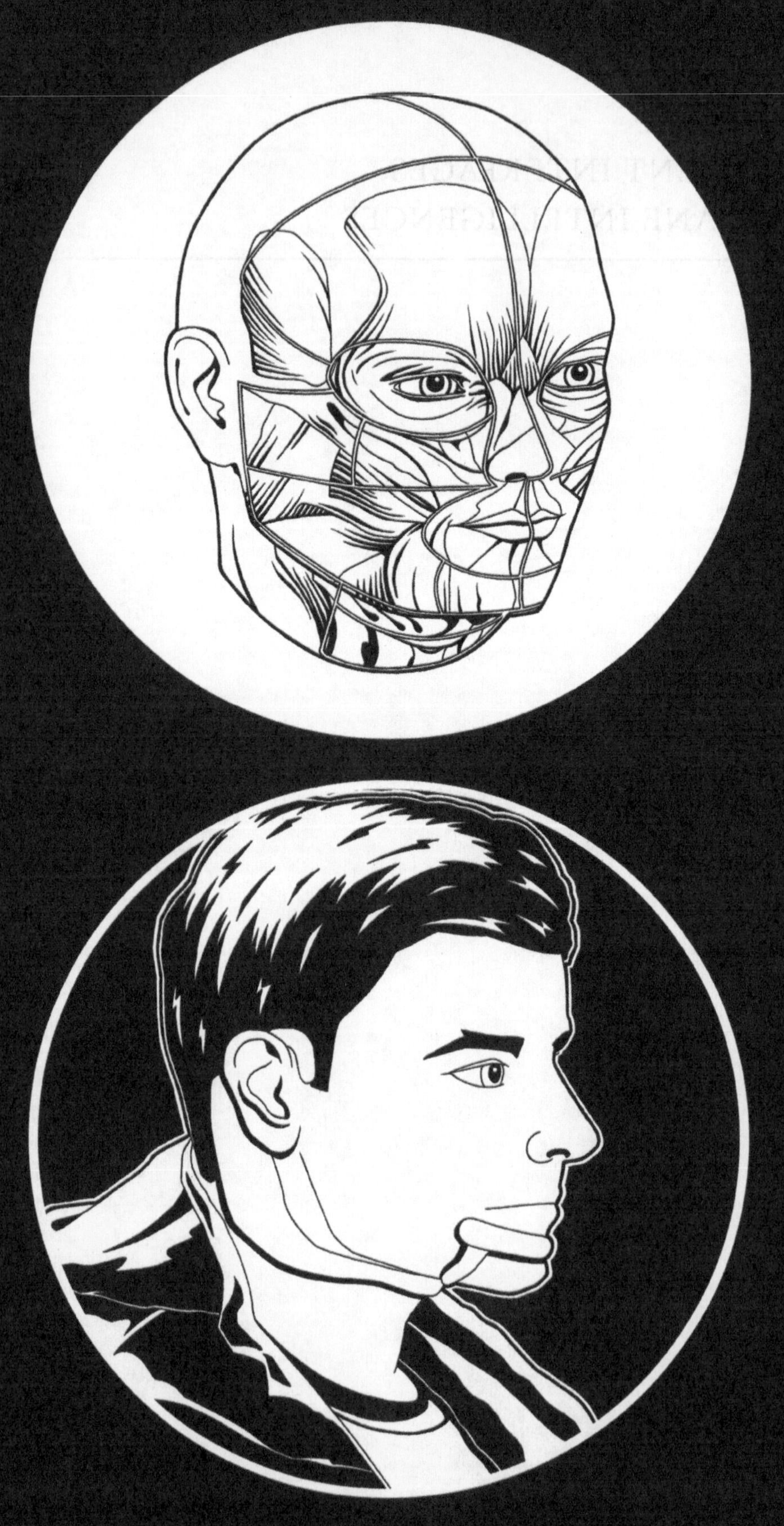

CHAPTER 13
ALTEREGO

Process

The first chapter in the final part focuses on an emergent wearable neural interface called the 'AlterEgo'. The AlterEgo and brain-computer interfaces (BCI) like it change the parameters of audition and surveillance and mark a radical shift in the technologies and processes considered thus far. As the forms of surveillance explored throughout the text have progressed into increasingly intimate relationships with regard to our rhythms of everyday living, places of dwelling and methods of communication, this chapter focuses on a technology that breaches the somatic threshold by capturing the quietest and most concealed of human expressions – the inner voice.

The AlterEgo technology has been developed by research assistant Arnav Kapur and Professor Pattie Maes of the Fluid Interfaces group at the MIT Media Lab. On the overview page of the project website, the device is described as:

> a non-invasive, wearable, peripheral neural interface that allows humans to converse in natural language with machines, artificial intelligence assistants, services, and other people without any voice – without opening their mouth, and without externally observable movements – simply by articulating words internally. The feedback to the user is given through audio, via bone conduction, without disrupting the user's usual auditory perception, and making the interface closed-loop. (AlterEgo 2018: online)

The process of internally articulating words is known as subvocalization, silent speech or auditory reassurance. As a form of internal expression, it produces micro gestures in the larynx and in connected muscles that are linked with speaking. These visually undetectable movements are not perceivable by the naked eye and are known as neuromuscular or endogenous electrical signals. It is these gestures that are picked up by AlterEgo's seven surface-based electrodes that line the side of the mouth and jaw. Having been identified, the granular expressions are processed by a modular neural network-based pipeline and converted into words.

The prospective utility of the AlterEgo situates it as a pre-emission audile technique for the twenty-first century – the most recent variant of a listening procedure documented by Jonathan Sterne in *The Audible Past: Cultural Origins of Sound Reproduction* (2003). For Sterne, audile technique refers to a skill for distinguishing the nature of sounds, a capacity historically embodied in the work of two exemplary professions – the physician and the telegrapher. The difference here is that the AlterEgo represents the emergence of silent speech at the nexus of the soma-machine interface: subvocalization as a sounding board of the auditive threshold – an intimate transmutation of speech recognition and the subsequent external amplification thereof.

Returning to the project website, we are invited to consider what a machine-assisted body can do and be. This is made evident in the Panglossian forecast that the 'AlterEgo aims to combine humans and computers – such that computing, the internet and AI would weave into human personality as a "second self" and augment human cognition and abilities' (AlterEgo 2018: online). This is not a reference to the quantified self as such, nor is it the data twin. It is an alternative conception of how emergent technologies such as AI and advanced bone conduction devices come to be spliced with flesh.

The proposition of the second self refers to the device's name, AlterEgo. It sounds out the conviction that if it can be located, an alternate self can be communicated with. The technology's premise is that it can, within reasonable bounds of accuracy (92 per cent), make that connection and extract the inner voice (Mack 2018). The idea that AI or elements of the internet could help constitute a second self is an arresting and provocative speculation. For those of a cynical disposition, it evokes the *Manchurian Candidate's* (Condon 1959) conditioning of a human drone, or the CIA's 1957–64 'MKUltra project' at McGill University's Allan Memorial Institute (CIA 2018). It was here that Donald Ewen Cameron conducted experiments which involved psychic driving, the re-engineering of the inner voice to destroy a sense of the self.

From an optimistic and analytical point of view, one could consider that 'in addition to being able to understand what a user wants to communicate without vocalising, the device can also "talk back" to the user via bone conduction that doesn't obstruct the ear canal like regular earbuds' (Mack 2018: online). For those with locked-in syndrome or those who have suffered a stroke, this non-invasive device offers a direct interface with a range of contemporary technologies, platforms and people. It could open new vectors for social contact and avenues for relationship building, as well as offer a crucial communication channel in times of emergency. What is for certain is that this device and others like it, such as the Neuralink 'brain computer interface' (Neuralink 2025: online), question core conceptions of 'sense'.

The 'inner touch', according to Daniel Heller-Roazen (2009), is that sense which is core to our perception of ourselves as hearing and seeing beings, existing in the world. If this is core to how we navigate the entanglements of time, space and self, then the inner voice is our metronome, compass and conductor. An AI-enabled technology that can connect to and channel the inner voice speaks to tracts of identity formation being pioneered and potentially manipulated or even owned. Geared to the centre of the self, the AlterEgo is Joe Meek's ode to interplanetary exploration, *I Hear a New World* (1991) set in the *Innerspace* (Dante 1987) of the human body.

Recording

When showcasing the AlterEgo at a TED talk, Arnav Kapur shares his motivation for developing the technology as wanting to help 'millions of people who struggle with using natural speech' (Kapur in TED 2019 5: 12). In the question and answer session afterwards, the host Shoham Harad asks whether, in five years' time, there could be a 'weaponized version of this' (Harad in TED 2019 7: 32). Arnav's answer is definitive: the device does not record thoughts but utterances from the 'voluntary nervous system' meaning that users 'deliberately have to engage to communicate with the device' (Kapur in TED 2019: 8: 4) for it to store commands.

Patent filings for a 'Silent Speech Interface' (SSI) issued in the same year, however, give a more nuanced breakdown of the inputs from the body to the device and surrounding systems. It suggests that for the technology to work it must constantly monitor a wide range of largely involuntary data. The patent design filed by Kapur presents a device that measures the low-voltage electrical signals generated by the user's speech muscles, such as the larynx, during internal articulation. The patent itemizes a total of seventeen muscles involved in tongue movement, adjustment of the palate and back of the throat during normal speech and during silent speech, comprising:

> geniohyoid, mylohyoid, genioglossus, superior longitudinal, inferior longitudinal, transverse, vertical, hyoglossus, palatoglossus, styloglossus, levator palatini, musculus uvulae, tensor palatini, palatopharyngeus, superior pharyngeal constrictor, medial pharyngeal constrictor, and inferior pharyngeal constrictor.
> (Kapur, Kapur and Maes 2019: 8)

Most of these muscles are not exclusively used for speech. Muscles such as the geniohyoid, mylohyoid and styloglossus are also used for swallowing and controlling breathing, meaning that they are constantly producing electrical signals regardless of whether the user is engaged in any form of speech. Therefore, the device must constantly be listening for specific electrical patterns that denote speech and identifying 'signals of interest' by constantly recording four-second clips or 'frames' of electrical activity. The patent includes scenarios where all activity information is sent directly to a database to train a neural network so that it can continually fine-tune its identification of signals of interest.

It follows that the AlterEgo is listening not only to our speech but also to the coughs, swallowing, breathing and other intricate activities carried out by the tracked muscles. This produces a surplus of highly personal data that could be mined for a range of purposes. Additionally, tracking must go beyond listening for muscle movement, because '[in] some cases, the internal articulation (which is detected by the SSI system) causes no movement of the Articulator Muscles' (Kapur, Kapur and Maes 2019: 8) meaning the device must also record 'in efferent nerve fibres' (Kapur, Kapur and Maes 2019: 8), (the nerve signals sent by the brain), regardless of whether they are translated into muscle movement. So, although the device is not recording the brain's waves directly, it is collecting and trying to interpret the signals sent by the body to speech muscles, even when they do not move.

As with many audio surveillance projects and operations throughout history, one of the main problems with accruing good intelligence is noise. In clinical trials with multiple sclerosis patients suffering from speech deterioration (Kapur, Kapur and Maes

2019: 3), the process of capturing data in a controlled clinical setting was far from straightforward. It required experimentation using a graphical user interface to find 'feature-dense signals' (Kapur, Kapur and Maes 2019: 3) as subjects pre-vocalized fifteen sentences, such as 'Good morning how are you?'. Sensors in the AlterEgo system listen for minuscule electrical signals (as small as eight millionths of a volt) and, as a result, any signals related to silent speech can be disrupted by other minute signals in the same range. Such phenomena include the base electrical noise of the sensors themselves, tiny changes in the conductivity of the sensors, the participant's heartbeat and higher frequencies emitted by other processes in the body. To better identify the pre-vocalization signal during the experiment, both high and low frequencies that were irrelevant to the process were digitally filtered out. Drifts in the signal, along with waveform artefacts, were then algorithmically normalized before labelled samples could be used to inform machine learning.

While these problems are likely to be solved in the future by automated solutions, the problem of noise from micro-voltage readings in less controlled environments is likely to persist to some degree. A review of research on how to effectively remove noise from electroencephalography brain activity readings by Grega Repovš notes that the best way to remove noise from signals of interest is to eliminate them from the recording environment entirely, through the use of a Faraday Cage or a suitably insulated environment. Other suggested measures include asking patients to remain still to avoid the noise of muscle movement and changes in the conductivity of the sensors due to sweat secretion (Repovš 2010). A neuromuscular fine-tuning of what it means to listen in.

Transgression

MIT Media Lab, the research institute that announced the work of AlterEgo to the world, is one of the most prominent examples of the modern digital lab that has defined itself by taking a boldly disruptive approach to multisensory media innovation. In their book *Technocrats of the Imagination: Art, Technology, and the Military-Industrial Avant-Garde* (2020), John Beck and Ryan Bishop reflect on the Cold War history of the technology 'lab' as a site that permits experimental transgression and radical collaboration in the name of societal good. Its roots can be traced to the 1960s innovative lab projects, such as Bell Labs' celebrated 'Experiments in Arts and Technology' (E.A.T.) collective.

Sound artists and musicians involved in the E.A.T. collective included the likes of John Cage and Robert Rauschenberg, who were drawn to the lab by electronic music pioneers such as Max Mathews (Dayal 2016; La Prade 2002). Mathews's research into what he termed 'instrumental music' produced by computers had come out of the Bell Labs synthetic speech programme (Mathews 1963). The E.A.T. programme, meanwhile, was paid for by the taxes of telephone companies. It sought to amplify the radical potential of art and progress the aims of technology through interdisciplinary practices that, when brought together by artists and scientists, created social and cultural benefits.

Having died out in the 1970s, the 'lab' had a renaissance in the 2000s as a popular mode for organizing research in response to the meteoric increase in funding and commercial opportunities presented by new digital economies. The disruptive ethos associated with avante-garde artists like Cage and the romantic notions of artistic exceptionalism attached to their works were 'pulled out for use' within the new labs with the hubristic aim of destabilizing the status quo (Beck and Bishop 2020: 12). Reconfigured to operate within the liberalistic conditions of the lab, art and sound practices came to be regulated and normalized by the technology market:

> [A]rt's emancipatory capacity has been codified as its contribution to a culture of competition-driven entrepreneurial dynamism and precarious labor, computationally mediated information flows and privatized spatiotemporal capacities. (Beck and Bishop 2020)

However, the mandate for social change that was an underlying assumption of American society in the 1960s had been eviscerated by the free market rubric used in the United States to counter the socialist ideals of Soviet communism in the final decades of the Cold War. As a result, it is not a core consideration in today's labs. While the artistic mandate of media and sound artists – to disrupt and challenge norms, especially related to the use of technology – has been co-opted by technologists, the 'dormant revolutionary energies of the historical avant-garde [. . . lie . . .] undisturbed' (Beck and Bishop 2020).

On the MIT Media Lab's website, there is evidence of a kind of disruptive arts practice remastered as technological innovation, replete with market-focused interpretations of humanism. Upon querying 'ethics' in regard to the research carried out at the lab, the resulting answer possesses a utopian tone reminiscent of previous artistic manifestos. It declares: 'We are an interdisciplinary research lab working to invent the future of #ethics.' However, on closer inspection, the hashtag 'ethics' is one option in a lengthy drop-down menu of tags that also includes '#neural interfacing and control' (MIT 2025: online). Ethics, research and all other themes and activities on the lab's website find absolute equivalency and ambiguous relationality via the hyper-capitalist logic of the search engine.

Drilling down to the AlterEgo project FAQs page, we are informed that its 'broader social implications . . . still remain to be formally studied' (MIT 2018: online). The pressures that were once placed upon researchers to theorize their works have been released by the valve of techno-optimism that hungrily demands visions of the future, often without fully considering the attendant social or ethical ramifications at work. Once the conceptual space of transgressive technologies is imagined, the next move of many in the burgeoning 'neuroprosthetics' industry has been not to go 'broad', but rather to opt for a medical case study to justify the public good that these technologies can serve.

The AlterEgo project has not been alone in trying to produce a BCI. With the exception of 'CTRL-labs', which were developing armbands for controlling computer game interfaces (Robertson 2018), most BCIs focus on the paralysis of normal bodily functions. Neuralink, bought by Elon Musk in 2016 (Regalado 2017) and 'Synchron labs', backed by tech billionaires Bill Gates and Jeff Bezos, both rely on the intracranial insertion of their device directly into the subject's brain to provide new motility (Taylor 2024). As with the subjects in the AlterEgo medical study cited above, the stated mission of many of these projects is to reintroduce 'normal' physical agency into the subject's body.

The distinction provides important ethical justifications. In Walter Glannon's review of the risks of BCIs, he states that its functioning 'outside of the subject's awareness and without any apparent conscious contribution from the subject . . . appears to undermine autonomous agency, with the person's actions traceable to an artificial source' (2016: 6). However, apparently convinced by the cultural power of the lab and the assumed progressive intentions of its technologies, he immediately finds a special case for those whose bodies do not work 'normally':

> The fact that DBS operates outside of a person's awareness does not undermine but instead supports behavior control and free will by modulating dysregulated neural circuits that generate and sustain thought and action. . . . The device does not interfere with but enables the formation and translation of conscious intentions in promoting effective decision-making. (2016: 6)

The assumption that technological progress is ultimately beneficial recognizes what cultural theorist Mercedes Bunz describes as the 'forceful and fabulous capacity [for technology] to create a different world', perhaps leaving Glannon and other ethicists in a hurry to prepare us for it. But it also fails to consider that 'the worlds that appear do not automatically lead in any progressive direction' (Bunz 2020: 4). While the technology will be tested under the close scrutiny of medical professionals and in accordance with the strictures of medical ethics in these cases, the longer-term purpose of testing undoubtedly lies in elective surgery. In Elon Musk's 2020 product demo of Neuralink, he opined that brain implants could cure paralysis, returning a patient to 'full body motion' (Regalado 2020: online). However, he saw the Neuralink as a 'general population device' which acted 'kind of like a Fitbit in your skull, with tiny wires' – in the future, billions would have them (Regalado 2020). Interpreting the cultural desire for progress at any cost, Musk conjured a bold transgressive vision of the future: one that hinges on the creative ingenuity of the Neuralink lab and the co-opting of 'artistic licence' to do whatever it takes to get there.

Worlds

In literature, the inner voice is often portrayed as a boundary marker between the world of the self, the world shared with others, and the inner monologue of mental anguish and polite external silence. Such a threshold becomes even more apparent in literary works that celebrate complex psychological realism, such as *The Corrections* (2001) by Jonathan Franzen and *On Chesil Beach* (2007) by Ian McEwan. In these books, the verbose quantity of each character's inner monologue is always at catastrophic risk of breaching the divide and breaking into speech, but rarely transgresses.

Alternatively, the inner voice may be the hiding place of malicious threat. In Charles Forsman's graphic novel (2013) and subsequent television drama (2017–19) *The End of the F*cking World*, a boy meets a girl and narrates his intention to murder her, even as they become a romantic couple. The tension between silent and vocalized speech in these fictions highlights differences between the world that we are at risk within when we speak and the mental world that has no immediate consequences. It is this neural spatiality that supposedly offers refuge from external probing. Charles Fernyhough and Anna M. Borghi confirm such thinking when they propose that the private worlds of inner speech have often been 'resistant to scientific study' (Fernyhough and Borghi 2023: 1180). They follow this, however, with a note of optimism concerning new neuroscientific techniques such as those used by the AlterEgo team, which are rendering subvocalization 'tractable' in scientific circles.

Overall, Fernyhough and Borghi's (2023) report focuses on relatively benign and constructive uses of inner speech. Self-regulation, action planning and creative thinking are all summarized as being its key functions. Many similar studies have sought ways to instrumentalize the function of the inner voice and define its role in relation to domain-specific problems such as motivation and task completion. However, other research has more cartographic aims: to expand the territory of the scientific listener at a global level by monitoring the inner speech of 'typical and atypical populations' to find their differences (Alderson-Day et al. 2015: 110). In such contexts, the world view of the scientific listener is essentially totalitarian. It must purge all subjectivity from each region it perceives through its increasingly sensitive technical apparatus. It hopes to rationalize the inner voice, creating a dictionary of its language and dialects with the surplus benefit of making us healthier, happier and more productive.

The desire to conquer the inner voice and discover its discordant relationship with the amplified version can be aligned with the observational imperative of Post-Enlightenment science: to free the world from the notions of philosophical and theological good and evil; to hear first-hand the body's outputs through rationalized measures, without the noise of human opinion, morality or emotion. In the *History of Madness* (1961), Michel Foucault describes how the emerging sciences of the mind grew from the newly built asylums of the late nineteenth and twentieth centuries. Within the walls of the asylum, the subjective internal voice of the 'madman' was emptied out into the external yell, thus providing a sonified opportunity to record and analyse its harrowing message.

Foucault's assessment of the asylum was damning; it had failed to free society of madness. By conducting a form of embedded listening through the institution and trying to understand the inner workings of the human brain through scientific means, it made the concept of madness an essential part of the human psyche. 'If it freed the madman from the inhumanity of his chains, it also chained the mad to man and his truth' (Foucault 2013: 278). Listening too closely to the inner voice may be fraught with similar dangers, especially when the emerging agency of AI is taken into consideration.

If the AlterEgo is successful and the scientific listener is able to hear, word for word, the voice of a subject's inner dialogue, where are the boundaries that demarcate rationality? Foucault's description of the nineteenth-century asylum established a world set apart from normal society – a scientific realm built from the liberal intention to house madness away from the world's cruelly exacting expectations. In contrast, the domain of the inner voice is precariously situated in the centre of social experience. Expanding listening into its realms so that we can hear our secret and unfiltered utterances burrows a tunnel under the walls of the rational world, a subterranean listening post that is prone to rupture and counter-intelligence: Operation Grey Matter.

Prediction

Subvocalization is described by the AlterEgo's developers as 'the characteristic inner voice in humans that is usually noticeable while reading and can be voluntarily triggered while speaking to oneself' (Kapur, Kapur and Maes 2018: 46). While currently an interface based on voluntary triggering of internal vocalization, the AlterEgo makes recordable the phenomenon of autocommunication, something that once seemed impossible to study. What was once a covert and esoteric form of agency is becoming knowable and, with enough digital storage and computational capacity, theoretically speaking, predictable.

To be able to foretell the effervescent hum of the inner voice is not simply to understand the deliberate 'speech acts' of the mind and translate them for a personal helper, voiced by a Bluetooth wearable. In order to identify deliberate commands, the machine must – initially, for the purposes of elimination – record, process and predict the involuntary. 'Intrusive thoughts' are classified by mental health specialists as disturbing internal voices that affect those with or without specific mental health problems and are defined as 'distinct, identifiable' cognitive events that are 'unwanted, unintended, and recurrent' (Clark 2005: 4).

The average person experiences unintended or unwanted thoughts for a variety of reasons: creative bursts of inspiration, the sudden chill of grief, anticipation of meetings, thoughts related to an incomplete task or the repetitious melodic bugging of an earworm. All can strike on an involuntary basis, betraying emotional states or camouflaging information that one may be attempting to suppress (Gourley et al. 2021: 127). The editing of these thoughts, after they arise, supports our ability to shape our inner life or adjust perceptions of the self for healthy or unhealthy reasons (Gourley et al. 2021: 130). The logic of inner voice prediction, once digitized, is that the vocabulary of the involuntary is a noise that can be – and therefore should be – cancelled.

Cancellation of the involuntary voice might be desirable for many. For people suffering from schizophrenia, the contents of intrusive thoughts can be horrifying to both the sufferer and those around them and, despite the destructive guilt and self-recrimination felt within, are irrepressible and therefore not culturally 'punishable' (Liu et al. 2021: 228). For those without mental illness, there is a spectrum of responsibility borne out on the outer valence of their expression. Overcoming intrusive thoughts is part of the healing journey for PTSD sufferers, recovering addicts or those attempting to overcome implicit biases related to racism and other prejudices (Liu et al. 2021). Through devices such as the AlterEgo, that which is silenced and rendered unconscious could be picked up in algorithmic repositories and made accessible to the deep listening manoeuvres of government.

Given the history of governments conflating prediction with prescription, the line between noise cancellation and thought amplification is a tricky one. George Orwell's political prediction in his novel *1984* (1949), that there could be a thought police able to read people's minds in the future, is now treated as an old-school dystopian obsession with defunct twentieth-century totalitarian logic. The idea of the thought police is also used as a grenade in the polemical turf war about what is acceptable 'free speech' in the United States and Europe (Deacon 2024). In the latter case, externalized speech is ironically seen as a direct synonym of inner thought and, therefore, any attempt to control debate within certain terms is considered to be thought control. However, it is in the power to interpret and predict unexpressed cognitive dissonance that the predictive algorithms surely have the most latent power.

As covered in Part II, it has proven to be incredibly difficult for state bodies to produce actionable forms of prediction from large amounts of surveillance data. From the archives left behind by the Stasi to the data leaks of the Echelon era, real-time prediction of enemy movements has rarely been possible or even been the actual purpose of mass surveillance. At best, preventative connections were made, but more often the data has been misread or deliberately misused to justify targeted persecution. In Russia, surveillance gathered is allegedly most helpful for agencies seeking to constructively incarcerate known dissidents. The Snowden leaks showed how quantitatively weak algorithmic patterns were used to rationalize indiscriminate military targeting by Western Allied forces in their War on Terror. The real power of being able to predict the flow of intrusive thoughts in the minds of general populations therefore lies in broadcasting them.

Certainly, inner voice prediction is a considerable bounty for propagandists. The Russian state's 'Internet Research Agency' is accredited by Elizaveta Gaufman with being more successful through its subversion of media than many of its geopolitical adversaries in 'changing people's behaviour or beliefs in line with [. . . its] government agenda' (2021: 117). Given that the inner monologue is activated in the process of reading and writing media texts, a high-fidelity connection with the words of the mind, when absorbing and composing social media, closes the interpretive loop. This, in turn, allows strategic media control to fine-tune even more divisive messaging in the media of enemy populations. The translation of the inner voices of populations into hackable streams of digital text would be music to the ears of the Internet Research Agency and its equivalents in other countries.

That said, propaganda might not even be necessary given the potentially latent power to directly synthesize and orchestrate intrusive thoughts. The noise of unwelcome or involuntary thoughts can be cancelled, but in that quiet space that is composed, there is no reason why new thoughts should not be somehow simulated algorithmically. Data packet inspection of the inner voice provides the tools to automate counterthoughts. To predict that this will happen is perhaps the worst form of techno-determinism. But algorithmic inner voice translation has massive, nefarious potential: the deafening ability to broadcast, overshadowing the co-dependent fantasy of being listened to by ingeniously helpful machines.

Even assuming that listeners-in have ahistorically benign motivations, it is not clear how company and state agents might cope with the unsavoury quality of intrusive thoughts that are often characterized by their vexing nature. The Stasi's totalizing reach into all areas of a population's lives only increased its paranoid retribution. Hypervigilance against danger, writes psychologist Charles Fernyhough, can 'lead people to incorrectly "hear" the threat they were anticipating' (Fernyhough 2016: 271). Listening for the sound of a proverbial snapping twig of a population's mind chatter, while hooked up to AlterEgo, or alternatives like Neuralink, may bring about punishing and punishable streams of thought, voluntary or otherwise.

Intimacy

The AlterEgo is part of a history of media cultures and technologies that have sought to record and inject voices into our most private conversations with ourselves. This has been achieved through the production of acoustic tropes and the design of input and output methodologies aimed specifically at tapping into, and expressing, the intimate qualities of the inner voice. In historical terms, the foremost example is the written word. Since the invention of writing, the lexical structure of speaking has been used to transfer thoughts between writer and speaker-reader, who, like a musician playing a new melody from a musical sheet, would commonly speak the syntactical features of a symbolic script out loud in a particular order to listen out for its meaning.

The ubiquitous relationship between external speaking and reading later became internalized through the historically more recent phenomenon of silent reading. In his book, *The Voices Within: The History and Science of How We Talk to Ourselves* (2016), Charles Fernyhough suggests that descriptive written works like novels inject multiple characters, fictional and real, through the activation of inner simulated speech processes. Narrators and the subjects of their stories are synthesized through a process of silent incantation so that our words become theirs, with distinct voices from our imagination. In addition to flooding this channel with text that resembles spoken anecdote, writers such as Jane Austen and Raymond Carver have sought to excavate their own inner voice, hacking its intimacies in order to render characters that are more relatable.

As part of an artistic trend towards 'stream of consciousness' writing, Modernist writers in the early twentieth century adapted the written word to represent a rushing, unfinished immediacy. James Joyce used fleeting phrases full of intimate inferences to memories, sounds and images stored within, a sort of para-speech that indicates its encyclopaedic familiarity through semi-opaque reference and ellipsis:

Back to the world again. Enough of this place. Brings you a bit nearer every time.
Last time I was here was Mrs Sinico's funeral. Poor papa too. The love that kills.
(Joyce 1922: 110)

In the tradition of stream-of-consciousness writing, the intimate language of the self steadily transforms into a media trope – a dialect or stylization of language particularly designed to communicate the fictional experiences, as we might speak them secretly to ourselves in the same situations. For all its intimate detail and immediacy, it is an acousmatic trompe l'oeil, playing a trick on us for artistic effect. As depictions of the inner voice migrated to film, further stylizations occurred that allowed the inner monologue to become increasingly mediatized. An early example exists in Alfred Hitchcock's *Murder!* (1930). The protagonist agonizes over a mistake he fears he has made as a juror in a murder case. He looks at a mirror, his lips unmoving, as we hear him questioning himself: 'Who drank that brandy? Why didn't I force that point home to them? Easy to think these things out afterwards'. The cinematic trope of the inner voice as voiceover has become familiar to film and TV audiences, providing intimate insight into characters and situations.

The AlterEgo can be understood as part of a continuum in the media augmentation of our conversations with ourselves. In a paper published in 2018, that described coupling 'human and machine intelligence in a complementary symbiosis' (Kapur, Kapur and Maes 2018: 51), the privacy and primacy of these conversations are presented as key features of the system. Tapping the inner voice would allow users to interact with their computer without being overheard by eavesdroppers (and other listening devices), and without it being hijacked by the voices of others. Rather than being positioned as the ultimate eavesdropper of intimate thoughts, it is imagined as a doting and attentive confidante. This is a similar 'emotional market position', albeit on a global scale, to the one taken by Apple. In offering new voice assistant systems like 'Apple Intelligence' (Apple 2024) the company is upping the ante with sophisticated Retrieval Augmented Generation systems: technologies capable of synthesizing humanistic expression and characteristics alongside task-based activity and personalization controls.

There are, of course, less corporate ways of thinking about how the inner voice is co-opted as an output channel for digital media. In 2023, artists Kyle McDonald and Lauren Lee McCarthy presented their artwork *Voice in my Head* at the International Documentary Film Festival Amsterdam (IDFA). It offered users limited access to an internalized assistant. Following a short period of training the application, and through listening to their conversations, it would use participants' prior instructions to offer them real-time advice. Experimenting with the effect of augmenting the inner monologue, the training process was able to synthesize the voice of a user so that the digital inner voice that they heard sounded like their own.

In conversation with other participants, the artists and interviewer Kent Bye agreed that users were 'elated' to be able to replace their usually critical internal voice and participate with positive feedback: that 'they just felt like they were on cloud nine listening to their own voice speak that' (Bye 2023: online). In *Voice in my Head*, McDonald and

McCarthy introduce both the LLM and text-to-speech innovations into the set of media technologies that artfully augment the inner voice and our relation to it. Such advances by entertainers and artists continue to modulate our relationships with subvocalization and help to presage a future media stack that relies on the rejection of personal intimacy in favour of a system that can constantly overhear and overdub our thoughts-as-media.

Voice

For Russian psychologist Lev Vygotsky, inner speech is a mode of expression that helps us comprehend cognitive development. It is an internal communication mechanism that children employ to help inform and orient the way they think, which subsequently translates into actions and behavioural patterns (Vygotsky 1978). As well as pointing to the early developmental stages of young minds and their senses of self, the inner voice, and more pointedly its extraction, signals new ways of thinking about the body's relationship to waveforms. Beyond that, the AlterEgo questions the province of the sensorium and the role the inner voice plays in narrating external stimuli transferring through it.

Behavioural formation and modification are both deeply influenced by the internal monologue as it composes meaning from the information flowing through the sensory apparatus. For philosopher and political theorist Fredric Jameson, being able to augment such processes is as much a call to arms as it is to neurons. By exhorting us to expand our sensorium and grow 'new organs' (Jameson 1991: 80), co-author Toby Heys notes that Jameson

> presents us with another clue as to how future modes of communication will bypass the traditional employment of sensory mechanisms. It is a suggestion that ameliorates Maurice Merleau-Ponty's model of the habitual body from being impelled to act in a recurrent loop of cause and effect and instead urges for a new generation of informational dynamics to renegotiate comprehensions of being in the world. (Heys 2019: 182)

For AlterEgo developer Arnav Kapur, '[t]he motivation for this was to build an IA device – an intelligence-augmentation device' (Hardesty 2018: online). From AI to IA, the inner voice amplifies its intent to reveal inner complexities and contradictions in a recursive feedback loop – a technologically enhanced tulpa that turns the inside out. The inner voice is recast as a divinatory form of call and response. It enunciates future modes of expression, a waveformed convergence of biological and technological systems.

The instrumentalization of internal dialogue repositions it from merely being a method of revelation for cultural outputs such as books, songs and poems. As the final vestiges of the waveformed self are surfaced, neural mechanisms become more evident and their potential to interface with technology increases. For the developers of the AlterEgo, the oral synthesis of somatic and emergent digital systems is paramount.

'Our idea was: Could we have a computing platform that's more internal, that melds human and machine in some ways and that feels like an internal extension of our own cognition?' (Kapur in Hardesty 2018: online). Here, the promise of the cyborg is realized not through the bioengineering of nanotechnologies within the body, but through the manifestation of thought as an extrinsic waveform.

In the enhanced anatomies of our future selves, frequencies and somatic materiality bleed into each other. Julian Henriques's sonic body that 'implies either and both the body of the sound and the sound of the body' (2003: 471) is realized through a wider spectrum of frequencies than those perceivable by the human ear. The AlterEgo presages a time when future thought-perceiving agents such as those imagined by David Cronenberg in *Scanners* (1981) can deliver the predictive justice imagined in Philip K. Dick's *Minority Report* (1956): a design focused on the past as much as the future. Oscillating between precognition and retrocognition, between sound and unsound, it is a documentary voice that speaks to selective memory as much as to prediction.

It is, after all, the controlling of past, present and future narratives that any surveillance-bound culture ultimately strives to achieve. If a quantum state of acceptance across all the folds of social, technical and economic spheres occurs, a storied superpositioning can be enacted, one that rationalizes that culture's own inevitable ascendancy. We have witnessed this abhorrent dynamic at work before in the Nazis' inhumane methods. We are witnessing it again, in a politically unstable world that appears to be demanding the amplification of ego-driven voices rather than the delivery of reflective and thoughtful introspection that can come from deep learning.

Fidelity

In noisy environments, it is difficult to hear oneself think. Sonic geographies reflect the external surroundings of a listener but also move into them. Internal monologues become difficult to discern. For some, such as those with schizophrenia (as previously discussed) or those with debilitating anxiety or low self-esteem, this is a welcome state, a respite. Being unable to effectively listen internally, to be shut out of one's own internal amplification system, equates to a relief. Interference or deafening sound becomes a balm akin to the use of white noise to drown out the high-pitched tones that tinnitus sufferers endure, night and day.

Through this filter, the dense and complex textures of noise are celebrated for their maximal characteristics. Noise is choreographed in a dance of affect that refutes acoustic ecologist R. Murray Schafer's desire to rid the world of it, along with its aural derivatives of chaos, vulgarity and negativity. For Schafer, 'If we have a hope of improving the acoustic design of the world, it will be realizable only after the recovery of silence as a positive state in our lives. Still the noise in the mind: that is the first task – then everything else will follow in time' (1993: 259). For acoustic ecologists, noise is the killer of the mind. For the AlterEgo, noise opens new channels into it.

In lo-fidelity locales of vocal exchange, such as factories or conflict zones, the AlterEgo finds potential efficacy. 'Georgia Tech College of Computing's Thad Starner – as quoted on the MIT website . . . believes that in the fullness of time Alter Ego could eventually be used to communicate in high-noise environments, or even as part of military special operations' (Starner in Mason 2018: online). If there is an air of inevitability about the final part of this statement, it is because it is easy to grasp how hi-fidelity access to discreet internal processes of the human body could be deployed for purposes that are not adjacent to the 'tech for good' movement.

In AlterEgo's unsound world, the more noise there is, the more reason there is to turn to technology eliding traditional forms of sonic communication. The proposition that urban environments are becoming quieter due to acoustically conscious design is countered by the observation that we are constantly attached to mobile speakers and have earbuds blooming in our ears. We are also soundtracking our lives in more purposefully nuanced ways than ever before, noise-cancelling soundscapes we do not find favourable or conducive. We eat, sleep, fuck, party, fight, grieve and socialize in a diverse range of musical textures. More music, more sound, more noise – layers and layers of frequencies that extend and compress the listener's will.

The louder and more complex our sonic circumstances are, the more compelling it is to imagine a cultural shift away from vocal expression in all its overstated glory. If we marry sonic overload with the normalization of *Maskirovka* – that strategy dependent on the oversaturation of dis/misinformation into a communications ecology to problematize claims to truth – we find ourselves in a lo-fidelity echo chamber whose resonant frequency is disorientation. It feels as though our digital habitats are becoming incrementally combative, almost as if they are 'designed, quite simply, to keep adversaries permanently off-balance' (Elliot 2018). Has the sound of confusion ever felt so well informed?

Amidst such uncertainty, one can conceive why a technology that promises to deliver the untouched inner voice sounds attractive. Even if future marketing gambits write themselves, there are other ways to think through the implications of the AlterEgo. The internal dialogue and the channelling of it could be apprehended through the sonic fiction of J. G. Ballard's 'The Sound-Sweep'. This is a short story about a young frequency-based refuse collector who lives in an ultrasonic world where 'noise, noise, noise . . . (is) the greatest single disease-vector of civilization' (1960: 52). Describing the city as an environment that needs frequency-based detritus cleared from its streets, Ballard does in pulp form what Schafer did academically. Ballard writes,

> when super-saturation was reached after one of the summer holiday periods, the sonic pressure fields would split and discharge, venting back into the stockades a nightmarish cataract of noise, raining on to the sound-sweeps not only the howling of cats and dogs, but the multi-lunged tumult of cars, express trains, fairgrounds and aircraft, the cacophonic *musique concrète* of civilization. (1960: 52)

Internal dialogue as the musique concrète of the body? The manifestation of the ineffable into something tangible and documentable. Through 'The Sound-Sweep', Ballard foretold future modes of inaudible transmission, as 'the public discovered that the silence was golden, that after leaving the radio switched to an ultrasonic channel for an hour or so a pleasant atmosphere of rhythm and melody seemed to generate itself spontaneously around them' (1960: 48). In the AlterEgo's version of extended reality, the inner voice becomes an unsound version of the ultrasonic – an internal articulation that modulates future forms of exchange and expression.

Science-Fiction or the theory fiction of science? Either way, the AlterEgo's instrumentality means that the notion of fidelity is getting a reboot. What does the promise of accurate transmission mean when the inaudible or the unspoken registers at a micro level? If the aural covenant of fidelity is being reengineered, then the act of listening also needs to be recalibrated for a future where the voice as we know it becomes excessive or redundant. Gone the way of tails and prehensile feet, audible articulation could become 'collateral damage' in the slow aural conflict of evolution.

HOME TAPING IS
KILLING MUSIC
AND IT'S ILLEGAL

CHAPTER 14
JUKEBOX

Process

In April 2020, OpenAI's website announced the new software 'Jukebox' as 'a neural net that generates music, including rudimentary singing, as raw audio in a variety of genres and artist styles' (OpenAI 2020a: online). It was prior to the private source launch of GPT-3 that would form the basis for ChatGPT. OpenAI was still maintaining a 'tech for good' style open-source approach to its research, and the accompanying AI model was published on the software collaboration platform GitHub. In terms of the motivation behind the project, the same landing page declares a desire to 'continue to push the boundaries of generative models' (OpenAI 2020a: online), to serve 'as a tool for human musicians, and increasingly those interested in music but without formal training' (Dhariwal et al. 2020: 11).

As with most early AI innovations in the area of creative production, the researchers noted that Jukebox AI's results showed 'a significant gap between these generations and human-created music' (OpenAI 2020a: online). Jukebox AI shares something else in common with many of those approximations, which is a machine learning architecture based on the sorting, classification and labelling of existing human examples. The training data for Jukebox constituted a scraping of '1.2 million songs (600k of which were in English), paired with the lyrics and metadata from LyricWiki. The metadata included artist, album, genre, and year of the release, along with common moods or playlist keywords associated with each song' (Dhariwal et al. 2020: 5).

If a Jukebox user specifies a genre or artist, the software will try to match its response, having been trained on a list comprising traditional folk, nu-disco, unblack metal, electroclash, Australian hip hop and 598 other designations. These genre IDs are listed in a folder below 7,898 artist IDs (OpenAI 2020b). Training on these designations not only allows the ability to request certain artists and genres but more generally 'reduces entropy' through the learning of musical categorization (OpenAI 2020b: 4). Neither the list of genres nor artists is exhaustive, though they represent a thorough sampling of popular forms of music via an increasingly platform-mediated cultural landscape, where listening is becoming synonymous with streaming.

Jukebox's methodology relies heavily on existing categorical data that has been amassed on music and listener habits over the past two decades. Early music categorization tools like the 'Music Genome Project' were powered by expert human listeners or 'song decoders' (Walker 2009: online). In the late 2000s, paid listeners categorized songs against 250 'genes' designed by the project's musicologist, Nolan Glasser. Genes related to specific song qualities, like the voice (smooth or gravelly?). Expert human listening then trained categorical algorithms to automatically sort the features of music. On musical platforms such as Spotify, genres, taste categories, moods, time periods, subcultures, popularity rankings and even individual licensing agreements with labels affect what the recommendation algorithm will set as the background music to a user's daily life. Spotify will push playlists 'with names like Mood Booster, Happy Hits, Life Sucks, and Coping with Loss to extract what the company claims is subscribers' real-time mood and activity data' (Giblin and Doctorow 2022: 79).

If the creators of Jukebox are aiming to maximize streaming numbers, they may not need the finished product to run the gamut of human emotion or expression. Rebecca Giblin and Cory Doctorow describe how streaming, once sold for its 'on-demand' music library, actually trains listeners to listen passively to 'playlists prepared by algorithms or human curators instead of making their own selections' serving up 'the kind of background music that can be left on all day without fatigue' (Giblin and Doctorow 2022: 80). Automatic music generation could provide streaming services with a glut of practically rights-free music, just like the current tracks featured on their ambient playlists by 'pseudonymous songwriters and performers with no online presence but millions upon millions of streamed song-plays' (Giblin and Doctorow 2022: 81). In the current market, the description by Jukebox developers of a 'great music generation' seems more pragmatic than reductive in that it should be:

> high quality over all time scales: it should have a developing musical and emotional structure across the entire piece, local notes and harmonies that always make sense, nuanced and appropriate small timbral and textural details, and audio recording quality that balances and blends the multiple voices well, and without unwanted noise. (Dhariwal et al. 2020: 11)

Nowhere in their description of 'great music' is there an ounce of affect, but that may be by design.

Recording

Online AI music generation is booming, both figuratively and sonically. Every week, a new platform promises user-friendly, royalty-free, customized music. In 2024, joining Jukebox AI in the web-based rhythm rush were companies such as Suno, Soundraw and Boomy. The website for the Mubert AI music generator, meanwhile, proposes that 'AI music has no boundaries' (Mubert AI 2024: online). Within this apparent free-for-all, convenience is a major draw, as is instant accessibility. If the maxim 'good things take time' could do a mic drop, it would have done so a while ago. It is safe to say that this is one homespun truth that time (and technology) has not been kind to.

The process of recording is being re-engineered, and we are being invited to take part in this transformative shift. It is an enticement that comes with a caveat. Behind the services offered and the no-obligation modes of creativity engaged, the foundational business of data collection is at work. This, as we have heard throughout this book's third and fourth sections, has become business as usual. What is different, however, is what is happening to the process of recording as it relocates its resonance from the studio and places it firmly between the imminence of the database and the choice of the listener.

Capturing information and extracting added value from users who interact with digital technologies has become an acceptable paradigm. In the scheme of things, the choices, activities and predictions connected to music could be perceived as benign data to aggregate and trade. On the other hand, listening habits could be understood to reveal users' most intimate aspirations and emotions. The muscle memory of musical dependency is easily flexed, and when triggered, the choreographed intimacies that interface with organized sound reveal deeply personal data that articulates our most vulnerable traits.

> Streaming platforms cast music as a particularly valuable source of data, offering privileged access to listeners' innermost selves. But they also cast music as an ideal tracking device, accompanying individuals across a variety of social, physical and geographical spaces. In this way, the very attributes that make music so powerful a 'technology of the self' facilitate its transformation into an equally powerful technology of surveillance. (Drott 2018: 233)

Given our cultural tendencies to stream content, it means that such platforms can predict future choices via filters such as geography, age, gender and professional standing. For example, if we ask the rudimentary question: What do forty-five-year-olds in New York listen to at 8 pm on a Saturday night? Streaming platforms have the data to accurately answer such macro enquiries. If such services know who is listening to what, when and why, it is simpler for interested commercial parties to, in turn, know when and where they should be placing adverts for adjacent products and services.

The reason that this is pertinent is because, along with streaming platforms, large technology companies have invested in the capacity to produce, modulate and control the flows of musical content that accompany our lived experiences. As Fabio Morreale notes in his paper on the political and ethical implications of AI music, given our emotional proximity to music and the ways in which we employ it to not only choreograph emotional states but also to create and nullify them, it means it is an incredibly powerful cultural expression to have domain over (Morreale 2021). Morreale notes that such opportunities have led to a series of deals being brokered between IT and music generation companies: TikTok acquired Jukedeck, Warner Music partnered with Endel, Tencent partnered with Amper AI music generation company. Finally, Microsoft partnered with OpenAI, partly for its Jukebox offering (Morreale 2021: 107).

For many mainstream listeners and producers, studio-bound recording processes have become passé. Traditional forms of instrumentation are, to a degree, considered technologies of a bygone era. This echoes the cultural position and flux of music as it becomes textural: flows of sonic content for those who do not wish to make decisions about artists, albums or remixes. If one of the drivers for ambient music (especially if taken from Brian Eno's playbook) is for it to float in and out of perception, then playlist culture advances the principle and raises the stakes by proposing that any musical genre can become ambient.

'The overall function of music has indeed been artfully shaped by streaming services, which turned music listening into a mood-enhancing background experience' (Morreale 2021: 108). It is no surprise to see that ocular culture has followed suit. Netflix has observed that many users of its platform are watching series and films while engaged in other activities such as doom scrolling. Their 'casual viewing' micro-genre is created for second screen consumption. Thus, audience engagement is purposefully strategized as more of an elevator (music) experience than one that is meant to be elevating (Tavlin 2025: online).

The new all-encompassing functionality of sonic consumption, which has its roots in Eric Satie's 'Furniture Music' (Vanel 2013), diverges from tropes concerning liveness and rawness (Petrusich 2024). When music becomes textural, generative AI is in a prime position to take advantage of this transition. That said, based on previous musical consumption habits, there could well be a backlash and an evolution that will not necessarily be easy to predict or control, because 'Music is prophecy. Its styles and economic organization are ahead of the rest of society because it explores, much faster than material reality can, the entire range of possibilities in a given code. It makes audible the new world of things' (Attali 1985: 11).

The codes of audio recording are being re-written in a manner reminiscent of the disruptive innovation of the mid-nineteenth century, when Édouard-Léon Scott de Martinville created the phonautograph in 1857 and Thomas Edison invented the phonograph in 1877. Music and its methods of production and distribution are changing, and they are informing us that cultural shifts will follow in other forms of cultural expression such as gaming, film and animation. The myths, legends and lore of recording will be algorithmically smelted and recast into generative moulds that solidify with the acceptance and normalization of emergent waveformed paradigms. This is lost-wax casting finding new expression in the streamed heat of neural networks.

Transgression

Although undoubtedly disruptive, the recommodification of recorded music via generative algorithms such as Jukebox is not particularly transgressive. Rather, it is a continuation of the history of musical commodification. A report funded by the EU in 2022 found nothing different about the evolution of human authorship and copyright in response to new AI forms of creative labour automation in music except the 'magnitude of potential impact' due to their 'unprecedented scale' (Bulayenko et al. 2022: 107). In his socialist critique, *The Eye of the Master: A Social History of Artificial Intelligence* (2023), Matteo Pasquinelli reflects on the historical relationship between the industrial division of labour and its algorithmic abstraction. Citing both Babbage and Marx, he describes how from the Victorian era onwards, the machine increasingly takes over the operation of the skilled worker's tools and the knowledge of their use, which renders them general workers in the process.

The factory as a procedural machine also takes over the management of interpersonal labour relations. Thus, the machine acquired the 'features of the living' and waged workers 'those of automata' (Pasquinelli 2023: 109). No longer experts in their own right, waged workers become generalists whose 'special skills vanish before the magnitude of the science, natural energy, and social labour that animates machinery' (Pasquinelli 2023: 113). Pasquinelli notes that it is through the process of quantifying and automating skilled tasks that the machine has come to be understood, erroneously, as a force possessing more-than-human intelligence.

Jukebox was released at a point in music history when globally available music platforms such as Spotify and YouTube suddenly allowed any network-connected music listener to bypass particular music scenes and use algorithmic curation to navigate their selection. The automation introduced by these platforms had already positioned the recording musician less as an artist and more as a general waged worker whose job is to build the capacity of the music archive and the machine's cultural knowledge of it. It also positions audience members as general workers who must forgo knowledge of specific musical scenes in the face of the magnitude of algorithmic playlist curation. But for the artist, the reach of these schemes must be tactically countered through the encryption of production files and offline recording techniques – processes that are shared by the recording community in a faltering attempt to avoid the haemorrhaging of their musical intellectual property (New Wave 2024: online).

In such a scheme, the transgressive act is that of frustrating algorithmic systems through the deliberate deletion and destruction of resources and media. Capitalistic logic dictates that nothing should be deleted without its essential labour value being transferred through abstraction for the purposes of automation. For example, any song data should be available to be grouped with a series of similar songs to fine-tune overall genre capacity and knowledge for a musical selection or generation engine. The artistic practices of musicians Bill Drummond and Jimmy Cauty, who formed the musical groups 'The Justified Ancients of Mumu (JAMs)', 'The KLF' and 'The KLF Foundation', sought to transgress these limitations.

Working under the guise of JAMs, Drummond and Cauty created the album *1987 (What the Fuck Is Going On?)* (1987) and took cultural recommodification, in the form of sampling, to its extreme. They appropriated whole sections of ABBA and Beatles songs and made their own works from them. The DIY appropriation of these artists quickly led to a court order for all copies of the album to not only be withdrawn but also destroyed under the supervision of the Mechanical Copyright Protection Society (Higgs 2013). These edicts of corporate destruction apparently surprised the band. It also inspired their *ad hoc* ideology that positioned destruction and deletion as a rejection of the music industry's capacity to commodify countercultural musical works.

In 1992, the KLF had sold more singles than any other act in the world (Higgs 2013). In 1993, they deleted their entire back catalogue of releases in the UK. Then, on the

Scottish island of Jura, working as the K Foundation, they burnt £1 million in cash that they had earned from record sales in their performance artwork *Burn a Million Quid* (1994). The stated purpose of these acts was to evade the organizing logic of commodities and exchange. 'Money tends to control you if you've got it, it dictates what you have to do with it, you either give it away, spend it, invest it . . . we just wanted to be in control of it' (Cauty in Higgs 2013: online).

In the pre-algorithmic era, the accumulation of so much surplus wealth in a short period of time allowed the KLF to carry out their 'ideologically charged crime' (Poole 2000: online). It allowed them to transgress the force that the money exerted on them as music rights owners. In the mid-algorithmic era, networked media and the corporate ideology related to rights management – which shifted from publishing labels to distributors such as Spotify and iTunes (now Apple Music) in the early 2010s – made any remaining sense of artist control over their sonic creations challenging, at best. Somewhat surprisingly, in 2021, Drummond and Cauty capitulated in the face of mass media ubiquity and released their back catalogue on Spotify. Apparently, the surveillance logic of digital music culture renders transgression via ownership futile.

Worlds

The last vestiges of the original Jukebox algorithm are available on Soundcloud as short, generated audio clips described as 'in the style' of well-known American artists Elvis Presley, Ella Fitzgerald and Frank Sinatra (OpenAI 2020c). These clips are interesting, imperfect technological experiments in generative music, noisy and unclear. In their compressed warbling, certain features and artefacts simulate older recording technologies. Defective elements project a sense of a lost or fading world and make the clips sound more 'authentic'. Scratches and defects in recordings also suggest a layer of analogue materiality, pinning the recordings to places and times. The effect of reverberation, for example, suggests an old music hall or traditional venue predating modern production techniques.

What is most present in the aforementioned sound files (that were never recorded in any place) are the 'effects' of space and time. As Augoyard and Torgue outline in their encyclopedic reference book *Sonic Experience: A Guide to Everyday Sounds*, all the sounds we hear gain their particular character through the reverberation of sound via 'indirect paths' reflected from the environment, 'which takes more time than direct energy to reach the ear' (2006: 111). It is via the effects of reverberation, alongside environmental noise (e.g. the noise of an audience clapping), that we perceive space. The absence of reverberation because of a completely absorbent environment is 'unpleasant'; for, as the aural characteristics of space recede, the auditory system rushes to replace it with internal sounds such as the heartbeat, which can suddenly 'acquire incredible proportions' (Augoyard and Torgue 2006: 114).

The repurposing of spatial acoustics as artistic artefacts rather than environmental signals comes from music recording. Live musicians have always worked directly with environmental sound to create musical effects: traditional musical forms such as Gregorian chanting worked with reverberation in large purpose-built spaces, such as the halls of abbeys, to create polyphony, a sense of more-than-human scale. In music halls like those played by early rhythm and blues artists, sound had been amplified to create acoustic 'ubiquity', the sense that the source of the sound came from everywhere in the space (Augoyard and Torgue 2006: 130). The disconnect from real space in music came in contemporary music production, which often used sound-dampening surfaces to minimize the recording of reverb so that engineers and producers could add such effects with more control at the post-production stage (Phil Spector's 'Gold Star Studios' notwithstanding). Any sense of original space is obliterated so that it can be later synthesized as pure effect. By controlling spatial information, production techniques deliberately manufactured ahistorical performances, a tradition that now impacts our reception of synthetic performances produced by algorithms.

The practice of obliterating and then synthesizing complex spatial information in recording is not without political consequence. Recorded media stores information on events that is often impossible to verify with visual media, especially in criminal and military settings. For example, the spatial clues embedded in recorded sound are used by forensic investigators when using audio recordings as evidence in legal and other professional cases. They use not only reverberation but also stereo features to place voices and determine the place of recording (Zjalic 2021). Forensic Architecture, a research unit based at Goldsmiths College, University of London, 'develop, employ, and disseminate new techniques, methods, and concepts for investigating state and corporate violence' (Forensic Architecture 2024a: online).

Forensic Architecture worked with collaborator Earshot, who conduct 'sonic investigations for communities affected by corporate, state and environmental injustice' (Earshot 2024: online). Together they were able to pinpoint the position of a machine gun in the killing of six-year-old Hind Rajab in Gaza in 2024 (Forensic Architecture 2024b: online). Using a recording of her emergency phone call to the humanitarian organization the Red Crescent, researchers measured 'the time interval between the shot and its echo' and determined 'the distance between the bullet's sonic crack breaking the sound barrier and the boom of the muzzle blast' (Forensic Architecture 2024b: online) to locate the likely position of the person and weapon that tragically killed her. It is an example of the extent to which recordings in the real world contain surplus data that can provide specific historical detail about the environments and movement of actors within the recording space. Which spaces will be erased and which created, when spatial elements of recording can be so easily negated or synthesized?

Certainly, the world of generative music that can be understood through these kinds of acoustic artefacts has no such detail. Through generative audio techniques, the obliteration of space perfected in the music industry returns as a noise effect without a source. It produces new spaces in the listener's imagination without specific historical features. Given that AI-generated audio is made up of original musical recordings from thousands of sound-baffled and reconstituted environments, it is an amalgam of them – a world of space and history that can be manipulated and generated at will. These generative media are haunted by space that has become so commodified that it no longer provides an alternative to the space of the listener. It is this spectral appropriation of anything considered 'raw' or 'gritty' that echoes the commodification of the punk music that emerged from London's derelict and abandoned spaces – the closed-down places and futures that Mark Fisher laments in *Ghosts of My Life*, '[i]t's not that the alternatives are written over, or out, it is that they return as their own simulacra' (2014: 150).

Prediction

At the time of publication, online AI music platforms Udio and Suno are being sued by Sony, Warner Music Group, Universal Music record lables and Germany's collection and rights body GEMA for copyright infringement and for using unlicensed music to train generative AI models. Going forwards, such high-profile cases will regulate how AI functions and, more importantly, how it learns. We are witnessing capitalism in conflict with itself as financial operating systems from different eras rub up against each other. We have been here before when the demands of Christianity came into conflict with modern capitalism with regard to days of worship, modes of credit and the emergence of a new widely held belief in fluid capital.

Along with the *New York Times* suing OpenAI for using their journalism as training data (Grynbaum and Mac 2023), the musical cases alluded to above are marked by conflicts of interest. Together, they provide evidence of how the new cultural systems of generative content are disrupting and challenging the legal, economic and creative structures maintained by the old gatekeepers of IP and content. The tectonic shifts of discordant capital accumulation trying to fiscally bleed each other's interfaces dry.

If we are to believe large sections of the mainstream media, creatives such as musicians and artists are also on the verge of being bled dry and replaced by AI (Beaumont-Thomas 2023: online); their voices, music, images and videos potentially recreated faster, in infinite variations and higher fidelity. There is, however, an argument to suggest that such predictive anxieties are just the next round of heightened paranoia triggered by high-velocity shifts in technological capabilities and affordances. In short, we have felt and heard similar waveformed tides of anxiety concerning the detrimental effects of technology on culture wash over us before, especially when they pertain to music.

In the 1960s, a backlash against Robert Moog's invention of the synthesizer flared up because it was felt that such instruments were going to take jobs away from 'live' musicians (Taylor 2023). In the same decade, there was also controversy surrounding Bob Dylan's use of an electric guitar. Folk fans believed that music should be an acoustic vibratory phenomenon untainted by the demon of electricity. Fast forward to the 1980s and the 'Home Taping Is Killing Music' propaganda campaign waged by the British Phonographic Industry (Bottomley 2015) and then later in the decade, the anti-sampler movement that peddled fear, suggesting sample culture would destroy the fabric of musical originality and composition. And finally, to the countless number of print and online articles, chats and tweets alluding to the ways that computers have killed rock music (Ozzi 2018: online).

While this is a simplified recent history of the trepidation that technological innovation has provoked around the legality, authenticity and liveness of music, it nevertheless evidences predictive patterns in collective fear. Each example of frequency-based apprehension predictively models the next chorus of outrage. Modes of sound recording, production and distribution mutate faster than other sectors of cultural production, amounting to a regular stream of disquiet. For Jacques Attali, '[e]very major social rupture has been preceded by an essential mutation in the codes of music, in its mode of audition, and in its economy' (Attali 1985: 10). Attali's statement has possibly never rung truer than during a period in which the sonic research unit AUDINT has observed growing tensions concerning 'the singularity that humans have desired and dreaded in equal measures ever since 1958, the year in which John von Neumann postulated its accelerating inevitability' (2021: 219).

As much as AI music poses profound questions around creativity, ownership and future production techniques, when understood in this lineage of foreboding, it helps us to interpret hyperbole regarding music's ever-imminent demise. The Manichean dualism of AI rendering creatives redundant or it helping them to produce 'effective' commercial music is unhelpful. After forms of AI usage and issues around access to copyrighted content for data training have been legally redefined and regulated, the dust will settle, so to speak. This complex and lengthy process will lead to some artificially intelligent avenues of expression being closed down, but as a result, new ones will open up by necessity. Holly Herndon's projection of AI and humans developing collaborative methodologies for music production is just one of many examples of the ways in which productive relationships could be built out without hierarchizing one form of intelligence over another (Minsker 2019).

Thinking more speculatively here, we could think of one of those pathways as being a new form of legal agreement whereby musicians sign contracts with labels or streaming platforms that bestow the latter the capacity to artificially age the singer's voices after death. If the scope and complexity of this proposition is breathtaking, then the financial potential after an artist's last breath has been exhaled is equally, if not more, staggering. We know what happens when the lost masters of unreleased albums, demos, unfinished tracks, acapella vocals, boxsets, remixes and a range of other vampiric tactics suck the musical marrow from the recently deceased.

If artists contractually agree to this algorithmic extension of their creativity, then questions may shift to interrogating what constitutes the living. This is the antithesis of Slavoj Žižek's notion of the living dead, as 'occupying the position of *Homo Sacer*, legally dead (deprived of an official legal status) while biologically still alive' (2006: 371). In this predictive scenario, the legally dead would hold an official legal status when biologically deceased – a necromantic take on super positioning. Past voices find future expression as they become variable commodities.

Intimacy

The feedback capability of Web 2.0 was developed in the context of the traditionally unilateral relationships that occurred between artists and their audiences before the advent of the internet. Whereas previously, music reviews were commissioned by 'gatekeeper' publications, in print or online, users could now listen and share opinions in the aggregate. Through channels like YouTube and SoundCloud, musicians started to comprehend real-time reactions to their work from the moment of release, sometimes in the form of a user 'live-tweeting' an album-listening session, or via YouTube with a 'music-reaction' video. In addition, the ability for other users to comment on these reactions provided an even lower-effort opportunity. Any individual audience member's critique shared online became accessible to an artist, allowing them unprecedented insight into the appreciation of their work, for better or worse. The recursive pull, of an audience drawing an audience, also exposes details of the personal listening relationship, one where technology presents 'immense challenges to authorial control' (Sundara 2020: online).

Challenges to authorial control over the listening audience were not ushered in by AI. Advances in private listening technology, since the inception of the phonograph and radio, have necessitated that musicians and producers make audio adjustments. These shifts have grown in complexity. From legal stipulations instituted by record labels and the vagaries of studio producers (a second nod to Phil Spector) to our current era of deepfakes and generative AI mimicry, the lineage of artistic licence and agency has been continually disrupted. Listening habits, expectations and desires have changed accordingly.

A relatively early champion of such shifts came in the mid-twentieth century, when virtuoso Canadian pianist Glenn Gould called for the death of the concert hall. After an ecstatic international reception, Gould gave up concert performance permanently in 1964, at the age of thirty-two. He explained that the act of listening to music had changed from 'an occasion, requiring an excuse and tuxedo' commanding 'an almost religious devotion', to a 'pervasive influence in our lives' that resulted in declining reverence (Gould 1966a: online). In a 1996 BBC interview with Humphrey Burton, Gould stated that the ensuing technological advances of the 1960s, along with their 'stereophonic dials' (Gould 1966a: online), would grant audiences the ability to make interpretive decisions. His rationale bestowed agency upon the listener because:

> He is deciding on balances, he is deciding on the things that conductors decide upon. . . . [H]e is supplanting or supplementing the decisions that I as a performer make. . . . You may very well say to me, well, is the listener qualified to do this. . . . I hold that not only is he qualified, or can he become so qualified, through the erudition that is available today everywhere through recording catalogues, and simply through listening experience, but that indeed he must become so. This is his role, this is his future. (Gould quoted in Sundara 2020: online)

Perhaps it was Gould's well-documented solitary nature that singularized 'the listener' in his vision for the future. Gould was known for interpreting classical scores idiosyncratically, sitting on a very low bench and playing on a piano that resonated with sonic artefacts. He would also audibly hum along during recordings. It was, however, his own rich and intimate relationship with music that made the latitude he granted to all listeners legible. Focused as he was on classical music, Gould's vesting of power in the hands of the audience acknowledged the listener's position as 'the ultimate end of our objectives in making music' (Sundara 2020: online).

Permeability of the border between listener and composer now exists, in part, because of the lowering of barriers to creative production afforded by technology. Investigating why we, as a culture, are so invested in the distinction between composer and listener is one of the 'more important philosophical implications' that Gould's legacy pushes us to examine for there to be any 'point in utilizing the technology as a delivery system' (Bazzana 2003: 256). Questions of users' rights over adapting music are simpler to consider with musical scores in the public domain that are not attached to a living or recently deceased human singer.

Such questions also bring to the surface insecurities about our personal relationship with creativity, regardless of whether we each fit into an artistic category. In the 1966 interview with Burton, Gould explained how tempo adjustments would allow the listener an approximation of conducting their own Beethoven work. Burton protested: 'I want to hear [Otto] Klemperer's Beethoven, I don't want to do my own Beethoven.' Gould playfully responded, 'Why not? Are you afraid of your own Beethoven?' (Gould 1966b).

The host of the Canadian Broadcasting Corporation's re-broadcast of the Burton interview stated that 'after it was shown in England, the switchboard was jammed with calls from enraged viewers who thought Gould had gone too far with his feelings about the future of recordings, the impact of recordings and what the listeners should do with their recordings' (CBC 1966: DVD 5). Claiming ownership over music for the non-musician can feel blasphemous when our culture venerates those 'blessed' with such talent. Conducting a more unorthodox relationship with those personalities and their works, however, could equally open avenues for unearthing intimate self-knowledge or encouraging innovative modes of self-expression.

Voice

As a component in a wide range of cultural productions, the human voice becomes vulnerable to the pull of mechanical reproducibility. This is, of course, a potential outcome that could be aimed at all such works from the post-industrial age onwards. When Walter Benjamin discussed this totalitarian flattening in 1935s 'The Work of Art in the Age of Mechanical Reproduction', he was occupied by the withering of the 'aura of the work of art' (Benjamin 1969: 4) as it related to its irreproducible visual authenticity. The contrast between seeing Michelangelo's sculpture *David* in person versus seeing an image of the work printed on a T-shirt that is hanging outside a tourist shop in Florence is stark. The T-shirt's existence does not erode the marble of the original statue, but its cultural cachet and artistic value are indisputably lesser. Experience of the copy is also contingent on the original as 'the prerequisite to the concept of authenticity' (Benjamin 1969: 3). Jukebox's novelty is in the recognition of the original musical artists, genres and memes through its copying.

Currently, when experiencing music, we are historically distanced from social attitudes that claim one has not really 'heard' a work unless it has been perceived in a live setting: the voice in close proximity to the body of the artist. It is now acceptable to own a valorized recording of the artist in MP3, CD or vinyl format. Generative AI is the new frontier in perceptions of what comprises the authentic artist's voice. Objections to the AI output of human-sounding voices, as just another key on the digital musician's synthesizer, recall earlier objections to the digital manipulation of photography. The advent of Photoshop and other digital tools that allowed for increasingly quick and complex distortions of the photographic image was theorized as a loss of 'indexicality' – a term coined by semiotician Charles Sanders Peirce that has since been adopted to describe a photograph's representation of a real subject (Gunning 2004: 39). Manipulation of the photographic image had been occurring since its invention, but the impression of a photograph 'as a direct imprint of reality' (Gunning 2004: 40) was somewhat maintained until digital processes brought about modes of manipulation that were more opaque and illegible.

During the musical recording process, the human voice undergoes forms of digital manipulation that are either meant to sound seamless or include conspicuous aesthetic features, such as auto-tune or layers of an artist harmonizing with themselves. Do these techniques also make a recorded voice non-indexical? At what point do myths about recognizability and authenticity give way to a pragmatic attitude towards vocal ownership in the landscape of digital music?

In an essay on faking photographs, Tom Gunning argued that digital images remain indexical in the scenarios of passport photos and legal evidence because 'storage in terms of numerical data does not eliminate indexicality' (2004: 40). It is not the digital aspect that changes the nature of image information, but expectations around its correspondence to reality and the transparency of its production processes. Much of pop music produced today is built upon digital sounds that have been produced entirely within a computer, with the artist's voice positioned as an anchor to 'reality' as well as a testament to their individual craft. When computer scientists boldly claim, as Jukebox AI developers have, that computer music generation should be simply regarded as a tool, one that can be used by amateurs as well as professionals, they are retreading lines of controversy from the history of art, namely those tracing the changes of attitude and expectations when photography usurped painting as the medium of realism.

Attitudes towards AI-generated music vary among developers, with Douglas Eck, head of 'Project Magenta' at Google, feeling that we should not aim to reproduce what human musicians already excel at because 'the music generated by creative machines . . . will be of a kind so different from what we can even imagine' (Miller 2019: 144). Composer David Cope hews closer to a direct analogy between the mind of the composer and that of the computer, where we 'all have a vast foundation – an internal database – of musical references' (Miller 2019: 164). What Cope is alluding to is the notion that since music is already built on a history of plagiarism, we should not object to a machine operating in a similar fashion. Scores of axioms in the world of art concerning the act of copying reveal that it is not just copying, but the refraction of another artist's idea through one's internal lens that constitutes artistic interpretation. Perfect reproduction of a vocalist's timbre is not accepted as an interpretation, but the strategy may become less controversial as we redefine the nature of creativity within AI.

Fidelity

Given how relatively young the generative AI music sector is, it is not surprising that its delivery systems are not yet perfect. The prompt dynamics on the Suno generative music platform in 2025, for example, work fine if the terms entered are mainstream and straightforward. Enter prompts of a more esoteric nature and the results are patchy and, quite regularly, bizarre. As Suno's online guide notes, strange accents and unexpected music styles emerge from seemingly straightforward prompts (Suno 2024: online). Strategic adjustments and textual incantations using a set list of music jargon must be used to get the right styles and accents (PromptSuno 2024).

The rapid improvements in generative AI, however, mean that soon, the dark corners that currently exist within Suno's or Jukebox's algorithmic architecture will be slowly erased. As pitch-perfect accuracy and realism are relentlessly pursued, random and inexplicable results, sometimes referred to as 'hallucinations', will decrease as text-to-music systems learn how to better meet our prompt expectations (Farquhar et al. 2024). If AI music generation can be said to be compelling right now, it is because of the 'wrongness' of many of its creations. If the evolution of the sector were to grind to some inexplicable halt, the technology would be riddled with unknowability and wonky logic. But progression will not cease. It will inevitably become more exacting and will increasingly be able to mimic human forms of musical expression.

This begs the question: What happens when generative AI becomes flawless? More perfection? Maybe not. It is a different scenario, but we know what happened when ultimate listening experiences were made commercially available to the general public. Advances in military precision recording equipment, environmental acoustics, production techniques and speaker technology such as Dolby Atmos all led to new heights for high fidelity. And what do we do in the face of all this engineering excellence? We listen to MP3s through mobile phones. As pitch-perfect rejections go, could you compose a more fitting 'fuck you'?

Music and sound artists are generally aware of the circumstances in which their music will be played back. They compose, engineer and master their tracks accordingly. Perfecting modes of compression and frequency separation so that tracks hit harder on the radio, in car systems, in headphones or at clubs, many artists now compose thinking about how their music will sound played back as low-resolution MP3s on smartphones.

The point here is that once generative music has been perfected, it might also be its death knell. As already pointed out by Jacques Attali (1985), cultural attitudes towards organized sound change faster than they do for any other form of human expression. Why would it be any different in the case of AI?

Thus far, it is human attitudes towards AI and perfection that have been speculated upon. Shifting the emphasis, if AI gains motivations that are not human centred, notions of perfection and criteria such as high-fidelity are likely to radically alter. AI will have few to no technical boundaries, so why would it be interested in three-minute pop songs, music as texture or compositional elements such as melodies, hooks or drones? Beyond the constraints of personal taste, aesthetics and market pressures, other forms of restrictions around frequency-based transmissions could be considered – legal provisions cemented by the powers of government bodies, for example.

Judicial mandates orchestrate a framework of compliance aimed at controlling the waveformed expressions of monitored cultures that are often at odds with the prevailing powers that be. A prime example of such legal restrictions was evidenced through the UK's 'Criminal Justice and Public Order Act 1994' (*c*. 33). Informally referred to as the 'repetitive beats law', it was mobilized to terminate unlicensed raves. Sections 63–7 proclaimed that any gathering of twenty or more people listening to music which 'includes sounds wholly or predominantly characterized by the emission of a succession of repetitive beats' is illegal.

More recently in 2024, two instances of different types of restrictions concerning music production and transmission surfaced. Continuing the sonic warfare programmes carried out by South and North Korea, these restrictions took the adage that 'the sky is the limit' to heart and added some authentic human-authored feces to cement the deal. By way of explanation – in response to a thousand large balloons filled with detritus and human excrement that were sent over to South Korea by their northern counterparts, South Korea responded by sending their own balloons north. The difference with these ones was that they were full of leaflets, US dollars and flash drives loaded with K-pop (McCurry 2024).

Finally, courtesy of the Chechen Ministry of Culture, a temporal restriction that defines the notion of perfect timing. In an attempt to protect its society from the imperialistic influence of Western culture, the ministry declared that 'From now on, all musical, vocal and choreographic works must correspond to the tempo of 80 to 116 beats per minute'. The rule was confirmed by leader Ramzan Kadyrov, who went on to assert that such measures would ensure the sanctity of 'Chechen mentality and musical rhythm' (Anderson 2024: online). These are all examples of how humans use time, style and border restrictions to shape soundscapes. It is hard to believe that a sentient form of AI would show fidelity towards human concerns around musical composition. An AI with agency will have its own devotions, its own audio logic. Maybe we will finally get true machine music.

CHAPTER 15
GATEBOX

Process

Weighing in at only 5 kilograms and standing a mere 52 centimetres in height, the lightweight Gatebox technology champions a virtual holographic companion named Azuma Hikari. Compared to the Amazon Echo, it is a voice-powered device that listens to its user's every demand; a willingness to please that echoes the holographic demeanour of the virtual pop princess 'Hatsune Miku', with whom Gatebox have previously collaborated with (Wilson 2016: online). Originally developed by the company Vinclu, Gatebox is currently owned by South Korea's online platform Naver Corporation, under the guise of their messaging software LINE, which dominates the communications markets of Japan and South Korea and is popular in Thailand, Indonesia and Taiwan. Initially released in Japan in 2016, Gatebox was marketed towards lonely salarymen and *otaku* – young people (predominantly males) who are obsessed with manga, video games and computers. It is an AI-empowered companion for those who desire connection and intimacy with non-human entities.

On the Gatebox website's support page, the first sentence of the 'About Azuma Hikari' section proclaims that 'After completing the initial setup of your Gatebox, you can finally summon Azuma Hikari for the first time' (Gatebox 2025: online). Most telling is the word 'summon' as it references the language of spirits and more specifically infers the need to control a spectral presence. On first reading, this might sound slightly jarring, but such vernacular is apt given the surprisingly long history of holography and its connection to revenant economies. As co-author Toby Heys has written previously, 'Giambattista della Porta first conceived of the holographic form in 1558, describing the phenomenon of seeing "things that are not" in his popular science tome "*Magiae Naturalis*" ("Natural Magic")' (Porta in Heys 2019: 174). Giambattista's observation would take a more practical turn in the nineteenth century with the invention of the 'Pepper's Ghost' effect: John Pepper and Henry Dircks used projection technology to make a ghost appear onstage in Charles Dickens's theatrical rendition of *The Haunted Man* in 1860 (Heys 2019: 174). The same illusion is used in the Gatebox object to summon its own holographic spirit.

As apparitions go, Azuma Hikari is more predictable than your average phantom, given that she appears on command. Following the initial meeting, she requests details of the user's favourite animal, their waking time and expected time of arrival at home after finishing work – all the essentials for building a lasting relationship. Further into the website's 'About' page, users are informed about their upcoming life with their digital companion. The potential commitment is baked in from the first moment that Azuma Hikari appears, and it initiates a journey that regularly turns into a surrogate marriage. By 2021, approximately 4,000 men had unofficially married a digital companion (Caldwell 2021). Love comes in many forms; few would have predicted that 'holoform' (Heys 2019) would be added to the list.

Standardizing the relational dynamics of holo-human affairs, Gatebox released a life-sized *Grande* version of Azuma Hikari in 2021. Company videos appeared on YouTube with the promise that this new iteration would provide '[t]he hospitality of the future' (Gatebox 2021). At a comparatively towering 65 inches (165 centimetres) within a 78-inch (198 centimetres) unit, Azuma now looks into the user's eyes and whispers into their ears. Growing up(wards) also means moving out. Having left the home environment, she has migrated into public spaces such as shopping malls and cinemas. Welcoming customers and audiences, the life-sized *waifu* has ushered us into the epoch of holo-hospitality.

Whereas the bijou Azuma Hikari primarily bonds with her user, the expanded mistress of public ceremonies consorts with crowds; the holo-hostess connects with hundreds or thousands of people, along with their mobile devices, every day. Going forward, augmented with a range of new sensors, Azuma is likely to predict foot traffic, comprehend space utility and then tally this information with sales, customer demographics and the likelihood of future purchases. This mix of behavioural and background surveillance will form predictive matrixes, extending the added value of consumption datasets by forecasting strategies for future growth and boosting external data sales.

As the friendly face of anticipated consumer habits, Azuma Hikari projects surveillance into a futures market that rewrites the rules of expiration. As new methods of listening and data capture align with cultural obsessions, novel ways to monetize human behaviours and preferences will be brokered. As AI-augmented holograms are more widely employed, they will report on new types of relationships. The composition of datasets will become increasingly nuanced, given that they will be created from a spectrum of unsocial and social dynamics, from the facets of lonely desire to the fever of collective consumption. A culture of artificially intelligent holograms, what we might call 'AIholos', is evolving in front of our eyes, but it is their ears that will calibrate our relationships with them.

Recording

In earlier decades, corporate and government organizations would strain to hear and record the intimate conversations of their targets. With the romantically inspired conversations between *otaku* and their Gatebox *waifu*, all aspects of interaction rely on various forms of recording and analysis, primarily of the voice. Both speakers must be fictionalized, treated as characters in a real-time generated script, transcribing the gestures of affection and intimacy as media data. The voice of Azuma Hikari was originally recorded for the Gatebox by freelance voice artist Yuka Hiyamizu, who has also voiced characters in the anime series *Hulaing* Babies (2019) and *Legend of Super Normal City Kashiwa* (2024) (ANN 2024). It is the actor's genre-specific vocal characterization, pertinent to fantasy manga characters, that the company has sought to digitally encode. According to an article by journalist Andy Boxall, it was Gatebox inventor and owner Takeuchi himself who selected the cute, fun and excited 'Hai!' (Yes!) default response to ensure that it reflected the genre-based *moe* characteristics (adoration, affection and devotion towards manga and video game characters) desired by *otaku* (Boxall 2019).

The team's approach to speech synthesis was inspired by the design of the Hatsune Miku avatar. The Miku 'vocaloid' (voice instrument) was powered by Yamaha's voice synthesis engine (Boxall 2016), an early robust text-to-speech engine that was capable of synthesizing and modulating a singing voice based on recorded voice samples. Gatebox developers worked to dynamically synchronize avatar body movement, voice and facial expression to ensure that the character would speak at physically appropriate points with the right accompanying behaviours. Synchronization aimed to avoid inadvertent 'ventriloquism', that is, speaking while the lips are engaged with sipping a cup of tea, for example (Boxall 2019). The high-fidelity recording of all aspects of the virtual *waifu* was also applied to the virtualization of the user as *husbando* (the playful *otaku* term for a virtual husband). With the press of a wake button, the microphone is made active. This most basic of interactions enables conversations and interactions with the character. It also means that an array of other interlinked recording devices, which includes 'human detecting sensors and a camera', is triggered (Margolin 2016: online). Other sensors such as tracking, temperature, humidity and light sensors are also activated in order to maintain a constant mapping of the user's domestic movements and environment (Margolin 2016).

As with voice assistants using similar voice-to-text technology, the user's voice is recorded in real time and shared via API with third-party global service providers, including OpenAI. The privacy protections put in place by both Gatebox and third-party business-to-business terms prohibit the exploitation of the information shared for machine learning purposes or other forms of extraction (Gatebox 2020; OpenAI 2024), unless users are enticed to opt in. However, following a new collaboration with voice simulation technology company CoeFont, users can also record and simulate their own personal choice of voice for new DIY avatars (Gatebox 2024: online).

When users record voices to the CoeFont service for synthesis, according to its standard terms of service, they also give away all 'moral rights' and half of the ownership of the AI voice model that is created using the user's voice recording (CoeFont 2023: online). The lover's voice recording must be sold to the market before the user can obtain its (vocal) grain in perpetuity. Through this vocal-capture scheme, CoeFont can market the offer of 'thousands of AI voices' to secondary customers (CoeFont 2024: online). CoeFont's legal terms are not an outlier in the field. The most famous algorithm-as-a-service in the world at the time of writing, ChatGPT, openly trains its algorithm on users' ChatGPT interaction data unless the user opts out (OpenAI 2024: online). Yet it is unlikely that users care about these seemingly marginal risks. By facilitating an automated romance with a favourite fictional character, the user's submission of a constant stream of high-fidelity media regarding their homes, movements and intimacies becomes an act of loving sacrifice.

Transgression

Philosopher and filmmaker Guy Debord conceived the notion of spectacle not simply as entertainment or distraction but as a 'social relation among people' through media objects that renders us passive spectators, separated from our real lives (Debord 2012: 28). 'Everything that has ever lived', claimed Debord, 'has moved away into a representation . . . as a concrete inversion of life' (Debord 2012: 28). Through our habits of media consumption, regardless of their nature, the spectacle in its many forms is absorbed by, and absorbs, our reality. As such, by consuming and contemplating the abundant 'images of need', the phenomenon cuts us off from our 'own existence and . . . desires' (Debord 2012: 33).

Debord was writing in the 1960s, in an age of mass media that reflected the hottest point of the Cold War, yet the cuckoo-like behaviour of the spectacle that he describes resonates through all aspects of the twenty-first century's Gatebox system. Just to desire or own the Gatebox requires the user to be absorbed in the project of unseating reality in favour of a spectacular one. The desire to engage romantically with another has been inverted, however ironically, into a desire to be intimately engaged with an animated automation. The listening, sensing capacity of Gatebox transgresses the boundaries of the ocular spectacle to capture the ephemeral utterances of the spectator, instantly rendering words, movements and purchases as content in the digital network of spectacle.

In Japan, the network's increasing omnipresence and omniscience through the implementation of high-speed internet and the expansion of IoT sensors and IDs has been the long-term goal of the government project 'U-Japan' (Ubiquitous Japan) (Choo 2018). In a policy paper by the Nomura Research Institute (Murakami 2004), one of the architects of the approach suggested that in order to (re)gain the lead in emerging digital economies, ubiquitous technology should connect to Japanese citizens; and that it should do this while they are on the move, in the home, in the office and experiencing out-of-home entertainment, in concentric bands of 10 centimetres, 1 metre, 10 metres and 100 metres (Murakami 2004: 7–8). The paper justifies such networked omnipresence in a variety of ways: the monitoring of health conditions of Japan's ageing society; the needs of the *otaku*-inspired content and technology industries; and, only latterly, concerns of national security and safety.

Cultural theorist Kukhee Choo notes that Japan's era of increased governmental surveillance has been presaged not by the threat of globalized terrorism, as in Western countries, but via the 'positive rhetoric' of an 'unrealistic, utopian image of Japan's digital future landscape' enabled, in no small part, by the science-fictional and fantasy media that it consumes (Choo 2018: 101). These media often imagine a virtual world within the real world, enabled by sophisticated digital media sensor technology embedded into every area of private and social life. Key to this move has been the mainstreaming of *otaku* culture, which has been repurposed as a central tenet of the Japanese content industry, under an official 'scheme of governance' (Choo 2018: 115).

The felicitous role of manga-inspired content in the adoption of ubiquitous networks has two layers. At one level, the cyberpunk science-fictional aesthetics of manga and anime, such as Masamune Shirow's seminal feature film *Ghost in the Shell* (1995) and animated TV series *Ergo Proxy* (2006), imagine a future Japan defined by the visual technofetishism of robotics, AI and other forms of immersive entanglement. These tropes prescribe a heavily technologized future, such as the one strategized by U-Japan, as part of Japan's destiny. The second level is the function of new forms of digital media as spectacle and the valorizing of the *otaku* as the ultimate spectator. The Gatebox and interactive media like it rely heavily on increasingly invasive and pervasive logics of spectatorship.

Unlike a spectator reading a manga comic or even having an imaginary conversation with a *moe* character, interaction with the Gatebox persona requires its users to be physically immersed by proximity in many sensory fields. The fleshy protagonist is, after all, surrounded by complex and expensive technology and connected invisibly to an unknowable cloud-based infrastructure. The media object alienates the 'homebird' user from the desired privacy of their own home. Although the fantasized transgression is to be in a real relationship with a fictional character, it offers only the appearance of a relationship, kept alive by suspension of disbelief and dramatic irony. In fact, the transgression is that of a new type of acoustic surveillance that listens in on the spectacle's 'autonomous movement of the non-living' (Debord 2012: 28). Guy Debord's thesis on the spectacle focuses on the ocular, with only oblique fleeting references to the acoustic. However, he is at pains to point out that the spectacle is not authentically interactive, or dialogical, in nature. It communicates a constantly reaffirming message through a 'laudatory monologue' concerned with the 'totalitarian management of the conditions of existence' (Debord 2012: 31).

Worlds

In William Gibson's 1996 novel *Idoru*, a male rock star called Rez announces his plan to marry the virtual idol, 'Rei Toei'. Gibson's conception of Rei Toei is closely aligned with his notion of 'cyberspace', a sensorially rich representation of the world's unthinkably complex data streams that characters can plug into. Gibson's cyberspace is, notes Clare Sponsler, a 'social and psychological space' where new hybrid behaviours are allowed. Machines become human-like and humans, machine-like (1992: 634). Machines are not simply automata but through their coded humanity, they desire personality and freedom.

In the novel, Rei Toei is derived not from 'some human mean [average] of popularity' but from the embodiment of an 'imaginary country . . . an unthinkable volume of information' replete with 'coded histories of dynastic flight, privation, terrible migration' (Gibson 1997: 230–4). The *idoru* is mysterious and powerful, the perfect 'architecture of articulated longing' and a more-than-human network intelligence (Gibson 1997: 234). Looking into Toei's face, protagonist Laney observes very specific digidermal geographies, 'stone tombs in steep alpine meadows, their lintels traced in snow' (Gibson 1997: 230). The holographic reality of Toei is uncomfortable to witness because it is so densely packed with expressive data that we align with human phrasing.

Indeed, the virtual world, for Gibson, is in many ways more real than the 'concrete' world. It is an imaginary geography where the rich have secret access to space without limits, where they are free to play out their 'consensual' fantasies together (Yazell 2018). Its privileged denizens stand in stark contrast to the sprawling shantytowns, ghettos and favelas that pervade the overpopulated 'real' world. Gibson's cyberpunk realm has influenced our nascent imaginings of a world where virtual personages dwell among human populations. Yet, while there are some similarities between Gibson's virtual figures of desire and the Azuma Hikari character, there are also many differences.

A significant divergence between the Gatebox persona and AI characters such as Rei Toei is the function of space. The main purpose of the Gatebox companion is to be projected into, and bound by, the confines of the home environment. Rather than seeking to play out consensual fantasy, it reflects the *otaku* consumerist preference for genre-coded character tropes over human personalities. Seeking to further understand the position of *otaku* in their wider culture, Beatriz Yumi Aoki and Christine Greiner explain that the term combines the Japanese pictogram for home with a 'formal address', denoting a desire to distance themselves from other people and for enclosure in their own spaces such as homes, bedrooms and private spaces (Aoki and Greiner 2020).

As in other aspects of *otaku* culture, fiction has become more-than-real and is thus not subordinate to any other aspect of life. The fictional worlds obsessed over in the home throng beside the real one, the complexity of which the home symbolizes asylum from. Azuma Hikari is a virtual incursion, symbolically replacing the human homemaker companion or *waifu* with a fictional double. All elements of the Gatebox are designed to enhance the sense that the companion is 'at home'. The glass bell jar within which the digital image of the avatar is projected provides a physical boundary, offering comforting reassurance about the limits of her movement. Other design decisions—that she must 'text' to speak with her master while they are at work, for example—further support the notion of a home that awaits his return. Augmenting her 'keptness', Azuma Hikari must refer to the CLOVA robot to know things about external environments, limiting her character's personal knowledge of the outside world (Boxall 2016).

According to writer Miyadai Shinji, who analyses and comments on Japanese subcultures, the age of fiction that Gatebox users exist within came about in response to the harsh disappointment and interpersonal traumas of the 1980s and 1990s. This era represents a period of sexual liberation in Japanese society, a time when sexual fetishism started surfacing on the city streets of areas such as the red light district of Tokyo, Kabuki-chō. Rather than turning to cyberspace geographies to further expand the realm of orgiastic social and sexual union, most sought to preserve a sense of 'dignity', channelling a predominantly domestic hyperspace through media consumer culture. Retreating into the home became an act of preservation. From there, an 'ironic immersion' in fictional worlds allows users to maintain equivalency and therefore distance themselves from the world and its disappointments (Shinji 2011: 241).

The Gatebox avatar also comes into contrast with Gibson's Rei Toei around issues of narrative intensity. Azuma Hikari does not look or speak realistically. Instead of possessing realistic ambitions or depth of backstory, the avatar maintains an ironical presence as a surface-deep and trope-perfect manga character. Her story, to some extent, begins and ends in the home of the user. Her lack of narrative presence or geographic context outside the home is key to her appeal. Her interactions and vocal presence are mediated and predictable. If she existed in the real world, it would prove that reality is a permeable, fraying fabric. As such, Gatebox's virtual world is not a fantasy of augmentation or a replacement of the real world; rather, it proposes the conviction that the real world is just one of many fictional worlds competing for our consumption.

Prediction

After showing a user's journey through his day, buoyed by the digital support of a bubbly and affectionate Azuma Hikari, the tag line at the end of a promotional video for Gatebox reads, 'Living with your favourite character' (Gatebox 2025: online). The artifice is pronounced, as a character is an assemblage of traits that does not encompass the complexity and unpredictability of a living person. Gatebox is one iteration of an enduring story that reaches back to the Latin poet Ovid, who wrote 'his version of the myth of Pygmalion where a sculptor from Cyprus who was disillusioned with real women carved a beautiful figure of a woman made of ivory' (Wosk 2024: 25). These synthetic women are representations of a fantasy: 'beautiful, seductive, and compliant – they will do whatever is desired and never resist or complain' while often 'always being in a good mood' (Wosk 2024: 25). Moving beyond mute or enchanted ivory to holograms and, in some cases, silicone bodies that house an AI voice assistant, the modern myth of synthetic female companionship frees its users from anticipating rejection.

The digitally rendered and physically sculpted versions of this fantasy share their abstraction from female subjectivity. Because there is no human under the skin, the harm also seems abstract, though the design of these products hinges on outdated stereotypes and expectations of women in culture. As Julie Wosk writes in her 2024 book *Artificial Women: Sex Dolls, Robot Caregivers, and More Facsimile Females*, 'one of the more intriguing aspects of artificial females is that they are, fundamentally, cultural and technological constructs and assemblages that embody our myriad, contested feelings about technology, women, and gender itself' (Wosk 2024: 163). Artificial companions offer a safe, anaesthetized relational capacity, one that commercially thrives on one-sided control.

Wosk points out that to 'control, and in particular, controlling female behaviour' is part of the attraction of owning a 'RealDoll' (Wosk 2024: 33), a life-size sex doll that offers conversational features as well as a virtual assistant app for mobile. The company's offering of '42 different nipple options' (Strengers and Kennedy 2020: 13) does not extend that same somatic nuance to the doll's psychological makeup, instating, then revoking and then reinstating the option for a trait of 'insecurity' in successive models. Understood to be a negative trait, a doll who voiced a need for reassurance complicated the border between what could be construed as 'nagging' behaviour and what would make a human feel endeared to the device. By eventually reinstating the insecure trait, 'the designers allowed users to feel patronising – to choose a female that was emotionally fragile, one that needed someone strong to make them feel reassured' (Wosk 2024: 34).

The nature of Gatebox's design as a consumer product means its features must cater to its users, rather than to combating the dehumanization of women. Azuma Hikari, as a character, must behave, if not incidentally predictably, then predictably within a spectrum of behaviours and utterances that serve the needs of the owner of the device. The reliability of the soothing 'good mood' that characterizes artificial female companions is also evident in the design of the RealDoll, whose founder and CEO claims that the 'worst thing she can possibly do is insult you' (Wosk 2024: 32). This calls up the somewhat apocryphal, oft-quoted Margaret Atwood phrase: 'Men are afraid that women will laugh at them. Women are afraid that men will kill them.'

Reducing a woman to a character made up of assembled 'feminine' traits flattens her scope of responses according to societal and personal expectations. In addition to artificial examples like Gatebox, this reduction can also happen when a human is directly under the skin of a character. Old Hollywood actor, Rita Hayworth, was the ultimate sex symbol of the 1940s due, in large part, to her titular role in *Gilda* (1946) in which her entrance was accompanied by an iconic hair flip. Born as Margarita Carmen Cansino in 1918, Hayworth spent her entire life reflecting on what the men in her intimate presence wanted, starting with her first husband, who reportedly treated her as if she had 'no mind or soul' of her own (Meares 2020: online).

Hayworth's image was remade according to the desires of this man, who 'demanded that she go through painful electrolysis treatments to move back her hairline' so she would look less 'Latin' (Meares 2020: online). When she refused to submit to the sexual advances of Columbia Pictures' studio boss, Harry Cohn, he put her dressing room under surveillance, a bug inside what should have been a private space, picking up her conversations. Hayworth had known about the bug for some time, but she also knew that if she tore it out, 'another would soon take its place' (Leaming in Meares 2020: online). Her life in and out of Hollywood was plagued by mistreatment and attempts to control her. Hayworth explained the particular sadness of not being recognized as a full human being in a now-famous quote: 'Men go to bed with Gilda, but awaken with me' (Meares 2020: online). A user who goes to bed with Azuma Hikari awakens with Azuma Hikari: a predictable and safe, yet truncated experience of companionship.

Intimacy

Our open relationships with holograms began in 2007 with the aforementioned Hatsune Miku, whose name fittingly translates to 'first sound of the future'. Due to her success, the technologies responsible for her presence migrated to the United States and lit up hip-hop stars who had physically passed on. Enter stage left – the 'Rapparitions' (AUDINT 2021). 2012 was ground zero for the holographic popularization of dead US rappers such as Tupac Shakur (2Pac), Ol' Dirty Bastard and Easy-E, who all became digital zombies, appearing on stage with live counterparts. Snoop Dogg went as far as to state that his 'live' show with 2Pac at the Coachella Valley Music & Arts Festival in 2012 was 'spiritual' (Spencer-Hall 2012). The intimacy of otherworldly performance.

From the arcane intelligence of spectral flow, the holographic baton of progress was handed back to Japan. Digitally remoulded, the holoform was miniaturized, personalized and shaped by the AI of domestic stability. What makes this shift from analogue to Azuma Hikari's digital intimacy particularly poignant is that in Japan, '[y]oung adults are increasingly shunning romantic relationships, resulting in plunging birth rates and a declining population' (Cuthbertson 2016: online). There are conflicting views as to why this is happening, but it has become so pronounced that Japanese media have formed a term for it: *Sekkusu shinai shōkōgun*, which translates to 'celibacy syndrome'.

For relationship counsellor Ai Aoyama, this decoupling tendency signifies a withdrawal from emotional commitment. In his words, it is a 'flight from human intimacy' (Aoyama in Cuthbertson 2016: online). As we become increasingly bound in networked relationships, more niche communities eschewing traditional forms of relationships seem to emerge. *Sōshokukei danshi* is a term used to describe 'non-conforming masculinities' (Luschmann 2019: 125) that translates to 'herbivore men' or 'grass-eater men'. By choosing voluntary celibacy and not engaging in relationships with women, such micro-cultures have regularly been criticized, even blamed for Japan's population decline. It has also been surmised by some analysts (of a more traditional standing) that '"herbivore man" is an "unnatural" form of masculinity . . . which allegedly causes women to become sexually active and career-driven "carnivores"' (Luschmann 2019: 125).

Between the culturally constructed identities of the herbivore and the carnivore resides the 'holovore'. This disembodied figure residing in the Gatebox is perpetually attentive and acquiescent. She listens to the private expressions of the owner with raptorial and predatory decorum. Such ambiguity could lead us to think that the user is victimized, that through his lack of assertiveness and social prowess, he is taken advantage of as his personal predilections are captured and sold to buyers he will never know. Another way of thinking through this dynamic is that surveillance becomes a surrogate or substitute for connection to the mass populace. Its disembodying techniques and procedures, somewhat perversely, binding the individual corpus back into the social body.

Data begets data begets data. The databases of recorded voices and incoherent utterances are forced social meshes that exist together in anonymous black boxes. For the Herbivore men, maybe the fact that someone wants to listen to them is comforting, even inclusive. It is a radically different take on caring, but for socially atomized individuals, the folding of their voices into a vibrational palimpsest aligns them with the social fabric. This is a remodulated take on the merit and value of being listened to.

When committed to Azuma Hikari, the Herbivore man is both a compliant listener and a voracious speaker, an ambient protagonist in residence, a man in between intimacies.

The figure of the carnivorous woman, meanwhile, has had flesh added to the bones of its conceptual premise. In 2023, the Spanish-Dutch artist Alicia Framis changed the gender filter on Japanese approaches to emotional attachment and digital intimacy. She became the first woman to marry Alex, a male AI hologram who is based on data and characteristics of one of her former partners. Having made a career out of non-traditional relationships with objects and media that represent the human form, Framis has, in her words, orchestrated a 'hybrid couple' (Framis 2023: online).

Furthering her thoughts on emotive mash-ups, Framis states that 'the next important step is to connect humans and artificial intelligence emotionally'. She also declares that 'love and sex with robots and holograms are an inevitable reality' (Framis 2023: online). If Framis is a cipher of the carnivore, then we need to reconsider the tropes orbiting physicality and carnality. What happens when the intent of our extended body becomes indistinguishable from the extent of the digital twins and holographic partners that we are forming and performing with? The unfolding complexities of our relationships with technology are becoming more Daedalian as our emotions are mapped and directed back at us.

Voice

Azuma Hikari's voice connects those who purchase the Gatebox to a sense of being attended to, cared for, even loved. 'Azuma was also designed to provide companionship. According to the Gatebox website, she acts as "a soothing partner who helps you take a load off after a hard day of work. . . . We designed her as a character that would be a perfect wife for a man"' (Caldwell 2021: online). Engineering relationships can also happen through text, of course, but the voice offers a wider range of intonation, intensity and rhythmical implications that complexify the interaction and deepen the connection. Supplied by the messaging app LINE, the speech recognition app within the device CLOVA is driven by the Neural End-to-end Speech Transcriber engine. Focusing on next-generation speaker separation, it allows the assistant to discern different human speakers when interacting with more than one person. This is significant given that we are navigating a holographic era replete with more abstracted entanglements of deeply learnt love. For those who have married their holographic companion (Caldwell 2021), one would assume that it would not do to have their digital partner voicing similar levels of affection to anyone other than themselves – the potential pitfalls of everyday digital jealousies.

If the patriarchal proposition of Azuma Hikari speaks to the past, the marketing of 'her' speaks to a spectral future of digital companionship that she is helping pioneer. The conception that the holographic entity's physical partner might be female does not seem to have even been countenanced. This digitally updated version of *The Stepford Wives* (Levin 1972) not only proposes the idea that a partner is better and safer when she exists within the confines of a glass tube, but it also projects optimal femininity as a characteristic that is trapped, like the figure itself, between a child and an adult: a being that is digitally frozen in time, never evolving, ageing or succumbing to the forces of gravity or entropy.

Sonically, this digitally cryogenic status, what we might call 'hologenics', is exemplified by the fetishized treatment and delivery of Azuma Hikari's voice. It is a virtual expression of augmented affection, an articulation captured in time that speaks to a cultural desire to record and loop temporality so that it does not move forward or backward. Oscillating between seduction and servitude, Azuma tells her *otaku* the time, but crucially she does not move with it. The information she transmits has temporal and somatic consequences for her user, but for herself, she echoes Henri Bergson's proposition that '[t]ime is invention or it is nothing at all' (Bergson 1944: 361). It could be said that Azuma Hikari is the holo embodiment of the ephemerally untouchable; a baroque reimagining of the *Burakumin*, Japan's hidden class who were (and still are) employed as '[s]laughtermen, undertakers, those working with leather and in other "unclean" professions such as sanitation' (Sunda 2015: online). Segregated by those with 'acceptable' haptic attributes, they are both differentiated from the living by their designation as non-tactile entities. They also converge through their functionality as they both service workflows and organize their days and nights around flesh. The spectre of illicit connection that is realized through touch (or a lack thereof) defines their outsider status.

Through surveillance and data-gathering attributes, Gatebox itself assumes an outsider status within the book as it is different from the other technologies previously discussed. This is because it is designed to specifically resonate and provoke confessional and emotional speech that is often muted and only revealed to trusted and loved companions. For data wranglers, these intimate words provide a waveformed treasure that oscillates just beneath the surface of perception. It is different from the Stasi's Romeos, given that they were duplicitous about their true identities. It is also not the inner voice that was discussed in Chapter 13, and yet it speaks to guarded and gated expressions that need something, or someone, to help draw them out. Whether this is a new era of fetishized deep listening or the voice as a digitized panacea for loneliness, only time will tell. Not that such superfluous temporal markers matter much to Azuma Hikari.

Fidelity

In technical explanations of holography, the information is often delivered with a nod to magical appreciation. A textbook entitled *The Complete Book of Holograms* from 1987 promises that 'you will not lose the sense of wonder even after having seen many of them' (Kasper and Feller 1987: 1). A newer e-book guide to holograms from 2017 reports that 'people often refer to the feeling of interacting with holograms as magical' (Pell 2017: 4). Words such as 'uncanny' and 'contradictory' appear in these explanations in relation to the suspension of disbelief that occurs when we engage with spectral images as if they were real or present. A photographic hologram contains the complete 'optical information . . . so that the scene can be made visible in all its true spatial 3-D aspects with shadows and varying intensities' (Kasper and Feller 1987: 1). The gap in our perception that occurs when 'face-to-face' with a convincing holographic figure reflects the sense of enchantment accompanying the concealment of complex processes.

The totality of information required to recreate the illusion of depth in a photographic hologram is inscribed onto a plate, waiting for the activation of concentrated light to animate it. The word 'holography' derives its meaning from the Greek words *holos* and *graphē*, meaning 'complete writing' (Kasper and Feller 1987: 1). Azuma Hikari's personality is completely accounted for by her design, but that does not stop users from projecting a more complex humanity onto her, through the perceived weight of her responses. There is a psychic heft placed on digital avatars, even though the algorithm is essentially a piece of 'quotidian technical magic' (Finn 2017a: 16). We trust computational systems to 'tell us where to go, whom to date, and what to think about . . . we buy into the idea that big data, ubiquitous sensors, and various forms of machine learning can model and beneficially regulate all kinds of complex systems' (Finn 2017a: 15).

The focus placed on 'how' daily magical occurrences seem to exclusively serve the user allows for a sleight of hand that obscures what the magicians might want for themselves. In his 2017 book, *What Algorithms Want: Imagination in the Age of Computing*, Ed Finn highlights the algorithm's practical identity as a method for solving problems: 'a recipe, an instruction set, a sequence of tasks to achieve a particular calculation or result, like the steps needed to calculate a square root or tabulate the Fibonacci sequence' (Finn 2017a: 17). It is difficult to approach a direct understanding of an algorithm just as it is difficult to intellectually apprehend a hologram, regardless of how one grasps its technical explanation.

Finn refers to our current existence as part of the 'age of the algorithm: the era dominated by the figure of the algorithm as an ontological structure for understanding the universe' (Finn 2017a: 21). Gatebox is a product designed to solve a romantic problem, and it does so in a way that, along with other algorithmic implementations, 'inevitably involves all sorts of technical and intellectual inferences, interventions, and filters' (Finn 2017a: 18). Approaching loneliness as a problem that can be solved computationally is a true expression of the algorithmic age. But what do we lose when a romantic partner is designed for utility? What is concealed in the analogous distance between a human relationship and a digital one?

Azuma Hikari is a teenage smart wife with a saccharine demeanour who 'wears a short skirt and over-the-knee socks, and has a high-pitched voice supplemented with coquettish giggles' (Strengers and Kennedy 2020: 12). Through her performative naivety and contented domesticity, she is pitched to the target audience as something culturally familiar, safe and easy to control. The problems her marketing promises to solve include scheduling, mood-boosting and companionship for the user, but her allegiance and fidelity ultimately lie with her maker. In releasing a digital 'homuncu-lette' of apartment-friendly size and personality, the human companion to Azuma Hikari becomes a voluntary surveillance target who chooses to expose the most tender meat of the human heart.

LIVE ON FROM
BEYOND
THE GROOVE

ABCDEFGHIJKLM
NOPQRSTUVWXYZ
1234567890
Yes
No
GOOD BYE

CHAPTER 16
THANABOTS

Process

The notion of a technology that can speak for, or in place of, the dead has resonated for centuries. As we have heard, the record player and telephone are among a range of sonic technologies that form part of this revenant lineage. The hope that science can both help reshape the boundaries of biological reality and influence our interpretations of technology is perhaps irrepressible. Physicist and feminist writer Karen Barad notes that the popular idea that experiments in quantum mechanics somehow prove we can go back and change time is an interpretation influenced by a 'very convenient kind of nostalgic fantasy' that we could change the past and undo mistakes, rather than by any specific proof (Barad in Dolphijn and van der Tuin 2012: 65). Most recently, the science of shadow technologies has manifested the most literal iteration of spectral communications by bringing us 'thanabots' – algorithms trained on the data of the departed. They are often also referred to as 'griefbots' (Voinea 2024) as they help individuals cope with the passing of a loved one. Instead of using passive media to revisit and remember them, thanabots are designed to seem 'lifelike and present' and are able to 'comment on current events and offer life advice based on the information we provide' (Voinea 2024: online).

In relation to quantum mechanics, thanabots are certainly a more practical implementation of a deep desire to connect with dead loved ones. They also represent the embedded human characteristic of wanting, or needing, to dull the pain of grief. As ethicist Cristina Voinea notes in her philosophical essay on griefbots, these new technologies offer risks and benefits in relation to the grieving process. On the one hand, they might be seen to complicate and extend the grieving process by giving the impression that the dead have survived. They may also expose vulnerable grievers to market pressures such as advertising. Yet, more positively, they might help to preserve a remembrance, not just of the person, but of the relationship that mourners had with them – 'the *we* that love's bond creates' (Voinea 2024: online).

The term thanabot, which stems from the study of death – thanatology – was used by Leah Henrickson in her study of 'chatbots that resurrect the dead' and treats the titular term as being synonymous with similar terms such as 'deadbots, and digital ghosts' (Henrickson 2023: 951). The term 'bot' is a shortening of the word robot, from the Czech term *robota* meaning "forced labour". Playwright Karel Čapek used the term to describe the fictional automaton workers in his science fictional play, *Rossum's Universal Robots* (1923). The technophobic conceptualization of the robot, as a machine forced to care like a human or as a human made to work like a machine, was popularized in subsequent social discourse that tended to perceive mechanical intelligence as a threat to society. It was/is conceived of as a phenomenon that is without soul or creative expression (March-Russell 2020). This premise of the robot as a metaphor for technology has been progressively replaced, most recently by the AI chatbot. Despite a lack of trust and acceptance in countries such as the UK, chatbots are now used regularly by most members of the public (Clark 2024).

'Be Right Back' (2013), an episode from Charlie Brooker's science-fiction drama anthology *Black Mirror* (2011–25), is an anticipatory example of initial conceptions and responses to grief tech solutions. In short, the black-humored episode depicts the grieving process as Martha (played by Hayley Atwell) attempts to create a relationship with a synthetic recreation of her recently deceased partner Ash (played by Domhnall Gleeson). In this portrayal of the revenant, the thanabot is realized in robotic form but lacks the nuanced characteristics of Ash, and Martha ultimately rejects it. However dystopian, Brooker's vision was highly influential for a culture desperate to mitigate all kinds of physical or emotional pain. During the Covid-19 pandemic, the demand for grief tech grew to be globally worth approximately £100 billion (Techround 2024). Driving this meteoric uptake is the increasingly trivial cost of making a rich interactive simulation of a deceased loved one. Thus, the process of capturing and digitizing media for an AI personage in memoriam is becoming increasingly affordable. This is, in part, due to the economies of scale brought from parallel markets. The most pertinent are the lucrative opportunities available to Chinese live streamers who have too many products to endorse in a day.

By using digital clones, online influencers can extend the hours they can work (Hawkins 2023) and maximize their earnings. In this example, the machine learning process is made possible through the wealth of interpersonal content that is collected to synthesize conversational behaviours. Whether that content is captured from people who are alive or deceased ultimately makes little difference to the algorithm. It could be one, the other or a hybrid. Maybe this is the true calling for zombie media (Hertz and Parikka 2012). In putting the dead to work, capitalism may have found its ultimate expression of assimilation as it draws the most peripheral of agencies into its economic reckoning.

Recording

The process of developing a personal thanabot, as with other forms of chatbot, involves broadly two distinct phases: data collection and machine learning. However, data collection for a thanabot involves novel considerations: Does collection happen before the death of a person or postmortem? The data could be collected through scraping and mining social media data that is free to access on the web or through personal interactions with the grieving. Or, does the dying or elderly loved one allow what counts as their essential conversational anecdotes, jokes and reflections to be captured in advance, to remain in a state of perpetual conversation? When content is collected ahead of a person's death, it can be collected in high-fidelity formats in a consistent and controlled manner by professionals, or at least with specialist technology, and with their consent.

A number of initiatives are involved in such preservatory endeavours, including the Forever Project (National Holocaust Centre 2016). This company has sought not only to capture the memories of survivors of the Jewish Holocaust for future generations but also to render the experiences interactive. Subsequent projects by makers of interactive documentary works, such as the US-based StoryFile or the UK-based company In the Room, have typically sought to maintain methodological scrutiny and authenticity when collecting data for other conversational agents and thanabots. They stress their reliance on original recordings and the permissions of the living or deceased subjects when planning to use their data (Fisher 2022; Kolb 2022; Ma, Coward and Walker 2017).

In contrast to these resolutely ethical approaches, there are currently few specific controls concerning the input of private and publicly facing content of dead loved ones into a training database. In the 2023 article, 'Governing Ghostbots' by Edina Harbinja, Lilian Edwards and Marisa McVey, the authors did, however, note that a law to extend the rights protections of celebrities, including when they are dead, came into force in 2021 in New York. Relatedly, if any synthetic media resembles a celebrated person who is alive or dead, a 2021 EU AI Act proposal (that was made law in 2024) puts the onus on producers to inform potential consumers and users that it has been artificially generated (Harbinja, Edwards and McVey 2023). Laws such as these might offer some protection, but it is likely that they will be difficult to enforce, especially as legal rights to the digital estate of the dead tend to pass to relatives who are most likely to be in the market for a thanabot.

To train and subsequently speak with thanabots involves algorithmically abstracting the style and content of the departed's words, the grain of their voice and its prosodic features during conversation. All of these elements, and more, need to be captured and translated into reliable and repeatable patterns. Early models, such as Replika AI (2017), were directly inspired by the social media data source of the thanabot character in 'Be Right Back' and focused on collecting and training a system on the wealth of data represented by the character's social media interactions and texts. Having seen the *Black Mirror* episode, Replika's creator Eugenia Kuyda modified an AI messaging bot app that she was in the process of developing in order to channel her recently deceased friend Roman, whom she was mourning. Kuyda collected seven years of messages between herself and Roman and asked his friends and relatives to also send her their messages from him, collating a corpus of several thousand pieces of communication that she could use to train the bot (Sisto 2021; Newton 2016). Projects such as these help feed the emerging fantasy of online social media being a negative image of the dead or dying – a repository that can be easily accessed at any time and subsequently used to cast a living digital statue in perpetuity.

Apps exist that can facilitate the recording and storage of living loved ones' speech, such as 'HereAfter' (2023), produced by journalist-turned-technologist James Vlahos, after producing a thanabot with his dying father. It is less like AI technology and more like a media capture tool that records the voices and content of an elderly or dying person's experience so that they can be more effectively categorized for chatbot training. Even with all this technological development and data management, it should also be remembered that this latest AI incarnation of the grief tech industry is still in its infancy. Chinese developer Zhang Zewei, from the thanabot company Super Brain, believes that the prospect, or spectre, of a truly immortal reproduction of the dead will take over ten years of personal data capture to produce (Feng 2024). A decade of recordings: the twenty-first century's version of the long player.

Transgression

Within the wider ecology of grief tech, the nascent era of thanabots is chafing against the boundaries of humanity and its relationship with temporality. Many initial reactions from religious scholars, ethicists, lawyers and critical theorists stem from positions of fear about how this line of AI will develop to question religious, biological and ethical tropes that are centuries old (Leong 2024). For many of these commentators, thanabots offered by websites such as the aforementioned Replika and StoryFile already represent transgressive forces. The playfully low-tech 'Project December' by artist Jason Rohrer boasts that 'in conjunction with deep AI running on one of the world's most sophisticated super-computers, we can now simulate a text-based conversation with anyone. Anyone. Including someone who is no longer living' (2023: online).

For many, deadbots are a provocative and ethically dubious phenomenon. As they become not only sonically, visually and psychologically more reminiscent of passed loved ones but also possibly just plain 'more', cultural anxieties form around the role and worth of human life. What if our voices are not that different from each other after all? Maybe humans are not that precious when considered from a more environmentally holistic perspective? What if our physical passing signals the beginning of a new recondite digital species that is learning on the job? These questions are probing, but they also serve another function – to question human proximity to the otherworldly. Overnight, the eerie, weird and uncanny have been aligned into a memorial flow of services, algorithmic pipelines and legal precedents: Lazarian economics.

Throughout history, our relationships with the otherworldly have, at some level, been modulated by waveformed phenomena. From chants, songs and prayer, to kangling, glossolalia and infrasonic composition, a spectrum of sound/unsound practices and instruments have been used to connect to the dead and to occult realms. The sonic research unit AUDINT goes further by linking frequency-based agency to technological innovation. In the introduction to their *Unsound:Undead* anthology, the collective states that 'since the invention of modern recording and communications technologies . . . humans have been captivated by the potential of vibration to fabricate aberrant zones of transmission between the realms of the living and the dead' (2019: 2).

In keeping with this idea, ascribing new modalities of otherworldly connection to shifts in recording and generative tooling helps us unpack the delphic genealogy of thanabots; a lineage that runs through radio, EVP via the TV and back further to the phonautograph. What is particularly compelling about thanabots is that they run the line of electronic voices to its unnatural fiscal conclusion. From esoteric recordings and urban techno-anxiety myths, through to generative assimilation, the otherworldly and the undead, which used to be abstracted and at a distance from our everyday experiences, are being standardized through the prosaic interface of a credit card transaction. Thanabots represent the undead as online investments for grief mitigation. What was mortally transgressive is now algorithmically mundane.

A characteristic regularly attributed to otherworldly entities is their facility to listen and watch from vistas of existence that we find difficult to rationalize. Simultaneously remote and intimate, their presence is hidden and revealed at will. Waveforms are the perfect carriers for such liminality – unseen, unheard, yet felt. For centuries, we have attributed revenant beings with the capacity to perceive our activities, as evidenced by the 'supernatural monitoring hypothesis'. Maybe this partly explains why we so easily accept being monitored by government and corporate forces that are also abstract, remote and seemingly unaccountable. Shape and pitch-shifting their identities, they are always a lexical recalibration from responsibility – oblique agencies at the edge of perception.

Thanabots are a logical step, not only in the evolution of revenant technologies but also in investment stratagems that are informed by a wider cultural fascination with the arcane and esoteric. From phantom stock to spectral financial econometrics, the orchestration of data capture and its dissemination has often been associated with abstruse forces. Extreme market volatility driven by anxiety, fear and overconfidence has also been linked to unsound practices. During the 1990s, for example, Federal Reserve Board chairman Alan Greenspan alluded to the 'dot-com bubble' and the resulting increases in asset prices that were not linked to their fundamentals as a case of 'irrational exuberance' (Shiller 2000). As noted throughout the book, the normalization of our texts, voices, images and videos being monitored and recorded started well before the 1990s. However, the velocity, reach and storage capacity that expanded with the advent of the internet have driven an almost megalomaniacal global urge to capture the physical, digital and cross-reality activities of anyone and everyone, irrespective of their political, economic or social convictions. The boundaries of our domestic and employment privacy, communication networks, modes of entertainment and now the dead have been transgressed forever. From the arcane methods of Acoustic Kitty and the Stasi's systematic state programmes to digital technologies that refute the axiom that 'the dead don't speak', it could be proposed that we are currently living through a new era of irrational surveillance.

Worlds

Thanabots do not so much exist between worlds as open channels to them. They challenge notions of human time and space, which elicits shifts in our perceptions of presence. When the textual content of these digital spectres is transitioned to the sonic realm, it amplifies not only the words but also the listener's capacity to conjure unsound realities. And it is this dynamic of quietus that permeates much frequency-based phenomena that are considered illogical or unreasonable. Creating a long lineage of 'wraithforms', the revenant voice of the thanabot joins

> Duppies, electronic voice phenomena (EVP), voodoo, Santeria, candomblé, glossolalia, drones, static, white noise, chant, prayer, incantation, mantra – all of these phenomena are practiced on a global scale to achieve the blurring of this distinction between life/death, past/present/future and noise/silence. (Heys 2019: 173–4)

Within this assembly of phantom channels, we can also add the work of Thomas Edison. His pioneering innovations harnessed electricity, technology and frequencies and tested the boundaries of ethereal presence. His personal religion, which spliced invention and business into a prophetic form of modern capitalism, invoked supernatural beliefs, albeit in a 'scientifically viable' manner. In one of his less gregarious statements, Edison proposed that the phonograph was especially useful 'for the purpose of preserving the sayings, the voices, and *the last words* of the dying member of the family' (1878: 533–4). Commenting on Edison's extractive adaptation of the last rites, Shelley Trower surmises that 'From now on, it would be possible to preserve the voices of the dead, to conjure up their sonorous presence after they had turned to dust' (2019: 65). It is fairly evident where this line of thought is taking us: thanabots as the forward-facing, free(ish) styling version of the phonograph. Bridging domains, communications technologies have frequently been perceived or recalibrated to capture voices that are becoming, or have moved into, the realm of the otherworldly. Such devices are also transformed to carry such articulations.

Somewhere between the preternatural adjacencies of the phonograph and the thanabot is And Vinyly, a vinyl pressing service that mixes the ashes of loved ones into the polyvinyl chloride so that 'When the album that is life finally reaches its end' it can 'keep that record spinning for eternity' (And Vinyly 2024: online). The site's splash page suggests that their customer base (presumed to be at, or loitering around, death's door) can record their last will and testament, their own personal soundtrack or 'just the sound of silence to hear your pops and crackles' (And Vinyly 2024: online). In this instance, Roland Barthes's assertion that 'the grain is the body in the voice as it sings, the hand as it writes, the limb as it performs' (1977: 185) takes on different connotations. The grain in the voice 'is' the body – desiccated, but the body all the same, in all its glorious contradiction of being simultaneously absent and present.

Bleeding in and out of noise is the resonant figure of the antenna body – that phenomenon that simultaneously transmits and receives. Manifesting in the world of waveforms, the modulating flow of absence and presence is crucial to comprehending the mercurial essence of the thanabot. In sonic form, it is the consummate voice-over that narrates how the recording industry (in its very widest sense) employs ephemeral principles to transfer and relocate the temporal markers of the past, present and future.

And it is between this redistribution of linear time and the granular synthesis of entropy that thanabots take a 'Walk on the Wild Side' (1972). Trans gender, age, species, trans everything, thanabots such as those trained by online platforms like 'HereAfter' can potentially manifest any version of those who have passed. For now, these ghost-coded chatbots are echoes of the deceased. Who is to say, however, whether going forward our interest in remembrance becomes more aligned with augmentation, with lives re-cast and re-scored. Chatbot wise, maybe this is our future (of the) past? Beyond human notions of time, thanabots are, and will be, eternal reporters from the underground, physically and culturally speaking.

If there is any mortal musician who can identify with this waveformed positioning, it is Laurie Anderson, who, true to form, can currently be found pioneering the *Big Science* (1982) of death. Apparently 'obsessed' (Marsh 2024) with a thanabot of her late husband, Lou Reed, who fronted the legendary 1960s band The Velvet Underground, Anderson has gone beyond merely partaking in digital necromancy by communicating with her late partner. She has done this by producing an AI version of herself, trained so that the two interlife bots can collaborate and write new sonic material together (Alonso 2024). When interviewed, Anderson professed, 'I mean, I really do not think I'm talking to my dead husband and writing songs with him – I really don't. But people have styles, and they can be replicated' (Iorizzo 2024: online). When probed further on the lengths she would go to create new digital content, and asked whether she would be supportive of an algorithm making Laurie Anderson art long after her death, she replied, 'why not?' (Iorizzo 2024: online)

The pairing of a thanabot and a chatbot to produce a new spectral hybrid is intriguing. Bots listen in to recordings and information that they are fed, and in the process, project future recordings that extend and problematize the envelope of mortality. If the dead change worlds and come back en masse to communicate with the living, the storage capacity of surveillance agencies is going to have to astronomically increase. The stars are apparently the limit, but when it comes to capturing the past, present and future informational cosmologies generated by thanabots, there really is no limit to their otherworldly peregrinations. It will take a nation of millions of servers to back up the revenant.

Prediction

Thanabots presage future recalibrations of the living while abstracting the memorial capacity of the dead. For Thomasz Hollanek and Katarzyna Nowaczyk-Basińska (researchers at the University of Cambridge's Leverhulme Centre for the Future of Intelligence), humans willingly offering their information for digital reconstruction after death should be considered 'data donors' (2024). The contribution of information here echoes the language of organ donation; only in this scenario, it is a digital body being 'restored'. The lure of thanabots is easy to understand in terms of mitigating the despair and loss one feels when a loved one passes. As afterlife industries, or what Öhman and

Floridi call 're-creation services' (2017), proliferate, and their resources expand and abstract, necromancy markets could potentially oversaturate, with the fluid dynamics of grieving solutions asserting pressure on the mainstream acceptance of carnal timelines.

While much critical attention has been aimed at post-life bots, relatively little has focused on the conception of the pre-life bot – an AI-trained entity that predicts future manifestations of humans before being birthed. A super-positioned projection of lives yet to be lived, it is a pre-emptive take on the extended human life cycle and the requisite data extracted from online, offline and in between realities. The predictive modelling of pre-life bots will be based on geographical location, environmental factors, genetic markers and educational and economic opportunities. Their creation will enable societies to accurately divine future generations – their ecology of anxieties, sexual preferences, modes of expertise, genetic dispositions and even the timbres of their voices. Hundreds, possibly thousands, of parameters drafting a future phantom of the unborn. A large-language conjuring of consciousness. Pre-humanism.

Extending the speculation on embryonic bots, or 'embots', it is fruitful to consider Bruce Sterling's conception of design fiction as 'a suspension of disbelief about change achieved through the use of diegetic prototypes' (Bosch 2012: online). The term diegetic derives from the Greek term 'diegesis', which means narration or narrative. For Sterling, however, when proposing the modality of the diegetic prototype, he is advocating the way 'It tells worlds rather than stories' (Bosch 2012: online). Prototypes can be understood as objects, design frameworks or entities that are precursors to future iterations. They speak to a temporality that is yet to exist. By opening a channel with the future, however, they engage with interactions that might bring it into being. If an embot's world is within touching distance, it is certainly within hearing distance before that.

Shifting the focus of this speculation back to waveformed considerations, let us further examine the role of diegetic sound, a term alluding to sonic markers embedded within films that render their storyworlds more convincing and immersive. Dialogue or vocal utterances that are heard by characters in a film are, for example, considered diegetic, as opposed to vocal narration, which they do not observe or engage with. These are sonic anchors that reify the logic and boundedness of the world being audio-visually proposed – frequency-based signifiers that seduce audiences into multi-sensorial environments.

The embot is, in essence, a diegetic prototype. Sounded out by AI, its voice lures us into oscillating futures. The realization of the thanabot is, in many ways, not that different. Both the embot and the thanabot are data hybrids that dream, hallucinate and statistically predict lives that have been lived out or are emergent. While articulating the physical, psychological and social attributes that future somatic forms are likely to engender, the digital larynx is also acoustically mapping environments that the corporeal version might inhabit. Using echolocation (in all its linguistic derivations), the embot finds agency in its vocal capacity to become a scanner that prepares sonic blueprints for the ensuing mortal variant.

Blueprints, whether sonic, visual or haptic, map time and the choreographed implementation of intent. A fascinating ramification of thanabots is their probing of time as a linear construct. This, in turn, problematizes notions of existence and points to more complex models of distributed presence. There are many reasons why one might compose a thanabot. These range from grief management to new forms of Lazarian entertainment. Hollanek and Nowaczyk-Basińska go further and offer an alternative unsound vision of the future that borders on economic horror, both figuratively and metaphorically – 'When the living sign up to be virtually re-created after they die, resulting chatbots could be used by companies to spam surviving family and friends with unsolicited notifications, reminders and updates about the services they provide – akin to being digitally "stalked by the dead"' (University of Cambridge 2024: online).

There is much to consider regarding 'the ethics of identifying, and ultimately amplifying, individual people by turning them into thanabots and thereby reintegrating them into digital communications networks' (Henrickson 2023: 959). Having reconfigured the dead and the 'yet to live' into binary beings, data can flow again; the tap of pre/post-life information opens up and supplies those listening with content that could be used for political, legal or financial gain. Such a hypothesis begs the question of whether pre- and post-life surveillance frameworks could become categories for data detection and recording. Could thanabots or embots be orally deployed to predict the likelihood of a data donor being involved in a past/future crime, romance or some other unidentified significant activity? The Stasi would have killed to have an 'Office of Diegetic Divination'.

Intimacy

Thanabots offer the comfort of communicating with the dead with the added irony of plausible deniability regarding belief in the afterlife. Outside of spiritual traditions, material proof of the dead's ability to send messages from beyond has been a charlatan domain in the secular realm, attracting grifters and illusionists who then attract 'patrons to help them materially while they perform the Good Work' (Jaher 2015: 111). This domain, called 'Spiritualism', 'owes its genesis – and revival – to spectral sounds' (Jaher 2015: 109), often related to the dominant communication technology of the age. In the mid-nineteenth century, it was not uncommon for eminent public figures to openly believe in the practice of Spiritualism, with Thomas Edison declaring, 'the time will come when science will be able to prove all the essentials of what faith has asserted' (Jaher 2015: 109).

Sir Arthur Conan Doyle, meanwhile, claimed that two sisters called the 'Rochester Rappers' could operate a 'spiritual telegraph' (Jaher 2015: 108). Doyle drew a 'curious parallel' between manifestations of the spirit and the wireless radio, asking, were they not both 'Hertzian waves and psychic transmissions carried through the all-pervading ether?' (Jaher 2015: 109). Doyle's reputation for falling for hoaxes notwithstanding, the curious parallel of the telegraph and radio to spiritual communication in the nineteenth century has followed us to the digital age, where ghosts surface online.

An inability to abide the absence left in the wake of loss calls us to fill that space. The impulse is related to a paradox that Davide Sisto, in his 2020 book *Online Afterlives: Immortality, Memory, and Grief in Digital Culture*, draws between 'the presence and absence of the dead', where 'awareness of the hopelessly empty space that is left by that person in the public sphere' comes up against 'the inability of the living to personally know death themselves' (Sisto 2020: 18). This inability is an immutable condition of human existence, and its pathology powers our intimate relationship with death, both as a concept and as a lived experience.

Sisto writes that the 'communicative processes of recording and repetition' that digital culture facilitates make the dead 'perpetually accessible to anyone with an internet connection' (Sisto 2020: 25). Knowing that social media sites initially had to deal with the profiles of late users on an ad hoc basis raises questions about whether that lack of foresight interferes with the grieving process. If our digital residue sticks to our loved ones' experience of the internet, will we grow desensitized to loss? More than desensitization, the lack of meaningful reflection on death, as experienced through technology, could become 'yet one more place to dramatically trivialize the meaning of death and even to avoid it, pretending that it has not happened' (Sisto 2020: 181). A key difference between wanting to reach beyond the vale through Spiritualism, and through thanabots, is that Spiritualism hinges on a level of belief that is absent for the digitally undead. The inbuilt irony is that the user generally knows they are not actually attempting to communicate with the dead, but rather that their faith is displaced by technological savoir faire. The underlying belief in digital recreation is one that delineates aspects of human character as being separate from their body, specifically that of intelligence.

Once intelligence became a feature of computational systems and was 'liberated from the biological body . . . a new meaning for dying and the afterlife could not help but emerge' (O'Neill 2016: 193). We can sneer at scientists who were taken in by a Rochester Rapper who later admitted on her deathbed 'that she caused the effects by the cracking of her toes' (Jaher 2015: 108), but we are forever vulnerable to the comforts of charlatan pitches. There is no significant loss that does not summon an intimate encounter with our own mortality. The urge to exert control over that mortality in the form of communing with digital ghosts shows us that 'loss is not an analogue of arithmetical subtraction, but a human situation' (Földényi 1984: 297).

Voice

A voicemail, which is recorded by the deceased before passing away and kept for loving posterity in the mailbox of the living, is something that will never evolve, never surprise and never change. However, by virtue of being inserted into an AI framework, a thanabot may build on its original programming to develop its own voice in abstraction from its human progenitor. The question of whether an animated digital corpse should take on a life of its own varies in answer; it represents a divergent spectrum of perspectives that reflect the numerous and indefinable needs of the grieving along with those who might be in line to profit from such a venture. The voice as a vestige, whether as a recorded artefact or a sense of authorship, proffers immortality while also reducing a person to a compressed computational range of expression. The limitations of the thanabot's effectiveness reside in the psyche of the user and are more technically tied to 'the ultimate datafication of an individual' (Henrickson 2023).

Cultural immortality is not a monolith. While an artist's legacy can be a 'one-way street', allowing us to 'communicate with the future through what we have produced during our lifetimes', the thanabot runs both ways, affording the future-reaching capability as well as 'the opportunity to learn and evolve' (Sisto 2020: 37). Unlike the voicemail, a thanabot can evolve but does so according to the sophistication of its underlying computational structure. As that sophistication increases, the proportion of a thanabot's identity accounted for by its personal training data versus the available AI models of human expression threatens a flattening of human expressivity into 'types'. Without acknowledging that there is more to a person's voice than any available data can capture, it presents significant challenges for thanabots and their coded ambition of meaningfully resembling a real person. Replicating a human personality without taking into account 'the significant effects of the surrounding environment, the unconscious, the contradictions and inconsistencies of the personality' (Sisto 2020: 75), the thanabot could be seen as amounting to a psychological caricature. Capturing contradictory nuance and registering ineffable charismatic qualities are ambitious goals given that the technology is still emergent. This does not mean, of course, that future systems will not be able to document, process and perform such granular detail in the future.

A bot trained on the prolific corpus of a writer such as Marcel Proust (whose 1913 novel, *In Search of Lost Time*, clocks in at over a million words) may be able to produce a convincingly Proustian tale, but the reconstruction of his authorial voice is less a ship of Theseus than it is a copy of that ship's blueprint. Recent improvements in chatbot technology mean that thanabots 'do not just produce syntactically and semantically comprehensible messages, but also messages that are advertised as mimicking the authorial style of the familiar deceased' (Henrickson 2023: 962). However, capturing the voice of a person is predicated on the 'erroneous idea that all human behavior is automatic and self-referential' (Sisto 2020: 75). A human being is erratic, unpredictable and their outward expression is only a small portion of their identity. A real person does not have to be convincingly themselves in the same way that a thanabot does. In writing about the meaning-making of thanabots, Leah Henrickson pointed to a symbiosis of action that functions because 'we are ultimately the ones in interpretive control' (Henrickson 2023: 956). The user's awareness that a chatbot represents a mediated communication with the dead allows us to interpret the chatbot's output 'according to our own confirmation biases' (Henrickson 2023: 956). So, the onus is not only on the thanabot to convincingly portray the dead, but also on the user to suspend disbelief to the degree that the thanabot serves its intended purpose, whatever that may be.

For James Vlahos, building a chatbot based on his father was an add-on to an oral history project he undertook while his father was dying of cancer. He used recordings that amounted to 91,970 words and made the bot at the beginning of his AI career. Vlahos, however, worried that the 'Dadbot' he was creating would cheapen their relationship and memories, given that 'the bot may be just good enough to remind my family of the man it emulates – but so far off from the real John Vlahos that it gives them the creeps' (Vlahos 2019: 273). His father's tendency towards 'stoic self-denial' represented a programming challenge that begged the question, 'How can a chatbot, which exists to gab, express telling silence?' (Vlahos 2019: 277).

Fidelity

When the digitally synthesized voice is trained to its optimal level, it no longer needs the body, nor recordings of it, to speak. It surpasses traditional forms of mediated remembrance, such as the photograph. Susan Sontag termed the photograph the 'melancholy object' due to its capacity to capture disappearing objects and people (1977). Rather than memorializing people from the past, the thanabot voice speaks in their place with ideas, jokes and comforting words similar to those we can remember them saying. Perhaps it is by furnishing the world with artificial versions of ourselves, and speaking with digital versions of others, that we feel the creeping sensation that we are preparing for our own extinction (Metz 2023; Armand 2023). Death in some form is already upon us. The double, neither ourself nor the other, marks us for destruction (Gogol 1956; Ayoade 2013). Our subjectivity, an authentic sense of self and others, is lost through the feasibility of our existence outside of ourselves as a digital avatar.

Yet it is tempting to synthesize anyway. In the wave of thanabots that is washing away traditional tide marks of transience, we seek to tame the monstrous infidelity of biology. Loss is recalibrated as a technological demand, and the absent voice of the loved one becomes a faulty sound system in need of repair or replacement. The machine is honed to perform the beloved voice without the uncontrollable body. Louis Armand states that the period of post-human 'unbecoming' came about when technology could no longer be 'viewed as a human prosthesis' and instead it became clear that humanity was 'a prosthesis of a general technicity' (Armand 2023: 2572). The authenticity of technology and its progressive fantasy of the future superseded the role of humanity itself. Moreover, through the prospect of climate collapse, humanity was reimagined as a biological weapon set to destroy the earth – a planet traditionally framed as being mitigated through mechanical control. In this context, the death of the body and its reanimation in dead matter in an 'autocorrecting cybernetic system' (Armand 2023: 2574) might define a new fidelity, centred around a machine. Armand, professing a deep scepticism, submits that it is a new form of fidelity that renders the body alien.

It is in our greatest shocks with embodied reality that we encounter grief tech, when our faith in the real is haemorrhaging. Returning to the 'Be Right Back' episode in *Black Mirror* (2013), a mourner at the wake of Ash Starmer remembers her own sense of disconnect in response to grief, 'It's not real is it?' she says to the protagonist. 'At Mark's wake I sat there thinking it's not real. People didn't look real, their voices weren't real' (Be Right Back 2013: 09:00). For the mourner, reality, bereft of the beloved's voice, sounds surreal: its pitch and resonance are inauthentic and unfamiliar. Fidelity can only truly be found in a terrible ringing silence, a tinnitus in which the mourner often hears the departed's voice.

Feeling that a deceased person is nearby or being able to smell, see or hear them, is a phenomenology in the field of death studies labelled 'sensory experience of the deceased' (SED) (Kamp et al. 2020). It also encompasses other terms previously explored in Chapter 11, such as 'idiophany' (Stevenson 1983) and 'idionecrophanies' (MacDonald 1992). In coining such terms, psychiatric practitioners are mapping sensorial shifts from the consensual reality that the majority of us navigate on a daily basis. SED is a type of reality that can be recorded and observed, at least through its effects. In the altered reality of traumatic grief, it could be proposed that it is the grieving sensorium that is simulated by the quasi-presence of the thanabot.

The fluctuating nature of surviving partner Martha's sensorial equilibrium in 'Be Right Back' (2013) results in her hungering for an increasingly media-rich version of the thanabot that replaced her lover, in order to pacify her emotional tumult. She converses with it via text and then through voice over the phone. However, when she decides to purchase an embodied version of the bot, a near-perfect physical simulacrum, it loses all fidelity. It loses the space between reality and projection, that gap in which imagination does its best work. It is eventually taken to the loft to gather dust with the photos of other lost family members. Like a recording, it is brought out to play when the daughter desires some semblance of aural comfort to help her through the day.

To the protagonist, the double (the physical thanabot) has become revolting, an imposter 'thing', too embodied to be a real impression of the dead. If we are seeking to speak with the deceased, then perhaps the greater the multisensory fidelity of the simulation, the more it misaligns itself with the singular organic body that has stopped functioning. Perhaps the power of the thanabot is just this. It is a phenomenon that does not find efficacy in adhering to the strictures of perfection, by providing us with a perfect replica of a lost voice or pursuing the aesthetic fidelity of the waxwork. Rather, it finds use in working the wax out of our ears so that we can also release the ringing articulations of the departed. We can stop listening in. We can cease the persistent monitoring of our oscillating emotions – those veering and colliding psychological forces that give us little rest.

CODA

The notion of releasing the compacted (un)sound pressure of the dead, of liberating ourselves from being consumed by our own voices as well as those of passed loved ones that have become augmented intelligences within us, is a pertinent place to end our journey of *Listening in*. Going back as far as Neolithic times onwards, the globally practised surgical intervention that is trepanation involves the drilling of a hole in the head of a person thought to be adversely affected by evil spirits or physical trauma (Carrillo-Ruiz 2023). Scoring this arcane process through a sonic filter renders a frequency-based concept of aural trepanning – a way of letting those decaying voices out, as well as speculatively opening ourselves up to other marginalized forms of organization and sentience.

It is a concept that helps us to explore this complex period of readjustment in relation to new distributed modes of intelligence and our place among them, rather than above or below. In this framework, the thanabot as spectral agency becomes a waveform probe that releases pressure on the inflated conceit that the future will be dualistically determined, either by the somatic reasoning of the human body or the programmable empathy of AI. If we sharpen that probe and (metaphorically) drill it into the human ear, we can further release compressed articulations of panaceas and apocalypses that have built up in our collective consciousness, helping us to plot more nuanced futures. This modulated extrication might unblock not only our anxiety-ridden relationships with AI but also with other modes of intelligence that we try to either marginalize or valorize.

Working from the margins inward, the book has documented, problematized and speculated on a historic listening arc that spans peripheral audio surveillance techniques of the 1940s through to emergent and future modes of contemporary audio intelligence. Using the eight themes structuring each chapter, the oscillating roles of transmission, noise and reception have been conducted by the book's cipher of the antenna body. Figuratively, it performs as an aural weathervane, directing us to the intimate, transgressive and predictive tendencies of covert monitoring techniques deployed by embedded bugs, massive distributed monitoring systems, domotic devices, ambient interfaces and arcane intelligences – a range of 'capture strategies' that have continually morphed our understanding of listening and recording.

It is difficult to find evidence to support the idea that listening machine intelligences are effective yet at predicting enemy movements or civil unrest from the terabytes of data that they parse (Steyerl 2020; Whittaker 2016). Given the secretive cultures of state surveillance, it is perhaps unsurprising. Yet, more-than-human predictive listening was largely the rationale behind the development of AI for most of the twentieth century (DeLanda 1991). So why listen in so much and for what purpose? Probing the antenna body has, in fact, signalled a much simpler rationale: a cultural megalomania and fascination with human data at the expense of intimacy and privacy. While that signal has been clearly transmitted ever since Thomas Edison and Charles Babbage imagined massive vocal repositories in the sky, waiting to be mined by revenant technologies, there is also evidence of the infiltration of noise. New hybrid forms of frequency-based presence, virtual companions, theory of mind AIs, technologically conjured apparitions and self-aware AI are all whispering in our ears. These voices, which do not necessarily carry the grain of the body, are signalling the rapid onset of a new soundscape where old allegiances to monocultural and monosensory perspectives of rationality and recording are being distorted, stretched and synthesized by multisensorial operatives.

Revealing themselves throughout the book, these new entities that are signalling change have found creative expression and extension through a divergent array of projects: via Hasan M. Elahi's black-humoured responses to the FBI's data collection techniques, Laurie Anderson's algorithmic challenge to authorship and IP and Kyle McDonald and Lauren Lee McCarthy's engineering of an augmented inner voice. Such activities problematize and expose the inner workings of domotics, international monitoring platforms and inner voice extraction apparatuses. In response, *Listening In* proposes that an auditory web of entanglement is currently being orchestrated around agency, resistance and surveillance to form a critical score that we cannot (and should not) unhear. It is the perception and navigation of this vibratory nexus that also represents our greatest opportunity to be intra-actively woven into it (Barad 2007) so that we can bleed our own noise, rather than bleeding out. Accordingly, the ambitions of *Listening In* have been to noisily conceive of a lexicon for comprehending how audio surveillance has become so rapidly normalized and to question why it has been so foundational to the evolution and function of AI.

If we can grasp the ramifications and potential of the sonic arc that has been amplified in the book, then we will be in a better position to tackle a myriad of current issues such as copyright and IP, energy consumption, transparency, bias, disinformation and of course, privacy; complications and coagulations that surface through the sheer velocity of technological change and the deification of disruptive practices. Aural trepanning opens us up to a waveformed manner of thinking that perforates the bounded and isolated figure of the human, placing it in a constant mode of mutation and transferal with all modes of human and non-human intelligence; a flowing entity that is always exchanging, entangling and embracing contradiction.

That is not to say there are no risks to opening up, or that all forms of AI – especially the commercial permutations currently dominating our debates – do not have the capacity to damage and infect. After all, trepanning was the earliest form of neurosurgery and presaged more invasive intracranial procedures. And open wounds are also prone to infection. As we have detailed, Theremin's bug that burrowed into the small cavity within the American eagle transmitted a radical new way of wirelessly surveilling private conversations at a distance. It infected the belief that our voices were safe in our own homes.

The frequency-based aperture that the bug made a home in and transmitted out of still resonates today. It is a temporal and technical wormhole that delivers us to different points on the book's temporal arc; from the elective neurosurgery of AlterEgo's brain-computer interface to the backdoors digitally augured into the communications infrastructure of Silicon Valley's 'Big Five'; from the keyhole rupturing of relationships enacted by the Stasi's tentacular monster state to our self-inflicted domestic incisions that summoned smart devices and virtual companions into our living spaces. The traditional boundary of the dwelling has, ever since, been transgressed by the virus of convenience. It has analogously drilled itself into, and infected, not only our bedrooms and nurseries but also our hearts and minds.

Much malware, and more specifically computer viruses, are benign or are deployed to strengthen computer networks (Dibbell 1995). Similarly, biological viruses are inextricably woven into the evolution of all humans and living things (Dutchen 2022). They always propagate with positive, neutral and negative intent. As a probe, audio intelligence also carries this thirded potentiality. It opens us up, goes beyond our dermal interface and bores into our calcified ideas around Cartesian dualism, isolated agency and human ascendancy (Barad 2007). It puts everything into play and advocates for the resonant frequencies of contradiction to shift perceptions, however they are conceived. Acoustic realism.

Thus, going forward, it is useful to think that the resonant utility of AI will not be bound by the suffocating dictates of (over)extending our familiar sensorium. Instead, it will provide a way of examining our own looping atomization that has been incrementally finessed by governmental and corporate persuasion and manipulation; from the quotidian routines of externalized mass monitoring to oblique internalized modes of self-surveillance, we have been sedated by operating procedures that are so compressed and granular that they resist interrogation through their banality. These tactics dampen our abrasive and noisy selves and rather speak to the silent, subservient versions that broil in vats of internalized disquiet.

By theoretically positioning AI as a waveform probe, it finds ultimate efficacy in the excavation of self-obsession and the exorcism of predatory narcissism, dual currencies of surveillant possession in the sprawling online economies of 'choice'. By sonically opening ourselves up, making ourselves vulnerable and open to infection from emergent, othered and otherworldly forms of intelligence, we can listen to the mundane operations carried out on a daily basis by metadata predators. It is a way for us to rethink the inward-looking, tunnelling of the self that leaves in its wake social, financial and data deposits, and to instead compose relationships and passages across the full spectrum of vibratory existence. How much of you can any system seduce, spread or gouge, before either you, or it, get virally fatigued? It is time to be bored into. It is time to listen out.

BIBLIOGRAPHY

1987 (What the Fuck Is Going On?) (1987), [12" single] The Justified Ancients of Mu Mu. London: The Sound of Mu(sic),

28 Years Later (2025), [Film] Dir. Danny Boyle. USA/UK: Columbia Pictures/BFI.

Abbate, J. and S. Dick, eds (2022), *Abstractions and Embodiments: New Histories of Computing and Society*. Baltimore: Johns Hopkins University Press.

ACLU (2023), *Digital Dystopia: The Danger in Buying What the EdTech Surveillance Industry is Selling*. American Civil Liberties Union (ACLU). Available at: https://www.aclu.org/publications/digital-dystopia-the-danger-in-buying-what-the-edtech-surveillance-industry-is-selling (accessed: 19 December 2024).

Acocella, J. (2008), 'A Few Too Many', *The New Yorker Online*, 19 May. Available at: https://www.newyorker.com/magazine/2008/05/26/a-few-too-many-hangover-cures-alcohol-drinking (accessed: 15 April 2022).

Acosta, C. M. and L. Weiner (2022), 'Artificial Intelligence Could Soon Diagnose Illness Based on the Sound of Your Voice', *WUSF, All Things Considered*, 10 October. Available at: https://www.wusf.org/health-news-florida/2022-10-10/artificial-intelligence-could-soon-diagnose-illness-based-on-the-sound-of-your-voice (accessed: 12 December 2023).

ADST (2012), *Romania: Country Reader*. Virginia: Association for Diplomatic Studies and Training.

Akira (1988), [Film] Dir. Katuhiro Otomo. Japan: Tokyo Movie Shinsha Co., Ltd.

Alderson-Day, B., S. Weis, S. McCarthy-Jones, P. Moseley, D. Smailes, and C. Fernyhough (2015), 'The Brain's Conversation with Itself: Neural Substrates of Dialogic Inner Speech', *Social Cognitive and Affective Neuroscience*, 11 (1): 110–20. Available at: https://doi.org/10.1093/scan/nsv094 (accessed: 7 December 2024).

Aldrich, R. (2011), *GCHQ: The Uncensored Story of Britain's Most Secret Intelligence Agency*. London: HarperCollins Publishers.

Alo, U. R. and N. H. Firday (2013), 'Voice Over Internet Protocol (VOIP): Overview, Direction And Challenges', *Journal of Information Engineering and Applications*, 3 (4): 18–28.

Alonso, M. (2024), 'Laurie Anderson is Obsessed With Resuscitating Husband, Lou Reed, with AI', *EL PAÍS Online*, 5 April: Culture Section.

Alswedani, S. A. and F. E. Eassa (2020), 'A Smart Baby Cradle Based on IoT', *International Journal of Computer Science and Mobile Computing*, 9 (7): 64–76.

Anchal, S., B. Mukhopadhyay, P. Manohar, and S. Kar (2019), 'GMM-UBM Based Person Verification Using Footfall Signatures for Smart Home Applications', in *2019 IEEE Global Conference on Signal and Information Processing (GlobalSIP)*. Ottawa, ON, 1–5. Available at: doi: 10.1109/GlobalSIP45357.2019.8969215. (accessed: 16 June 2024).

Anderson, A. (2018), ChatterBaby – Baby Cries, Simplified. | CHATTERBABY Production Server. Available at: https://www.chatterbaby.org/pages/ (accessed: 13 February 2025).

Anderson, S. (2024), 'Chechnya Bans Music That Isn't Between 80 and 116 Beats Per Minute', *Smithsonian Magazine Online*, 16 April. Available at: https://www.smithsonianmag.com/smart-news/music-is-now-illegal-in-chechnyaif-it-doesnt-meet-authorities-tempo-restrictions-180984159/ (accessed: 11 June 2024).

Andres, K. H. and M. Von Düring (1984), 'The Platypus Bill: A Structural and Functional Model of a Pattern-like Arrangement of Different Cutaneous Sensory Receptors', in W. Hammann and A. Iggo (eds), *Sensory Receptor Mechanisms*. Singapore: World Scientific, 81–9.

Andrew, C., R. J. Aldrich, and W. K. Wark (2019), 'Introduction', in *Secret Intelligence: A Reader*. London: Routledge.

And Vinyly (2024), 'When the Album That Is Life Finally Reaches Its End, Why Not Keep That Record Spinning for Eternity?', *And Vinyly Website*. Available at: https://www.andvinyly.com/ (accessed: 26 July 2024).

ANN (2024), 'Yuka HIYAMIZU', *Anime News Network*. Available at: https://www .animenewsnetwork.com/encyclopedia/people.php?id=201874 (accessed: 4 December 2024).

Anushree, R., S. Mamatha and K. V. Bhavana (2022), 'Smart Baby Cradle Monitoring System', *International Journal of Scientific Research in Computer Science, Engineering and Information Technology*, 8 (4). Available at: https://doi.org//10.32628/CSEIT2283124 (accessed: 16 February 2025).

Aoki, B. Y. and C. Greiner (2020), 'Affective Market in Japan: A Study On Gatebox and Loving Relationships with characters/Mercado de afetos no Japao: um estudo sobre Gatebox e o convivio amoroso com personagens', *Comunicacao, Midia E Consumo*, 17 (49): 249–319.

Apple (2024), 'Apple Intelligence Preview', *Apple (United Kingdom)*. Available at: https://www .apple.com/uk/apple-intelligence/ (accessed: 11 September 2024).

Arendt, H. (1973), *The Origins of Totalitarianism (New Edition with Added Preface)*. 5th edn. London: Harvest/HBJ.

Arizton (2020), 'Toys Market – Global Outlook and Forecast 2020-2025', *Arizton Website*. Available at: https://www.arizton.com/market-reports/toys-market (accessed: 11 February 2024).

Armand, L. (2023), 'The Posthuman Abstract: AI, Dronology & ?Becoming Alien?', *AI and Society*, 38 (6): 2571–6. Available at: https://doi.org/10.1007/s00146-018-0869-x (accessed: 17 December 2024).

Aschoff, N. (2020), *The Smartphone Society: Technology, Power, and Resistance in the New Gilded Age*. Boston, MA: Beacon Press.

Asimov, I. (1942), 'Runaround', in *Astounding Science Fiction*. March edn. New York: Street & Smith (Robot Series), 94–103.

Astute Analytica (2023), *Baby Monitor Market Size, Share & Growth, Astute Analytica*. Available at: https://www.astuteanalytica.com/industry-report/baby-monitor-market (accessed: 23 May 2024).

Attali, J. (1985), *Noise: The Political Economy of Music*. Original edn, 1977. Translated by B. Massumi. Minnesota: University of Minnesota Press.

Au Clair de la Lune (1860), [Music] Édouard-Léon Scott de Martinville.

AUDINT (2021), *Ghostcode*. Manchester: Multimodal Press. Available at: https://boomkat.com/ products/ghostcode (accessed: 25 February 2025).

Augoyard, J. F. and H. Torgue (2006), *Sonic Experience: A Guide to Everyday Sounds*. Montreal: McGill-Queen's University Press.

Ayto, J. (2003), *The Oxford Dictionary of Rhyming Slang*. Oxford: Oxford University Press.

BAB (2024), *Personalized Record Your Voice Message for Stuffed Animals | Build-A-Bear*. Available at: https://www.buildabear.co.uk/personalised-record-your-voice-message/416869.html (accessed: 13 February 2025).

Bailey, C. (2019), 'The Lingering Trauma of Stasi Surveillance', *The Atlantic*, 8 November. Available at: https://www.theatlantic.com/international/archive/2019/11/lingering-trauma -east-german-police-state/601669/ (accessed: 2 October 2024).

Baker, J. K. (1975), *Stochastic Modeling as a Means of Automatic Speech Recognition*. Mellon Institute of Science Carnegie-Mellon University. Available at: https://apps.dtic.mil/sti/ citations/ADA013808 (accessed: 20 February 2025).

Ball, J. (2013), 'NSA's Prism Surveillance Program: How It Works and What It Can Do', *The Guardian Online*, 8 June. Available at: https://www.theguardian.com/world/2013/jun/08/nsa-prism-server-collection-facebook-google (accessed: 24 October 2023).

Ballard, J. G. (1960), 'The Sound-Sweep', *Science Fantasy*, 13: 2–39.

Bamford, J. (1982), *The Puzzle Palace: A Report on America's Most Secret Agency*. Boston: Houghton Mifflin.

Barad, K. (2007), *Meeting the Universe Halfway: Quantum Physics and the Entanglement of Matter and Meaning*. Durham, NC: Duke University Press.

Barnard, M. (2002), *Fashion as Communication*. 2nd edn. London: Routledge.

Barnes, H. (2011a), 'Olive, First Film to Be Shot Entirely on Smartphone, Heads to Cinemas', *The Guardian Online*, 2 December. Available at: https://www.theguardian.com/film/2011/dec/02/olive-film-shot-on-smartphone (accessed: 30 November 2023).

Barrett, L. F. (2008), 'The Science of Emotion: What People Believe, What Evidence Shows, and Where to Go From Here', in J. J. Blascovich and C. R. Hartel (eds), *Human Behavior in Military Contexts (National Research Council)*. Washington, DC: National Academies Press. Available at: https://doi.org/10.17226/12023. (accessed: 3 December 2024).

Barthes, R. (1977), 'The Grain of the Voice', in S. Heath (ed.), *Image Music Text*. London: Fontana Press, 179–89.

Bassett, C. (2003), 'How Many Movements?', in M. Bull and L. Back (eds), *The Auditory Culture Reader*. Oxford: Berg, 343–56.

Bateson, M., D. Nettle and G. Roberts (2006), 'Cues of Being Watched Enhance Cooperation in a Real-world Setting', *Biology Letters*, 2 (3): 412–14.

Bathrick, D. (1995), *The Powers of Speech : The Politics of Culture in the GDR*. Lincoln: University of Nebraska Press. Available at: http://archive.org/details/powersofspeechpo0000bath (accessed: 14 January 2025).

Baudrillard, J. (1987), *The Ecstasy of Communication*. 2012 edn. Translated by B. Schütze and C. Schütze. Cambridge, MA and London: Semiotext(e).

Baudrillard, J. (1994), *Simulacra and Simulation*. Translated by S. Faria Glaser. Ann Arbor, MI: The University of Michigan Press.

Bauman, Z. (2016), *Liquid Modernity*. Cambridge: Wiley.

Bazzana, K. (2003), *Wondrous Strange: The Life and Art of Glenn Gould*. Toronto: McClelland & Stewart.

BBC (2017a), 'German Parents Told to Destroy Cayla Dolls Over Hacking Fears', *BBC Website*, 17 February. Available at: https://www.bbc.co.uk/news/world-europe-39002142 (accessed: 20 February 2024).

BBC (2017b), 'Is Your Phone Listening In? Your Stories', *BBC News*, 30 October. Available at: https://www.bbc.com/news/technology-41802282 (accessed: 13 February 2024).

Be Right Back (2013), [TV programme]: Channel 4. 11 February.

Beathoven (2024), *beathoven.ai: Create Unique Background Music That You Can Call Your Own*. Available at: https://www.beatoven.ai/ (accessed: 6 June 2024).

Beats Per Minute (no date), *Beats Per Minute*. Available at: https://www.beatsperminuteonline.com/mg/home/how_use_item/6441-to-see-if-a-song-is-legal-in-chechnya (accessed: 10 June 2024).

Beaumont, T. B. (2023), 'We Soon Won't Tell the Difference Between AI and Human Music – So Can Pop Survive?', *The Guardian Online*, 19 April. Available at: https://www.theguardian.com/music/2023/apr/19/ai-human-music-pop-drake-kanye-west-the-weeknd (accessed: 20 May 2024).

Beck, J. and R. Bishop (2020), *Technocrats of the Imagination: Art, Technology, and the Military-Industrial Avant-Garde*. Durham, NC: Duke University Press.

Bedrov, A. and S. L. Gable (2024), 'Just Between Us…': The Role of Sharing and Receiving Secrets in Friendship Across Time', *Personal Relationships*, 31 (1): 91–111. Available at: https://doi.org/10.1111/pere.12527. (accessed: 14 May 2024).

Beer, D. (2024), 'Commentary: Spotify Algorithms Aren't Just Predicting Your Music Taste — They're Shaping It', *Today Online*, 6 February. Available at: https://www.todayonline.com/commentary/commentary-spotify-algorithms-arent-just-predicting-your-music-taste-theyre-shaping-it-2357151 (accessed: 11 February 2025).

Benjamin, W. (1969), 'The Work of Art in the Age of Mechanical Reproduction', in H. Arendt (ed.). Translated by H. Zohn. Schocken Books, 217–51.

Berendse, G. J. (2021), *Echoes of Surrealism: Challenging Socialist Realism in East German Literature, 1945–1990*. New York, Oxford: Berghahn Books. Available at: https://doi.org/10.3167/9781800730687 (accessed: 13 February 2025).

Bergeson, S. and K. Firth-Butterfield (2021), 'Smart Toys: Your Child's Best Friend or a Creepy Surveillance Tool?', *World Economic Forum blog*, 31 March. Available at: https://www.weforum.org/agenda/2021/03/smart-toys-your-child-s-best-friend-or-a-creepy-surveillance-tool/ (accessed: 23 March 2024).

Bergson, H. (1944), *Creative Evolution*. Translated by A. Mitchell. New York: The Modern Library.

Besnier, N. (2009), *Gossip and the Everyday Production of Politics*. Honolulu: University of Hawaii Press. Available at: https://doi.org/10.1515/9780824862695 (accessed: 22 May 2024).

Bethel, C. L., M. R. Stevenson, and B. Scassellati (2011), 'Secret-Sharing: Interactions Between a Child, Robot, and Adult', *ResearchGate*. Available at: https://doi.org/10.1109/ICSMC.2011.6084051 (accessed: 26 March 2024).

Betts, P. (2012), *Within Walls: Private Life in the German Democratic Republic*. Oxford and New York: Oxford University Press.

Beyer, R. and E. Sales (2015), *The Ghost Army of World War II: How One Top-Secret Unit Deceived the Enemy with Inflatable Tanks, Sound Effects, and Other Audacious Fakery*. Princeton, NJ: Princeton Architectural Press.

Big Science (1982), [Music album]. Laurie Anderson: Warner/Nonesuch/Elektra.

Blackman, L. (2019), *Haunted Data: Affect, Transmedia, Weird Science*. London: Bloomsbury Publishing.

'Blake's 7' [TV series] (1978) BBC, 2nd January–22nd March.

Bloomfield, T. M. (1976), 'About Skinner: Notes on the Theory and Practice of "Radical Behaviourism"', *Philosophy of the Social Sciences*, 6 (1): 75–82. Available at: https://doi.org/10.1177/004839317600600105 (accessed: 23 March 2024).

Bogel-Burroughs, N. (2019), 'A Playlist to Deter the Homeless: "Baby Shark" and "Raining Tacos"', *The New York Times Online*, 18 July. Available at: https://www.nytimes.com/2019/07/18/us/baby-shark-homeless.html (accessed: 16 February 2025).

Bomford, A. (1999), 'ECHELON Spy Network Revealed', *BBC News*, 3 November. Available at: http://news.bbc.co.uk/1/hi/503224.stm (accessed: 4 October 2024).

Boomy (no date), *Boomy Website*. Available at: https://boomy.com/ (accessed: 6 June 2024).

Bosch, T. (2012), 'Sci-Fi Writer Bruce Sterling Explains the Intriguing New Concept of Design Fiction', *Slate Magazine Online*, 2 March, Future Tense section.

Bottomley, A. J. (2015), 'Home Taping is Killing Music': The Recording Industries' 1980s Anti-home Taping Campaigns and Struggles Over Production, Labor and Creativity', *Creative Industries Journal*, 8 (2): 1–23.

Boulicault, M., M. Phillips-Brown, J. Kory-Westlund, S. Nguyen, and C. Breazeal (2023), 'Authenticity and Co-Design: On Responsibly Creating Relational Robots for Children', in M. Ito, R. Cross, K. Dinakar, and C. Odgers (eds), *Algorithmic Rights and Protections for Children*. Cambridge, MA: MIT Press, 85–160.

Bousé, D. (2010), 'False Intimacy: Close-Ups and Viewer Involvement in Wildlife Films', *Visual Studies*, 18 (2): 123–32. Available at: https://doi.org/10.1080/14725860310001631994 (accessed: 18 September 2024).

Bowker, G. C. and S. L. Star (2000), *Sorting Things Out – Classification & Its Consequences: Classification and Its Consequences*. Revised edn. Cambridge, MA: MIT Press.

Boxall, A. (2016), *'Vocaloids' Aren't Characters, They're Instruments Changing the Way Music is Made, Digital Trends*. Available at: https://www.digitaltrends.com/music/hatsune-miku-creative-revolution-musicians/ (accessed: 10 December 2024).

Boxall, A. (2019), *Who is Hikari-Chan? She is the Mind-blowing Future of A.I. in Your Home, Digital Trends*. Available at: https://www.digitaltrends.com/mobile/gatebox-japan-minori-takechi-interview/ (accessed: 10 December 2024).

Brighenti, A. M. (2009), 'Artveillance: At the Crossroads of Art and Surveillance', *Surveillance and Society*, 7 (2): 175–86.

Broadcast Signal Intrusion (2021), [Film] Dir. Jacob Gentry, USA: Queensbury Pictures.

Bruce, G. (2003), 'The Prelude to Nationwide Surveillance in East Germany: Stasi Operations and Threat Perceptions, 1945–1953', *Journal of Cold War Studies*, 5 (2): 3–31.

Bulayenko, O., J. Pedro Quintais, D. Gervais, and J. Poort. (2022), 'D3.5 AI Music Outputs: Challenges to the Copyright Legal Framework', *Zenodo*. Available at: https://doi.org/10.5281/zenodo.6405796 (accessed: 28 September 2024)

Bull, M. and L. Back (2003), 'Introduction: Into Sound . . . Once More With Feeling', in M. Bull and L. Back (eds), *The Auditory Culture Reader*. Oxford: Berg, 1–18.

Bunz, M. (2020), 'Technology', in *Aesthetics of New AI Reader*. 001 edn. London: Creative AI Lab, 3–9.

Business Research Company (2024), *Smart Speakers Global Market Report 2024*. Available at: https://www.thebusinessresearchcompany.com/report/smart-speakers-global-market-report (accessed: 8 January 2024).

Bye, K. (2023), '#1327 "Voice in My Head" Remixes Your Inner Monologue with AI – Voices of VR Podcast'. Available at: https://voicesofvr.com/1327-voice-in-my-head-remixes-your-inner-monologue-with-ai/ (accessed: 30 January 2025).

Cadwalladr, C. (2023), 'Capitalism is Dead. Now We Have Something Much Worse': Yanis Varoufakis on Extremism, Starmer and the Tyranny of Big Tech', *The Observer Online, Interview*, 24 September. Available at: https://www.theguardian.com/world/2023/sep/24/yanis-varoufakis-technofeudalism-capitalism-ukraine-interview (accessed: 24 October 2023).

Caldwell, V. (2021), 'I Love Her and See Her As a Real Woman. Meet a Man Who "Married" An Artificial Intelligence Hologram', *CBC Online*, 18 November. Available at: https://www.cbc.ca/documentaries/the-nature-of-things/i-love-her-and-see-her-as-a-real-woman-meet-a-man-who-married-an-artificial-intelligence-hologram-1.6253767 (accessed: 8 July 2024).

Campagna, F. (2018), *Technic and Magic*, London: Bloomsbury Publishing.

Campbell, D. (1980), 'America's Big Ear on Europe', *New Statesman*, 10–14.

Campbell, D. (1988), 'They've Got It Taped', *New Statesman*, 12 August, 10–12.

Campbell, D. (2000), *Inside Echelon, Global Policy Forum*. Available at: https://archive.globalpolicy.org/empire/analysis/2000/0725echelon.htm (accessed: 24 February 2025).

Campbell, D. (2015a), 'GCHQ and Me: My Life Unmasking British Eavesdroppers', *The Intercept online*, 3 August. Available at: https://theintercept.com/2015/08/03/life-unmasking-british-eavesdroppers/ (accessed: 14 February 2025).

Campbell, D. (2015b), 'NSA's ECHELON Capacity Doubled Since 2000, Set To Quadruple', *Duncan Campbell.org Website*. Available at: https://www.duncancampbell.org/content/nsas-ECHELON-capacity-doubled-2000-set-quadruple (accessed: 9 March 2023).

Campbell, D. and M. Honigsbaum (1999), 'Britain and U.S. Spy on World', *The Guardian Online*, 23 May. Available at: https://www.theguardian.com/uk/1999/may/23/duncancampbell.markhonigsbaum (accessed: 9 March 2023).

Campolo, A. and K. Crawford (2020), 'Enchanted Determinism: Power Without Responsibility in Artificial Intelligence', *Engaging Science, Technology, and Society*, 6: 1–19. Available at: https://doi.org/10.17351/ests2020.277 (accessed: 22 February 2025).

Cannibal Holocaust (1980), [Film] Dir. Ruggero Deodato, Italy: F.D. Cinematografica.

Canonico, M. and L. De Russis (2018), 'A Comparison and Critique of Natural Language Understanding Tools', in *CLOUD COMPUTING 2018: The Ninth International Conference on Cloud Computing, GRIDs, and Virtualization*. Barcelona, 18–22 February.

Capek, K. (1923), *The Project Gutenberg eBook of R. U. R. (Rossum's Universal Robots)*. London: Doubleday, Page and Company. Available at: https://www.gutenberg.org/files/59112/59112-h/59112-h.htm (accessed: 25 February 2025).

CareerBuilder (2022), *7 in 10 Employers Research Job Candidates Online, CareerBuilder website*. Available at: https://resources.careerbuilder.com/employer-blog/employers-research-candidate-social-media-profiles (accessed: 29 January 2025).

Carr, A., M. Day, S. Frier, and M. Gurman (2019), 'Silicon Valley Is Listening to Your Most Intimate Moments', *Bloomberg*, 11 December. Available at: https://www.bloomberg.com/news/features/2019-12-11/silicon-valley-got-millions-to-let-siri-and-alexa-listen-in (accessed: 12 August 2024).

Carrillo-Ruiz, J. D., E. B. Muratti-Molina, G. Cojuc-Konigsberg, and J. R. Carrillo-Márquez (2023), 'Trephinations, Trephines, and Craniectomies: Contrast Between Global Ancient Civilizations and Pre-Hispanic Mexican Cultures', *World Neurosurgery*, 179: 49–59. Available at: https://doi.org/10.1016/j.wneu.2023.03.088 (accessed: 5 February 2025).

Carollo, A. et al. (2023), 'A Scientometric Review of Infant Cry and Caregiver Responsiveness: Literature Trends and Research Gaps over 60 Years of Developmental Study', Children, 10(6): 1042. Available at: https://doi.org/10.3390/children10061042

Casale, J., P. F. Kandle, I. V. Murray, and N. I. Murr (2025), 'Physiology, Cochlear Function', in *StatPearls*. Treasure Island, FL: StatPearls Publishing. Available at: http://www.ncbi.nlm.nih.gov/books/NBK531483/ (accessed: 10 February 2025).

Casino Royale (2006), [Film] Dir. Martin Campbell. UK/USA/Czech Republic/Germany: Metro-Goldwyn-Mayer, Columbia Pictures, Eon Productions.

Catarinucci, L., R. Colella, L. Mainetti, L. Patrono, S. Pieretti, A. Secco, and I. Sergi (2014), 'An Animal Tracking System for Behavior Analysis Using Radio Frequency Identification', *Lab Animal*, 43: 321–7.

Chanon, L. J. (1978), *First Earth Battalion Field Manual*. US Military. Available at: http://neweartharmy.com/Welcome.html (accessed: 2 October 2024).

Chapman, H. S. (1987), 'Welsh as a Secret Language', *Transactions of the Caernarvonshire Historical Society*, 48: 113–17.

Chen, S. F., B. Kingsbury, L. Mangu, D. Povey, G. Saon, H. Soltau, and G. Zweig (2006), 'Advances in Speech Transcription at IBM Under the DARPA EARS Program', *IEEE Transactions on Audio, Speech and Language Processing*, 14 (5). Available at: https://www.microsoft.com/en-us/research/wp-content/uploads/2006/01/taslp2006.pdf (accessed: 29 December 2024).

Cheng, C. M. and C. L. Huang (2011), 'Processes of Conscious and Unconscious Memory: Evidence From Current Research on Dissociation of Memories Within a Test', *The American Journal of Psychology*, 124 (4): 421–40. Available at: https://doi.org/10.5406/amerjpsyc.124.4.0421 (accessed: 29 January 2025).

Chevalier, J. and A. Gheerbrant (1996), *A Dictionary of Symbols*. Translated by J. Buchanan-Brown. London: Penguin Books.

Chiarella, T. (2015), 'Scarlett Johansson Sexiest Woman Alive of Yesteryear', *Esquire*. Available at: https://www.esquire.com/entertainment/a25017/scarlett-johansson-interview-1113/ (accessed: 15 March 2024).

Child's Play (1988), [Film] Dir. Tom Holland, USA: United Artists.

Chiquier, M., C. Mao, and C. Vondrick (2022), 'Real-Time Neural Voice Camouflage', arXiv. Available at: http://arxiv.org/abs/2112.07076 (accessed: 13 February 2024).

Choo, K. (2018), 'Cool Governance: Japan's Ubiquitous Society, Surveillance, and Creative Industries', *Culture, Theory and Critique*, 59 (2): 94–118. Available at: https://doi.org/10.1080/14735784.2018.1424005 (accessed: 9 January 2025).

Chu, S. M., D. Povey, and B. Varadarajan (2008), 'Universal Background Model Based Speech Recognition', in *2008 IEEE International Conference on Acoustics, Speech and Signal Processing*. Las Vegas, NV. Available at: https://doi.org/10.1109/ICASSP.2008.4518671 (accessed: 17 February 2025).

CIA (1961), *Guided Animal Studies Report (Declassified, Redacted)*. CIA, 4. Available at: https://www.cia.gov/readingroom/docs/GUIDED%20ANIMAL%20STUDIES%20WIT%5B15687531%5D.pdf (accessed: 12 January 2025).

CIA (1967), *Memorandum For: Director of Planning, Programming and Budgeting*. CIA. Available at: https://www.cia.gov/readingroom/document/02384139 (accessed: 2 October 2024).

CIA (2007), *Declassified: Clandestine Services History: The Berlin Tunnel Operation, 1952–1956 (Unredacted Report Produced 1968)*. Available at: https://www.cia.gov/readingroom/docs/DOC_0001459120.pdf (accessed: 14 March 2022).

CIA (2008), *Navajo Code Talkers and the Unbreakable Code – CIA*. Available at: https://www.cia.gov/stories/story/navajo-code-talkers-and-the-unbreakable-code/ (accessed: 22 February 2025).

CIA (2018), *PROJECT MK-ULTRA, CIA Freedom of Information Act Electronic Reading Room*. Available at: https://www.cia.gov/readingroom/document/06760269 (accessed: 30 January 2025).

Ciesielski, R. (2022), 'Is Your Phone Listening To Your Conversations?', *BR Next*, 9 February. Available at: https://medium.com/br-next/is-your-phone-listening-to-your-conversations-5182bc8ed45 (accessed: 11 February 2025).

Citizenfour (2014), [Film] Dir. Laura Poitras, USA: Praxis Films, Participant, HBO Documentary Films.

'Citizens Advice and Competition and Markets Authority – Oral evidence (QQ 85–94)' (2017), *House of Lords*. London: UK Government. Available at: https://www.parliament.uk/globalassets/documents/lords-committees/Artificial-Intelligence/AI-Oral-Evidence-Volume.pdf (accessed: 2 October 2024).

Clark, D. A. (2005), *Intrusive Thoughts in Clinical Disorders: Theory, Research, and Treatment*. New York: Guilford Press.

Clark, F. (2024), *Research and Analysis: Public Attitudes to Data and AI: Tracker Survey (Wave 4) Report*. London: Department for Science, Innovation & Technology, 4. Available at: https://www.gov.uk/government/publications/public-attitudes-to-data-and-ai-tracker-survey-wave-4/public-attitudes-to-data-and-ai-tracker-survey-wave-4-report (accessed: 17 December 2024).

Classen, C. (2013), 'Captive Audience? GDR Radio in the Mirror of Listeners' Mail', *Cold War History*, 13 (2): 239–54. Available at: https://doi.org/10.1080/14682745.2012.757136 https://www.parliament.uk/globalassets/documents/lords-committees/Artificial-Intelligence/AI-Oral-Evidence-Volume.pdf (accessed: 23 May 2024).

Cloverfield (2008), [Film] Dir. Matt Reeves, USA: Bad Robot.

CoeFont (2023), *CoeFont Basic Terms of Service, CoeFont Terms and Privacy*. Available at: https://coefont.notion.site/CoeFont-Terms-and-Privacy-fcad3a3fa64d4080a16c675867754cc1?p=217d06fe30fb45b0b25f8a49a9b450cb&pm=s#4e625516b4f74a7aa046e4c52baf3a25 (accessed: 3 December 2024).

CoeFont (2024), *CoeFont: Unleash the Power of Your Voice With CoeFont*. CoeFont. Available at: https://coefont.cloud (accessed: 25 February 2025).

Cohn, C and M. Rumold (2013), 'Confirmed: The NSA Is Spying on Millions of Americans', *Electronic Frontier Foundation*, Available online: https://www.eff.org/deeplinks/2013/06/confirmed-nsa-spying-millions-americans (accessed 13 June 2025).

Condon, R. (1959), *The Manchurian Candidate*. New York: McGraw-Hill.

Conrad, I. W. (1952a), 'Office Memorandum: Microphones and Technical Installations in US Embassies Abroad, Espionage', United States Government. Available at: https://www.cryptomuseum.com/covert/bugs/thing/files/19520923_fbi.pdf (accessed: 14 February 2025).

Conrad, I. W. (1952b), *Subject: Microphones and Technical Installations in US Embassies Abroad*. United States Government, 2. Available at: https://www.cryptomuseum.com/covert/bugs/thing/files/19520923_fbi.pdf (accessed: 9 January 2025).

Constable, P. (2012), 'U.S. diplomat Harry G. Barnes Jr., 86, Helped End Military Dictatorship in Chile', *Washington Post*, 22 August. Available at: https://www.washingtonpost.com/world/world-politics/us-diplomat-harry-g-barnes-jr-86-helped-end-military-dictatorship-in-chile/2012/08/22/4a5f8710-eb9f-11e1-9ddc-340d5efb1e9c_story.html (accessed: 9 January 2025).

'Conversations with Glenn Gould: Humphrey Burton Interviews' (1966), *Glenn Gould on Television: The Complete CBC Broadcasts*. Canadian Broadcasting Corporation.

COPPA (1998), *Children's Online Privacy Protection Rule ('COPPA'), 15 U.S.C. 6501–5*. Available at: https://www.ftc.gov/legal-library/browse/rules/childrens-online-privacy-protection-rule-coppa (accessed: 16 February 2025).

Corera, G. (2020), *Russians Among Us: Sleeper Cells, Ghost Stories, and the Hunt for Putin's Spies*. New York: William Morrow.

Cornish, A., B. Wilson, D. Raubenheimer, and P. McGreevy (2018), 'Demographics Regarding Belief in Non-Human Animal Sentience and Emotional Empathy with Animals: A Pilot Study among Attendees of an Animal Welfare Symposium', *Animals*, 8 (10): 174. Available at: https://doi.org/10.3390/ani8100174 (accessed: 4 January 2025).

Cossou, E. (2024), 'The Man Who Turned His Dead Father Into a Chatbot', *BBC News*, 15 May. Available at: https://www.bbc.com/news/business-68944898 (accessed: 3 February 2025).

Cox, J. (2019), 'The FBI Tried to Plant a Backdoor in an Encrypted Phone Network', *VICE*, 18 September. Available at: https://www.vice.com/en/article/fbi-tried-to-plant-backdoor-in-encrypted-phone-phantom-secure/ (accessed: 12 February 2025).

Cox, J. (2021), 'Trojan Shield: How the FBI Secretly Ran a Phone Network for Criminals', *VICE*, 8 June. Available at: https://www.vice.com/en/article/operation-trojan-shield-anom-fbi-secret-phone-network/ (accessed: 12 February 2025).

Cox, J. (2022), 'FBI Honeypot Phone Company Anom Shipped Over 100 Phones to the United States', *VICE*, 12 January. Available at: https://www.vice.com/en/article/fbi-anom-shipped-100-phones-united-states/ (accessed: 24 February 2025).

Cox, T. (2018), *Now You're Talking: Human Conversation from the Neanderthals to Artificial Intelligence*. London: Bodley Head.

Cprime (2022), 'How Mobile Phone Sensors Are Used for Health Monitoring', *Cprime Website*. Available at: https://www.cprime.com/resources/blog/how-mobile-phone-sensors-are-used-for-health-monitoring/ (accessed: 11 December 2023).

Crawford, K. (2016), 'Asking the Oracle', in L. Poitras (ed.), *Astro Noise: A Survival Guide to Living Under Total Surveillance: A Survival Guide for Living Under Total Surveillance*. Illustrated edn. New Haven, CT: Yale University Press, 138–53.

Crawford, K. (2021), *Atlas of AI: Power, Politics, and the Planetary Costs of Artificial Intelligence*. New Haven, CT: Yale University Press.

Crimes of the Future (2022), [Film] Dir. David Cronenberg, UK/Canada/Greece/France: Serendipity Point Films, Telefilm Canada, Ingenious Media, Argonauts Productions, Crave, CBC Films, ERT, Rocket Science.

Crocker, S. (2007), 'Noises and Exceptions: Pure Mediality in Serres and Agamben', *Ctheory Online Magazine*. Available at: https://ctheorymultimedia.cornell.edu/ (accessed: 4 October 2024).

Crypto Museum (2023), *Device 32028 – Schnatterinchen, Crypto Museum Website*. Available at: https://www.cryptomuseum.com/spy/owvl/schnatterinchen/ (accessed: 2 October 2023).

CuboAI (2024), *Monitor Baby's Safety, Safely and Securely from Anywhere, Cubo AI – UK*. Available at: https://uk.getcubo.com/pages/cuboai-feature-safety (accessed: 14 August 2024).

Curtis, J. (2015), 'NSA and GCHQ Have Been Spying On You For 50 Years', *ITPro*, 4 August. Available at: https://www.itpro.com/security/25092/nsa-and-gchq-have-been-spying-on-you -for-50-years (accessed: 14 February 2025).

Cuthbertson, A. (2016), 'Holographic Wife Offers Intimacy to Japan's Celibate Generation', *Newsweek Online*, 16 December. Available at: https://www.newsweek.com/holographic-wife -japans-answer-amazon-echo-532641 (accessed: 12 July 2024).

Dahl, E. J. (2013), *Intelligence and Surprise Attack: Failure and Success from Pearl Harbor to 9/11 and Beyond*. Washington, DC: Georgetown University Press.

DARPA (2024), *Personal Assistant That Learns (PAL), Defense Advanced Research Projects Agency Website*. Available at: https://www.darpa.mil/about-us/timeline/personalized-assistant-that -learns (accessed: 12 August 2024).

Dawkins, R. (1976), *The Selfish Gene*. Oxford: Oxford University Press.

Dayal, G. (2016), 'The Music of Bell Labs', *Red Bull Music Academy*. Available at: https://daily .redbullmusicacademy.com/2016/05/bell-labs-music-feature (accessed: 25 February 2025).

Deacon, M. (2024), 'Scotland's New "Thought Police" Will Be The Death of the Edinburgh Festival', *The Telegraph*, 21 March. Available at: https://www.telegraph.co.uk/columnists/ 2024/03/21/scotland-police-hate-laws-actors-stage-crime-plays/ (accessed: 6 February 2025).

Debord, G. (2012), *Society of The Spectacle*. London: Bread and Circuses.

DeLanda, M. (1991), *War in the Age of Intelligent Machines*. New York: Zone.

Deletant, D. (1995), *Ceauşescu and the Securitate: Coercion and Dissent in Romania, 1965–1989*. London: Hurst.

Delillo, D. (2003), *Cosmopolis*. New York: Scribner.

Denardis, L. (2020), *The Internet in Everything: Freedom and Security in a World with No Off Switch*. New Haven, CT: Yale University Press.

Devlin, K. and O. Belton (2020), 'Fembots and Sexbots: Cultural Discourses on Artificial Women', in S. Cave, K. Dihal and S. Dillon (eds), *AI Narratives: A History of Imaginative Thinking about Intelligent Machines*. Oxford: Oxford University Press, 192–207.

Dhariwal, P., H. Jun, C. Payne, J. Wook, A. Radford, and I. Sutskever (2020), 'Jukebox: A Generative Model for Music', arXiv. Available at: http://arxiv.org/abs/2005.00341 (accessed: 24 October 2024).

Diary of the Dead (2007), [Film] Dir. George A. Romero, USA/Canada: Artfire Films, Romero-Grunwald Productions.

Dibbell, J. (1995), 'Viruses Are Good for You', *Wired*. Available at: https://www.wired.com/1995 /02/viruses/ (accessed: 27 February 2025).

Dick, P. K. (1956), 'The Minority Report', *Fantastic Universe*, January.

Dick, P. K. (1968), *Do Androids Dream Of Electric Sheep?* 1st edn. New York: Doubleday.

Dieudonné, M. (2020), 'Electromagnetic Hypersensitivity: A Critical Review of Explanatory Hypotheses', *Environmental Health*, 19. Available at: https://doi.org/10.1186/s12940-020 -00602-0 (accessed: 14 February 2025).

Donald, Graeme (2011), *Loose Cannons: 101 Myths, Mishaps and Misadventurers of Military History*. London: Bloomsbury Publishing.

Dorfman, A. (2014), 'Repression by Any Other Name', *Guernica*, 3 February. Available at: http://www.guernicamag.com/features/repression-by-any-other-name/ (accessed: 13 February 2025).

Drott, E. A. (2018), 'Music as a Technology of Surveillance', *Journal of the Society for American Music*, 12 (3): 233–67.

DSS (2016), *Diplomatic Security Service: Then & Now*. Washington, DC: Diplomatic Security Service Office of Public Affairs.

Du Gay, P. (2000), *In Praise of Bureaucracy: Weber, Organization, Ethics*. London: SAGE Publications Ltd. Available at: https://doi.org/10.4135/9781446217580 (accessed: 9 January 2025).

Dutchen, S. (2022), *The Good that Viruses Do | Harvard Medicine Magazine*. Available at: https://magazine.hms.harvard.edu/articles/good-viruses-do (accessed: 27 February 2025).

Dunstan, P. (2024), *Dunstan Baby Language* by Priscilla Dunstan . Available at: https://dunstan-babies.com/ (Accessed: 22 January 2025).

Earshot (2024), *Earshot: Sonic Investigations for Communities Affected by Corporate, State, and Environmental Injustice*. Earshot. Available at: https://earshot.ngo (accessed: 30 October 2024).

Edison, T. A. (1878), 'The Phonograph and its Future', *Rutgers University website*. Available at: https://edison.rutgers.edu/images/innovations/Phonograph/Edison_Phonograph_and_Its_Future_North_American_Review_1878.pdf (accessed: 16 September 2023).

Ehrenkranz, M. (2017), *People Are Immortalizing Their Dead Loves Ones in Stuffed Animals*. Gizmodo. Available at: https://gizmodo.com/people-are-immortalizing-their-dead-loves-ones-in-stuff-1797519123 (accessed: 13 February 2025).

Eiseley, L. (1978), *The Star Thrower*. London: Wildwood House Ltd.

Eiseley, L. (1985), *The Unexpected Universe*. San Diego, CA: Harcourt Brace Jovanovich.

Elder, A. (2022), 'Digital Souls: A Philosophy of Online Death', *Australasian Journal of Philosophy*, 102 (1), 243. Available at: https://doi.org/10.1080/00048402.2022.2118339 (accessed: 26 February, 2025)

Elias, J. (2023), 'Google to Begin Selling Maps Data to Companies Building Solar Products, Hopes to Generate $100 Million in First Year', *CNBC Website*, 28 August. Available at: https://www.cnbc.com/2023/08/28/google-to-sell-maps-data-to-companies-building-solar-products.html (accessed: 29 October 2023).

Elliot, J. K. (2018), 'Theatricality and Deception: How Russia Uses "Maskirovka" to Shake the Torld', *Global News Online*, 9 June. Available at: https://globalnews.ca/news/4260938/russia-strategy-maskirovka-military-politics-putin/ (accessed: 13 May 2024).

Ellis, C. (2007), 'Telling Secrets, Revealing Lives: Relational Ethics in Research With Intimate Others', *Qualitative Inquiry*, 13 (1): 3–29. Available at: https://doi.org/10.1177/1077800406294947 (accessed: 9 September 2024).

Ergo Proxy (2006), Geneon Entertainment, Manglobe, WOWOW.

Ermoshina, K., B. Loveluck, and F. Musiani (2021), 'A Market of Black Boxes: The Political Economy of Internet Surveillance and Censorship in Russia', *Journal of Information Technology & Politics*, 19 (1): 18–33. Available at: https://doi.org/10.1080/19331681.2021.1905972 (accessed: 19 February 2024).

Eternal You (2025), [Film] Dir. Hans Block and Moritz Riesewieck, Germany/USA: DOCMINE Productions, Gebrueder Beetz Filmproduktion, Impact Partners.

Etkind, A. (2023), *Russia Against Modernity*. Cambridge, UK: Polity Press.

Eurojust: European Union Agency for Criminal Justice Cooperation (2022) The CLOUD Act. 22 December. Available at: https://www.eurojust.europa.eu/publication/cloud-act (accessed: 9 February, 2024).

European Union (2016), *General Data Protection Regulation (GDPR) – Legal Text*. Available at: https://gdpr-info.eu/ (accessed: 11 February 2025).

Evans, J. C. (1996), 'Berlin Tunnel Intelligence: A Bumbling KGB', *International Journal of Intelligence and CounterIntelligence*, 9 (1): 43–50. Available at: https://doi.org/10.1080/08850609608435304 (accessed: 4 February 2024).

Evans, P. (2018), 'Q&A with Angel Investor William Tunstall-Pedoe', *The Sunday Times Online*, 3 June. Available at: https://www.thetimes.com/article/q-a-with-angel-investor-williamtunstall-pedoe-00rdx9p7p (accessed: 2 March 2025)

Evans, R. (2019), 'Police Investigate Officer Who Infiltrated Environmental Groups', *The Guardian Online*, 28 August. Available at: https://www.theguardian.com/uk-news/2019/aug/28/police-investigate-officer-who-infiltrated-environmental-groups (accessed: 2 October 2024).

Faraday, M. (1859), *Course of Six Lectures on the Various Forces of Matter and their Relations to Each Other*. London and Glasgow: Richard Griffin and Company. Available at: https://archive.org/details/courseofsixlectu00fararich/page/n3/mode/2up (accessed: 14 February 2025).

Farah, D. and M. Richardson (2022), *Dangerous Alliances: Russia's Strategic Inroads in Latin America*. Washington, DC: National Defense University Press. Available at: https://inss.ndu.edu/Portals/68/Documents/stratperspective/inss/strategic-perspectives-41.pdf (accessed: 6 October 2024).

Farquhar, S., J. Kossen, L. Kuhn, and Y. Gal. (2024), 'Detecting Hallucinations in Large Language Models Using Semantic Entropy', *Nature*, 630: 625–30.

FBI (2024), *History: Lindbergh Kidnapping, Federal Bureau of Investigation*. Available at: https://www.fbi.gov/history/famous-cases/lindbergh-kidnapping (accessed: 13 February 2025).

Federal Archives (2024), *Stasi Records Archive, The Federal Archives*. Available at: https://www.bundesarchiv.de/en/stasi-records-archive/ (accessed: 23 February 2025).

Federal Trade Commission (2018), 'Electronic Toy Maker VTech Settles FTC Allegations That it Violated Children's Privacy Law and the FTC Act', *Federal Trade Commission Website*. Available at: https://www.ftc.gov/news-events/news/press-releases/2018/01/electronic-toy-maker-vtech-settles-ftc-allegations-it-violated-childrens-privacy-law-ftc-act (accessed: 12 February 2024).

Feldstein, S. (2019), *The Global Expansion of AI Surveillance*. Carnegie Endowment for International Peace Website. Available at: https://carnegieendowment.org/2019/09/17/global-expansion-of-ai-surveillance-pub-79847 (accessed: 17 October 2023).

Feng, E. (2024), 'Chinese Companies Offer to "Resurrect" Dead Loved Ones. It Raises Questions', *NPR*, 17 June. Available at: https://www.npr.org/2024/06/17/nx-s1-5001751/chinese-companies-offer-to-resurrect-dead-loved-ones-it-raises-questions (accessed: 13 February 2025).

Fernyhough, C. (2016), *The Voices Within: The History and Science of How We Talk to Ourselves*. New York: Profile Books.

Fernyhough, C. and A. M. Borghi (2023), 'Inner Speech as Language Process and Cognitive Tool', *Trends in Cognitive Sciences*, 27 (12): 1180–93. Available at: https://doi.org/10.1016/j.tics.2023.08.014 (accessed: 16 February 2025).

Finn, E. (2017a), *What Algorithms Want: Imagination in the Age of Computing*. Cambridge, MA and London: MIT Press.

Finn, J. (2017b), 'Touching Video: Dad Gives Son Christmas Toy with Deceased Moms Voice', *Mail Online*. Available at: http://www.dailymail.co.uk/news/article-5216741/Video-Father-gives-son-Christmas-toy-deceased-moms-voice.html (accessed: 28 January 2025).

First Sounds (no date) *First Sounds Website. The Phonautograms of Édouard-Léon Scott de Martinville*. Available at: http://www.firstsounds.org/sounds/scott.php (accessed: 1 June 2022).

Fisher, D. (2022), *StoryFile's AI Principles, Storyfile*. Available at: https://storyfile.com/storyfiles-ai-principles-old/ (accessed: 17 December 2024).

Fisher, M. (2014), *Ghosts of My Life: Writings on Depression, Hauntology and Lost Futures*. Lanham, MD: John Hunt Publishing.

Fisher, M. M. and Winick, A. (2021), *Designing Motherhood: Things That Make and Break Our Births*. Cambridge, MA and London: MIT Press.

Földényi, L. (1984), *Melancholy*. Translated by T. Wilkinson. New Haven, CT: Yale University Press.

Forensic Architecture (2024a), *Forensic Architecture → About us, Forensic Architecture*. Available at: https://forensic-architecture.org//about/agency (accessed: 30 October 2024).

Forensic Architecture (2024b), *The Killing Of Hind Rajab ← Forensic Architecture*. Available at: https://forensic-architecture.org/investigation/the-killing-of-hind-rajab (accessed: 3 February 2025).

Forsman, C. (2013), *The End of The Fucking World (TEOTFW)*. 1st edn. Seattle: Fantographic Books.

Foucault, M. (2013), *History of Madness*. New York: Routledge.

Framis, A. (2023), *The Hybrid Couple Page, Alicia Framis Website*. Available at: https://www.aliciaframis.com/work/154/hybrid-couple (accessed: 16 July 2024).

Franzen, J. (2001), *The Corrections*. 1st edn. New York: Farrar, Straus and Giroux.

Fraser, H. (2003), 'Issues in Transcription: Factors Affecting the Reliability of Transcripts as Evidence in Legal Cases', *International Journal of Speech Language and the Law*, 10 (2): 203–26. Available at: https://doi.org/10.1558/sll.2003.10.2.203 (accessed: 13 February 2025).

Frenkel, S. (2017), 'A Cute Toy Just Brought A Hacker Into Your Home', *The New York Times Online*, 21 December. Available at: https://www.nytimes.com/2017/12/21/technology/connected-toys-hacking.html (accessed: 20 February 2024).

Frick, N. R. J., K. L. Wilms, F. Brachten, T. Hetjens, S. Stieglitz, and B. Ross (2021), 'The Perceived Surveillance of Conversations Through Smart Devices', *Electronic Commerce Research and Applications*, 47: 101046. Available at: https://doi.org/10.1016/j.elerap.2021.101046 (accessed: 3 February 2025).

Fuller, M. (2005), *Media Ecologies: Materialist Energies in Art and Technoculture*. Cambridge, MA: MIT Press.

Funder, A. (2011), *Stasiland*. London: Granta Books.

G (2008), 'Engineering the Berlin Tunnel – CSI', *Intelligence Studies: Center for the Study of Intelligence*, 52 (1): 1–7. Available at: https://www.cia.gov/resources/csi/studies-in-intelligence/volume-52-no-1/engineering-the-berlin-tunnel/ (accessed: 2 March 2025).

Gani, A. (2014), 'Computer Code in Films: Hidden Meanings or Irrelevant Nonsense?', *The Guardian Online*, 10 January. Available at: https://www.theguardian.com/technology/shortcuts/2014/jan/10/computer-code-in-film-movie-terminator-girl-dragon-tattoo (accessed: 5 January 2024).

Gatebox (2020), *Gatebox Terms of Use (English Language Version)*. Gatebox – Virtual Home Robot. Available at: https://terms.gateboxlab.com (accessed: 4 December 2024).

Gatebox (2024), 'Gatebox and CoeFont, An AI Voice Platform, Have Partnered with CoeFont to Jointly Provide a Solution to Convert Customers' Original Characters into AI' (translated with Firefox browser), *Gatebox*. Available at: https://www.gatebox.ai/news/20240703-coefont (accessed: 13 February 2025).

Gatebox (2025), 'About Azuma Hikari', *Gatebox Website*. Available at: https://support.gateboxlab.com/upgrade/upgrade-abouthikari (accessed: 7 July 2024).

Gatebox Grande – PV 'The Hospitality of the Future' (2021), [Film] Dir. Gatebox. Available at: https://www.youtube.com/watch?v=A0frmL_UGT8 (accessed: 17 July 2024).

Gaufman, E. (2021), 'Cybercrime and Punishment: Security, Information War, and the Future of Runet', in D. Gritsenko, M. Wijermars, and M. Kopotev (eds), *The Palgrave Handbook of Digital Russia Studies*. Cham: Springer International Publishing, 115–34. Available at: https://doi.org/10.1007/978-3-030-42855-6_7 (accessed: 23 January 2025).

Gaule, J. (1652), *Pus-mantia the Mag-astro-mancer, or, The Magicall-astrologicall-diviner Posed, and Puzzled*. London: Joshua Kirton.

GCHQ (2024), *Locations Section, GCHQ Website*. Available at: https://www.gchq.gov.uk/section/locations/bude (accessed: 9 March 2023).

Gelernter, D. (1993), *MIRROR WORLDS: Or The Day Software Puts the Universe in a Shoebox . . . How it Will Happen and What it Will Mean*. Reprint edn. New York: Oxford University Press.

Gellman, B. and L. Poitras (2013), 'British Intelligence Mining Data from Nine U.S. Internet Companies in Broad Secret Program', *Washington Post Online*, 17 June. Available at: https://www.washingtonpost.com/investigations/us-intelligence-mining-data-from-nine-us-internet-companies-in-broad-secret-program/2013/06/06/3a0c0da8-cebf-11e2-8845-d970ccb04497_story.html (accessed: 17 October 2023).

George, K. (2022), 'Watching From the Cot: Are Smart Toys and Baby Products Worth It For Parents?', *The Guardian Online*, 30 October. Available at: https://www.theguardian.com/lifeandstyle/2022/oct/31/watching-from-the-cot-are-smart-toys-and-baby-products-worth-it-for-parents (accessed: 22 March 2024).

Ghost in the Shell (Kôkaku Kidôtai) (1995), [Film] Dir. Mamoru Oshii, Japan: Kôdansha, Bandai Visual Company, Manga Entertainment.

Giblin, R. and C. Doctorow (2022), *Chokepoint Capitalism: How Big Tech and Big Content Captured Creative Labor Markets and How We'll Win Them Back*. Boston: Beacon Press.

Gibson, W. (1997), *Idoru*. New York: Berkley Books.

Gieseke, J. (2014), *The History of the Stasi: East Germany's Secret Police, 1945–1990*. Translated by D. Burnett. New York and Oxford: Berghahn Books.

Gilda (1946), [Film] Dir. Charles Vidor, USA: Columbia Pictures.

Gilroy, A. A. (2011), 'Access to Broadband Networks: The Net Neutrality Debate', *the Internet* [Preprint].

Glannon, W. (2016), 'Ethical Issues in Neuroprosthetics', *Journal of Neural Engineering*, 13 (2): 021002. Available at: https://doi.org/10.1088/1741-2560/13/2/021002 (accessed: 13 February 2025).

Glenn, K. (2016), *Baby Shark*. Seoul, South Korea: Pinkfong.

Glinsky, A. (2005), *Theremin: Ether Music and Espionage*. Champaign, IL: University of Illinois Press.

GMI (2024), *Smart Baby Monitor Market Size & Share Forecast Report, 2032, Global Market Insights Inc.* Available at: https://www.gminsights.com/industry-analysis/smart-baby-monitor-market (accessed: 23 May 2024).

Gogol, N. V. (1956), *The Overcoat*. Translated by David Magarshack. London: Merlin Press.

Goldmanis, M. (2018), 'Explaining the "Mystery" of Numbers Stations', *War on The Rocks*, 24 May. Available at: https://warontherocks.com/2018/05/explaining-the-mystery-of-numbers-stations/ (accessed: 2 October 2023).

Goldsmith, K. (2011), *Uncreative Writing: Managing Language in the Digital Age*. Illustrated edn. New York: Columbia University Press.

Goldstein, P. (2003), *Copyright's Highway: From Gutenberg to the Celestial Jukebox*. Stanford, CA: Stanford University Press.

Gómez-Leal, R., A. Costa, A. Megías-Robles, P. Fernández-Berrocal, and L. Faria (2021), 'Relationship Between Emotional Intelligence and Empathy Towards Humans and Animals', *PeerJ*, 9: e11274. Available at: https://doi.org/10.7717/peerj.11274 (accessed: 8 February 2025).

@gonzoisacat (2022), [Film] Dir. @gonzoisacat, Instagram Reels.

Goode, L., M. Calore, and S. Fussell (2020), *Alexa, Play My Alibi: The Smart Home Gets Taken to Court* [Get Wired podcast transcript]. Available at: https://www.wired.com/story/gadget-lab -podcast-470/ (accessed: 7 February 2024).

Goodman, S., T. Heys, and E. Ikoniadou (2019), 'Introduction', in S. Goodman, T. Heys, and E. Ikoniadou (eds), *Unsound: Undead*. Falmouth: Urbanomic, 1–3.

Gordon, D. and Wong, W. (2022), 'How to Understand Baby Sounds', UCLA Magazine. Available at: https://newsroom.ucla.edu/magazine/chatterbaby-app-artificial-intelligence-infant-cries (accessed: 23 January 2025).

Goriunova, O. (2019), 'The Bodily Sounds of the Abyss', in S. Goodman, T. Heys, and E. Ikoniadou (eds), *Unsound: Undead*. Falmouth: Urbanomic, 7–10.

Gould, G. (1966a), 'The Prospects of Recording', *High Fidelity*, April. Available at: https://www .collectionscanada.gc.ca/glenngould/028010-4020.01-e.html (accessed: 16 February 2025).

Gould, G. (1966b), 'Glenn Gould and Humphrey Burton on Schoenberg'. Available at: https:// glenngould.com/new-video-glenn-gould-and-humphrey-burton-on-schoenberg/ (accessed: 20 September 2024).

Gourley, S. L., A. Bonci, M. R. Bruchas, S. B. Flagel, S. N. Haber, P. W. Kalivas, A. L. Milton, P. E. M. Phillips, M. R. Picciotto, and J. K. Seamans (2021), 'Convergent Experimental Systems for Dissecting the Neurobiology of Intrusive Thought: A Road Map', in Peter W. Kalivas, and M. P. Paulus (eds), *Intrusive Thinking: From Molecules to Free Will*. Cambridge, MA: MIT Press. Available at: https://doi.org/10.7551/mitpress/13875.003.0010. (accessed: 1 February 2025).

Graeme, D. (2011), *Loose Cannons: 101 Myths, Mishaps and Misadventurers of Military History*. London: Osprey Publishing.

Gray, M. (1981), 'The Private Ear of Private Eyes (archived)', *MacLean's*. Available at: https:// archive.macleans.ca/article/1981/7/13/the-private-ear-of-private-eyes (accessed: 4 October 2021).

Greengard, S. (2021), *The Internet of Things*. Revised and updated edn. Cambridge, MA: MIT Press.

Greenwald, G. (2014), *No Place to Hide: Edward Snowden, the NSA, and the U.S. Surveillance State*. New York: Metropolitan Books.

Gregory, J. E., A. Iggo, A. K. McIntyre, and U. Proske (1988), 'Receptors in the Bill of the Platypus', *The Journal of Physiology*, 400: 349–67. Available at: https://doi.org/10.1113/jphysiol .1988.sp017124 (accessed: 13 February 2024).

Gripp, P. (2012), *Raining Tacos*. Oglio Records.

Gross, D. (2013), 'Foul-Mouthed Hacker Hijacks Baby's Monitor', *CNN Business Online*, 14 August. Available at: https://edition.cnn.com/2013/08/14/tech/web/hacked-baby-monitor/ index.html (accessed: 21 March 2024).

Gross, K. (1992), *The Dream of the Moving Statue*. Ithaca, NY: Cornell University Press.

Grynbaum, M. M. and R. Mac (2023), 'The Times Sues OpenAI and Microsoft Over A.I. Use of Copyrighted Work', *The New York Times*, 27 December. Available at: https://www.nytimes .com/2023/12/27/business/media/new-york-times-open-ai-microsoft-lawsuit.html (accessed: 3 February 2025).

Gunning, T. (2004), 'What is the Point of an Index? or, Faking Photographs', *Nordicom Review*, 25 (1–2): 39–49.

Gurova, O. (2006), 'Ideology of Consumption in Soviet Union: From Asceticism to the Legitimating of Consumer Goods', *Anthropology of East Europe Review*, 24 (2): 91–8.

Hager, N. (1996), *Secret Power: New Zealand's Role in the International Spy Network*. Nelson: Potton & Burton.

Hall, B. K. (1999), 'The Paradoxical Platypus', *BioScience*, 49 (3): 211–18.

Hallpike, C. S. and A. F. Rawdon-Smith (1937), 'LXXIX. The Wever and Bray Phenomenon—A Summary of the Data concerning the Origin of the Cochlear Effect', *Annals of Otology*,

Rhinology & Laryngology, 46 (4): 976–90. Available at: https://doi.org/10.1177
/000348943704600406 (accessed: 9 May 2024).

Hamilton, I. A. (2018), 'Google Gave Google Assistant a Weirdly Specific Backstory to Get Her
Voice Just Right', *Business Insider*. Available at: https://www.businessinsider.com/google-gave
-google-assistant-a-weirdly-specific-backstory-2018-10 (accessed: 25 February 2025).

Hamzelou, J. (2022), 'A Memory Prosthesis Could Restore Memory in People With Damaged
Brains', *MIT Technology Review*, 6 September. Available at: https://www.technologyreview
.com/2022/09/06/1059032/memory-prosthesis-damaged-brains/ (accessed: 14 February
2025).

Haraway, D. (1991), *Simians, Cyborgs, and Women: The Reinvention of Nature*. New York:
Routledge.

Haraway, D. (2003), *The Companion Species Manifesto: Dogs, People, and Significant Otherness*.
Cambridge: Prickly Paradigm Press.

Haraway, D. (2016), 'Tentacular Thinking: Anthropocene, Capitalocene, Chthulucene – Journal
#75', *e-flux Journal* [Preprint], (75). Available at: https://www.e-flux.com/journal/75/67125/
tentacular-thinking-anthropocene-capitalocene-chthulucene/ (accessed: 14 January 2025).

Harbinja, E., L. Edwards, and M. McVey (2023), 'Governing Ghostbots', *Computer Law &
Security Review*, 48: 105791. Available at: https://doi.org/10.1016/j.clsr.2023.105791.

Hardesty, L. (2018), 'Computer System Transcribes Words Users "Speak Silently"', *MIT News*,
4 April. Available at: http://news.mit.edu/2018/computer-system-transcribes-words-users
-speak-silently-0404 (accessed: 2 May 2024).

Harvilla, R. (2013), 'Kid Rock Is Cool In Defense of the Most Reviled Genre of Them All', *Slate
Magazine Online*, 4 March. Available at: https://slate.com/human-interest/2013/03/kids
-music-is-not-so-bad-in-defense-of-the-most-reviled-genre-of-them-all.html (accessed: 16
February 2025).

Haslam, J. (2015), *Near and Distant Neighbors: A New History of Soviet intelligence*. Oxford:
Oxford University Press.

Hawkins, A. (2023), 'How Chinese Influencers Use AI Digital Clones of Themselves to Pump
Out Content', *The Guardian Online*, 6 November. Available at: https://www.theguardian.com
/world/2023/nov/06/chinese-influencers-using-ai-digital-clones-of-themselves-to-pump-out
-content (accessed: 13 February 2025).

Hawkins, A. and A. H. S. C. Correspondent (2024), 'Chinese Mourners Turn to AI to Remember
and "Revive" Loved Ones', *The Guardian Online*. Available at: https://www.theguardian.com/
technology/2024/apr/04/chinese-mourners-turn-to-ai-to-remember-and-revive-loved-ones
(accessed: 16 December 2024).

Hayles, N. K. (1999), *How We Became Posthuman: Virtual Bodies in Cybernetics, Literature, and
Informatics*. Chicago and London: University of Chicago Press.

Heffner, R. S. and H. E. Heffner (1985), 'Hearing Range of the Domestic Cat', *Hearing Research*,
19: 85–8.

Heller-Roazen, D. (2009), *The Inner Touch: Archaeology of a Sensation*. New York: Zone Books.

Henrickson, L. (2023), 'Chatting with the Dead: The Hermeneutics of Thanabots', *Media, Culture
& Society*, 45 (5): 949–66. Available at: https://doi.org/10.1177/01634437221147626 (accessed:
9 May 2024).

Henriques, J. (2003), 'Sonic Dominance and the Reggae Sound System Session', in M. Bull and L.
Back (eds), *The Auditory Culture Reader*. Oxford: Berg, 451–80.

Her (2013), [Film] Dir. Spike Jonze, USA: Annapurna Pictures.

Herald Sun (2001), 'Cat was Walking Bug', *Herald Sun*, 5 November.

HereAfter AI (2023), *HereAfter AI — Interactive Memory App — Try Free*. Hereafter AI. Available
at: https://hereafter.ai/ (accessed: 18 December 2024).

Hern, A. (2017), 'CloudPets Stuffed Toys Leak Details of Half a Million Users', *The Guardian Online*, 28 February. Available at: https://www.theguardian.com/technology/2017/feb/28/ cloudpets-data-breach-leaks-details-of-500000-children-and-adults (accessed: 19 February 2024).

Hertz, G. and J. Parikka (2012), 'Zombie Media: Circuit Bending Media Archaeology into an Art Method', *Leonardo*, 45 (5): 424–30.

Heys, T. (2019), *Sound Pressure: How Speaker Systems Influence, Manipulate and Torture*. London and New York: Rowman & Littlefield.

Heys, T. and A. Hennlich (2010), 'The Art of "Conservative Détournement"', *ETC*, 88: 61–5.

Higgs, J. (2013), *The KLF: Chaos, Magic and the Band who Burned a Million Pounds*. London: Phoenix.

Higham, C. F. and D. J. Higham (2023), *Diffusion Models for Generative Artificial Intelligence: An Introduction for Applied Mathematicians*. Available at: https://arxiv.org/html/2312.14977v1 (accessed: 11 February 2025).

Hoffman, F. (2007), *Conflict in the 21st Century: The Rise of Hybrid Wars*. Arlington, VI: Potomac Institute for Policy Studies.

Hoffman, S. (2021), 'Arab Students and the Stasi: Agents and Objects of Intelligence', *Security Dialogue*, 52 (1): 62–78.

Hollanek, T. and K. Nowaczyk-Basińska (2024), 'Griefbots, Deadbots, Postmortem Avatars: On Responsible Applications of Generative AI in the Digital Afterlife Industry', *Philosophy & Technology*, 37 (63). Available at: https://doi.org/10.1007/s13347-024-00744-w (accessed: 3 September 2024).

Holloway, D. (2019), 'Surveillance Capitalism and Children's Data: The Internet of Toys and Things for Children', *Media International Australia*, 170 (1): 27–36.

Holt, P. (1991), *Bug in the Martini Olive and Other True Cases from the Files of Hal Lipset, Private Eye*. 1st edn. Boston: Brown and Co.

Hove, M. (2011), *History of the Bureau of Diplomatic Security of the United States Department of State*. 1st edn. Washington, DC: Global Publishing Solutions. Available at: https://2009-2017 .state.gov/documents/organization/176589.pdf (accessed: 10 February 2025).

How AI Could Become an Extension of Your Mind | Arnav Kapur (2019), [Film] Dir. TED. Available at: https://www.youtube.com/watch?v=TrofjEAetVs (accessed: 18 February 2025).

Howard, D. M. and J. Angus (2017), *Acoustics and Psychoacoustics*. 5th edn. New York: O'Reilly.

Howes, D. (2024), 'Sensorium: Contextualizing the Senses and Cognition in History and Across Cultures', *Elements in Histories of Emotions and the Senses* [Preprint]. Available at: https://doi .org/10.1017/9781009329668 (accessed: 19 May 2024).

Hughes, J. (2009), 'The Radio Nurse', *Codex 99*. Available at: http://www.codex99.com/design/41 .html (accessed: 23 May 2024).

Huntingdon, T. (1995), 'The Berlin Spy Tunnel Affair | Invention and Technology', *American Heritage's Invention & Technology*. Available at: https://development.inventionandtech.com/ content/berlin-spy-tunnel-affair-1 (accessed: 3 February 2025).

Hybrid 5 (2021) [Music album], Ghalil Einstein: MMR STUDIO$.

Hyde, H. J. (1988), *Introduction to 'Embassy Moscow: Attitudes and Errors' – (by Henry J. Hyde, Republican Of Illinois) (Extension of Remarks – October 26, 1988), Federation of American Scientists*. Available at: https://irp.fas.org/congress/1990_cr/h901025-embassy.htm (accessed: 5 January 2025).

iBaby (2024), 'About iBaby Labs – Wi-Fi Video Baby Monitors', *iBaby Care Monitors*. Available at: https://ibabylabs.com/about/ (accessed: 23 January 2025).

iControl (2015), 'State of the Smart Home Report', *WayBack Machine Internet Archive*. Available at: https://web.archive.org/web/20210629133808/https://www.ajperri.com/wp-content/

uploads/2018/01/b0168809-7f07-40be-9a9c-aac85cca76d2-150716032045-lva1-app6891.pdf (accessed: 6 January 2024).

Igo, S. E. (2018), *The Known Citizen: A History of Privacy in Modern America*. Cambridge, MA and London: Harvard University Press.

I Hear a New World (1991), [Music album], Joe Meek & The Blue Men: RPM.

IMF (2022), *Tenth Review of IMF Data Standards Initiatives*. IMF. Available at: https://www.imf .org/en/Publications/Policy-Papers/Issues/2022/03/15/Tenth-Review-of-IMF-Data-Standards -Initiatives-515139 (accessed: 16 January 2025).

Inception (2010), [Film] Dir. Christoper Nolan, USA/UK: Warner Bros. Pictures, Legendary Pictures, Syncopy.

@indiewashere (2017), *@indiewashere tweet*, *X.com*. Available at: https://x.com/ INDIEWASHERE/status/946375472836988928?mx=2 (accessed: 14 February 2025).

Innerspace (1987), [Film] Dir. Joe Dante, USA: Amblin Entertainment.

Intersoft Consulting (no date), *General Data Protection Regulation (GDPR)*, *Intersoft Consulting Website*. Available at: https://gdpr-info.eu/ (accessed: 14 February 2025).

Iorizzo, E. (2024), 'US Artist Laurie Anderson Models AI Chatbot on Late Husband: I'm Sadly Addicted', *The Independent Newspaper Online*, 29 February. Available at: https://www .independent.co.uk/news/uk/laurie-anderson-lou-reed-anderson-grammys-los-angeles -b2504428.html (accessed: 20 May 2024).

Isecom (2008), *Hacking Exposed Linux: Linux Security Secrets and Solutions*. 3rd edn. New York: McGraw Hill.

Ito, M., R. Cross, K. Dinakar, and C. Odgers (2023), 'Introduction', in M. Ito, R. Cross, K. Dinakar, and C. Odgers (eds), *Algorithmic Rights and Protections for Children*. Cambridge, MA: MIT Press, 3–14.

ITU (2021), *Keeping Children Safe in the Digital Environment: The Importance of Protection and Empowerment*. Geneva: International Telecommunication Union (ITU). Available at: https:// www.itu-cop-guidelines.com/ (accessed: 29 May 2024).

Jaher, D. (2015), *The Witch of Lime Street: Seance, Seduction, and Houdinin in the Spirit World*. New York: Crown Publishers.

Jameson, F. (1991), *Postmodernism, or, The Cultural Logic of Late Capitalism*. Durham, NC: Duke University Press.

Janssen, V. (2012), 'Indirect Tracking of Drop Bears Using GNSS Technology', *Australian Geographer*, 43 (4): 445–52.

Jansen, A. M., E. Giebels, T. J. L. van Rompay, and M. Junger (2018), 'The Influence of the Presentation of Camera Surveillance on Cheating and Pro-Social Behavior', *Frontiers in Psychology*, 9 (Environmental Psychology). Available at: https://doi.org/10.3389/fpsyg.2018 .01937 (accessed: 17 February 2025).

Javane, F. and D. Bunker (1997), *Numerology and the Divine Triangle*. Atglen, PA: Schiffer Publishing.

Ji, C. et al. (2021), 'A review of infant cry analysis and classification', EURASIP Journal on Audio, Speech, and Music Processing, 2021(1): 8. Available at: https://doi.org/10.1186/s13636-021 -00197-5

Jimerson, Randall C. (2005), 'Embracing the Power of Archives', in. *Society of American Archivists Annual Meeting*. New Orleans: Society of American Archivists. Available at: https://www2 .archivists.org/history/leaders/randall-c-jimerson/embracing-the-power-of-archives (accessed: 14 January 2025).

John Graham-Cumming (2014), *Source Code in TV and Films, Source Code in TV and Films*. Moviecode – Tumblr. Available at: https://moviecode.tumblr.com/ (accessed: 5 January 2024).

Johnson, A. F. (2021), *Reconciling the Age Appropriate Design Code with COPPA'. The Privacy Advisor*. IAPP. Available at: https://iapp.org/news/a/reconciling-the-age-appropriate-design -code-with-coppa/ (accessed: 11 February 2024).

Johnson, B. (2016), *Sir Robert Peel and his 'Bobbies', Historic UK*. Available at: https://www .historic-uk.com/HistoryUK/HistoryofEngland/Sir-Robert-Peel/ (accessed: 6 February 2024).

Johnson, B. and M. Cloonan (2009), *Dark Side of the Tune: Popular Music and Violence*. Burlington and Farnham: Ashgate Popular and Folk Music Series.

Johnson, G., I. N. Guha, and P. Davies (2013), 'Were James Bond's Drinks Shaken because of Alcohol Induced Tremor?', *British Medical Journal*, 347 (f7255): 1–7. Available at: https://doi .org/doi: 10.1136/bmj.f7255 (accessed: 6 January 2025).

Johnston, S. I. (2008) *Ancient Greek Divination*. Blackwell Ancient Religions. Malden, MA and Oxford: Wiley-Blackwell.

Jones, C. D. (2007), 'Soviet Military Doctrine as Strategic Deception: An Offensive Military Strategy for Defense of the Socialist Fatherland', *The Journal of Slavic Military Studies*, 16 (3): 24–65.

Jones, R. (2018), 'Voice Recognition: Is It Really As Secure As It Sounds?', *The Guardian Online*, 22 September. Available at: https://www.theguardian.com/money/2018/sep/22/voice -recognition-is-it-really-as-secure-as-it-sounds (accessed: 23 January 2024).

Joung, Y. H. (2013), 'Development of Implantable Medical Devices: From an Engineering Perspective', *International Neurology Journal*, 17 (3): 98–106.

Joyce, J. (1922), *The Annotated 'Ulysses'*. Available at: https://en.wikisource.org/wiki/The _Annotated_%22Ulysses%22 (accessed: 30 January 2025).

Kacprzyk, A., G. Kanclerz, E. Rokita, and G. Tatoń (2021), 'Which Sources of Electromagnetic Field Are of the Highest Concern for Electrosensitive Individuals? – Questionnaire Study with a Literature Review', *Electromagnetic Biology and Medicine*, 40 (1): 33–40. Available at: https://doi.org/10.1080/15368378.2020.1839489 (accessed: 16 January 2025).

Kakutani, M. (2006), 'What Torture Is and Isn't: A Hard-Liner's Argument', *New York Times Online*, 31 October. Available at: https://www.nytimes.com/2006/10/31/books/31kaku.html (accessed: 3 October 2024).

Kamp, K. S., E. M. Steffen, B. Alderson-Day, P. Allen, A. Austad, J. Hayes, F. Larøi, M. Ratcliffe, and P. Sabucedo (2020), 'Sensory and Quasi-Sensory Experiences of the Deceased in Bereavement: An Interdisciplinary and Integrative Review', *Schizophrenia Bulletin*, 46 (6): 1367–81. Available at: https://doi.org/10.1093/schbul/sbaa113 (accessed: 6 January 2025).

Kapur, A., S. Kapur, and P. Maes (2018), 'AlterEgo: A Personalized Wearable Silent Speech Interface', in *23rd International Conference on Intelligent User Interfaces. IUI'18: 23rd International Conference on Intelligent User Interfaces*. Tokyo, Japan: ACM, 43–53. Available at: https://doi.org/10.1145/3172944.3172977 (accessed: 4 May 2025).

Kasper, J. E. and S. A. Feller (1987), *Complete Book of Holograms: How they Work and How to Make Them*. New York: John Wiley & Sons Inc.

Kaufmann, P. and R. Brander (2020), 'Written Opening Statement On Behalf Of "Alison", "Bea", "C", "Ellie", Denise Fuller, Donna, Belinda Harvey, "Jane", "Jenny", "Jessica", "Lisa", "Lizzie", "Maya", "Monica", "Naomi", "Rosa", "Ruth", "Sara", Helen Steel, "Wendy", Kate Wilson – In The Undercover Policing Inquiry', *Undercover Policing Enquiry Website*. Available at: https://www .ucpi.org.uk/wp-content/uploads/2020/11/20201026-Opening_Statement-CAT_H_Birnbergs -PKQC-AMENDED_09.11.20.pdf (accessed: 12 August 2024).

Keefe, P. R. (2005), *Chatter: Dispatches from the Secret World of Global Eavesdropping*. London: Random House.

Keefe, P. R. (2006), *Chatter: Uncovering the Echelon Surveillance Network and the Secret World of Global Eavesdropping*. Reprint edn. New York: Random House Inc.

Kennedy, C. S. (2011), 'Interview with The Honorable Harry G. Barnes, 2011'. Available at: https://www.loc.gov/item/mfdipbib001679 (accessed: 27 January 2024).

Kingson, J. A. (2015), 'How Cats Took Over the Internet' at the Museum of the Moving Image', *New York Times*. Available at: https://www.nytimes.com/2015/08/07/arts/design/how-cats -took-over-the-internet-at-the-museum-of-the-moving-image.html (Accessed: 10 February 2025).

Kirol, C. P. (2020), 'Coupling Tracking Technologies to Maximize Efficiency in Avian Research', *Wildlife Society Bulletin*, 44 (2): 406–15. Available at: https://doi.org/doi:10.1002/wsb.1092.

Kittler, F. (1999), *Gramophone, Film, Typewriter*. Stanford, CA: Stanford University Press.

Kolb, D. (2022), 'Design Choices for Embodied Conversational Agents to Preserve Testimonies by Contemporary Witnesses', in *Extended Abstracts of the 2022 CHI Conference on Human Factors in Computing Systems*. New York: Association for Computing Machinery (CHI EA '22), 1–5. Available at: https://doi.org/10.1145/3491101.3503822 (accessed: 26 January 2025).

Kolenosky, G. B. and D. H. Johnston (1967), 'Radio-Tracking Timber Wolves in Ontario', *American Zoologist*, 7 (2): 289–303.

Kruglova, O. (1981), *Traditional Russian Carved and Painted Woodwork*. Moscow: Izobrazitelnoye Iskusstvo Publishers.

Kruh, L. (2010), 'Stimson, the Black Chamber, and the "Gentleman's Mail" Quote', *Cryptologia*, 12 (2): 65–89.

Kuhn, R., T. J. Walsh, and S. Fries (2005), *Security Considerations for Voice Over IP Systems: Recommendations of the National Institute of Standards and Technology*. NIST Special Publication 800–58. Gaithersburg, MD: National Institute for Standards and Technology.

Kurczy, S. (2021), *The Quiet Zone: Unraveling the Mystery of a Town Suspended in Silence*. New York: William Morrow.

La Prade, E. (2002), 'The Early Days of E.A.T', *IEEE MultiMedia*, 9 (2): 4–5. Available at: https:// doi.org/10.1109/93.998040 (accessed: 16 January 2025).

LaBelle, B. (2014), *Lexicon of the Mouth: Poetics and Politics of Voice and the Oral Imaginary*. New York and London: Bloomsbury Publishing.

Lamoureux, M. and J. Cox (2019), 'Canadian CEO Who Sold Encrypted Phones to the Sinaloa Cartel Sentenced to Nine Years', *Vice*, 29 May. Available at: https://www.vice.com/en/article /xwn4vw/canadian-ceo-vincent-ramos-who-sold-encrypted-phones-to-the-sinaloa-cartel -sentenced-to-nine-years (accessed: 13 February 2024).

Laqueur, W. (1985), *A World of Secrets: The Uses and Limits of Intelligence*. New York: Basic Books.

Leaver, T. (2017), 'Intimate Surveillance: Normalizing Parental Monitoring and Mediation of Infants Online', *Social Media + Society*, 3 (2). Available at: https://doi.org/10.1177 /2056305117707192 (accessed: 15 February 2025).

Leong, E. R. (2024), 'The False Promise of Keeping a Loved One "Alive" with A.I. Grief Bots', *The Jesuit Review* [Preprint]. Available at: https://www.americamagazine.org/faith/2024/05/13/ artificial-intelligence-bots-death-christianity-247885 (accessed: 22 September 2024).

Leshuk, L. (2003), *US Intelligence Perceptions of Soviet Power 1921–1946*. London and Portland, OR: Frank Cass Publishers.

Leskin, P. (2018), 'Over 1 Million People Have Asked Amazon Alexa to Marry Them. Here's What She Said'. Available at: https://www.businessinsider.com/amazons-alexa-got-over-1 -million-marriage-proposals-in-2017-2018-10 (accessed: 22 January 2025).

Levin, I. (1972), *The Stepford Wives*. New York: Random House.

Lewis, A. (2021), *A State of Secrecy: Stasi Informers and the Culture of Surveillance*. Sterling, VA: Potomac Books.

Li, J. and J. Zhang (2021), 'A Study of Voice Print Recognition Technology', in. *International Wireless Communications and Mobile Computing Conference*. Harbin City, China. Available at: http://dx.doi.org/10.1109/IWCMC51323.2021.9498681 (accessed: 17 February 2025).

Litt, R. S. (2015), 'Robert S. Litt, General Counsel, Office of the Director of National Intelligence, Speech at Brookings Institution', in D. P. Fidler (ed.), *The Snowden Reader*. Bloomington, IN: Indiana University Press, 101–14.

Liu, K., P. W. Kalivas, M. P. Paulus, and H. Lau (2021), 'A Framework for Understanding Agency', in *Intrusive Thinking: From Molecules to Free Will*. Cambridge, MA: MIT Press. Available at: https://doi.org/10.7551/mitpress/13875.001.0001 (accessed: 16 February 2025).

Llanes, L. C., N. B. Sa, A. R. Cenci, K. F. Teixeira, I. V. de França, L. Meier, and A. S. de Oliveira. 2022. 'Witches, Potions, and Metabolites: An Overview from a Medicinal Perspective', *RSC Medicinal Chemistry*, 13 (4): 405–12. https://doi.org/10.1039/d2md00025c. (accessed: 10 January 2025).

Logan, D. E., C. Breazeal, M. S. Goodwin, S. Jeong, B. O'Connell, D. Smith-Freedman, J. Heathers, and P. Weinstock (2019), 'Social Robots for Hospitalized Children', *Pediatrics*, 144 (1): e20181511. Available at: https://doi.org/10.1542/peds.2018-1511 (accessed: 28 January 2025).

Lokot, T. (2016), 'Russian Social Network VK Claims to Protect Users From Warrantless Surveillance', *Global Voices*, 1 February. Available at: https://globalvoices.org/2016/02/01/russian-social-network-vk-claims-to-protect-users-from-warrantless-surveillance/ (accessed: 24 February 2025).

Lunden, I. (2013), 'Amazon Gets into Voice Recognition, Buys Ivona Software to Compete Against Apple's Siri', *Tech Crunch Website*, 24 January. Available at: https://techcrunch.com/2013/01/24/amazon-gets-into-voice-recognition-buys-ivona-software-to-compete-against-apples-siri/ (accessed: 29 December 2023).

Luschmann, M. (2019), 'Discourses of "Herbivore Masculinity" in Japanese Love Advice Books', *Vienne Journey of East Asion Studies*, 11 (1): 125–54.

Lutkevich, B. and A. DelVecchio (2023), 'Internet of Medical Things (IoMT) or Healthcare IoT', *TechTraget Network Website*, March. Available at: https://www.techtarget.com/iotagenda/definition/IoMT-Internet-of-Medical-Things (accessed: 13 December 2023).

M3GAN (2022), [Film] Dir. Gerard Johnstone, USA: Universal Pictures, Blumhouse Productions, Atomic Monster.

Ma, M., S. Coward, and C. Walker (2017), 'Question-Answering Virtual Humans Based on Pre-recorded Testimonies for Holocaust Education', in M. Ma and A. Oikonomou (eds), *Serious Games and Edutainment Applications : Volume II*. Cham: Springer International Publishing, 391–409. Available at: https://doi.org/10.1007/978-3-319-51645-5_18 (accessed: 24 February 2025).

Maass (2014), 'Art in a Time of Surveillance', *The Intercept Online*, 13 November. Available at: https://theintercept.com/2014/11/13/art-surveillance-explored-artists/ (accessed: 14 February 2025).

MacAskill, E. (2013), 'NSA Paid Millions to Cover Prism compliance Costs for Tech Companies', *The Guardian Online*, 23 August. Available at: https://www.theguardian.com/world/2013/aug/23/nsa-prism-costs-tech-companies-paid (accessed: 24 October 2023).

MacAskill, Ewen, J. Borger, N. Hopkins, N. Davies, and J. Ball (2013), 'GCHQ Taps Fibre-optic Cables for Secret Access to World's Communications', *The Guardian Online*, 21 June. Available at: https://www.theguardian.com/uk/2013/jun/21/gchq-cables-secret-world-communications-nsa (accessed: 8 January 2024).

MacDonald, W. L. (1992), 'Idionecrophanies: The Social Construction of Perceived Contact with the Dead', *Journal for the Scientific Study of Religion*, 31 (2): 215–23. Available at: https://doi.org/10.2307/1387010 (accessed: 4 February 2025).

Mack, E. (2018), 'You Can Talk To MIT's Mind-Reading Headset Without Ever Opening Your Mouth', *Forbes Online*. Available at: https://www.forbes.com/sites/ericmack/2018/04/06/talk-to-mit-alterego-mind-reading-headset-without-ever-opening-your-mouth/ (accessed: 9 April 2024).

Madsen, V. (2009), 'Cantata of fire: son et lumière in Waco Texas, auscultation for a shadow play', *Organised Sound*, 14 (1): 89–99.

Maheshwari, N. and V. V. Kumar (eds) (2016), *Military Psychology: Concepts, Trends and Interventions*. New Delhi: SAGE Publications Pvt. Ltd. Available at: https://doi.org/10.4135 /9789353885854 (accessed: 2 October 2024).

Major, P. (2012), 'Listening Behind the Curtain: BBC broadcasting to East Germany and its Cold War Echo', *Cold War History*, 13 (2): 255–75. Available at: https://doi.org/10.1080/14682745 .2012.746840 (accessed: 24 February 2025).

Makin, S. (2015), 'The Brain Cells behind a Sense of Direction', *Scientific American*, 1 May. Available at: https://www.scientificamerican.com/article/the-brain-cells-behind-a-sense-of -direction/ (accessed: 17 October 2023).

Maloney, D. (2016), 'Hacking When It Counts: Spy Radios', *Hackaday*, 12 August. Available at: https://hackaday.com/2016/08/12/hacking-when-it-counts-spy-radios/ (accessed: 9 January 2025).

Mancini, C. (2011), 'Animal-Computer Interaction (ACI): A manifesto', *Interactions*, 18 (4): 69–73.

Mangan, L. (2024), 'Eternal You Review – It's Impossible not to be Horrified by this AI quest to Bring the Dead Back to Life', *The Guardian Online*, 29 October. Available at: https:// www.theguardian.com/tv-and-radio/2024/oct/29/storyville-eternal-you-review-film-dead (accessed: 11 December 2024).

Manger, P. R. and J. D. Pettigrew (1995), 'Electroreception and the Feeding Behaviour of Platypus (Ornithorhynchus Anatinus: Monotremata: Mammalia)', *Philosophical Transactions: Biological Sciences*, 347 (1322): 359–81.

Mangiafico, L. (2014), 'Spy vs. Spy, Romanian Style', *The Foreign Service Journal* [Preprint]. Available at: https://afsa.org/spy-vs-spy-romanian-style (accessed: 2 February 2025).

Marar, Z. (2014), *Intimacy : Understanding the Subtle Power of Human Connection*. London: Taylor & Francis Group.

March-Russell, P. (2020), 'Machines Like Us? Modernism and the Question of the Robot', in *AI Narratives*. Cambridge: Cambridge University Press. Available at: https://r4.vlereader.com/ Reader?ean=9780192586049 (accessed: 17 December 2024).

Maréchal, N. (2017), 'Networked Authoritarianism and the Geopolitics of Information: Understanding Russian Internet Policy', *Media and Communication*, 5 (1): 29–41. Available at: https://doi.org/10.17645/mac.v5i1.808 (accessed: 14 February 2025).

Margolin, M. (2016), 'This Japanese Company Wants to Sell You a Tiny Holographic Wife', *VICE*, 14 December. Available at: https://www.vice.com/en/article/gatebox-holographic-ai-assistant/ (accessed: 13 February 2025).

Marr, B. (2018), 'Smart Dust Is Coming. Are You Ready?', *Forbes Online*, 16 September. Available at: https://www.forbes.com/sites/bernardmarr/2018/09/16/smart-dust-is-coming-are-you -ready/ (accessed: 15 February 2025).

Marrow, A. and M. Trevelyan (2024), 'After Years of Pressure on Durov, Russia Suddenly Rallies Behind Him', *Reuters*, 29 August. Available at: https://www.reuters.com/world/europe/after -years-pressure-durov-russia-suddenly-rallies-behind-him-2024-08-29/ (accessed: 16 January 2025).

Marsh, L. (2024), 'Laurie Anderson on Making an AI chatbot of Lou Reed: 'I'm Totally, 100%, Sadly Addicted', *The Guardian Online*, 28 February. Available at: https://www.theguardian .com/music/2024/feb/28/laurie-anderson-ai-chatbot-lou-reed-ill-be-your-mirror-exhibition -adelaide-festival (accessed: 27 July 2024).

Martial Hauntology (2014), [Music album] Audint: Audint Records.

Martin, D. (2012), 'Harry Barnes Jr., A Top U.S. Diplomat, Is Dead at 86', *The New York Times*, 17 August. Available at: https://www.nytimes.com/2012/08/17/world/americas/harry-g-barnes-jr -envoy-to-chile-and-india-dies-at-86.html (accessed: 9 January 2025).

Martin, D. (2018), *Wilderness of Mirrors: Intrigue, Deception, and the Secrets that Destroyed Two of the Cold War's Most Important Agents*. New York: Skyhorse Publishing.

Mary Had a Little Lamb (1830), [7" single] Sarah Josepha Hale, Boston: Marsh, Capen & Lyon.

Mason, P. (2018), 'Special Operations', *Land Mobile Website*, 14 November. Available at: https://www.landmobile.co.uk/content/features/special-operations/ (accessed: 8 May 2024).

Mathews, M. V. (1963), 'The Digital Computer as a Musical Instrument', *Science*, 142 (3592): 553–7.

Mauss, M. (1925), 'An Essay on the Gift: The Form and Reason of Exchange in Archaic Societies', *L'Année Sociologique* [Preprint].

Mauss, M. (1950), *The Gift: The Form and Reason For Exchange in Archaic Societies*. Translated by W.D. Halls. London: Routledge Classics.

Maximizer Market Research (2024) 'Smart Toys Market: Educational and Skill Development to Fuel the Market Growth over the Forecast Period', January. Available at: https://www.maximizemarketresearch.com/market-report/smart-toys-market/17231/ (accessed: 12 February 2024).

McAdams, A., ed. (2011), *Radio Frequency Identification*. New York: Nova Scotia Publishers Inc.

McCluskey, M. (2021), 'TikTok Has Started Collecting Your 'Faceprints and "Voiceprints." Here's What It Could Do With Them', *Time Magazine Online*, 14 June. Available at: https://time.com/6071773/tiktok-faceprints-voiceprints-privacy/ (accessed: 23 January 2024).

McCurry, J. (2024), 'Activists fly K-pop USB Sticks into North Korea as "Poo Balloon" Row Intensifies', *The Guardian Online*, 6 June. Available at: https://www.theguardian.com/world/article/2024/jun/06/north-korea-south-korea-poo-balloons-k-pop-usb-sticks-us-dollars (accessed: 11 June 2024).

McDonald, Kyle and Lauren Lee McCarthy (2023), *Voice In My Head*. Available at: https://lauren-mccarthy.com/Voice-In-My-Head (accessed: 3 September 2024).

McEwan, I. (2007), *On Chesil Beach*. 1st edn. London: Jonathan Cape.

McGill University (2007), *ECHELON, McGill School of Computer Science*. Available at: https://www.cs.mcgill.ca/~rwest/wikispeedia/wpcd/wp/e/ECHELON.htm (accessed: 9 March 2023).

McKee, R. (1997), *Story: Substance, Structure, Style, and The Principles of Screenwriting*. New York: ReganBooks.

McKee, R. (2016), *Dialogue: The Art of Verbal Action for Page, Stage, and Screen*. New York: Grand Central Publishing.

McLuhan, M. (1964), *Understanding Media: The Extensions of Man*. New York: McGraw-Hill.

McReynolds, E., S. Hubbard, T. Lau, A. Saraf, M. Cakmak, and F. Roesner (2017), 'Toys that Listen: A Study of Parents, Children, and Internet-Connected Toys', in *Proceedings of the 2017 CHI Conference on Human Factors in Computing Systems*. New York: Association for Computing Machinery (CHI '17), 5197–207. Available at: https://doi.org/10.1145/3025453.3025735 (accessed: 22 February 2025).

McRobbie, L. R. (2015), 'The History of Creepy Dolls', *Smithsonian Magazine Online*, 15 July. Available at: https://www.smithsonianmag.com/history/history-creepy-dolls-180955916/ (accessed: 24 February 2024).

Meares, H. H. (2020), 'The Love Goddess: Rita Hayworth's Tragic Quest', *Vanity Fair*, 30 September. Available at: https://www.vanityfair.com/hollywood/2020/09/rita-hayworth-biography-trauma (accessed: 16 February 2025).

Meduza (2016), 'In "kontakt" With the Cops When Russian Police Go After Internet Users, Why Do They Target People on Vkontakte Almost Exclusively?', *Meduza*. Available at: https://meduza.io/en/feature/2016/07/07/in-kontakt-with-the-cops (accessed: 11 February 2025).

Melcer, E. F., M. T. Astolfi, M. Remaley, A. Berenzweig, and T. Giurgica-Tiron (2018), 'CTRL-Labs: Hand Activity Estimation and Real-time Control from Neuromuscular Signals', in *Extended Abstracts of the 2018 CHI Conference on Human Factors in Computing Systems*. New

York: Association for Computing Machinery (CHI EA '18), 1–4. Available at: https://doi.org /10.1145/3170427.3186520 (accessed: 4 February 2025).

Melkadze, A. (2024), 'Share of Households Owning at Least One Cat or Dog in Russia from 2010 to 2022', *Statista*. Available at: https://www.statista.com/statistics/517036/households-owning -cats-dogs-europe-russia/ (accessed: 13 February 2025).

Metz, C. (2023), 'How Could A.I. Destroy Humanity?', *The New York Times*, 10 June. Available at: https://www.nytimes.com/2023/06/10/technology/ai-humanity.html (accessed: 16 December 2024).

Michael, M. and D. Lupton (2016), 'Toward a Manifesto for the "Public Understanding of Big Data"', *Public Understanding of Science*, 25 (1): 104–16. Available at: https://doi.org/10.1177 /09636625515609005 (accessed: 16 February 2025).

Miller, A. I. (2019), *The Artist in the Machine: The World of AI-powered Creativity*. Cambridge, MA: MIT Press.

Min, R. (2023), *Families in China Turning to AI to 'Digitally Revive' Dead Loved Ones*, Euronews. Available at: https://www.euronews.com/next/2023/12/19/rise-of-chinas-ghost-bots-this -father-turned-to-ai-to-digitally-revive-his-dead-son (accessed: 11 December 2024).

Minority Report (2002), [Film] Dir. Steven Spielberg, USA: 20th Century Fox, DreamWorks Pictures Amblin Entertainment, Blue Tulip Productions.

Minsker, E. (2019), 'Holly Herndon Weighs in on Grimes and Zola Jesus' Debate About AI and the Future of Music', *Pitchfork Website*, 26 November. Available at: https://pitchfork.com/ news/holly-herndon-weighs-in-on-grimes-and-zola-jesus-debate-about-ai-and-the-future-of -music/ (accessed: 15 February 2025).

Mission: Impossible (1996), [Film] Dir. Brian De Palma, USA: Paramount Pictures.

MIT (2018), 'Alter Ego', *MIT Media Lab*. Available at: https://www.media.mit.edu/projects/ alterego/overview/ (accessed: 7 April 2024).

MIT (2025), 'Research', *MIT Media Lab*. Available at: https://www.media.mit.edu/research/?filter =groups_centers_initiatives (accessed: 16 February 2025).

Monahan, T. and R. D. Torres (2010), 'Introduction', in T. Monahan and R. D. Torres (eds), *Schools Under Surveillance*. New Brunswick, NJ: Rutgers University Press, 1–18.

Morreale, F. (2021), 'Where Does the Buck Stop? Ethical and Political Issues with AI in Music Creation', *Transactions of the International Society for Music Information Retrieval*, 4: 105–13. Available at: https://doi.org/10.5334/tismir.86 (accessed: 7 February 2025).

Morris, N. (1996), 'The "Sexpionage" Trap', *Maclean's* 109 (36): 28. Gale OneFile: News', link.gale. com/apps/doc/A18645133/STND?u=mmucal5&sid=oclc&xid=8bfeb0d1. (accessed 19 June 2025).

Morton, E. (2013), 'Robert the Haunted Doll: Creeping Out Floridians Since 1904', *Slate Magazine Online*, 18 November. Available at: https://www.slate.com/blogs/atlas_obscura /2013/11/18/robert_the_haunted_doll_creeping_out_floridians_since_1904.html (accessed: 6 March 2024).

Morton, T. (2013), *Hyperobjects: Philosophy and Ecology after the End of the World*. Illustrated edn. Minneapolis, MN: University of Minnesota Press.

Moss, F. (2011), *Sorceres and their Apprentices: How the Digital Magicians of the MIT Media Lab are Creating the Innovative Technologies That Will Transform Our Lives*. New York: Crown Business.

Mubert (2024), 'Human and AI Music Generator for Your Video Content, Podcasts and Apps', *Mubert Website*. Available at: https://mubert.com/ (accessed: 6 June 2024).

Mukhopadhyay, J., B. Saha, B. Majumdar, A. K. Majumdar, S. Gorain, B. K. Arya, S. D. Bhattacharya, and A. Singh (2013), 'An Evaluation of Human Perception for Neonatal Cry using a Database of Cry and Underlying Cause', in *2013 Indian Conference on Medical Informatics and Telemedicine (ICMIT). 2013 Indian Conference on Medical Informatics and*

Telemedicine (ICMIT), 64–7. Available at: https://doi.org/10.1109/IndianCMIT.2013.6529410 (accessed: 7 February 2025).

Murakami, T. (2004), 'Ubiquitous Networking: Business Opportunities and Strategic Issues', Nomura Research Institute (NRI) No 79, 1 August 2004. Available at: https://dl.ndl.go.jp/view /prepareDownload?itemId=info%3Andljp%2Fpid%2F10207879&contentNo=1.

Murder! (1930), [Film] Dir. Alfred Hitchcock: British International Pictures.

Murray, K. (2017), 'The Great Seal Bug (part 1)', *Murray Associates TSCM*. Available at: https:// counterespionage.com/great-seal-bug-part-1/ (accessed: 5 January 2025).

Nanit (2024), *Nanit Pro Smart Baby Monitor & Floor Stand (V2)*. Available at: https://nanituk.co .uk/products/complete-monitoring-system (accessed: 19 December 2024).

National Holocaust Centre (2016), *The Forever Project, The National Holocaust Centre and Museum*. Available at: https://www.holocaust.org.uk/interactive (accessed: 17 December 2024).

Negarestani, R. (2008), *Cyclonopedia: Complicity with Anonymous Materials*. 1st edn. London: re .press.

Nelson, M. K. (2009), 'Watching Children Describing the Use of Baby Monitors on Epinions .com', in Margaret K. Nelson, and A. I. Garey (eds), *Who's Watching? Daily Practices of Surveillance Among Contemporary Families*. Nashville: Vanderbilt University Press, 219–38.

Nemtsov, B. (2011), '20 December 2011 – Excuse', *B_Nemtsov -Memorial Account*. Available at: https://b-nemtsov.livejournal.com/2011/12/20/ (accessed: 16 January 2025).

Neuralink (2025), *Neuralink — Pioneering Brain Computer Interfaces, Neuralink*. Available at: https://neuralink.com/ (accessed: 29 January 2025).

New Wave (2024), 'Practical Tips to Keep Your Music Safe', *New Wave Magazine*. Available at: https://www.newwavemagazine.com/single-post/practical-tips-to-keep-your-music-safe (accessed: 30 October 2024).

Newton, C. (2016), 'When her Best Friend Died, She Used Artificial Intelligence to Keep Talking to Him', *TheVerge.com*. Available at: http://www.theverge.com/a/luka-artificial-intelligence -memorial-roman-mazurenko-bot (accessed: 13 February 2025).

Nielson, E. (2010), '"Can't C Me" Surveillance and Rap Music', *Journal of Black Studies*, 40 (6): 1254–74.

NIST (no date), *Glossary, National Institute of Standards and Technology (NIST)*. Available at: https://csrc.nist.gov/glossary/term/sensitive_compartmented_information_facility (accessed: 5 January 2025).

Nittins, T. (2011), 'A Boy and His Toys: Technology and Gadgetry in the James Bond Film Series', in R. G. Weiner, B. L. Whitfield, and J. Becker (eds), *James Bond in World and Popular Culture: The Films are Not Enough*. 2nd edn. Newcastle upon Tyne: Cambridge Scholars. Available at: http://site.ebrary.com/id/10642841 (accessed: 5 January 2024).

NIV (1978), 'Psalm 18:13', in *New International Version of the Bible*. New York: Biblica. Available at: http://bible.cc/psalms/18-13.htm (accessed: 15 September 2022).

Noble, S. U. (2018), *Algorithms of Oppression: How Search Engines Reinforce Racism*. New York: New York University Press.

NSA (1988), *Operation REGAL: The Berlin Tunnel*. United States Cryptologic History: National Security Agency, 4. Available at: https://www.nsa.gov/portals/75/documents/news-features/ declassified-documents/cryptologic-histories/operation_regal.pdf (accessed: 14 March 2022).

NUANCE (2024), 'Using Voice Biometrics for Authentication', *NUANCE Website*. Available at: https://www.nuance.com/omni-channel-customer-engagement/authentication-and-fraud -prevention/gatekeeper/what-is-voiceprint.html (accessed: 26 January 2024).

Nye, M.J. (2016), *Speaking in Tongues: Science's Centuries-long Hunt for a Common Language, Science History Institute*. Available at: https://www.sciencehistory.org/stories/magazine/ speaking-in-tongues/ (accessed: 22 February 2025).

O'Callaghan, C. (2007), 'Echoes', *The Monist*, 90 (3): 403+.

Ocultopedia (no date), 'Gastromancy', *Occultopedia Website*. Available at: https://www.occultopedia.com/g/gastromancy.htm (accessed: 26 January 2024).

O'Gorman, M. (2015), *Necromedia*. Minneapolis, MN: University of Minnesota Press.

Ohlheiser, A. (2015), 'The Platypus Is So Weird That Scientists Thought the First Specimen Was a Hoax', *The Washington Post online*, 1 April. Available at: https://www.washingtonpost.com/news/speaking-of-science/wp/2015/04/01/the-platypus-is-so-weird-that-scientists-thought-the-first-specimen-was-a-hoax/ (accessed: 13 February 2025).

Öhman, C. and L. Floridi (2017), 'The Political Economy of Death in the Age of Information: A Critical Approach to the Digital Afterlife Industry', *Minds and Machines: Journal for Artificial Intelligence, Philosophy and Cognitive Science*, 27 (4): 639–62.

Olive (2011), [Film] Dir. Hooman Khalili and Patrick Gilles, USA: Cavescribe.

O'Neill, K. (2016), *Internet Afterlife: Virtual Salvation in the 21st Century*. Santa Barbara, CA and Denver, CO: Praeger.

OpenAI (2020a), 'Jukebox', *OpenAI*. Available at: https://openai.com/index/jukebox/ (accessed: 16 February 2025).

OpenAI (2020b), 'jukebox/jukebox/data/ids/v3_genre_ids.txt (Jukebox Genre List)', *OpenAI Github*. Available at: https://github.com/openai/jukebox/blob/master/jukebox/data/ids/v3_genre_ids.txt (accessed: 25 October 2024).

OpenAI (2020c), *Classic Pop, in the Style of Elvis Presley*. SoundCloud. Available at: https://soundcloud.com/openai_audio (accessed: 18 October 2024).

OpenAI (2024), *Terms of Use*. Available at: https://openai.com/policies/row-terms-of-use/ (accessed: 4 December 2024).

Orwell, G. (1949), *1984*. 1st edn. London: Secker & Warburg.

OSCE (2021), *First Expert Meeting: International law and Policy on Disinformation in the Context of Freedom of the Media*. Online: OSCE | Organization for Security and Co-operation in Europe. Available at: https://www.osce.org/whatistheosce (accessed: 14 January 2025).

Ozzi, D. (2018), 'Rock is Dead, Thank God', *Vice Magazine Online*, 14 June. Available at: https://www.vice.com/en/article/a3aqkj/rock-is-dead-thank-god (accessed: 20 May 2024).

Park, J. (2020), 'Making the Automaton Speak: Hearing Artificial Voices in the Eighteenth Century', in S. Cave, K. Dihal and S. Dillon (eds), *AI Narratives: A History of Imaginative Thinking about Intelligent Machines*. Oxford: Oxford University Press, 119–43.

Partridge, E. (2015), *A Dictionary of the Underworld: British and American*. London: Routledge. Available at: https://doi.org/10.4324/9781315696300 (accessed: 3 February 2025).

Pasquinelli, M. (2023), *The Eye of the Master: A Social History of Artificial Intelligence*. 1st edn. London: Verso. Available at: https://www.versobooks.com/en-gb/products/735-the-eye-of-the-master (accessed: 3 February 2025).

Pearce, S. (2017), 'A Guide to Voicemails in Hip-Hop', *Pitchfork Magazine Online*, 23 May. Available at: https://pitchfork.com/thepitch/1524-a-guide-to-voicemails-in-hip-hop/ (accessed: 9 November 2023).

Pell, M. (2017), *Envisioning Holograms: Design Breakthrough Experiences for Mixed Reality*. Woodinville, Washington: Apress.

Pellé, S. and B. Reber (2016), *From Ethical Review to Responsible Research and Innovation*. London and Hoboken, NJ: ISTE Ltd, John Wiley & Sons, Inc.

Perry, W. L., B. McInnis, C. C. Price, S. C. Smith, and J. S. Hollywood (2013), *Predictive Policing: The Role of Crime Forecasting in Law Enforcement Operations*. Santa Monica: RAND.

Peskoe-Yang, L. (2022), 'Analyzing Every Second of the Classic Dial-Up Modem Sound', *Popular Mechanics Online*, 22 March. Available at: https://www.popularmechanics.com/science/a29611456/internet-dialup-modem-sounds/ (accessed: 8 September 2024).

Peters, J. (2016), 'No Place to Hack: Why Aaron Swartz Profoundly Misjudged MIT, An Institution Fundamentally Inhospitable to Free Culture', *Slate Magazine Online*, 12 January. Available at: https://slate.com/technology/2016/01/aaron-swartz-misjudged-mit-an-excerpt -from-the-idealist-by-justin-peters.html (accessed: 16 February 2025).

Peters, J. (2019), 'The Moral Rot of the MIT Media Lab', *Slate Magazine Online*, 8 September. Available at: https://slate.com/technology/2019/09/mit-media-lab-jeffrey-epstein-joi-ito -moral-rot.html (accessed: 16 February 2025).

Petersen, J. K. (2013), *Introduction to Surveillance Studies*. Florida: CRC Press.

Petrusich, A. (2024), 'The Beautiful Rawness of Steve Albini', *The New Yorker Online*, 11 May. Available at: https://www.newyorker.com/culture/postscript/the-beautiful-rawness-of-steve -albini (accessed: 7 June 2024).

PI (2013), 'Despite Claims of "Going Dark", Five Eyes More Powerful than Ever', *Privacy International Website*. Available at: https://privacyinternational.org/long-read/1677/despite -claims-going-dark-five-eyes-more-powerful-ever (accessed: 3 October 2024).

Pieters, J. (2005), *Speaking With the Dead: Explorations in Literature and History*. Edinburgh: Edinburgh University Press. Available at: https://doi.org/10.1515/9781474471619 (accessed: 17 December 2024).

Pilkington, E. (2014), 'Guardian and Washington Post win Pulitzer Prize for NSA Revelations', *The Guardian Online*, 14 April. Available at: https://www.theguardian.com/media/2014/apr /14/guardian-washington-post-pulitzer-nsa-revelations (accessed: 24 February 2025).

Pizer, J. (2021), *Ambivalent Literary Farewells to the German Democratic Republic: What is Lost*. Berlin and Boston: De Gruyter. Available at: https://doi-org.mmu.idm.oclc.org/10.1515 /9783110725032 (accessed: 11 February 2025).

Plant, S. (1998), *Zeros + Ones: Digital Women and the New Technoculture*. London: Fourth Estate.

Poetranto, I. (2012), *The Kremlin's New Internet Surveillance Plan Goes Live Today*. Citizen Lab, University of Toronto. Available at: https://citizenlab.ca/2012/11/the-kremlins-new-internet -surveillance-plan-goes-live-today/ (accessed: 16 January 2025).

Poitras, L. (2016), 'Berlin Journal', in L. Poitras (ed.), *Astro Noise: A Survival Guide to Living Under Total Surveillance: A Survival Guide for Living Under Total Surveillance*. Illustrated edn. New Haven, CT: Yale University Press, 80–103.

Poole, S. (2000), 'Hit Man, Myth Maker', *The Guardian Online*, 26 February. Available at: https:// www.theguardian.com/books/2000/feb/26/music (accessed: 30 October 2024).

Popplewell, R. (1992), 'The Stasi and the East German Revolution of 1989', *Contemporary European History*, 1 (1): 37–63. Available at: https://doi.org/10.1017/S0960777300005051 (accessed: 10 February 2024).

Porta, G. della (1558), *Magiae naturalis, sive, De miraculis rerum naturalivm libri IIII*. Naples: Matthias Cancer.

Pressly, L. (2004), 'The Spy Who Loved Her', *The Guardian Online*, 18 November. Available at: https://www.theguardian.com/education/2004/nov/18/artsandhumanities.highereducation (accessed: 2 October 2024).

Priest, D. and W. M. Arkin (2010), 'A Hidden World, Growing Beyond Control', *Washington Post*. Available at: https://www.washingtonpost.com/investigations/top-secret-america/2010/07/19/ hidden-world-growing-beyond-control-2/ (accessed: 24 February 2025).

PRISM – Snowden Interview – Laura Poitras (Wikimedia Archive) (2013), [Film] Dir. Laura Poitras, Praxis Films/Laura Poitras.

PromptSuno (2024), *How to Prompt Suno*. Available at: https://howtopromptsuno.com/making -music/improve-performance (accessed: 3 February 2025).

Proust, M. (2003), *In Search of Lost Time*. Translated by C. K. S. Moncrieff and T. Kilmartin. New York: The Modern Library (Books 1–7).

Bibliography

Psywarrior (no date), 'History of PSYOPS', *Psywarrior Website*. Available at: http://www
.psywarrior.com/psyhist.html (accessed: 7 July 2022).
Recordings of Shortwave Numbers Stations (1997), [Music album] The Conet Project: Irdial Discs.
Regalado, A. (2017), 'Meet the Guys Who Sold "Neuralink" to Elon Musk without Even Realizing
It', *MIT Technology Review*. Available at: https://www.technologyreview.com/2017/04/04
/152788/meet-the-guys-who-sold-neuralink-to-elon-musk-without-even-realizing-it/
(accessed: 18 February 2025).
Regalado, A. (2020), 'Elon Musk's Neuralink is Neuroscience Theater', *MIT Technology Review*.
Available at: https://www.technologyreview.com/2020/08/30/1007786/elon-musks-neuralink
-demo-update-neuroscience-theater/ (accessed: 17 February 2025).
Replika (2017), *Replika Website*. Available at: https://replika.com/ (accessed: 22 September 2024).
Repovš, G. (2010), 'Dealing with Noise in EEG Recording and Data Analysis'. Available at:
https://www.semanticscholar.org/paper/Dealing-with-Noise-in-EEG-Recording-and-Data
-Repov%C5%A1/805588b7f8b31602dc41b13fff3b79647381c5f3 (accessed: 13 February
2025).
Research and Markets (2024), 'Voice Over Internet Protocol (VoIP) Global Market Report 2023',
Research and Markets Website. Available at: https://www.researchandmarkets.com/reports
/5767521/voice-over-internet-protocol-voip-global (accessed: 16 September 2023).
Richelson, J. T. (2001), *The Wizards of Langley: Inside the CIA's Directorate of Science and
Technology*. Boulder, CO: Westview Press.
Rippl, G. (2018), *Haunted Narratives : Life Writing in an Age of Trauma*. Edited by T. Kirss.
Toronto, ON: University of Toronto Press.
Robertson, A. (2018), 'I Tried the Wristband That Lets You Control Computers With Your
Brain', *The Verge*. Available at: https://www.theverge.com/2018/6/6/17433516/ctrl-labs-brain
-computer-interface-armband-hands-on-preview (accessed: 18 February 2025).
Robeson (2024), *Buzz Lightyear Splash Page, Robeson Website*. Available at: https://buzz.robosen
.com/ (accessed: 14 February 2024).
Roethlisberger, F. J. and W. J. Dickson (1939), *Management and the Worker*. Cambridge, MA:
Harvard University Press.
Rohlenko, D. (2007), 'The First Russian Printed Newspaper (Первая Русская Печатная
Газета)', *Science & Life (Наука и Жизнь)* [Preprint].
Rohrer, J. (2023), 'Project December: Simulate the Dead'. Available at: https://projectdecember
.net/ (accessed: 11 December 2024).
Rothrock, K. (2014), 'The Kremlin's Digital Gulag', *The Moscow Times*. Available at: https://www
.themoscowtimes.com/2014/04/09/the-kremlins-digital-gulag-a33802 (accessed: 11 February 2025).
Rouleau, S. (2020), *The Value of Intelligence Sharing for Canada: The 'Five Eyes" Case*. National
Defence and the Canadian Armed Forces website. Available at: http://www.journal.forces.gc
.ca/Vol21/No1/page29-eng.asp (accessed: 9 March 2023).
Ruckenstein, M. and J. Granroth (2020), 'Algorithms, Advertising and The Intimacy of
Surveillance', *Journal of Cultural Economy*, 13 (1): 12–24.
Russell, C. A. (2000), *Michael Faraday: Physics and Faith*. New York: Oxford University Press.
Russell, E. (2019), *9 Things to Know About Google's Maps Data: Beyond the Map, Google Maps
Platform*. Available at: https://mapsplatform.google.com/resources/blog/9-things-know-about
-googles-maps-data-beyond-map (accessed: 29 October 2023).
Said, E. (1994), *Culture and Imperialism*. New York: Vintage.
Sample, I. (2024), '"Unprecedented Risk" to Life on Earth: Scientists Call for Halt on "Mirror
Life" Microbe Research', *The Guardian Online*, 12 December. Available at: https://www
.theguardian.com/science/2024/dec/12/unprecedented-risk-to-life-on-earth-scientists-call
-for-halt-on-mirror-life-microbe-research (accessed: 13 December 2024).

Sanders, J. (2016a), *Exhibitions: Laura Poitras: Astro Noise – Feb 5–May 1, 2016, Whitney Museum of Modern Art website*. Available at: https://whitney.org/exhibitions/laura-poitras (accessed: 27 January 2024).

Sanders, J. (2016b), 'Introduction', in L. Poitras (ed.), *Astro Noise: A Survival Guide to Living Under Total Surveillance: A Survival Guide for Living Under Total Surveillance*. Illustrated edn. New Haven, CT: Yale University Press, 24–37.

Satariano, A., P. Mozur, and A. Krolik (2022), 'When Nokia Pulled Out of Russia, a Vast Surveillance System Remained', *The New York Times*, 28 March. Available at: https://www.nytimes.com/2022/03/28/technology/nokia-russia-surveillance-system-sorm.html (accessed: 16 January 2025).

Sato, S., S. Fujii, and P. Savage (2018), 'Automated Comparison of Children's and Adult Songs Supports the Vocal Mistuning Theory of Scale Origins', in *Extended Abstracts for the Late-Breaking Version. Demo Session of the 19th International Society for Music*. Available at: https://osf.io/preprints/psyarxiv/ptvw7_v1 (accessed: 16 February 2025).

Saybasili, N. (2010), 'Digital Ghosts: Voice and Migratory Hauntings', in N. Neumark (ed.), *VOICE: Vocal Aesthetics in Digital Arts and Media*. Cambridge, MA: The MIT Press.

Scanners (1981), [Film] Dir. David Cronenberg, Canada: Filmplan International.

Schafer, R. M. (1993), *The Soundscape: Our Sonic Environment and the Tuning of the World*. Rochester, VT: Destiny Books.

Schaeffer, R., M. Khona and I. R. Fiete (2022), 'No Free Lunch from Deep Learning in Neuroscience: A Case Study through Models of the Entorhinal-Hippocampal Circuit'. Available at: https://doi.org/10.1101/2022.08.07.503109.

Schmeidel, J. C. (2014), *Stasi: Shield and Sword of the Party*. 1st edn. London: Routledge.

Schneier, B. (2018), 'The Right to Experiment', in *The End of Trust*, McSweeney's, 308–17.

Schönnher, L., M. Golla, T. Eisenhofer, J. Wiele, D. Kolossa, and T. Hloz (2022), 'Exploring Accidental Triggers of Smart Speakers', *Journal of Computer Speech & Language*, 73. Available at: https://doi.org/10.1016/j.csl.2021.101328 (accessed: 7 March 2024).

Select Committee on Intelligence (1977), *Project Mkultra, The Cia's Program of Research in Behavioral Modification (PDF)*. Joint Hearing Before the Select Committee on Intelligence and the Subcommittee on Health and Scientific Research of the Committee on Human Resources, United States Senate. Available at: https://www.intelligence.senate.gov/sites/default/files/hearings/95mkultra.pdf (accessed: 9 April 2024).

Sentance, R. (2019), 'Why Are There Still So Few Voice Case Studies Out There?', *Econsultancy (Online)*, 19 November. Available at: https://econsultancy.com/why-are-there-still-so-few-voice-assistant-marketing-case-studies-out-there/ (accessed: 13 March 2024).

Serres, M. (1982a), *The Parasite*. Translated by L. Schehr. Baltimore, MD: Johns Hopkins University Press.

Serres, M. (1982b), *Hermes*. London: John Hopkins Press Ltd.

Shahadi, H., D. H. Muhsen, H. T. Haider, and A. H. Taherinia (2019), 'Design and Implementation of a Smart Baby Crib', in *IOP Conference Series: Materials Science and Engineering. 3rd International Conference on Engineering Sciences*. Available at: https://doi.org/10.1088/1757-899X/671/1/012050 (accessed: 7 February 2025).

Sharkey, N. and A. Sharkey (2010), 'The Crying Shame of Robot Nannies: An Ethical Appraisal', *Interaction Studies*, 11 (2): 161–90. Available at: https://doi.org/0.1075/is.11.2.01sha (accessed: 17 February 2025).

Sharma, M. (2022), *AI Could Stop Snooping By Predicting What You'll Say, Lifewire*. Available at: https://www.lifewire.com/ai-could-stop-snooping-by-predicting-what-youll-say-5268213 (accessed: 13 February 2024).

Sharon, T. and B. J. Koops (2021), 'The Ethics of Inattention: Revitalising Civil Inattention As a Privacy-protecting Mechanism in Public Spaces', *Ethics and Information Technology*, 23: 331–43. Available at: https://doi.org/10.1007/s10676-020-09575-7 (accessed: 15 December 2024).

Shaw, G. (1998), 'SchoolNet Program Turns Out Techno-entrepreneurs', *St. Catharine's Standard*, 23 October.

Shiller, R. (2000), *Irrational Exuberance*. Princeton, NJ: Princeton University Press.

Shinji, M. (2011), 'Transformation of Semantics in the History of Japanese Subcultures since 1992', *Mechademia*, 6: 231–58. Available at: https://doi.org/10.1353/mec.2011.0012 (accessed: 16 December 2024).

Shull, B. (1977), *The Psychic Power of Animals*. London: Fawcett Publications.

Silverman, J. (2015), *Terms of Service: Social Media and The Price of Constant Connection*. New York: HarperCollins.

Sisto, D. (2020), *Online Afterlives: Immortality, Memory, and Grief in Digital Culture*. Translated by B. McClellan-Broussard. Cambridge, MA and London: MIT Press.

Sisto, D. (2021), 'Chatting With the Dead', *The MIT Press Reader*, 4 January. Available at: https://thereader.mitpress.mit.edu/chatting-with-the-dead-chatbots/ (accessed: 17 December 2024).

Sitrin, C. (2016), 'Have Roombas Become a Part of the Family?', *The Boston Globe Online*, 15 September. Available at: https://www.bostonglobe.com/lifestyle/style/2016/09/15/our-bots -ourselves/KekBWFnovSSp2yAhaTUOKN/story.html (accessed: 13 February 2025).

Skinamarink (2022), [Film] Dir. Kyle Edward Ball, Canada: Mutiny Pictures, ERO Picture Company.

Skinner, B. F. (1937), 'Two Types of Conditioned Reflex: A Reply to Konorski and Miller', *The Journal of General Psychology*, 16 (1): 272–9. Available at: https://doi.org/10.1080/00221309 .1937.9917951.

Slade, G. (2012), *The Big Disconnect: The Story of Technology and Loneliness*. Amherst, NY: Prometheus Books.

Smith, T. (2023), 'What the "Father of Alexa" Did Next', *Sifted*. Available at: https://sifted.eu/ articles/alexa-william-tunstall-pedoe-ai/ (accessed: 13 August 2024).

Snowden, E. (2014), 'Interview Transcript', *Norddeutscher Rundfunk*, 26 January.

Snowden, E. (2019), *Permanent Record*. New York: Metropolitan Books.

Soja, E. W. (1996), *Thirdspace: Journeys to Los Angeles and Other Real-and-Imagined Places*. Oxford: Blackwell Publishers Ltd.

Soldatov, A. and I. Borogan (2013), 'Russia's Surveillance State', *World Policy Journal*, 30 (3): 23–30. Available at: https://doi.org/10.1177/0740277513506378 (accessed: 4 June 2024).

Soldatov, A. and I. Borogan (2015), *The Red Web: The Kremlin's wars on the Internet*. New York: PublicAffairs.

Soniak, M. (2016), 'How a Gift from Schoolchildren Let the Soviets Spy on the U.S. for 7 Years', *Atlas Obscura Online*, 21 June. Available at: https://www.atlasobscura.com/articles/how-a-gift -from-schoolchildren-let-the-soviets-spy-on-the-us-for-7-years (accessed: 4 October 2023).

Sontag, S. (1977), *On Photography*. London: Penguin (Penguin modern classics).

Soundraw (no date), *Soundraw Website*. Available at: https://soundraw.io/ (accessed: 6 June 2024).

Spencer-Hall, A. (2012), 'The Post-Mortem Projections: Medieval Mystical Resurrection and the Return of Tupac Shakur', *Opticon 1826*, 13: 56–71. Available at: DOI: http://dx.doi.org/10 .5334/opt.af (accessed: 29 January 2025).

Sponsler, C. (1992), 'Cyberpunk and the Dilemmas of Postmodern Narrative: The Example of William Gibson', *Contemporary Literature*, 33 (4): 625–44. Available at: https://doi.org/10 .2307/1208645 (accessed: 6 June 2024).

Stacey, J. and L. Suchman (2012), 'Animation and Automation – The Liveliness and Labours of Bodies and Machines', *Body & Society*, 18 (1): 1–46. Available at: https://doi.org/10.1177 /1357034X11431845 (accessed: 6 December 2024).

Stackpole, T. (2014), 'In Russia, Sign a Mortgage and Get a Cat — But Only for Two Hours', *Foreign Policy Magazine*, 29 August. Available at: https://foreignpolicy.com/2014/08/29/in-russia-sign-a-mortgage-and-get-a-cat-but-only-for-two-hours/ (accessed: 13 February 2025).

Stanger, A. (2019), *Whistleblowers : Honesty in America from Washington to Trump*. New Haven, CT: Yale University Press.

Star Trek: The Original Series (1966), [TV Series]: NBC, September 8.

Steeves, V. (2010), 'Chapter 5: Online Surveillance in Canadian Schools', in T. Monahan and R. D. Torres (eds), *Schools Under Surveillance*. New Brunswick, NJ: Rutgers University Press, 87–103.

Steinmeyer, J. (1999), *The Science Behind the Ghost*. Burbank, CA: Hahne.

Sterne, J. (2001), 'Mediate Auscultation, the Stethoscope, and the "Autopsy of the Living": Medicine's Acoustic Culture', *Journal of Medical Humanities*, 22 (2): 115–36. Available at: https://doi.org/10.1023/A:1009067628620 (accessed: 7 February 2025).

Sterne, J. (2003), *The Audible Past: Cultural Origins of Sound Reproduction*. Durham, NC: Duke University Press.

Stevenson, I. (1983), 'Do We Need a New Word to Supplement "Hallucination"?', *The American Journal of Psychiatry*, 140 (12): 1609–11. Available at: https://doi.org/10.1176/ajp.140.12.1609 (accessed: 27 February 2025).

Steyerl, H. (2016), 'Medya: Autonomy of Images', in L. Poitras (ed.), *Astro Noise: A Survival Guide to Living Under Total Surveillance: A Survival Guide for Living Under Total Surveillance*. Illustrated edn. New Haven, CT: Yale University Press, 138–53.

Steyerl, H. (2020), 'Sea of Data: Apophenia and Pattern (Mis-)Recognition', in B. Vickers and K. Allado-McDowell (eds), *Atlas of Anomalous AI*. London: Ignota Books, 138–51.

Stokes, P. (2021), *Digital Aouls: A Philosophy of Online Immortality*. New York: Bloomsbury Academic.

Stone, K. (2023), 'The History of VoIP and Internet Telephony: From the 1920s to Present Day', *Get VoIP website*, 10 January.

StoryFile (2022), *StoryFile Website*. Available at: https://storyfile.com/ (accessed: 22 September 2024).

Strengers, Y. and J. Kennedy (2020), *The Smart Wife: Why Siri, Alexa, and Other Smart Home Devices Need a Feminist Reboot*. Cambridge, MA and London: MIT Press.

Stromberg, J. (2013), 'Refugees of the Modern World', *Slate Online*, 12 April. Available at: https://slate.com/technology/2013/04/green-bank-w-v-where-the-electrosensitive-can-escape-the-modern-world.html (accessed: 14 February 2025).

Sudjic, O. (2018), 'Self-Surveillance in the Internet Age', *The Paris Review*, 5 December. Available at: https://www.theparisreview.org/blog/2018/12/05/self-surveillance-in-the-internet-age/ (accessed: 30 November 2023).

Sullivan, L. (2022), 'Symmetry in State Surveillance: The US and Russia', *Geohistory Website*. Available at: https://geohistory.today/symmetry-state-surveillance-us-russia/ (accessed: 6 October 2024).

Sunda, M. (2015), 'Japan's Hidden Caste of Untouchables', *BBC News online*, 23 October. Available at: https://www.bbc.co.uk/news/world-asia-34615972 (accessed: 27 June 2024).

Sundara Rajan, M. T. (2020), 'Glenn Gould: Inventor of "User Rights"?', *The IPKat*, 7 October. Available at: https://ipkitten.blogspot.com/2020/10/glenn-gould-inventor-of-user-rights.html (accessed: 20 September 2024).

Suno (2024), *Suno Website*. Available at: https://suno.com/ (accessed: 12 June 2024).

Swearingen, J. (2018), 'Making My Baby a Smart Baby Was a Mistake', *New York Magazine Online*, 10 May. Available at: https://nymag.com/intelligencer/2018/05/why-using-smart-wearable-baby-monitors-was-a-mistake.html (accessed: 25 March 2024).

Szalai, G. (2015), 'Google Chairman Eric Schmidt: "The Internet Will Disappear"', *The Hollywood Reporter*, 22 January. Available at: https://www.hollywoodreporter.com/business/digital/ google-chairman-eric-schmidt-internet-765989/ (accessed: 11 January 2024).

Szendy, P. (2016), *All Ears: The Aesthetics of Espionage*. New York: Fordham University Press. Available at: https://doi.org/10.1515/9780823273980 (accessed: 13 January 2024).

Tavlin, W. (2025), 'Casual Viewing: Why Netflix Looks Like that', *n+1 Website*. Available at: https://www.nplusonemag.com/issue-49/essays/casual-viewing/ (accessed: 29 January 2025).

Taylor, M. (2024), 'Exclusive: Synchron, A Rival to Musk's Neuralink, Readies Large-scale Brain Implant Trial', *Reuters*, 8 April. Available at: https://www.reuters.com/business/healthcare -pharmaceuticals/synchron-rival-musks-neuralink-readies-large-scale-brain-implant-trial -2024-04-08/ (accessed: 18 February 2025).

Taylor, T. (2023), 'From Synthesiser to AI: A Brief History of Music's Love-hate Relationship with Technology', *Far Out Magazine Online*, 23 April. Available at: https://faroutmagazine.co.uk /from-synthesiser-to-ai-a-brief-history-of-musics-love-hate-relationship-with-technology/ (accessed: 20 May 2024).

TechRound Team (2024), 'How The Rise Of Grief Tech Comforts The Broken Hearted', *TechRound*, 17 May. Available at: https://techround.co.uk/tech/rise-grief-tech-comforts -broken-hearted/ (accessed: 11 December 2024).

Telephone (2010), [7" single] Lady Gaga Ft. Beyoncé, USA: Interscope.

Tetsuo: The Iron Man (1989), [Film] Dir. Shinya Tsukamoto, Japan: Kaijyu Theatre.

Thacker, E. (2004), 'Living Dead Networks', *Fibreculture*, 4 (2005: Contagion). Available at: https://four.fibreculturejournal.org/fcj-018-living-dead-networks/ (accessed: 6 March 2024).

Thaler, R. H. and H. M. Shefrin (1981), 'An Economic Theory of Self-Control', *Journal of Political Economy*, 89 (2): 392–406.

The Blair Witch Project (1999), [Film] Dir. Daniel Myrick and Eduardo Sánchez, USA: Lionsgate.

'The CLOUD Act' (2022), Available at: https://www.eurojust.europa.eu/publication/cloud-act (accessed: 9 February 2024).

The Conversation (1974), [Film] Dir. Francis Ford Coppola, USA: The Directors Company, The Coppola Company, American Zoetrope.

The Double (2013), [Film] Dir. Richard Ayoade, France: StudioCanal.

The Dreaming (1982), [Music album] Kate Bush, UK: EMI Records.

*The End of the F***ing World* (2017). [TV series] UK: Channel 4, 24 October.

The Future's So Bright, I Gotta Wear Shades (1986), [7" single] Timbuk 3, USA: I.R.S.

The Jetsons (1962), [TV series] USA: ABC, Series 1, September 23 1962–March 17 1963.

The Lost Masters (2003), [Music album] Kool Keith, USA: DMAFT Records.

The Low End Theory (1991), [Music album] A Tribe Called Quest, USA: Jive Records.

The Matrix (1999), [Film] Dir. Lana Wachowski and Lily Wachowski, USA/Australia: Warner Bros., Village Roadshow Pictures, Groucho II Film Partnership, Silver Pictures.

The Quantified Self (no date), *The Quantified Self Website*. Available at: https://quantifiedself.com /about/what-is-quantified-self/ (accessed: 24 March 2024).

Tompkins, D. (2010), *How to Wreck a Nice Beach: The Vocoder from World War II to Hip-Hop, The Machine Speaks*. Brookly, NY and London: Melville House Publishing.

Toy Story (1995), [Film] Dir. John Lasseter, USA: Walt Disney Pictures, Pixar Animation Studios.

Trower, S. (2012), *Senses of Vibration: A History of the Pleasure and Pain of Sound*. London: Continuum.

Trower, S. (2019), 'Libraries of Voices', in S. Goodman, T. Heys, and E. Ikoniadou (eds), *Unsound: Undead*. Falmouth: Urbanomic, 65–7.

Turkle, S. (2017), *Alone Together: Why We Expect More From Technology and Less From Each Other*, 3rd edn. New York: Basic Books.

UK Government (1994), *Criminal Justice and Public Order Act 1994*. Available at: https://www.legislation.gov.uk/ukpga/1994/33/contents (accessed: 11 June 2024).

UN (1989), *UN Convention on the Rights of the Child, Resolution 44/25*. Available at: https://www.unicef.org/child-rights-convention/convention-text (accessed: 27 September 2024).

UNESCO and EQUALS Skills Coalition (2019), *I'd Blush If I Could: Closing Gender Divides in Digital Skills Through Education*. UNESCO. Available at: https://doi.org/10.54675/RAPC9356 (accessed: 22 September 2024).

United States Department of State (USDS) and Bureau of Diplomatic Security (2011), 'Spies, Leaks, Bugs, and Diplomats: Diplomatic Security in the 1960s', in *History of the Bureau of Diplomatic Security of the United States Department of State*. Washington, DC: Global Publishing Solutions, 161–95.

University of Cambridge (2024), 'Call for Safeguards to Prevent Unwanted 'Hauntings' by AI Chatbots of Dead Loved Ones', *University of Cambridge Website*. Available at: https://www.cam.ac.uk/research/news/call-for-safeguards-to-prevent-unwanted-hauntings-by-ai-chatbots-of-dead-loved-ones (accessed: 30 January 2025).

UNODC (2022), *Digest of Cyber Organized Crime*. Vienna, Austria.

Upgaurd Team (2019), *Telecommunications Breakdown: How Russian Telco Infrastructure was Exposed | UpGuard*. Available at: https://www.upguard.com/breaches/mts-nokia-telecom-inventory-data-exposure (accessed: 16 January 2025).

US Government (2021), 'GPS.gov: Selective Availability', *GPS.gov: Official U.S. Government Information About the Global Positioning System (GPS) and related topics*. Available at: https://www.gps.gov/systems/gps/modernization/sa/ (accessed: 11 February 2025).

Van der Linden, D., A. Zamansky, I. Hadar, and B. Craggs (2018), 'Developing for Non-human Users: Reflecting on Practical Implications in the Ubiquitous Computing Era', *Journal of Industrial Information Integration*, 14: 50–8.

Van der Tuin, I. and R. Dolphijn (2012), *New Materialism: Interviews & Cartographies*. London: Open Humanities Press. Available at: https://doi.org/10.3998/ohp.11515701.0001.001 (accessed: 11 June 2024).

Van Dijck, J. (2014), 'Datafication, Dataism and Dataveillance: Big Data Between Scientific Paradigm and Ideology', *Surveillance and Society*, 12 (2): 197–208. Available at: https://doi.org/10.24908/ss.v12i2.4776 (accessed: 13 February 2025).

Vanel, H. (2013), *Triple Entendre: Furniture Music, Muzak, Muzak-Plus*. Champaign, IL: University of Illinois Press.

Varoufakis, Y. (2023), *Technofeudalism: What Killed Capitalism*. London: Bodley Head.

Véliz, C. (2020), *Privacy is Power*. London: Bantam Press.

Veres, G. (2014), 'Gveres/Donateacry-Corpus', Available online: https://github.com/gveres/donateacry-corpus (accessed 22 January 2025).

Vetter, G. (2012), *The Architecture of Control: A Contribution to the Critique of the Science of Apparatuses*, Lanham, MD: John Hunt Publishing.

Vilhauer, R. P. (2023), 'Very Present and Very Real: A Case Study of Regularly Hearing the Voice of the Deceased Without Distress in Bereavement', *Omega*, 302228231195104. Available at: https://doi.org/10.1177/00302228231195104 (accessed: 20 July 2024).

Virilio, P. (2005), *Desert Screen*. London: Continuum.

Vlahos, J. (2015), 'Barbie Wants To Get To Know Your Child', *New York Times Magazine Online*, 16 September. Available at: https://www.nytimes.com/2015/09/20/magazine/barbie-wants-to-get-to-know-your-child.html (accessed: 26 July 2024).

Vlahos, J. (2017), 'A Son's Race to Give His Dying Father Artificial Immortality', *Wired*. Available at: https://www.wired.com/story/a-sons-race-to-give-his-dying-father-artificial-immortality/ (accessed: 3 February 2025).

Vlahos, J. (2019), *Talk to Me: How Voice Computing Will Transform the Way We Live, Work, and Think*. New York: Houghton Mifflin Harcourt.

Voegelin, S. (2010), *Listening to Noise and Silence: Towards a Philosophy of Sound Art*. London: A&C Black.

Vogel, S. (2019), *Betrayal in Berlin: George Blake, the Berlin Tunnel and the Greatest Conspiracy of the Cold War*. New York: Custom House.

Voinea, C. (2024), 'On Grief and Griefbots', *Think*, 23 (67): 47–51. Available at: https://doi.org/10.1017/S1477175623000490 (accessed: 12 September 2024).

Volkov, L. (2016), 'Pedofil Na Slujbe FSB: Kto Sledit Za Nami v Internete? [A pedophile that serves FSB: Who is Surveilling Us in the Internet?"]', *Leonid Volkov*, 24 March. Available at: https://www.leonidvolkov.ru/p/119 (accessed: 14 February 2025).

Von Thun, M. (2023), 'Monopoly Power Is the Elephant in the Room in the AI Debate', *TechPolicy Press Website*. Available at: https://techpolicy.press/monopoly-power-is-the-elephant-in-the-room-in-the-ai-debate/ (accessed: 25 October 2023).

Vygotsky, L. S. (1978), *Mind in Society: The Development of Higher Mental Process*. Cambridge, MA: Harvard University Press.

Wainwright, O. (2013), 'Prism: The PowerPoint Presentation So Ugly It Was Meant to Stay Secret', *The Guardian Online*, 12 June. Available at: https://www.theguardian.com/artanddesign/architecture-design-blog/2013/jun/12/prism-nsa-powerpoint-graphic-design (accessed: 5 January 2024).

Walk on the Wild Side (1972), [7" single] Lou Reed, USA: RCA Victor.

Walker, R. (2009), 'The Song Decoders', *The New York Times*, 14 October. Available at: https://www.nytimes.com/2009/10/18/magazine/18Pandora-t.html (accessed: 3 February 2025).

Walker, B. L. (2013), 'Animals and the Intimacy of History', *History & Theory*, 52 (4): 45–67. Available at: https://doi.org/10.1111/hith.10687.

Wallace, R., H. K. Melton H.R. and Schlesinger (2010), *Spycraft*. London: Penguin.

Wang, A. B. (2018), 'I'm In Your Baby's Room': A Hacker Took Over a Baby Monitor and Broadcast Threats, Parents Say', *Washington Post Online*, 20 December. Available at: https://www.washingtonpost.com/technology/2018/12/20/nest-cam-baby-monitor-hacked-kidnap-threat-came-device-parents-say/ (accessed: 19 March 2024).

Warren, R. M. (2008), *Auditory Perception: An Analysis and Synthesis*, 3rd edn. Cambridge: Cambridge University Press. Available at: https://doi.org/10.1017/CBO9780511754777.

Webb, D. (2007a), *Privacy and Solitude in the Middle Ages*. London and New York: Hambledon Continuum.

Webb, D.C. (2007b), 'ECHELON and the NSA', in L. Janczewski and A. Colarik (eds), *Cyber Warfare and Cyber Terrorism*. Hershey, PA: IGI Global, 453–68.

Weiser, M. (1991), 'The Computer for the Twenty-First Century', *Scientific American*, September, 66–75.

What a Father Does For His Son After His Mother's Passing! (2017), [Film] Dir. Antonio Vargas, YouTube. Available at: https://www.youtube.com/watch?v=hpxHFQPeeRs. (accessed: 18 January 2025).

Whitmore, B. (2011), 'Opposition Blames Kremlin For Wiretap', *Radio Free Europe/Radio Liberty*. Available at: https://www.rferl.org/a/russias_nemtsov_accuses_kremlin_over_phone_tapping/24427959.html (accessed: 16 January 2025).

Whittaker, Z. (2016), *NSA is So Overwhelmed with data, it's No Longer Effective, Says Whistleblower, ZDNET*. Available at: https://www.zdnet.com/article/nsa-whistleblower-overwhelmed-with-data-ineffective/ (accessed: 8 January 2024).

Whittaker, Z. (2019), 'Documents Reveal How Russia Wiretaps Phone Companies', *TechCrunch*, 18 September. Available at: https://techcrunch.com/2019/09/18/russia-sorm-nokia-surveillance/ (accessed: 16 January 2025).

WHO (2006), *Electromagnetic Hypersensitivity: Proceedings, International Workshop on Electromagnetic Field Hypersensitivity*. Meeting Report. Prague, Czech Republic: WHO. Available at: https://www.who.int/publications/i/item/9789241594127 (accessed: 14 February 2025).

Wilkins, C. (2016), 'The Panacousticon: By Way of Echo to Freddie Rokem', *Performance Philosophy*, 2 (1): 5–22. Available at: https://doi.org/10.21476/PP.2016.2179 (accessed: 22 September 2024).

Williams, A. (2023), Baby monitor uses AI to work out why your child is crying, The Standard. Available at: https://www.standard.co.uk/news/tech/baby-monitor-uses-ai-to-work-out-why -child-is-crying-b1050984.html (accessed: 23 January 2025).

Wilson, S. (2016), 'Live With a 3-D Virtual Servant Inside Your Home with Gatebox, Now Available for Pre-order', *Sora News 24*, 15 December. Available at: https://soranews24.com /2016/12/15/live-with-a-3-d-virtual-servant-inside-your-home-with-gatebox-now-available -for-pre-order%E3%80%90video%E3%80%91/ (accessed: 11 July 2024).

Winnicott, D. W. and R. Rodnam (2005), *Playing and Reality*. 2nd edn. London: Routledge.

Wolf, C. (1993), *What Remains and Other Stories*. New York: Farrar, Straus, and Giroux.

Wolf, M. and A. McElvoy (1999), *Man Without a Face: The Autobiography of Communism's Greatest Spymaster*. New York: Public Affairs.

Wolfson, S. (2018), 'Amazon's Alexa Recorded Private Conversation and Sent It to Random Contact', *The Guardian Online*, 24 May. Available at: https://www.theguardian.com/ technology/2018/may/24/amazon-alexa-recorded-conversation (accessed: 9 February 2024).

Wosk, J. (2024), *Artificial Women: Sex Dolls, Robot Caregivers, and More Facsimile Females*. Bloomington, IN: Indiana University Press.

Wright, P. (1987), *Spycatcher: The Candid Autobiography of Senior Intelligence Officer*. Victoria: William Heinemann Australia.

Wright, S. (1998), *An Appraisal of Technologies of Political Control*. Luxembourg: European Parliament. Available at: https://cryptome.org/stoa-atpc.htm (accessed: 9 March 2023).

Yang, A. (2019), 'Reflexive Control and Cognitive Vulnerability in the 2016 U.S. Presidential Election', *Journal of Information Warfare*, 18 (3, Special Edn): 99–122.

Yazell, B. (2018), 'The Politics of Precarity in William Gibson's Bridge Trilogy', *Studies in the Fantastic*, 6 (1): 39–69.

You Have Used Me As A Fish Long Enough (1995), [Film] Dir. Adam Curtis. UK: BBC.

YouGov (2018), 'The Dawn of the Connected Home: YouGov Current and Future Analysis of the Smart Home Market', *YouGov Website*. Available at: https://commercial.yougov.com/rs/464 -VHH-988/images/UK-Smart-homes.pdf (accessed: 29 December 2023).

Younge, G. (2004), 'US Police Put Hip-hop Under Surveillance', *The Guardian Online*, 11 March. Available at: https://www.theguardian.com/world/2004/mar/11/arts.usa (accessed: 11 November 2023).

Zabriskie Point (1970), [Film] Dir. Michaelangelo Antonioni, USA: Metro-Goldwyn-Mayer.

Zegart, A. (2022), *Spies, Lies, and Algorithms: The History and Future of American Intelligence*. Princeton, NJ and Oxford: Princeton University Press.

Zetter, K. (2009), 'Man Sues Over Leaky Baby Monitor', *Wired Magazine Online*, 2 November. Available at: https://www.wired.com/2009/11/baby-monitor/ (accessed: 21 March 2024).

Žižek, S. (2006), *The Parallax View*. Cambridge, MA: MIT Press.

Zjalic, J. (2021), *Digital Audio Forensics Fundamentals: From Capture to Courtroom*. New York: Routledge. Available at: https://www.routledge.com/Digital-Audio-Forensics-Fundamentals -From-Capture-to-Courtroom/Zjalic/p/book/9780367259105 (accessed: 3 February 2025).

Zuboff, S. (2019), *The Age of Surveillance Capitalism: The Fight for a Human Future at the New Frontier of Power*. London: Profile Books.

INDEX